Teaching Elementary Social Studies

Principles and Applications

JAMES J. ZARRILLO
California State University, Hayward

MERRILL, AN IMPRINT OF PRENTICE HALL

Upper Saddle River, New Jersey

Columbus, Ohio

Library of Congress Cataloging-in-Publication Data

Zarrillo, James.
   Teaching elementary social studies : principles and applications /
James J. Zarrillo.
     p.   cm.
   Includes bibliographical references (p.) and indexes.
   ISBN 0–02–431352–1
   1. Social sciences—Study and teaching (Elementary)—United
States.   2. Multicultural education—United States.   I. Title.
LB1584.Z27 2000
372.83′044′0973—dc21
                                                 99-40309
                                                  CIP

Editor: Bradley J. Potthoff
Developmental Editor: Linda Ashe Montgomery
Production Editor: JoEllen Gohr
Editorial Assistant: Mary Evangelista
Design Coordinator: Diane C. Lorenzo
Photo Coordinator: Nancy Harre Ritz
Production Coordination: Betsy Keefer
Text Designer: Kate Nichols Design
Cover Designer: Allen Bumpus
Cover Photo: FPG International
Production Manager: Pam Bennett
Director of Marketing: Kevin Flanagan
Marketing Manager: Meghan Shepherd
Marketing Coordinator: Krista Groshong

This book was set in ITC Garamond Light by The Clarinda Company, and was printed and
bound by R.R. Donnelley & Sons Company. The cover was printed by Phoenix Color Corp.

© 2000 by Prentice-Hall, Inc.
Pearson Education
Upper Saddle River, New Jersey 07458

Photo credits are listed on page v.

Printed in the United States of America

10 9 8 7 6 5 4 3 2

ISBN: 0–02–431352–1

Prentice-Hall International (UK) Limited, *London*
Prentice-Hall of Australia Pty. Limited, *Sydney*
Prentice-Hall of Canada, Inc., *Toronto*
Prentice-Hall Hispanoamericana, S.A., *Mexico*
Prentice-Hall of India Private Limited, *New Delhi*
Prentice-Hall of Japan, Inc., *Toyko*
Prentice-Hall (Singapore) Pte. Ltd., *Singapore*
Editora Prentice-Hall do Brasil, Ltda., *Rio de Janeiro*

and the performing arts should play prominent roles in elementary social studies. Applying a variety of instructional strategies and resources will increase the chances that every child in your room will be successful and be better prepared for a productive life in the 21st century.

Acknowledgments

I wish to thank the elementary school teachers from whom I borrowed ideas for this book: my colleagues in Burbank, California; the teachers I observed during research projects from school districts in Los Angeles County; the cooperating teachers in the ABC and Long Beach Unified School District who guided my student teachers; and my students at California State University, Hayward. Many thanks also to Linda Montgomery, developmental editor at Merrill/Prentice Hall; Betsy Keefer, the production coordinator, and Linda Poderski, the copyeditor for this book.

Photo credits include page 246 by Bill Bachmann/Photo Researchers; page 73 by Canadian Tourism Commission; pages 33, 119, 159, 209, 267, 281, 295, 312, and 336 by Scott Cunningham/Merrill; page 46 by Laura Dwight; page 139 by Buddy Endress/Silver Burdett Ginn; page 221 by Exxon Corporation; page 142 by Tony Freeman/Photo Edit; pages 1, 63, 95 (middle), 126, 183, 210, 216, and 324 by Anthony Magnacca/Merrill; page 87 by National Museum of American Art, Washington DC/Art Resource, NY; page 275 by Pearson Education/PH College; pages 7, 20, 27, 78, and 136 by Barbara Schwartz/Merrill; pages 110 and 255 by Silver Burdett Ginn; pages 52, 95 (top and bottom), 153, 164, and 225 by Anne Vega/Merrill; page 101 by Tom Watson/Merrill.

The outside reviewers of the book made many important suggestions: Jo Anne Buggey, University of Minnesota; Duane M. Giannangelo, The University of Memphis; Felipe V. Golez, California State University, Long Beach; Thomas B. Goodkind, University of Connecticut; Phillip A. Heath, The Ohio State University at Lima; Bruce E. Larson, Western Washington University; John H. Litcher, Wake Forest University; Wayne Mahood, SUNY-Geneseo; Jay A. Monson, Utah State University; and Kenneth C. Schmidt, University of Wisconsin-Eau Claire. I am grateful. Thank you.

While I was in the final stages of finishing this book, my mother, Lois Zarrillo, passed away after a long and happy life. She taught junior high and senior high school social studies in Missouri and California, beginning her career in 1937 and retiring in 1981. One of her principals called her a "quintessential teacher," who believed all her students had the potential to succeed. I hope some of her spirit survives in these pages.

J.J.Z.

Discover the Companion Website Accompanying This Book

The Prentice Hall Companion Website: A Virtual Learning Environment

Technology is a constantly growing and changing aspect of our field that is creating a need for content and resources. To address this emerging need, Prentice Hall has developed an online learning environment for students and professors alike— Companion Websites—to support our textbooks.

In creating a Companion Website, our goal is to build on and enhance what the textbook already offers. For this reason, the content for each user-friendly website is organized by chapter and provides the professor and student with a variety of meaningful resources. Common features of a Companion Website include:

For the Professor—

Every Companion Website integrates **Syllabus Manager**™**,** an online syllabus creation and management utility.

- **Syllabus Manager**™ provides you, the instructor, with an easy, step-by-step process to create and revise syllabi, with direct links into Companion Website and other online content without having to learn HTML.
- Students may logon to your syllabus during any study session. All they need to know is the web address for the Companion Website and the password you've assigned to your syllabus.
- After you have created a syllabus using **Syllabus Manager**™**,** students may enter the syllabus for their course section from any point in the Companion Website.

- Class dates are highlighted in white and assignment due dates appear in blue. Clicking on a date, the student is shown the list of activities for the assignment. The activities for each assignment are linked directly to actual content, saving time for students.
- Adding assignments consists of clicking on the desired due date, then filling in the details of the assignment—name of the assignment, instructions, and whether or not it is a one-time or repeating assignment.
- In addition, links to other activities can be created easily. If the activity is online, a URL can be entered in the space provided, and it will be linked automatically in the final syllabus.
- Your completed syllabus is hosted on our servers, allowing convenient updates from any computer on the Internet. Changes you make to your syllabus are immediately available to your students at their next logon.

For the Student—

- **Chapter Objectives**—outline key concepts from the text
- **Interactive self-quizzes**—complete with hints and automatic grading that provide immediate feedback for students
- After students submit their answers for the interactive self-quizzes, the Companion Website **Results Reporter** computes a percentage grade, provides a graphic representation of how many questions were answered correctly and incorrectly, and gives a question by question analysis of the quiz. Students are given the option to send their quiz to up to four email addresses (professor, teaching assistant, study partner, etc.).
- **Message Board**—serves as a virtual bulletin board to post—or respond to—questions or comments to/from a national audience
- **Net Searches**—offer links by key terms from each chapter to related Internet content
- **Web Destinations**—links to www sites that relate to chapter content

To take advantage of these and other resources, please visit the *Teaching Elementary Social Studies* Companion Website at

www.prenhall.com/zarrillo

Brief Contents

Contents

Lesson Plans and Other Instructional Activities

More than 150 instructional activities appear in this book in a variety of formats. Many are described briefly, usually as examples of instructional strategies discussed in the text. Following is a list of the lessons, projects, units, and other activities presented in detail:

Part I

The Foundations of
Social Studies Teaching

Chapter 1

An Introduction to the Social Studies: Linking the Past and the Present

n a kindergarten classroom, the teacher reads aloud the picture book *A Chair for My Mother*. Afterward, the children discuss how characters in the story cooperated to solve a problem. Then the children help their teacher make a list of ways they can work together to make their classroom a happier, more productive place.

A first-grade teacher wants his students to engage in a simple form of critical thinking—comparing and contrasting—so he has gathered one set of photographs of people doing things in winter (in a region where winters are cold and snowy) and another set showing people doing things in summer. His first graders will work in small groups to identify how weather affects the way people live.

Twenty-three second graders follow their teacher on a "walking" field trip around the playground of their school and the adjoining streets. They look at signs that state rules people must follow. Afterward, the children will be asked to provide a rationale for each rule they observed. Then a group of five students will devise a set of new signs that will make their school safer. They will present their suggestions to the school principal and PTA.

As part of a year-long study of their community, six third graders undertake a bold project: to compile an oral history of their school. During this project, they will interview former students, teachers, and community leaders.

In a fourth-grade classroom, one Chinese American girl is working with her mother to learn to write in Chinese. She shares examples of her writing, and her classmates want to learn more. Her teacher prepares a 4-day mini-unit that will allow all students in the room to learn about the logographic Chinese system and to write a few Chinese characters.

Working in small groups, fifth graders read the first-person narratives of former enslaved people found in the book *To Be a Slave*. Later, each group will share with their classmates what they have learned about American slavery.

A sixth-grade classroom is alive with many activities as students learn about ancient Greece. Some students rehearse a play on the myth of Daedalus, others paint a mural of the Acropolis, a third group works on a CD-ROM presentation on the Greeks, and three students explore an Internet Web site with photographs of the Parthenon.

▲　　▲　　▲

All this and much more is social studies in the elementary school. During social studies, children learn about people—people who lived long ago and people who live today. It is when children become more proficient as thinkers, researchers, readers, writers, speakers, listeners, artists, and technologists. It is the time when they use what they have learned to become good citizens in our democratic society.

In this chapter, you will read about:

▶ Perspectives that currently define social studies
▶ Two historical, influential movements that still characterize the discipline of social studies—Progressive Education and the New Social Studies
▶ Three components that frame a responsible social studies curriculum: content, processes, and values

Definitions of Social Studies

In 1992, the National Council for the Social Studies (NCSS) adopted the following definition of *social studies:*

> Social studies is the integrated study of the social sciences and humanities to promote civic competence. Within the school program, social studies provides coordinated, systematic study drawing upon such disciplines as anthropology, archaeology, economics, geography, history, law, philosophy, political science, psychology, religion, and sociology, as well as appropriate content from the humanities, mathematics, and natural sciences. The primary purpose of social studies is to help young people develop the ability to make informed and reasoned decisions for the public good as citizens of a culturally diverse, democratic society in an interdependent world. (NCSS Task Force on Standards for Teaching and Learning in the Social Studies, 1993, p. 213)

The NCSS, the professional organization of social studies educators, has played an essential role since 1921. The NCSS definition seems to be a good place to start our discussion of how to teach social studies in an elementary school classroom. The existence of an "official" definition is somewhat misleading because authorities in the field have long debated the dimensions of an appropriate definition of social studies (Barr, Barth, & Shermis, 1977; Barth & Shermis, 1970; Dougan, 1988; Griffith, 1991). The NCSS definition states the topics covered in social studies and clarifies the purposes of social studies teaching and learning. Barth (1993) provides a simpler definition of social studies:

> Social studies is the interdisciplinary integration of social science and humanities concepts for the purpose of practicing problem solving and decision making for developing citizenship skills on critical social issues. (p. 57)

I think this is a useful definition. It emphasizes the ultimate goal of social studies teaching: to help students think critically *and to use what they know to be active citizens.* I have a definition too:

> Social studies is the study of people. Social studies should help students acquire knowledge, master the processes of learning, and become active citizens.

A closer look at my definition and a discussion of those provided by the NCSS and Professor Barth should bring social studies into sharper focus.

Social Studies Is the Study of People. People are the domain of social studies. This includes people as nearby as family and as far away as those who live in the most distant nations. It includes people living now, those who lived long ago, and those who will live in the future. Social studies has the potential to be the best part of the school day because it is when children connect with other people. As children learn about others, they will be fascinated by differences among cultural groups, while at the same time they will find the commonalities that create a shared sense of humanity. It is a complex task to teach about people, and information must come from many fields of study. The NCSS definition points out that the various disciplines of the social sciences and the humanities provide the content for what is taught during social studies. Too often, we as educators think that social studies is limited to history and geography, and over the last 20 years, the trend nationally has been to emphasize those two areas (Bradley Commission on History in the Schools, 1988; California Department of Education, 1987; National Commission on Social Studies in the Schools, 1989). It is imperative, however, that the other social sciences (anthropology, economics, philosophy, political science, psychology, and sociology) not be neglected; they should be a significant part of every social studies program.

The humanities (literature, the performing arts, and the visual arts) are an important part of social studies too (Eisner, 1991). The arts serve two functions. First, they help children better understand the people, places, and ideas they study. Stories, songs, dances, plays, paintings, statues, and other works of art allow children to become acquainted with the people who created them. Second, children can show us what they know by expressing themselves through the arts. As Barth (1993) points out, social studies involves *integration* of the social sciences and the humanities. A good social studies unit of study pulls information and ideas from several different fields.

Social Studies Should Help Students Acquire Knowledge, Master the Processes of Learning, and Become Active Citizens. The knowledge children acquire as a part of social studies tends to be the highest priority for teachers, parents, and the children. The common perception is that this is what social studies is all about—knowing things such as the location of the Rocky Mountains, the conditions aboard a slave ship, and the purpose of a mailbox. This is too limited a view because social studies must be a vehicle for children to become better communicators, thinkers, researchers, computer users, and artists (Natoli, 1992). Finally, all three definitions state that the ultimate goal of social studies is active citizenship in our society, as children *use* the knowledge they have acquired and the processes they have mastered to make communities, the nation, and the world better places (Field, 1997).

In the end, there probably will never be one universally accepted definition of social studies. This lack of consensus reflects fundamental disagreements on the primary purpose of social studies. Consider the following points of view on social studies teaching and learning:

- Social studies should be issues centered as children search for answers to problems and dilemmas confronted by people today and in the past (R. W. Evans, 1992).

- Social studies should develop democratic citizens who are more than loyal and patriotic; good citizens are also critics of, and participants in, their government (Engle & Ochoa, 1988).
- Social studies should focus on the big ideas of the social science disciplines, and the essential activity for children is problem solving (Fenton, 1967).
- Social studies should concentrate on history and geography and give all children a shared view of the past (Finn & Ravitch, 1988; U.S. Department of Education, 1991).
- Social studies should be child centered and permit children to pursue topics of personal interest (Goodman, 1986; Kilpatrick, 1918).

Perhaps a good way to conclude our discussion of the definition of social studies is through example. The following is from field notes I took while visiting Mrs. Denise Winslow's sixth-grade classroom one Tuesday afternoon.

Classroom Vignette / Grade 6

Multiple Activities Day During a Unit—"Ancient Greece"

There is a lot going on here! Some students rehearse a play they have written on the myth of Daedalus. Another group is busy painting the Acropolis for a large mural on ancient Greeks. Some kids are in their seats reading books. Mrs. Winslow has brought several to class from the local library. Matt reads Margaret Hodges' *The Arrow and the Lamp,* a retelling of the myth of Eros and Psyche. Julie examines an information book, *The Parthenon,* written by Susan Woodford. Ricardo and Thuy, working on a computer, are looking at photographs of the Parthenon through an Internet Web site ("History/Social Studies Web Site for K–12 Teachers"). Mrs. Winslow works with a group of students who are producing a CD-ROM on ancient Greece. This "electronic encyclopedia" will have photographs, maps, charts, and written text (Ouch! The students know much more about this technology than I do!)

I also copied a page from Mrs. Winslow's plan book. This is what she wrote for the day I observed:

1:05–2:00 Social Studies
Ancient Greek unit, Day 10, Multiple Activities:

1. "Daedalus" play group—read through second part of script—first walk-through tomorrow
2. Mural group—paint Acropolis

3. CD-ROM encyclopedia group—I will spend most of my time with this group—edit rough drafts of text, answer questions
4. Computer/Internet—view photographs of the Parthenon available through "History/Social Studies Web Site for K–12 Teachers"
5. Other students—read independently

Let's consider these activities in the context of the definitions presented earlier. Both the NCSS definition and Barth's definition stress that social studies must integrate the social sciences and the humanities. The focus of the unit was historical, but Mrs. Winslow did a good job of integrating the arts with the historical content of the unit. The play on Daedalus and books like *The Arrow and the Lamp* were just a few of the ways she introduced her students to Greek myths. Development of the mural helped students understand Greek architecture and would be followed with lessons showing Greek influence on American architecture. The arts were also a means for student expression. Rather than limit her students to written assignments, Mrs. Winslow provided opportunities for expression through the visual and performing arts. My definition stresses that social studies should help students master several processes; and in this one day, I saw students reading, writing, acting, talking, cooperating, drawing, painting, and "computing" (using the computer to gather and present information). Remember, each definition states that the ultimate purpose of social studies is good citizenship. Mrs. Winslow's unit on the ancient Greeks provided

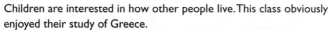

Children are interested in how other people live. This class obviously enjoyed their study of Greece.

her students with knowledge of the link between ancient Greece and contemporary America and the influence of their democratic governments on society.

 Effective Teaching in Today's Diverse Classroom: It is important to note that the multiple-activity approach used by Mrs. Winslow is essential in a classroom with diverse students. While engaging in different types of experiences, each student in her room was learning more about ancient Greeks. Some students will learn more through the visual arts, others through reading and writing, and others through the performing arts. Howard Gardner (1983) describes the "multiple intelligences" that people possess, and our teaching should allow children to learn social studies content in a variety of ways. Also, the multiple activities that Mrs. Winslow planned provided for both group and individual work. Even though all students need to work with their classmates in small-group formats, it was good to see that she provided an opportunity for students to choose to work individually or with their peers.

A Brief History of Social Studies Teaching

Now that we have some sense of what social studies is, let's turn to another topic that will help establish a foundation for our teaching. Over the last 100 years, some of the greatest educational thinkers have turned their attention to social studies. Indeed, the history of social studies, regarding both *what* should be taught and *how* to teach it, makes fascinating reading for anyone interested in teaching and learning. This is too large a topic for a thorough discussion in a methods text, however, so I suggest that you read other sources for a more comprehensive treatment: Atwood (1991), Cremin (1961), Douglass (1967), Hertzberg (1981), Jenness (1990), Lybarger (1991), and Saxe (1991). I focus on two curriculum theorists and educational "movements." We can learn a great deal from Francis Parker, Jerome Bruner, and the best ideas from Progressive Education and the New Social Studies.

Colonel Parker and Progressive Education

From Colonial times to the end of the 19th century, social studies was a dreary, unimaginative business. The term *social studies* was not used to refer to what was taught in elementary schools until 1897 (Saxe, 1992). In the place of integrated social studies, time was devoted to the separate topics of history, geography, and *civics* (the study of how federal, state, and local governments work). Malcolm Douglass (1967) gives a concise summary of how social studies was taught in most 19th-century classrooms: "Prior to 1900, the teaching of history, geography, and civics was dominated by memoriter methods. Drill and recapitulation of the textbook in class was the method of instruction" (p. 41). Children memorized isolated facts like "the two principal crops of the Plains states are corn and wheat." The teacher called on a student, who stood and recited the answer. It is worth considering how much of this style of teaching has remained unchanged over the years. In far too many classrooms, the textbook and memorization continue to dominate social studies teaching and learning (Cuban, 1991; Finklestein, Nielsen, & Switzer, 1993; Goodlad, 1984; Haas, 1986; Ochoa, 1986).

Fortunately, the late 19th century brought great changes to social studies curriculum and instruction. This was the period of *progressivism,* the social and political movement that reformed American life between 1880 and 1920. Women gained the vote, large corporations were regulated through antitrust legislation, corruption was weeded out in city halls and statehouses, and organizations were created to enrich the life of the urban poor. Social studies was born during this period as reformers wanted students to play an active role in solving society's problems. Social studies would include information from several of the social sciences, especially anthropology, sociology, and economics. Civics would be redirected from memorization to the use of knowledge to make the world a better place (Saxe, 1992).

During this period, many educators decided that the schools, too, should be changed. The movement known as *Progressive Education* encouraged individual expression, promoted a variety of instructional activities, used several instructional resources, and based teaching on the belief that children learn from interesting activities (Cremin, 1961). Francis W. Parker's (1883, 1894) ideas were an essential part of Progressive Education.

Parker began his career as a schoolmaster before the Civil War. He was wounded while serving as a Union soldier (part of his windpipe was shot off), was given a promotion in recognition of his heroism, and adopted the title of "Colonel." In 1873, he was chosen superintendent of the Quincy, Massachusetts, schools by a school board dissatisfied with the academic performance of the city's students. Later, Parker continued his innovations at the Cook County Normal School in Chicago. His ideas were revolutionary (the best summary is in Cremin, 1961). He modified the curriculum and de-emphasized textbooks. He introduced teacher-made materials, field trips, and what we call today "hands-on experiences." Students wrote books for their classmates to read and made their own science equipment. Drawing, painting, music, drama, and physical education were no longer viewed as frills; they became important parts of the curriculum. Parker wrote that "we learn to do by doing, to hear by hearing, and to think by thinking" (1883, p. 115).

Geography, always a part of social studies, was transformed by Parker. Study in geography began with trips to the surrounding countryside. Children observed and described what they saw. Following this firsthand experience, children made maps by molding sand. Later, they would draw their own maps. When studying history, Parker believed, children should think. In history, he believed, children should learn different points of view and not rely on the textbook as the sole source of information. Parker sought to develop each child's "power of organized inference" (1894, p. 269). "Children should be allowed to compare and contrast, speculate, and find generalizations," stated Colonel Parker. Teachers led this process by planning activities, asking questions, and suggesting places where answers could be found.

Francis Parker's reforms were among the most significant in the history of American education. John Dewey (1900, 1902), however, gave Progressive Education a unifying, underlying philosophy. One key element of Dewey's philosophy was the importance of "child-centered" education. Children, he argued, will receive the best education if they are given choices over what they learn and when they learn it. Dewey also stressed the importance of "activity-based" learning, calling for a challenging curriculum that provides children with many opportunities to build things, manipulate things, and create things. While at the University of Chicago, Dewey put his ideas into practice, creating a laboratory school where his theories of Progressive Education were implemented. The practical reforms of Francis Parker and the educational philosophy of John Dewey became part of a larger movement that changed many aspects of the elementary school curriculum. Eventually, every school in the United States adopted some ideas of the Progressives. We as today's teachers should remember four ideas from Colonel Parker and Progressive Education:

1. Social studies is more than the memorization of facts. It is where children learn to think, to make hypotheses, and to find answers.
2. Social studies should be activity based. Learning requires firsthand experiences. Children need to act, sing, build, dance, take field trips, and have hands-on activities.
3. Social studies requires the use of many instructional materials. Textbooks can play an important role in social studies teaching, but many other learning resources must be used.
4. Social studies should build on the interests of children. This is not to say that children should make all the decisions. It is important, however, that children be allowed to make some choices. To put this in practical terms, every instructional unit should be structured so that children select some of their learning activities.

Jerome Bruner and the New Social Studies

Now let's turn to another important educational theorist—Jerome Bruner—and another significant educational movement—the New Social Studies. During the first 20 years of the 20th century, the influence of Progressive Education was considerable. Some Progressive ideas had problems, however. For example, some Progressive schools were too permissive; any activity that children decided to pursue was viewed as worthwhile. Between 1920 and 1960, the influence of the Progressives steadily weakened. Perhaps the most influential critic was Arthur Bestor (1953, 1955), who thought Progressive schools too unstructured and their curricula void of important content. He also called for abandoning the term *social studies* because it led to "educational confusion" (1955, p. 126).

In the 1960s, social studies was reexamined. In 1959, the National Academy of Sciences sponsored a summer study group at Woods Hole on Cape Cod. It was a small group (only 35 participants) of scientists, scholars from other fields, and educators. The purpose of the gathering was to discuss how science education could be improved in elementary and secondary education. The results of this meeting would play an influential role not only in science education but in social studies as well. Jerome Bruner, a cognitive psychologist from Harvard, was the chairperson. Bruner's *The Process of Education* (1960), a little book reporting on the conference, sounded the keynote for a period of considerable reform in elementary education. *The Process of Education* provided the theory for instructional programs that became known as the "New Social Studies" (and for the "New Math"). The federal government provided millions of dollars for reform-oriented social studies projects during the 1960s (Hertzberg, 1981).

Theory Becomes Practice: MACOS. In 1961, Bruner moved from the theoretical to the practical and began work on a fifth-grade curriculum called "Man: A Course of Study" (MACOS). Eventually, MACOS was used in 1,700 elementary schools in 47 states by more than 320,000 children.

MACOS centered on three questions: (a) What is human about human beings? (b) How did they get that way? and (c) How can they be made more so? The first half of the year-long program focused on the life cycles and behaviors of salmon, herring gulls, and baboons. The second half required students to study the culture of the Netslik Eskimos. Five subjects associated with the evolution of humans provided the organizing concepts of MACOS: (a) toolmaking, (b) language, (c) social organization, (d) management of childhood, and (e) man's urge to explain his world. The program provided a variety of materials: films, poems, stories, and games. Activities were structured to "encourage students to discover on their own" (Bruner, 1966, p. 96).

Although MACOS was received enthusiastically by educators and social scientists, the program eventually died in a storm of public controversy. Conservatives found MACOS's depiction of Eskimo life repugnant and a challenge to their values. By the early 1970s, three congressional committees were investigating MACOS (Bruner, 1966, 1983; Dow, 1991; Schaffarzick, 1979).

Bruner's Two Key Ideas. Bruner's ideas were at the heart of MACOS and many other New Social Studies programs. Bruner believed that the subject matter for social studies should be organized around two concepts: (a) the "structure of the disciplines" and (b) "the spiral curriculum" (both are explained in *The Process of Education*). Although neither was a new idea, both have considerably influenced those who plan social studies programs. Bruner (1960) thought that what children learn about any subject "should be determined by the most fundamental understanding that can be achieved of the underlying principles that give structure to that subject" (p. 31). Thus, if we wanted elementary students to learn from the field of economics, we would first define the most important principles of economics and then develop materials and activities to teach them.

Bruner also believed that the curriculum should "spiral"; that is, these important concepts or principles would be taught at several grade levels, and as the children grew older, the principles would be covered with greater sophistication. And Bruner believed that *any* concept could be simplified and taught to a child at *any* age. He wrote that "we begin with the hypothesis that any subject can be taught effectively in some intellectually honest form to any child at any stage of development" (1960, p. 33). The task for authors of social studies textbooks and curriculum guides and for teachers who use them was to take big ideas and present them so that small children would understand them. The instructional programs developed as part of the New Social Studies attempted to teach children the fundamental principles from many social science disciplines, especially anthropology and sociology. Bruner had strong ideas about which learning activities should dominate social studies. He thought that social studies should be based on inquiry learning (*inquiry* is a process of solving problems and answering questions). He wrote that one purpose of social studies was "the development of an attitude toward learning and inquiry, toward guessing and hunches, toward the possibility of solving problems on one's own" (1960, p. 96). He believed that the best way for students to learn how to solve problems was for them to do the same type of activities as grown-up practitioners. If children were studying history, they should go about answering questions the same way real historians do. Bruner (1961) did not believe that discovery or inquiry activities were an end in themselves; he believed that their purpose was to teach children about the world around them.

Today, we as teachers should remember three ideas from Jerome Bruner and the New Social Studies:

1. Social studies should introduce children to the important principles of several social science disciplines (especially anthropology, economics, and sociology). Social studies should go further than teach children important information. For example, second graders will learn a considerable amount of information when they learn how food moves from farms to markets. They also should be introduced to the concept of *economic interdependence*—how people rely on others for their basic needs.

2. Social studies should include the *doing* of social science; that is, children should do the same things historians, geographers, anthropologists, and political scientists do. For example, children can examine primary sources, such as diary entries and old newspapers, just like historians.

3. Social studies should involve many opportunities for children to solve problems and to answer complex questions. This is one factor that distin-

guishes effective teachers: They challenge their students to use the facts they have learned to complete tasks that require critical thinking. For example, a group of second graders could use what they have learned about their community to propose a location for a new park.

Toward the Future

The programs created as part of the New Social Studies were popular during the 1960s and 1970s. Whereas Bruner focused on teaching the basic principles of the social sciences through inquiry, others created programs built on solving social problems (Oliver & Shaver, 1966; Rossi, 1992). Unfortunately, by the late 1970s, most New Social Studies programs had been abandoned. Scholars still discuss the reasons why the New Social Studies curricula were dropped in favor of traditional textbook-centered approaches (Engle, 1986; R. W. Evans, 1989b; Fenton, 1991). The debate continues over what social studies should be, regarding both what is taught and how to teach it (Cardis & Risinger, 1994). Recently, a great deal of controversy has surrounded the historical component of social studies. First, some authorities want historical content to be virtually the sole focus of social studies programs. This point of view is far from unanimous, however, and a history-based social studies has been roundly criticized (Cherryholmes, 1990; R. W. Evans, 1989a; J. L. Nelson, 1991). Second, attempts to define the history that children will learn, both at the state and the national level, have been controversial. It seems that any historical scope and sequence becomes a political document, subject to criticism from either the Left or the Right or both! (See Grant, 1997, for a discussion of New York's proposed curriculum; and Nash & Dunn, 1995, for a summary of the debate over national history standards.)

A National Curriculum: Goals and Standards. Another trend of great importance is the "nationalizing" of the social studies curriculum. The United States is one of the few nations that leaves most important educational decisions to state and local governments. Compared with European ministries of education, for example, the U.S. Department of Education has had little control over school curriculum and decisions governing it. States allow communities to create school districts (except for Hawaii, which does not have local school districts). The school district, through an elected school board and appointed administrators, controls its schools. Any social studies curriculum, though influenced by several factors, in almost every case is determined by the school district. Just in the previous decade, however, the federal government has exerted more influence over curriculum and instruction. The Bush administration's *America 2000: An Education Strategy* (U.S. Department of Education, 1991) showed the increased federal interest in curricular issues. *America 2000* defined five core subjects that should be emphasized from kindergarten through Grade 12: English, mathematics, science, history, and geography. *America 2000* called for national examinations at Grades 4, 8, and 12 to test student knowledge in those five areas. *America 2000* did not mandate change; rather, it suggested a course of action. In 1994, President Clinton signed into law the Goals 2000: Educate America Act. Earlier legislation, passed in 1992, authorized the creation of "national curriculum standards." The U.S. Department of Education funded the development of curriculum standards in the arts, civics and government, economics, English, foreign language, geography, history, mathematics, physical education, science, and vocational education. The proposed standards would define what children should know and be able to do and state at what age those goals should be accomplished. The Goals 2000 legislation set as a national goal that all children will leave Grades 4, 8, and 12 having mastered the objectives established in the standards. Unfortunately, Goals 2000 did not call for national standards in social studies. The National Council for the Social Studies (NCSS) created a task force to write national standards for social studies.

All these standards projects have now been completed:

- Standards for social studies generally, *Expectations of Excellence: Curriculum Standards for the Social Studies* (NCSS, 1994), available on the Internet at *http://www.ncss.org*
- Standards for civics and government, *National Standards for Civics and Government* (Center for Civic Education, 1994), *http://www.civiced.org*
- Standards for economics, *National Content Standards in Economics* (National Council on Economic Education, 1997), *http://www.nationalcouncil.org*
- Standards for geography, *Geography for Life: National Geography Standards* (Geography Education Standards Project, 1994), *http://www.ncge.org*
- Standards for history, *National Standards for History: Basic Edition* (National Center for History in the Schools, 1996), *http://www.ucla.edu/nchs*

Let's take a brief look at the national social studies standards developed by the NCSS (1994). *Expectations of Excellence: Curriculum Standards for the Social Studies* presents a unique perspective on the social studies curriculum. Curriculum standards "specify what students should know and when they should know it" (p. viii). Rather than proposing topics for each grade level K–12, the standards are organized under 10 themes. Each theme has "performance standards" for the early grades, the middle grades, and high school. The national social studies standards also include examples of exemplary instructional activities. The 10 themes are shown in Table 1.1.

For example, the theme of Culture has five performance standards for the early grades. The first two are as follows:

Social studies programs should include experiences that provide for the study of culture and cultural diversity, so that the learner can:

(a) explore and describe commonalties and differences in the ways groups, societies and cultures address similar human needs and concerns;

Table 1.1 Ten Organizational Themes for Social Studies

Themes	Theme Descriptions
1. *Culture*	Students will learn the common characteristics and significant differences among the world's cultural groups. The content related to this theme comes primarily from the social science field of anthropology.
2. *Time, Continuity, and Change*	Students will learn how to reconstruct the past and develop a historical perspective to interpret the present. The content related to this theme comes primarily from the social science field of history.
3. *People, Places, and Environments*	Students will learn to understand the significance of place and develop a geographic perspective to interpret current social conditions. The content related to this theme comes primarily from the social science field of geography.
4. *Individual Development and Identity*	Students will learn how culture, social groups, and institutions shape personal identity. The content related to this theme comes primarily from the social science field of psychology.
5. *Individuals, Groups, and Institutions*	Students will learn how institutions such as schools, churches, families, and government influence people's lives. The content related to this theme comes primarily from the social science field of sociology.
6. *Power, Authority, and Governance*	Students will learn how forms of government distribute power and authority. The content related to this theme comes primarily from the social science field of political science.
7. *Production, Distribution, and Consumption*	Students will learn that resources are limited and that people must make decisions on what things will be produced, how those things will be distributed, and the rate at which they will be consumed. The content related to this theme comes primarily from the social science field of economics.
8. *Science, Technology, and Society*	Students will learn that new technology changes the way people live. The content related to this theme comes from several social sciences fields.
9. *Global Connections*	Students will learn about the global connections among the world's societies. The content related to this theme comes from social science fields.
10. *Civic Ideals and Practices*	Students will learn the importance of civic participation in a democratic society. The content related to this theme comes primarily from political science.

(b) give examples of how experiences may be interpreted differently by people from diverse cultural perspectives and frames of reference . . . (NCSS, 1994, p. 33)

The national social studies curriculum standards were written as a starting point for educators planning social studies curriculum. It is important to remember that all the standards are advisory and that at the time this book went to press it was too early to judge their impact on social studies teaching and learning. They could have a considerable impact on the development of elementary social studies, forming the backbone of programs developed by textbook publishers and others who create instructional materials (Alter, 1995b; Handley & Adler, 1994).

A Diverse Student Population and an Information Age. During the 1990s, two societal phenomena played increasingly significant roles in social studies teaching and learning: diversity and technology. Teachers were working with students who were increasingly diverse, especially regarding language and culture. Technology has transformed all aspects of contemporary life, and the classroom was no exception.

The national social studies standards, published in 1994, require curricula that teach about both diversity and technology. The first theme, Culture, states that "social studies programs should include experiences that provide for the study of culture and cultural diversity." The eighth theme of Science, Technology, and Society challenges students to understand the "relationship among science, technology, and society" (NCSS, 1994, pp. 21, 28). An increasing number of articles in social studies journals and presentations at social studies conferences address either diversity or technology. For example, the theme of the December 1998 issue of *Social Education* is Social Studies and the New Immigration, whereas the theme of the March 1998 issue is Technology 101: Teaching in the Information Age. It seems safe to say that, in the 21st century, successful teachers will be those who are able to educate a diverse student population for the reality of the information age.

Social Studies: The Curriculum

Although using the themes of social studies is an important part of curriculum planning, it is essential to structure the social studies curriculum within the framework of three organizational components: content, processes, and values.

Content

Scope and Sequence. Given the domain of social studies, the study of people, there is far more content than can be presented in the seven elementary grades. Therefore, anyone planning a social studies curriculum must design a scope and sequence. A *scope and sequence* is an outline of the content studied at each grade level. *Scope* refers to the topics covered, *sequence* to the order of their presentation. The scope and sequence of any curriculum is organized around grade levels. The topics chosen and the concepts related to those topics are dependent on the developmental level of students. Thus, simpler concepts are usually chosen for earlier grade levels. For the purposes of this textbook, I provide lesson examples for Grades K–6, a more traditional breakout of grades.

One scope and sequence has dominated elementary social studies: the *expanding environments* approach (also called *expanding communities* or *expanding horizons*). Some authorities question when this framework was first implemented; social studies programs from as far back as 1900 in some ways resemble it (LeRiche, 1987). Paul Hanna (1963, 1987a, 1956/1987b) first advocated it as a distinct theory in 1956. The essence of expanding environments is that children first should learn about what is nearest to them and then, as they grow older, about people and places that are progressively more remote. A good example is the 1989 framework adopted by the Virginia State Department of Education:

Kindergarten: Self, Family, School
First Grade: Family and School
Second Grade: Neighborhood and Community
Third Grade: Our Community and Other Communities
Fourth Grade: Virginia Studies
Fifth Grade: United States History
Sixth Grade: World Studies

The expanding environments scope and sequence has been criticized for its lack of substance in the primary grades and for its too narrow scope (Akenson, 1989; Larkins & Hawkins, 1990). Young children need to learn about the many cultural groups in the United States and around the world. Devoting four grades to family, school, and community provides children with too limited a view. Certainly, in a time of increased cultural diversity in the United States and of interdependence internationally, the expanding environments concept needs to include cross-cultural and global perspectives whenever possible. The *Social Studies Framework* of the Gwinnett County, Georgia, Public Schools is an example of an innovative, internationalized scope and sequence (Blankenship, 1994). An outline of the framework is included in Table 1.2.

The expanded environments concept, however, remains a strong influence on curriculum planners. Alternative outlines, while emphasizing other themes and presenting new topics, generally reflect the self–family–school–neighborhood–community–state–nation–world sequence of expanding environments. For example, the influential California *History-Social Science Framework* (California Department of Education, 1987) introduced a few different topics in the primary grades and redefined the historical focus in the upper grades. An ad hoc committee of the NCSS

Table 1.2 Social Studies Scope and Sequence: Three Perspectives

	NCSS Ad Hoc Committee 1989	California 1987	Gwinnett County 1994
Kindergarten	Awareness of self in a social setting	Learning and working now and long ago	Discovering our world
Grade 1	Individual in primary social groups: School and family life	A child's place in time and space (social skills, geography of neighborhood, folktales)	Exploring our world: The Americas and Antarctica
Grade 2	Meeting basic needs of nearby social groups: The neighborhood	People who make a difference (suppliers of food, family history, biographies)	Exploring our world: Europe, Asia, Africa, Oceania/Australia
Grade 3	Sharing earth space with others: The community	Continuity and change (local history, U.S. history through biography and folklore)	Civilizations long ago and far away
Grade 4	Human life in varied environments: The region	California history and geography	Our nation: New beginnings
Grade 5	The people of the Americas: The United States and its neighbors	United States history (to about 1850)	Our nation: New frontiers
Grade 6	People and cultures: Eastern hemisphere and Latin America	World history: Ancient civilizations (to about A.D. 500)	International perspectives: Europe, the Americas, Oceania

produced an outline that is consistent with expanded environments although different in the way each grade level's topic is approached (National Council for the Social Studies Task Force on Scope and Sequence, 1989). Table 1.2 compares the scope and sequence outlines of the NCSS Ad Hoc Committee, the California Department of Education, and the Gwinnett County Public Schools.

Scope-and-sequence outlines can be found in several places. Curriculum frameworks prepared by state departments of education have them, as do school district curriculum guides (which typically reflect the state framework). Each series of social studies textbooks has one. Finally, curriculum theorists and committees from organizations like the NCSS produce scope-and-sequence outlines. As teachers, we are expected to follow the scope and sequence in our school district curriculum guide. We and our students should have the freedom to pursue topics of interest, however, both within the context of the grade-level curriculum and beyond it. For example, suppose a third-grade class is studying community workers. If a child shows a keen interest in firefighters, then she should be encouraged to complete unique activities relating to fighting fires while other children do other things.

Here's one other point related to scope and sequence: The elementary school is the ideal place for us as teachers to plan cross-curricular units of instruction. These units combine one or more of the following: social studies, science, mathematics, literature, language arts, the performing arts, and the visual arts. Two factors brought renewed interest in cross-curricular units of instruction during the 1980s: (a) the whole language philosophy of language arts (Vacca & Rasinski, 1992) and (b) the reorganization of junior high schools into middle schools, where sixth and seventh graders frequently are taught in "humanities blocks," 2-hour periods with an integrated curriculum of social studies and language arts (Kellough, 1995; K. A. Young, 1994).

Concepts, Generalizations, and Facts. A scope and sequence defines what is to be covered, but the large question remains: What specific content are students expected to acquire? If fourth graders study their state, what should they learn about their state? The content that students learn consists of concepts, generalizations, and facts. This three-level categorization of the content component of social studies is based on the work of Hilda Taba (Frankel, 1992; Taba, 1967). Note that other authorities in the social studies offer different definitions for generalizations and concepts. Here, though, I use Taba's system:

- *Concepts* are ideas. They may be stated in a variety of ways. They tend to be broad and somewhat fuzzy. Conflict, justice, and family are all concepts. Perhaps the easiest way to think of concepts is as the big ideas we want children to understand.
- *Generalizations* are content-specific statements. They are more specific than concepts and are based on the factual content of the social studies curriculum.
- *Facts* support concepts and generalizations.

It is essential that we understand the relationship among concepts, generalizations, and facts. Children learn facts so that they can make generalizations. Several generalizations, when understood in concert, explain a concept. Generalizations and concepts enable children to make sense of what they study; facts, if unconnected to larger ideas, are of little value. Taba (1967) points out that the purpose of teaching facts "is to explain, illustrate, and develop main ideas" (p. 19). Figure 1.1 shows the hierarchical relationship among concepts, generalizations, and facts for one part of a third-grade social studies curriculum.

Some social studies concepts are relatively easy to understand while others are more difficult. Effective teachers provide assistance to those students who need it.

Processes

In addition to teaching children concepts, generalizations, and facts, social studies programs should improve children's ability in several processes. A *process* involves doing; it usually can be stated in a single word ending with *-ing*. National standards,

Figure 1.1 Concepts, Generalizations, and Facts for "Coming to Our City" in a Third-Grade Curriculum

Concept: Movement (A geographic concept—that people, products, and ideas move across political and natural borders.)

Generalization: People have come to our city throughout its history.

Facts:
▶ In about A.D. 1000, Native Americans first settled in what was to become our city.
▶ In 1792, the Franciscan missionaries built a mission near our city.
▶ During the 10 years after World War II (1945–1955), the population of our city doubled, from 40,000 to 80,000 people.
▶ From 1975 to 1990, 9,500 immigrants from Southeast Asia moved to our city.

state frameworks, district curriculum guides, and textbooks all list the processes that children should undertake as they learn the content of the curriculum. The processes related to social studies can be categorized as follows:

- *Inquiry processes,* in which children formulate questions, gather data, analyze what they have found, and share what they learned
- *Thinking processes,* in which children develop the ability to apply, analyze, synthesize, and evaluate information
- *Language arts processes,* especially as they relate to the social science disciplines, as children read, write, speak, and listen
- *Visual and performing arts processes,* which are of two kinds, as children learn to *appreciate* the arts and learn to *use* the arts for expression
- *Technology processes,* in which children manipulate computer-based resources
- *Participation processes,* as children express personal views, work cooperatively with others toward common goals, and become active citizens

Values

Content is the *what* of social studies; processes are the *how-to*. That's not all there is to social studies. Recall from the definitions in the first part of this chapter that an important part of social studies is teaching values. The NCSS Task Force on Scope and Sequence (1989) provides this definition of *values:*

> Values constitute the standards or criteria against which individual behavior and group behavior are judged. Beliefs represent commitments to those values. (p. 378)

Honesty, for example, is a value. If we are honest, then we will adopt a certain way of living and expect others to behave in a way that reflects that value. The set of values that social studies emphasizes is *civic values,* beliefs that lead to active citizenship. It is not enough that children acquire content and become skillful in a variety of processes. Children should *use* what they know to make their families, school, community, state, nation, and world a better place. This part of the elementary curriculum has existed since Colonial times and is fundamental to public schooling in a democratic society. Democracies must have citizens who are both knowledgeable and active. Other than civic values, social studies should teach children to value themselves by nurturing positive self-concepts. Along with the rest of the elementary curriculum, social studies programs should help children adopt healthy values toward school and learning (National Council for the Social Studies Task Force on Early Childhood/Elementary Social Studies, 1989).

It should be stressed from the beginning, however, that values education should not be a process of indoctrination. Rather, children should adopt civic values because they understand the importance of them in a free society. As children learn to treasure our democratic system, they must concurrently learn of the differences in all aspects of life in a democratic society. In other words, diversity is inevitable in a democracy. The values component of the social studies curriculum can be difficult to teach, but we should not shy away from it. Engle and Ochoa (1988) state it nicely:

> It is much easier and more straightforward to ask what are the facts than to ask what value or values should we subscribe to in a given instance. Despite the difficulty, a social studies program that neglects to deal with value problems stops far short of teaching students how to think intelligently about the real world. (p. 120)

Following is a lesson that has objectives from each component of the social studies curriculum: content, processes, values.

LESSON PLAN

Kindergarten: Cooperation and *A Chair for My Mother*

Overview: This is a lesson for kindergarten. It is part of a unit titled "Happy Together—Family and Friends." It is planned for 25 children.

Resources and Materials: (a) one copy of *A Chair for My Mother* by Vera B. Williams, (b) paint and paper for bulletin board illustrations, (c) 25 sheets of primary-level drawing/writing paper, (d) chart paper and marker.

Content Objectives: Children will see how members of a family and their friends help each other in a time of need. They will consider how they can cooperate in our classroom. They will build their understanding of the concepts of cooperation and family. One theme in the national social studies standards is Individuals, Groups, and Institutions. One performance expectation for the early grades is that children can "show how groups and institutions work to meet individual needs and promote the common good, and identify examples of where they fail to do so" (NCSS, 1994, p. 38).

Process Objectives: Children will (a) *listen* to the book read aloud, (b) *respond* orally to the teacher's questions, (c) *identify* how several characters help Rosa and her family, and (e) complete one of three postreading optional activities.

Values Objectives: Children acquire the value Consideration for Others, that we should help people who have suffered from something unexpected.

Teaching Sequence:

1. Before the lesson begins, be sure all materials and resources are ready; on the chalkboard, write the names of the following characters: Rosa, Grandmother, Aunt Ida and Uncle Sandy, Neighbors.

2. On a sheet of chart paper, write the following postreading options: (a) Go with Ms. Sanchez (the instructional aide). Draw pictures for *A Chair for My Mother* section of "Our Favorite Books" bulletin board. (b) Go to your seat. Draw and write anything you want about *A Chair for My Mother.* (c) Stay with Mr. Wong (the teacher). Talk about what makes working together difficult and what makes it easy.

3. Ask children to sit on the carpet. Read aloud *A Chair for My Mother.*

4. Ask children whether they would like to say anything about the book (use what children say as a basis for further discussion).

5. Discuss with children how Rosa, Grandmother, Aunt Ida and Uncle Sandy, and the neighbors helped. Refer back to illustrations in the book.

6. Lead a discussion group on how class members can work together and help each other. Begin by listing all the classroom chores that are easier to complete if members of the class work together. Ask what things other than classroom tasks members of the class can do for each other (many things should come to mind, such as sharing supplies, cheering up classmates who are sad). Record the children's ideas on a sheet of chart paper.

7. Explain options to the class (see #2 above).

8. Be sure all children are working with Ms. Sanchez, in their seats, or still on the carpet.

9. Later, bring the group together. Have children share their pictures, dictated narratives, and the results of the discussion.

Evaluation: At the kindergarten level, evaluation is often informal. The pictures children draw and the texts they write or dictate can be saved in student portfolios.

Effective Teaching in Today's Diverse Classroom: Mr. Wong's class included several Spanish-speaking English language learners. These children spoke some English. The excellent illustrations in the book Mr. Wong read to the class allowed the English language learners to understand the story even though they did not know the meaning of every word in the story's text. Like most kindergarten teachers, Mr. Wong modified his speech when talking to his 5-year-olds. He slowed down, repeated things, and avoided big words. This, too, helped the English language learners understand what he was saying. If the class had included English language learners who spoke almost no English, then the activity would need the assistance of a bilingual person (the teacher, an instructional aide, a parent volunteer, an older student). Each of the following adjustments could be added: (a) Someone should explain the plot of the story in the native language of the English language learners (in this case, Spanish), and (2) the postreading discussion could be conducted in the English language learners' native language. We want children to understand the concept of cooperation and to see its importance in the story and in the classroom. To achieve this objective, it might be necessary to conduct all or part of the lesson in a language other than English.

No one can tell what the future will bring for social studies. It seems safe to say that debates about both curricular and instructional issues will be ongoing. As elementary schoolteachers, we will become a part of the history of social studies as we guide our students to become active citizens.

SUMMARY OF KEY POINTS

▶ Social studies is integrated and interdisciplinary in that ideas and information come from many fields of study.
▶ Social studies goes beyond the textbook and rote memorization of facts.
▶ Social studies adopts the best ideas from the period of Progressive Education, including hands-on experiences, student selection of activities, thematic units, and the integration of social studies with the arts.
▶ Social studies continues the innovations of the New Social Studies, such as teaching children fundamental concepts of the social sciences through inquiry learning.
▶ National standards defining what children should know and be able to do have been written for social studies, civics and government, economics, geography, and history. Although in the future these standards may define the social studies curriculum, at this point they are merely advisory.
▶ Social studies content includes concepts, generalizations, and facts.
▶ Social studies processes fall into the following categories: inquiry, thinking, language arts, visual arts, performing arts, technology, and participatory.
▶ Social studies emphasizes acquisition of civic values, the set of beliefs that leads to active citizenship.

FOR FURTHER READING

General Sources of Information on Social Studies

▶ The technology revolution is changing many things, including how you can find information on the topics presented in this book. The Internet already has far too many Web sites to mention. Three of note: *http://www.ncss.org* (the address of the NCSS), *http://execpc.com/~dboals/boals.html* ("History/ Social Studies Web Site for K–12 Teachers"), and *http://score.rims.k12.ca.us* ("Schools of California Online Resources for Education").

- Many special issues of journals have been devoted to articles on technology and social studies. See, for example, the March 1997 and March 1998 issues of *Social Education* (Simpson, 1997, 1998).
- Of course, the best way to find more "traditional" sources of information on topics in education is through the ERIC system (Educational Resources Information Center of the U.S. Department of Education). The process is really easy because ERIC's *Current Index to Journals in Education* (CIJE) and *Resources in Education* (RIE) are both on CD-ROM. The computer disc is easy to use and saves a great deal of time.
- Many journals focus on social studies. Most of my references are from three journals: *Social Education, Social Studies and the Young Learner,* and *The Social Studies*.
- If you want to get acquainted with research on social studies, start with the 660-page *Handbook of Research on Social Studies Teaching and Learning* (Shaver, 1991). Another book with essays reviewing research is *Elementary School Social Studies: Research as a Guide to Practice* (Atwood, 1991).

Definitions of Social Studies

- Interested in reading more definitions of social studies? A good book, though dated, is *Defining the Social Studies* (J. Barr et al., 1977). Engle and Ochoa (1988) provide an excellent critique of the confusion over social studies definitions in chapter 7 of their book.

Social Studies: A History

- We can all learn a great deal by exploring classrooms of the past. Lawrence Cremin's *The Transformation of the School* (1961) is about Progressive Education and is fascinating reading. *How Teachers Taught* (Cuban, 1984) is another excellent book with a general focus. On social studies specifically, I suggest Cuban (1991), Hertzberg (1981), Jenness (1990), and Saxe (1991). For a closer look at social studies in Dewey's laboratory school, see Dewey (1897/1976) and Mayhew and Edwards (1936). A great deal has been written about MACOS. Inkpen (1974) compiled a bibliography. See, too, Dow (1976, 1991), Herlihy (1974), and Cort and Peskowitz (1977).

Social Studies: The Curriculum

- Most topics mentioned here are covered elsewhere in this book, so refer to the "For Further Reading" sections in the relevant chapters. For more on scope and sequence, see the chapter in the *Handbook of Research on Social Studies Teaching and Learning* by W. W. Joyce, Little, and Wronski (1991). For a scope and sequence with a more global perspective than that provided by the expanding environments approach, see Kniep (1989). For a survey of what scope and sequences school districts were adopting more than a decade ago, see Herman (1988).

Instructional Activities

▶ For more picture books with the theme of Working Together With Family and Friends, take a look at chapter 5 of *Multicultural Literature, Multicultural Teaching* (Zarrillo, 1994). Flouris (1988) provides a model instructional unit on ancient Greece.

Photographs of the Parthenon on the Internet

▶ Mrs. Winslow checked the "History/Social Studies Web Site for K–12 Teachers" (*http://execpc.com/~dboals/boals.html*). Photographs of the Parthenon were found by clicking on "European History Sources," "Ancient and Classical," "Urban History—#13 Ancient City of Athens." This excellent photograph archive is maintained by Indiana University.

Chapter 2

Children, Diversity, and Learning: Understanding Your Students

Matt Marcella's second-grade class reflected the diversity of his community. Twelve children were Hispanic, five were Vietnamese American, four were African American, and nine were European American. Eight children were immigrants to the United States. Mr. Marcella wanted to start the year with a social studies unit that incorporated the diversity of his students and at the same time introduced the children to each other. He planned a unit called "Families and Friends." During the unit, the children listened while he read picture books about friendship and families. The children's favorites were *Abuela,* Arthur Dorros's charming fantasy about a Latina girl and her grandmother who fly above New York; *Peter's Chair,* Ezra Jack Keats's story about an African American boy who runs away from home because of the arrival of his new sister; and *The Lost Lake,* Allen Say's beautifully illustrated tale about a Japanese American father and son who go backpacking.

Mr. Marcella's class sang songs about families and friendship. His favorite was "Five People in My Family," a song he had learned when he was a boy (from the *Sesame Street Song Book,* Raposo & Moss, 1971). The children liked "I Live in the City," by Malvina Reynolds, a song about how people of many colors build a city. Throughout the unit, the children worked in small groups to define friendship, focusing on a list of things friends do for their friends. During the unit, Mr. Marcella gave the children many opportunities to write about their families, their feelings, and their friends. Then, because Mr. Marcella knew that autobiographies would help the children appreciate the diverse backgrounds of their classmates, he made the creating of autobiographies a culminating activity. Some children were able to bring photographs from home to illustrate their books; others drew pictures. Mr. Marcella helped each student organize her or his book around such topics as celebrating holidays, starting school, moving to a new apartment, and enjoying summer vacations. First, the children drew pictures or used their photographs to help recall details. Then, they wrote descriptive sentences that related what was happening in their photographs. Although most children were able to write a few sentences about each illustrated event, some needed to dictate their text, and three wrote in Spanish. When completed, the autobiographies were shared with the whole group as each child, alone or with Mr. Marcella's help, read his or her book aloud.

▲   ▲   ▲

In this chapter, you will read about:

- ▶ Constructivism, a learning theory that encourages teachers to guide students into constructing their own meaning from daily lessons
- ▶ The zone of proximal development, a theoretical perspective that identifies the importance of social interaction for learning
- ▶ The ideas of Stephen Krashen and James Cummins on linguistic diversity and language acquisition, important to lesson planning for students acquiring English as a second language
- ▶ The advantages of planning social studies programs that meet the needs of culturally diverse classrooms

Acknowledging Student Differences

Like Mr. Marcella, we teach social studies in the context of an increasingly diverse society. We need to adapt our teaching to fit the backgrounds, abilities, interests, and needs of our students. In fact, our success as teachers depends on our ability to plan an instructional program that accounts for the diversity of our students. This is a tall order, so let's take a look at how students in our classrooms might differ.

Dictionary definitions of *diversity* use words like "different," "varied," or "diversified," and these are good descriptors of the students we teach. Capitalizing on the diversity of our students will enhance our joy of teaching. Every year, we will work with a group of different individuals, each with unique challenges and gifts, so each class we teach will be delightfully different.

How will our students differ? Students in all elementary school classrooms vary in a number of ways. Both girls and boys will be assigned to our rooms, and some will be older (or younger) than most of their classmates. Although students usually are assigned to classes by age, a variety of factors can result in a group with significant age differences, and the "higher" the grade we teach (e.g., fourth, fifth, sixth), the greater the span between our oldest and youngest students. Some of our students will be well adjusted, confident, and happy. Others, however, will struggle with personal issues and the effects of difficult past experiences. Most public elementary schools reflect the concept of the neighborhood school, and the level of homogeneity in family income status among students will be high. There is a good chance, however, that some of our students will be significantly more affluent (or impoverished) than their classmates.

Students will differ widely in their native talents and abilities, with variation in all areas of mental and physical performance. If we are good teachers, we will be able to develop instructional programs that allow each student to develop the full limit of his or her ability. Public Law 94–142, the Education for All Handicapped Children Act of 1975 (now called the Individuals with Disabilities Education Act [IDEA]), established the requirements for children with special needs in public schools. Among these requirements is that each child be placed in his or her "least restrictive environment." This requires schools to educate students with disabilities with nondisabled students, to the maximum extent appropriate for the student with disabilities (Turnbull, Turnbull, Shank, & Leal, 1999). Thus, we might teach children with exceptionalities for part or all of the school day. By the time they reach our classrooms, our students will have clearly defined tastes, interests, and preferences. Without any special effort on our part, many of our students will be interested in the topics presented in social studies. Others, though, only will become engaged if the activities we plan and the resources we select are exciting and challenging.

An ever-increasing percentage of students acquire first a language other than English. These students will face the challenge of learning social studies content, mastering social studies processes, and adopting social studies values *at the same time* they are learning to read, write, speak, and listen in English. The United States is a pluralistic society. Our cultural identity plays a primary role in shaping our values and behaviors. Research shows important differences in the ways children of different cultural groups communicate, interact, and learn. This chapter focuses on these two aspects of diversity—language and culture. Before we look at how language and culture affect the way children learn, it would be a good idea to examine two perspectives on how all people learn.

How People Learn: Two Perspectives

Our social studies teaching should be consistent with how children learn. It would simplify things if psychology could offer us a single, universally accepted theory on what takes place when learning occurs. This cannot be done, however, as there are many theoretical positions on how people learn. Two perspectives seem to provide practical perspectives for us as we plan elementary social studies lessons.

Constructivism

One learning theory with current popularity is *constructivism* (Scheurman & Yell, 1998; Steffe & Gale, 1995). Constructivists argue that learning is an active process, that knowledge is acquired as learners interact with the environment and modify what they already know. When children encounter new information, ideas, and things, they relate it to the knowledge they have. Here are four useful summaries of constructivism:

> Knowledge is something that the learner must construct for and by himself. There is no alternative. Discovery, reinvention, or active reconstruction is necessary. (Blais, 1988, p. 3)

> Constructivists posit that learning is a process whereby new meanings are created (constructed) by the learner within the context of her or his current knowledge. (Poplin, 1988, p. 404)

> Constructivism refers to a set of related theories that deal with nature of knowledge. The common denominator linking these theories is a belief that knowledge is created by people and influenced by their values and culture. (Scheurman, 1998, p. 6)

> Students develop new understandings through a process of active construction. They do not passively receive or copy curriculum content: they actively process it by relating it to what they already know (or think they know) about the topic. (NCSS Task Force on Standards for Teaching and Learning in the Social Studies, 1993, p. 219)

Jean Piaget provided a description of how this "active construction" of knowledge takes place. Piaget received his academic training as a zoologist and described learning in biological terms. People, like all animals, strive to maintain harmony with their environment. It is a challenge to achieve this balance, or *equilibrium*. It is accomplished through the mental process of *equilibration,* which is how people learn (Piaget & Inhelder, 1969; Vuyk, 1981). It works like this:

When something new is introduced to us, we are temporarily placed in a state of *disequilibrium*. To regain our balance, we rely on the related functions of *assimilation* and *accommodation*. Assimilation involves an attempt to make new phenomena (ideas, words, objects) fit the patterns of knowledge we already have. If new knowledge does not readily fit in with what we already know, we accommodate and modify our patterns to fit the new phenomenon. These functions occur together, working in concert, and as they do, we learn.

For example, consider how Sheila, a fifth grader, constructed an understanding of the concept of slavery. Sheila was presented with images of slavery in a film. She then read *To Be a Slave* (Lester, 1968), which comprises autobiographical accounts of the capture, transport, sale, and daily life of enslaved people. Sheila viewed the film and read the book during the first part of a fifth-grade unit on slavery. This new information threw Sheila into disequilibrium. Before the unit, she had a vague idea of the meaning of slavery and was aware that, at some time in the past, African Americans were slaves in the United States. She had a small, incomplete mental file on slavery (psychologists call these files *schemata* [sing., *schema*]). These classroom activities on slavery introduced her to information that was challenging and disquieting.

At first, Sheila may have attempted to assimilate what she saw and read. She may have tried to make the facts of slavery fit into other schemata, like what she knew about travel on boats and work on a farm. That wouldn't work because the slave experience was much more dreadful than the experiences of people who were not enslaved. So, she mentally accommodated the new information. Sheila modified her schema on slavery so that her mental file was significantly transformed. It became larger and more accurate. She has learned, and what she has learned is more than a random set of facts. Her slavery schema, or mental file, now includes a richer understanding of a concept (slavery), several generalizations (e.g., enslaved people were a commodity, no different from cotton or cattle), and many facts (e.g., the first African slaves were brought to Virginia in 1619). Keep in mind that Sheila's conceptual understanding of slavery is not complete. In subsequent grades, she will learn about slavery in ancient Greece and Rome, and as she grows older, she will also learn more about slavery in the United States.

This pattern is true for all learners: Concepts become more complete over time. Learning is an evolutionary process, and according to constructivist theory, all growth is the result of something new being added to a person's prior knowledge.

Perhaps the two principles stated below will clarify the implications of constructivism:

1. *Learning is an individualized process.* We learn in "a manner that allows us to individually select and determine what is to be learned" (Poplin, 1988, p. 406). Different children learn different things from the same experience. This occurs because what we learn depends on what we know and what we consider interesting. Imagine the individual differences during a third-grade unit on boats. Some children will have traveled on several types of boats, whereas others will have no firsthand experience with boats at all. To state it another way, differences will exist in the depth of conceptual knowledge children have about boats. For the concept of boats, some children will have vague understandings, whereas some of their classmates will have more complete knowledge. As the unit progresses, differences will exist in the depth of conceptual knowledge each child possesses about boats. At the same time, some children will be fascinated by the topic, others will be mildly interested, and a few will be bored (if the unit is designed and implemented with skill and enthusiasm, they won't *stay* bored). Although we can be sure that almost all the children will learn some of the same things, differences in interest and ability will mean that each child will learn unique things from the unit.

2. *To learn, children must be active.* As one teacher told me, "Children must do lots of things that end with *-ing*." To acquire facts, generalizations, and concepts, children must be reading, writing, speaking, listening, gathering, analyzing, sharing, producing, acting, singing, dancing, and "arting" (drawing, painting, sculpting). Learning is a matter of "personal experiencing" (Douglass, 1989, p. 40). To sum it up, constructivist learning theory tells us that two factors will determine how much children learn during a social studies unit of instruction: (a) what they already know and (b) the quality of their involvement in the unit's activities. All children require new information that is close to what they know, and all children need experiences that demand engaging physical and mental activity.

Vygotsky's Zone of Proximal Development

Another important perspective on learning, especially for teachers, was provided by Lev Vygotsky (1934/1962, 1935–66/1978), a Russian psychologist. Vygotsky was one of the first psychologists to understand the importance of social activity in learning. He believed that a gap exists between what children can do independently and what they can do if they have help. In his words, "with assistance every child can do more than he can do by himself" (1934/1962, p. 103). Vygotsky described a *zone of proximal development* (ZPD): "It is the distance between the actual development level as determined by independent problem solving and the level of potential development as determined through problem solving under adult guidance or in collaboration with more capable peers" (1935–66/1978, p. 86).

In the 21st century, the student population in our classrooms will be increasingly diverse. Small-group work gives children from different cultural groups the opportunity to develop positive attitudes towards each other.

Like most educational psychologists who accept the challenge of dealing with complex topics, Vygotsky is difficult to understand. All children can do school-related tasks with help that they cannot do on their own. Vygotsky argued that when children interact with other people and work in cooperation with them, "a variety of internal developmental processes" begin to operate that do not engage when children work independently (1935–66/1978, p. 90). When children work with others, they see things differently. New mental and physical processes, both of which might take years for children to master on their own, are "awakened." Through collaboration, the children enter their Zones of Proximal Development. Certain learning processes occur in the ZPD, and after they are done repeatedly, the children can do them on their own.

All of us have the potential to learn more if we are assisted by others. Yes, some things we can learn on our own without much help. Yes, some things beyond our grasp we will not learn even if we have a great deal of help. But between what we can learn by ourselves and what is "over our heads" lies the ZPD. There, with the help of others, we can realize our full potential as learners. Fifty years before co-operative learning became popular in elementary classrooms, Vygotsky provided a sound theoretical foundation for it. One of the best examples of the ZPD occurs during small-group work. Think how many times you have participated in a group discussion during which someone said something that triggered in you a sudden understanding of something new or pinpointed a solution to a previously unsolvable problem. It is as if someone had turned on the lights, the change in your perception was that great. This will happen when we work with students in our classes; they will say something like, "Oh, yeah!" "Now I get it!" or, "OK, I can do it now." I hope your course instructor allows you to discuss the ideas in this book in a group. If so, your classmates will help you enter a personal ZPD!

Linguistic Diversity

Constructivism and the zone of proximal development provide an explanation of how all people learn. Our social studies teaching should be consistent with both perspectives. Other factors, however, make learning a process that differs from child to child. Language and culture are two such factors; they are strong influences on how children learn, and they contribute significantly to the differences in how our students go about learning what we teach them. First, let's look at the challenge children face when they are learning social studies at the same time they are learning English as a second language.

English Language Learners

Students with native languages other than English may be called "language minority students." Those language minority students who have not achieved a level of English language proficiency (reading, writing, and speaking) comparable to a monolingual student of the same age have been classified as "limited English proficient" (LEP). Remember, not all language minority students have LEP status; some will come to our classrooms fully bilingual. They will astound us with their ability to use their native language and English. There will be a wide range of English competency among our LEP students: Some will have virtually no English, whereas others will be on the threshold of becoming fluent English proficient (FEP). The level of each student's English proficiency will be a key factor in our designing appropriate social studies instruction.

I find the label *limited*-English proficient unfortunate and misleading because all of us grow as language users over a lifetime. The extent of our language proficiency is without limits, so all of us are to some degree "limited." The use of *limited,* with its negative connotation, is unfair to students who are classified as LEP. I prefer the descriptor "English language learners" to describe students of limited English proficiency, and I use it instead of "limited-English proficient" in this book.

The number of English language learners in U.S. schools has increased dramatically in the last 20 years. In 2000, more than 3.5 million English language learners were attending public schools in the United States. From 1980 to 1990, Hispanic en-rollments increased 48%, whereas Asian American enrollments increased 85% (Lara, 1994). The 1990 census revealed soaring numbers of Americans who speak languages other than English. More than 17 million people living in the United States speak Spanish ("Language Mirrors Immigration," 1993). Since 1960, the pattern of immigra-tion has shifted from immigrants from Europe to immigrants from Asia and the Spanish-speaking Americas. Thus, many schools have significant populations of Korean-speaking, Vietnamese-speaking, and Khmer-speaking English language learners (Khmer is the language of Cambodia).

Second Language Acquisition and Learning in Social Studies

The ideas of Stephen Krashen and James Cummins provide a theoretical framework for effective social studies teaching with English language learners.

Krashen: Second Language Acquisition. Stephen Krashen is a linguist who has developed a model of second language acquisition that has been adopted widely in the United States by second language teachers (1981, 1982, 1985, 1986; Krashen & Biber, 1988; Krashen & Terrell, 1983). Although his ideas are controversial among linguists, his perspectives are consistent with the principles of constructivism and have helped teachers be more effective in teaching their English language learners (McLaughlin, 1987). There is no need in a book about social studies teaching and learning to explore all of Krashen's theory of second language acquisition, but two of his ideas are essential: (a) the concept of *comprehensible input* and (2) the impact of the *affective filter*.

Krashen believes that second languages are acquired when persons are exposed to *comprehensible input in a low-anxiety environment*. We acquire a second language by listening to spoken language and reading written language that is slightly more advanced than what we know. The goal of English-speaking teach-ers is to make the English understandable, and this requires teachers to modify what they say and how they say it. Also, English language learners should read materials with English words, phrases, and ideas that are just slightly beyond what they know. If we want English language learners to understand what we say and at the same time acquire English, then our goal must be to provide comprehensible input.

For example, a teacher working with English language learners during a social studies lesson will repeat certain key words and phrases, slow his or her speech, and refrain from using difficult vocabulary not essential in the lesson. Although the teacher's speech will be simplified, it will not change to the point where it seems ar-tificial. The key, of course, is for the teacher to communicate with the students. Social studies textbooks are often not comprehensible input for English language learners. So, we as teachers may read the text aloud to students or present the material through charts and graphs, illustrations, or films. Some of us rewrite important sections of the textbook in simplified English so that our English language learners have a version to read that they can understand.

Krashen argues that an *affective filter* can make it difficult for students to acquire a second language. The affective filter is an attitude or feeling that works as a mental block. Anxiety, fear, and lack of motivation can operate as affective filters. To put it simply, if we want to make it difficult for students to understand something, scare them or bore them. Even if we or the students are providing comprehensible input, the input might not get through if a student is worried, upset, frightened, or disinterested. Worry, anxiety, fear, and boredom work as filters, and the input we so carefully offered is wasted. Consider the following examples: In one classroom, most of the social studies "talk" is among students working in small groups. These conversations are among peers, and there are no affective filters; all the comprehensible input an English language learner hears will "get through." In another classroom, in contrast, the teacher asks questions from the textbook and randomly calls on students to answer. The affective filter will be "thick" as the fear of being called on blocks the available comprehensible input. The implication for social studies teaching with English language learners is quite clear: Our teaching must provide comprehensible input in a situation where students' "affective filters are low enough to allow the input in" (Krashen, 1986, p. 62).

Cummins: Dimensions of Language Proficiency. Canadian linguist James Cummins has had an immense influence on educators in the United States (1979, 1986a, 1986b, 1989, 1992). As with Krashen, our discussion of Cummins's ideas must be selective. Most significant to the teaching of social studies is Cummins's description of the *dimensions of language proficiency*. His discussion of "cognitive demand" and "contextual support" provides us with a useful framework for planning effective lessons for all students, particularly for students whose first language is not English.

Cummins has noted that ability to use language has "dimensions"; that is, there are differences between the language people use in social situations and the language required in school settings. Cummins has used the descriptors "BICS" (**b**asic **i**nterpersonal **c**ommunication **s**kills) and "CALP" (**c**ognitive **a**cademic **l**anguage **p**roficiency). *BICS* refers to the speaking and listening we do in casual, interpersonal settings. In a situation where BICS are used, we usually support what we are saying with familiar gestures and refer to objects that both speaker and listener can see and touch (e.g., a conversation about a birthday gift). Also, we usually are talking about an experience we have shared with the persons who are listening (e.g., discussing a meal we have shared). The conversations students have on the playground are good examples of basic interpersonal communication. *CALP*, in contrast, refers to the language, usually processed by reading and writing, demanded by difficult school assignments. Students who have CALP can read and understand their social studies textbook, retrieve information from an encyclopedia, write essays about complex political issues, and complete standardized tests.

Cummins argues that educators frequently make judgments about a person's ability to use a language solely on his or her ability to communicate with BICS. Even though many English language learners can speak English effectively on the playground or in a store, they cannot use English fluently enough to do challenging social studies or science activities.

Cummins has expanded on the distinction between BICS and CALP, noting that any system that has only two categories "inevitably oversimplifies reality" (1992, p. 17). He has pointed out the two key factors in completing any task that requires the use of language—cognitive demand and contextual support. *Cognitive demand* is the level of thinking a person must do to complete a task. Cognitively *undemanding* tasks include writing a description of a new pair of shoes, asking to borrow a pair of scissors, or reading the television program listings in the Entertainment Section of a newspaper. At the other end of the continuum are cognitively *demanding* tasks, which require complex thinking, such as discussing the relative merits of capitalism and socialism, reading and understanding information about the Russian monetary system, or writing an essay on comprehensive health care. In social studies, students should be asked to complete tasks at all points along the cognitive demand continuum, from the most facile to the most difficult.

Contextual support is the level of help a person has to complete a task. Many language tasks have a great deal of contextual support. The person performing the task can ask questions, seek help from other people, and refer to illustrations or real objects. At the other end of the continuum are tasks for which the person who is to perform them has little, if any, support. Any task, regardless of its cognitive demand, can have either a great deal of contextual support or very little, depending on how teachers structure the situation. For example, a group of students are asked to compare and contrast a Mohawk long house and a Sioux tipi. If the students can work together to write their answer, if they can ask the teacher for help, if they have several accurate illustrations to examine, then the task has a high level of contextual support. In contrast, if students must work individually, are given 15 minutes to write their answers, and are not permitted to ask anyone for help, then there is no contextual support to complete the task.

Cummins developed a diagram to help educators understand the roles of cognitive demand and contextual support in school-related tasks (1986b, 1992). The diagram, consisting of four quadrants, classifies the way language is used. My students have found it easier to understand and apply these concepts if they are presented in a four-level chart. Figure 2.1 places social studies activities in four categories, explains the level of cognitive demand and contextual support in each of the categories, and provides an example in each category of an activity from a third-grade unit on boats (the full unit appears in chapter 10). Following are explanations of the categories.

Category 1: Activities Are Cognitively Undemanding, Completed with Contextual Support. During the instructional unit, the teacher read aloud an illustrated book

Figure 2.1 Social Studies Activities: Cognitive Demand and Contextual Support

CATEGORY 1

Activities are cognitively undemanding, completed with contextual support.

▶ The topic is simple and easily understood.

▶ Students are asked to do things that require relatively simple thinking (e.g., recalling, summarizing).

▶ Completion of the activity is supported by cooperative learning, visual aids, real things, and hands-on experience. Materials that students read or view are easy to understand.

▶ These are the "easiest" activities to complete. All students should be successful.

▶ Example from a third-grade unit on boats: Pantomime—Life on a New England fishing island.

CATEGORY 2

Activities are cognitively undemanding, completed with little, if any, contextual support.

▶ The topic is simple and easily understood.

▶ Students are asked to do things that require relatively simple thinking (e.g., recalling, summarizing).

▶ Students complete the activity individually, with little support of any kind.

▶ Even though the topic is easy and the required thinking is simple, the lack of contextual support will make it difficult for some students to be successful.

▶ Example from a third-grade unit on boats: Independent reading of picture books.

CATEGORY 3

Activities are cognitively demanding, completed with contextual support.

▶ The topic is complicated and difficult to understand.

▶ Activities in this category require complex thinking (e.g., analyzing, synthesizing, evaluating).

▶ Completion of the activity is supported by cooperative learning, visual aids, real things, and hands-on experience. Materials that students read or view are easy to understand.

▶ The topic and level of thinking will challenge students, but the contextual support will help them be successful.

▶ Example from a third-grade unit on boats: Lesson on the history of boats.

Figure 2.1 *(Continued)*

CATEGORY 4

Activities are cognitively demanding, completed with little, if any, contextual support.

▶ The topic is complicated and difficult to understand.

▶ Activities in this category require complex thinking (e.g., analyzing, synthesizing, evaluating).

▶ Students complete the activity individually, with little support of any kind.

▶ These are the most difficult activities to complete successfully.

▶ Example from a third-grade unit on boats: Student-authored encyclopedia.

---

titled *Surrounded by Sea: Life on a New England Fishing Island* (Gibbons, 1991). Before reading the book, the teacher wrote on the chalkboard some of the jobs people on the island perform: repairing sails, loading equipment, bringing in the catch, unloading the fish or shellfish for processing. The photographs in the book are excellent and make it easy for all children to see what is involved in each task. Also, the teacher modeled each job through a slow and somewhat exaggerated pantomime. Finally, the children joined their teacher in pretending to do each job through a group pantomime experience. The teacher's objective was simple and appropriate: She wanted her students to have a basic understanding of the work the people on the island do as part of an economy based on fishing.

This activity is a good example of those falling in Category 1 because the information the children were expected to learn (the different jobs related to island fishing) was relatively simple, and the behavior expected of the children (to listen, to pantomime) was easy, fun, and performed in a group. The photographs and the modeling by the teacher provided the children with a great deal of support. If, however, the children had been expected to complete a chart, answer questions, or work independently, then the level of cognitive demand would increase and the activity would belong in Category 3.

Category 2: Activities Are Cognitively Undemanding, Completed with Little, if any, Contextual Support. Few instructional activities fall into Category 2. Here, the topic or material requires simple thinking (cognitively undemanding), and little, if any, help is provided for children (which makes it context reduced). During the unit, children read picture books independently. Each story, of course, was related to the unit's topic, boats. The stories were simple, so cognitive demand was minimal. Because the children read on their own, the level of contextual support was reduced. Storybooks, however, are not the best example of a cognitively undemanding learning activity. The least demand occurs when children read, write, or talk about their personal experiences.

Category 3: Activities Are Cognitively Demanding, Completed with Contextual Support. In Category 3, I placed a lesson the teacher presented on the history of boats, emphasizing how methods of propulsion have changed over the years (sails, oars, engines). The specific learning objective was "children will learn that although the functions of boats have remained constant, their design and capacity (e.g., speed, size) have changed radically." This was cognitively demanding material, especially because most of the third graders knew very little about boats when the unit began. So, it was important that the teacher provide contextual support for her students. Below is a description of how she designed the lesson to provide the support for her English language learners (in Cummins's words, how the activity became more "contextually embedded"):

1. Early in the unit, children participated in a field trip to a harbor to see boats in action. This gave them a "firsthand" experience. This activity provided a knowledge base for all the lessons that followed.

2. When selecting her materials, the teacher chose books with excellent illustrations: *The Book of Fantastic Boats* (Bernard, 1974), *Oars, Sails, and Steam: A Picture Book of Ships* (Tunis, 1952), and *Ships, Sailors, and the Sea* (Humble, 1991). The English language learners in this classroom would not have been able to read any of these books. It wasn't necessary, however, because the content could be presented through the illustrations.

3. The teacher made good use of maps and charts. The lesson was supported with a timeline and a map; these showed when and where the following boats were built and used: a Roman trireme (powered by sail and oar), a Haida canoe (sail and oar), "Old Ironsides" (the *Constitution,* sail), the *Great Eastern* (sail and steam engines), the *Queen Mary* (engines), and the *Nautilus* (first atomic-powered submarine).

4. During the lesson, the teacher modified the way she talked so that her presentation was comprehensible. She slowed down, watched her choice of words, and repeated certain descriptions and explanations. At no time, however, did her speech sound artificial. This modification is very important for English language learners because, without it, other materials in the lesson (illustrations, maps, charts) will be less effective.

5. At the end of the lesson, teacher and children completed a large data retrieval chart as a summary of the material that had been presented. The chart included the name of each boat in the presentation, the source of power of each boat, and when and where each boat was built. It is important to provide clear summaries of essential material for English language learners.

6. The children worked in cooperative groups to answer three questions: (a) What are the advantages of ships that have engines? (b) If a ship has oars and sails, what conditions make it difficult for the ship to move in the water? (c) Why might it be more fun to sail than to go on a boat with an

engine? It is unlikely that the English language learners could complete this task individually. To use Vygotsky's words, working in groups allowed the children to move into a "zone of proximal development."

7. After the lesson was over, the Spanish-speaking aide worked with children who needed primary language support. The aide reviewed the essential information in the lesson and answered any questions the children asked. Thinking back to Krashen's ideas for a moment, we can further understand why Categories 1 and 3 are best for English language learners. The contextual support increases the chances that students will receive comprehensible input. The chance to work together, the use of visual aids and real things, and opportunities for hands-on experiences make subject matter easier to understand. This type of contextual support also lowers the affective filter. Schoolwork in Categories 1 and 3 is less stressful, it is more pleasant, and it is where most social studies activities should fall.

Category 4: Activities Are Cognitively Demanding, Completed with Little, if any, Contextual Support. Activities that fall into Category 4 are the most difficult for children to complete successfully. Cummins claims that one reason why English language learners have difficulty in school is that we ask them to do Category 4 activities before their level of English proficiency is adequately developed. Category 4 has a high level of cognitive demand because the topic is challenging, the material is new, or the activity requires complex thinking. It is important that English language learners be confronted with this type of intellectual challenge. The problem is that, in Category 4, the task lacks contextual support. The child is left to do the most difficult type of activity with the least amount of help! In the unit on boats, some children chose to compile a small encyclopedia on boats. They wrote and illustrated several "entries," each summarizing what they knew about the entry (e.g., "submarine," "clipper," "starboard.") The task, for a third grader, was challenging because the children could not simply copy information from an encyclopedia. They had to synthesize and condense what they knew about each item to fit the restricted space available on each page of their homemade "encyclopedia." Most social studies lessons using the textbook, unless they make use of other resources, fall into Category 4 and will be frustrating experiences for second language learners.

All this adds up to a simple conclusion: Social studies activities for English language learners should have a great deal of contextual support (those that fall into Categories 1 and 3). Second language acquisition theory, especially the ideas of Krashen and Cummins, helps define appropriate social studies teaching. This type of teaching, wherein we use a variety of strategies to help support our students as they learn social studies, science, and mathematics, is called different things. The most popular descriptor is "sheltered instruction" (Chung, 1992; D. Freeman & Freeman, 1988; Echevarria & Graves, 1998; Krashen, 1985; Mohan, 1986). In California, however, the phrase "specially designed academic instruction in English" (SDAIE) is being used (Diaz-Rico & Weed, 1995). This is an emerging methodology, and many issues are yet to be resolved in teaching social studies to English language learners (M. King, Bratt, & Baer, 1992; Short, 1994).

Cultural Diversity

In addition to differences in native language, our classrooms are culturally diverse. Remember, native language and cultural identity are not synonymous. Among our Spanish-speaking students, we could have Ecuadoran Americans, Nicaraguan Americans, as well as Mexican Americans. African American and Native American children come to our schools with rich cultural identities. The challenge of educating children from many backgrounds has always been a facet of American public schooling. The fact is that schools in the United States have done a poor job of educating Native Americans, African Americans, children of poverty, and immigrant children (Beatty, Reese, Persky, & Carr, 1996; Gay, 1997; Langer, Applebee, Mullis, & Foertsch, 1990; U.S. Department of Education, 1992). All too frequently, culture and native language have been ignored, with the unfortunate results of lower achievement and high dropout rates (J. A. Banks & Banks, 1997; Garcia, 1994).

Definitions of Key Words and Descriptors

It would probably be a good idea to clarify some terms related to culture because they are used throughout this book. I prefer to use an anthropological definition of *culture:* "Culture encompasses the learned behaviors, beliefs, attitudes, values, and ideas that are characteristic of a particular society or population" (Ember & Ember, 1990, p. 17). Thus, culture is commonly shared and learned by a group of people. Remember, though, people are not members of a culture. Each person belongs to a *cultural group;* the group shares a culture.

The NCSS Task Force on Ethnic Studies, *Curriculum Guidelines for Multicultural Education* (1992) considers an *ethnic group* a special kind of cultural group. Authors of the guidelines believe that some ethnic groups are defined by different things, like religion (Jewish Americans) or national origin (Polish Americans). James Banks (1997b) believes that a "core" culture in the United States includes things almost all Americans share, such as baseball and income taxes. Thus, every American is a member of a core U.S. cultural group and an ethnic group. This description gets even more complicated because each person also identifies with other types of groups (e.g., gender: woman; social class: upper; religion: Unitarian). Finally, every individual adopts certain behaviors, beliefs, and values that are the result of personal decisions rather than of culture, gender, religion, or social class.

In this book, I use *cultural group* and always try to be absolutely clear about the identity of the group (e.g., Vietnamese Americans). I also use the term *minority groups,* which includes African Americans, Asian Americans, Hispanic Americans, and Native Americans. One other point that is tricky: I refer to those of us who are "White" or "Anglo" or "mainstream" or "majority" as European Americans. I acknowledge problems with this descriptor (Kleg, 1993). As I noted earlier in the text, the combined total of "minority" groups will constitute the majority of the K–12 student population in the United States sometime early in the 21st century. Each year, the minority population rises, both in total numbers and as a percentage of the total. For instance, 10.4 million minority students were in Grades K–12 in 1985–86; 13.7 million in 1994–95 (Garcia, 1994). Preparing for the changing demographics of the school population is important because culture shapes how children learn.

How Culture Shapes Learning

A great deal of research has been conducted on the different styles of learning, communication, and participation of minority students (Gay, 1991; Ladson-Billings, 1995; Losey, 1995; Shade & New, 1993; Stone, 1991). For example, studies have been conducted on African Americans (Boykin, 1982; Ladson-Billings, 1995; Shade, 1986), Native Hawaiians (Au, 1980; Boggs, Watson-Gegeo, & McMillen, 1985), Mexican Americans (Heath, 1986; Losey, 1995; Ramirez & Castaneda, 1974), the larger Hispanic community (Grossman, 1984), and Native Americans (Greenbaum, 1985; Phillips, 1972). These studies indicate differences in the way children of different cultural groups communicate, learn, and interact. Our goal as teachers should be to create a "cultural congruence" between our classrooms and the homes of our students (Au & Kawakami, 1994).

Before proceeding, one important caution is in order. Although researchers can describe a norm, a typical way of thinking or behaving among members of a cultural group, these are generalizations. For some individuals within the group, these generalizations will not be accurate. Let me provide an example from an observation I made while supervising two university students who were participating in a second-grade bilingual (Spanish-English) classroom. All the children were Hispanic. Research has shown that Hispanic students have a preference for social learning, for working in groups [Losey, 1995]. The children in this classroom decided to stay indoors during recess because the temperature had climbed to 100. All the children were drawing pictures of the fire station they had visited earlier in the week. They were free to work where they wished. Of the 28 children, 20 worked in small groups, chatting happily as they drew. This was consistent with the research. Eight children, however, did not follow the norm, choosing to work individually. My afternoon in that classroom provided me with a good example of how a cultural norm will not define the behavior of every member of a cultural group.

It would be impossible in a book of this size to summarize all the conclusions reached on each cultural group, but here are examples of these cultural differences:

- *European American* teachers and parents will expect students to ask questions and express personal opinions. Many *Korean American* students, however, will be hesitant to demonstrate these classroom behaviors. In traditional Korean culture, student behavior of this sort is considered rude; it shows disrespect for the teacher. In Korea, students refrain from asking questions because it indicates the teacher did a poor job. It is not appropriate for a child to express an opinion to an adult (California Department of Education, 1992a).

- *Native Hawaiians* have a strong tradition of group storytelling, called "talkstory." It is no wonder, then, that many of these students thrive in activities that require cooperation and a lot of talking. Many Native Hawaiian students become frustrated with activities that ask for silence and that are completed individually (Au, 1993).

- Some teachers claim that their *African American* students give no answers, give single-word answers, or give short, flippant answers to questions asked in front of the whole class. The same students on the playground talk in an animated manner and speak at great length when explaining things and describing events. Shade and New (1993) note that this behavior occurs because "in the traditional African American community, children are not usually expected to be information givers and are infrequently asked direct questions" (p. 320). Communication among African Americans is passionate and less formal than among European Americans. We as teachers should expect our African American students to differ from our European American students in each of the following aspects of language use: (a) turn taking (when people speak, European Americans follow a more rigid structure during a conversation), (b) tone (European Americans speak in less audible tones), (c) gestures (European Americans use few gestures), and (d) pace (European American speech is slower). Research shows that African American students do better in school when (a) teachers plan participatory learning experiences in which students move around, such as dramatic role play; (b) students have many opportunities to talk with classmates in informal, conversational settings; (c) students have a chance to think out loud and work in small groups; and (d) teachers present material auditorily through music, rhymes, and chants (Gay, 1991, 1997; Hollins, Smiler, & Spencer, 1994; Ladson-Billings, 1995; Shade & New, 1993).

- Prior to coming to school, *Native American* children learn by observation and direct experience. This stands in stark contrast to European American children, whose caretakers spent a great deal of time talking to and with the children. Native American children have learned not to respond quickly to questions because such a response is disrespectful. This hesitance to respond is often misinterpreted by teachers from other cultural groups (Gilliland, 1992; Stokes, 1997).

Good teachers respect the diversity of their students. We should use the resources of our local community to learn about the cultural identities of our students. We should understand the level of English proficiency of our English language learners. We should get to know our students as individuals and have a good sense of each student's interests and abilities. The methodology for today's classroom must reflect the diversity of our students, must be multidimensional, and must include a wide variety of instructional resources and strategies. This book describes that methodology.

One way to "celebrate" the cultural diversity of our students is to use their experiences as a basis for social studies teaching. The following mini-unit does just that.

Grade 4: "Chinese Writing"

MINI-
UNIT

This mini-unit was planned for a fourth-grade class in which the majority of students were English language learners. One girl in the class, Chimei, was learning to write Chinese. Chimei's mother was teaching her. During a time when students could "show and tell," Chimei talked about what she had learned. Other students expressed interest when Chimei showed them the beautiful examples of Chinese writing she had produced. The teacher saw Chinese writing as an excellent opportunity for a mini-unit and used the NCSS (1994) standards for social studies as an organizing framework for unit objectives.

Part I: Organizing Framework

NCSS Thematic Strand (1): Culture

Performance Expectation (a): The learner can compare similarities and differences in the ways groups, societies, and cultures meet human needs and concerns. The common need is to communicate.

This mini-unit answers one question:

Unit Question: How Is Chinese Writing Like English Writing, and How Is It Different?

Part II: Instructional Activities

Overview: Because the English writing system and the Chinese writing system meet this need in very different ways, this mini-unit answers one question. The activities designed for this mini-unit are focused on helping students answer that question.

Resources and Materials: (a) children's books: *Chinese Writing: An Introduction* (Wolf, 1975) and *Lóng Is a Dragon: Chinese Writing for Children* (Goldstein, 1991); "China the Beautiful" Web site on the Internet *(http://chinapage.com/china-rm.html)*; (c) a member of the community who can write and speak Chinese (not absolutely necessary, but a real plus); (d) blank paper, fine-tipped paintbrushes, and black tempera paint

The world's people share certain basic needs, like communication. Your students should learn that cultural groups develop unique ways of meeting those needs. Students here experience the challenge of writing in Chinese.

Content Objectives: Students will learn that the English system of written language differs from the Chinese system in two ways: form and number of characters. They will also learn that the function of the Chinese written system is the same as English.

Process Objectives: After students *listen* to their teacher read aloud *Lóng Is a Dragon: Chinese Writing for Children* (Goldstein, 1991), they will *observe* the logographic system of Chinese writing, *compare* the Chinese letter forms to English letter forms, *reproduce* the basic strokes of Chinese writing, *recognize* the tonal system of Chinese oral language, and *write* five Chinese characters.

Values Objectives: Students will develop an appreciation for the beauty and sophistication of the Chinese system of writing. It is hoped that students will abandon ethnocentric attitudes they might have toward languages other than English and see that other languages are neither better nor worse than English, just different.

Day I

1. Read aloud *Lóng Is a Dragon: Chinese Writing for Children.* Be sure students understand that Chinese writing is logographic: Each character represents something (a thing, a person, a place, an idea). A good way to do this is to compare the English representation of a word (e.g., *water*) with the single symbol for it in Chinese. Note the origins of the characters as pictographs (pp. 4–8 of *Lóng Is a Dragon*). Stress the artistic, almost spiritual nature of writing in Chinese.

2. Use an LCD (liquid crystal display) projector to display computer images of certain Chinese characters produced by Chinese grand masters of calligraphy. (You may need to define *calligraphy* for your students.) The Web site "China the Beautiful" has excellent descriptions and examples of Chinese calligraphy from A.D. 900 to the present *(http://chinapage.com/china-rm.html)*. If you cannot enlarge the images that appear on the computer monitor, then consider other ways to share these stunning images. Students could view the images in small groups, for example. You may want to point out to students that there are really five styles of Chinese calligraphy and that, within each style, there is room for artist expression. The samples of Chinese writing available on the Web site identified here dramatically illustrate the artistry of the calligrapher.

3. Begin the writing instruction in the basic strokes (pp. 9–10 of *Lóng Is a Dragon*). The ideal situation is to have a person who is familiar with writing Chinese to demonstrate these strokes for the class. (Chimei's mother could not visit this class, but Zhou's mother did.) Any teacher, however, can demonstrate the basic strokes with practice (true mastery takes time). Stress the importance of moving the brush in the correct direction. Students should begin to understand that drawing Chinese characters takes considerable skill and practice.

Day 2

1. Read aloud parts of *Chinese Writing: An Introduction* or have a class visit from a person who speaks a Chinese dialect. Although Chinese has many spoken dialects, it has only one written form. This is one advantage of a logo-graphic writing system: Speakers of different dialects are able to understand the same system of writing. Students are fascinated to learn that spoken Northern Chinese has four "tones" (other dialects have as many as nine tones) and that each tone gives an utterance a different meaning. Thus, *tung* can mean "to succeed," "together," "to govern," or "painful," depending on the vocal pitch of the speaker (see p. 13 of *Chinese Writing*).
2. Teach students how to make five characters (see *Lóng Is a Dragon,* pp. 11–26). Students should first draw the character in pencil and then, if you think they are ready, trace with fine-tipped paintbrushes and black tempera paint.

Day 3

1. Stress again the mental state of the calligrapher (pp. 23–24 of *Chinese Writing*).
2. Continue to work on painting the characters. Today, try a sentence (p. 27 of *Lóng Is a Dragon;* p. 18 of *Chinese Writing*)!
3. Ask the class the unit question: "How is Chinese writing like English writing, and how is it different?" Pair students with partners to answer the question by using the cooperative learning structure called Think-Pair-Share (see chap. 5). If students have trouble with the question, help them by suggesting two categories of comparison: (a) function—the languages serve the same function, they are used to communicate; and (b) form—the written languages look different.

Day 4 and Beyond

The mini-unit will be just the beginning! Depending on students' response, the entire class might benefit from a longer unit that looks at other aspects of China, such as the visual art, music, and religions of the Chinese people. Perhaps small groups of students will want to learn more about the history, geography, and current political status of China. They could share what they have learned with their classmates.

Evaluation: You can use two sources of data to assess your students. First, keep some sort of record of the Think-Pair-Share activity on Day 3. It might be a good idea to make a chart listing each set of partners and containing a place to write comments. Circulate around the room as students figure out how Chinese writing and English writing are the same and different. Note the level of success students have in answering the question. Another alternative is to have each student write an answer after the Think-Pair-Share experience concludes. These written answers could serve as a simple test.

Second, it is important to keep anecdotal notes during the first 2 days of the unit. The notes should record some of the questions students ask and summarize your assessment of which students seem to grasp the similarities and differences between the two language systems. The comments students make as they work during the unit should give you an idea whether or not they have adopted the values you proposed in the objectives section of the mini-unit. Interestingly enough, the samples of Chinese writing painted by each student would have little value in assessment; this writing experience, though essential to achieve the mini-unit's objectives, provides little evidence to determine whether or not students understand the differences between the two writing systems (e.g., a student could make an elegant copy of a Chinese character yet not understand the logographic nature of that character).

Effective Teaching in Today's Diverse Classroom: This mini-unit was a great success. It was also a perfect chance to raise the self-esteem of Chimei and the five other Chinese American students in the classroom. The mini-unit is a good example of what can happen when a teacher chooses to avoid a "deficit" model of teaching in a diverse classroom. Rather than view cultural diversity as a hurdle that must be overcome, this teacher used the cultural identity of one of her students to enrich the curriculum. Also of note, even though many students in the room were in the beginning stages of acquiring English, all were successful. The unit made strong use of visual aids (the illustrations in the books, the demonstrations by Zhou's mother). Full participation did not require the use of English.

SUMMARY OF KEY POINTS

- ▶ Students will differ in gender, age, language status, cultural identity, challenging condition, psychosocial status, family income, ability, interest, and physical characteristics.
- ▶ Constructivism explains how children learn. Knowledge is constructed (or "built") through an active process as children relate new things to what they already know.
- ▶ Vygotsky defined a zone of proximal development, wherein children can expand what they are able to learn and what they can do by working cooperatively with others.
- ▶ English language learners will be learning social studies at the same time they are acquiring a second language.
- ▶ Social studies teaching should present comprehensible input to students in a low-anxiety environment.
- ▶ Most social studies activities, especially those planned for a diverse class, should have a great deal of contextual support.
- ▶ Cultural identity shapes learning. Methodology must account for the learning styles, ways of communicating, and participation preferences of several cultural groups.

FOR FURTHER READING

Learning

► I presented a simple description of constructivism. Actually, constructivism has several theoretical strands: social constructivism, radical constructivism, and sociocultural constructivism. I think the best source is the book edited by Steffe and Gale (1995), which has 27 essays, including contributions by most leading constructivists. Another excellent source is the January 1998 issue of *Social Education,* which has several articles on constructivist social studies teaching (Scheurman & Yell, 1998). Two good books on Piaget's theories are those by Donaldson (1978) and Ginsburg and Opper (1979). A book by Trueba (1989) has a good discussion of Vygotsky in relation to culturally diverse children. Frank Smith (1988) is best known for his work on how children learn to read. During the 1980s, he broadened his perspectives to examine the conditions that promote the learning of any subject or process (1986a, 1986b). I think that what he has written makes a great deal of sense, especially for social studies.

► Constructivism provides one perspective on how children learn. Other researchers and theorists, for example, have looked at how children acquire concepts (Alleman & Rosaen, 1991; Wyner & Farquhar, 1991). Most of this research applies to specific areas of knowledge, such as history, geography, economics, friendship, civic understanding, race, gender, and moral reasoning. It appears that young children can learn more difficult concepts than most social studies programs have offered (NCSS Task Force on Early Childhood/Elementary Social Studies, 1989). A great deal has been written about the use of specific instructional techniques for teaching concepts (Beyer & Penna, 1971; Eggen & Kauchak, 1995; Martorella, 1991a, 1991b; Taba, 1967).

Diversity

► If you want to know more about social studies and challenged students, start with Curtis's (1991) review of the literature. For gifted children, see Delisle (1991).

► All of us as teachers should understand our African American students; see the several insightful chapters in *Teaching Diverse Populations* (Hollins, King, & Hayman, 1994). I also recommend books by Hale-Benson (1986), Kochman (1981), Paley (1979), and Smitherman (1977). Gay (1991) reports that surprisingly little research has been conducted on the social studies achievement of minority children. One interesting study showed that African American students were greatly influenced by their teachers—so much so that many identified their favorite school subject as the one taught by their favorite teacher (Hollins et al., 1994).

► The educational achievement of immigrant children is a primary concern for public school educators. Caplan, Choy, and Whitmore (1991) wrote a book about the success of the children of Southeast Asian "boat people." An ongoing process called "democratic dialogues" was very successful with ninth-grade immigrant students; it certainly could be used with upper elementary students too (Pezone & Singer, 1997).

▶ Good books on Hispanic students include those by Keefe and Padilla (1987) and Grossman (1984).

▶ The California Department of Education has published a series of excellent books on Asian American students, with separate books on Cantonese-speaking students, Japanese Americans, Filipino Americans, Hmong Americans, Vietnamese Americans, and Korean Americans. You can get a complete list by calling (916) 445–1260 or by writing to the Department's Publications Office at P.O. Box 271, Sacramento CA 95802–0271. Also of note, Kleg (1993) disagrees with the NCSS Task Force on Ethnic Studies Curriculum Guidelines on the issue of what constitutes an ethnic group.

Krashen and Cummins

▶ The best summary of Krashen's ideas is in his book *Inquiries and Insights* (1985). Cummins is most accessible in his chapter in the edited book *The Multicultural Classroom: Readings for Content-Area Teachers* (1992).

▶ Also of interest here is a book by Christian Faltis, *Joinfostering: Adapting Teaching Strategies for the Multilingual Classroom* (1993); it has a good chapter on teaching content to English language learners. Many good books have been published in the last 15 years on teaching content (social studies and science) to English language learners. My favorite is by Echevarria and Graves (1998). Mohan's book (1986) is very good, with an excellent description of how language is used in the classroom.

China

▶ Many instructional units on China are available in the ERIC system. Use the descriptors "China," "Units," and "Social Studies." Of particular interest are units prepared by participants in the Fulbright-Hays Seminars Abroad Program (1993). Two more recent participants in the Fulbright-Hays program, Stephanie Wasta and Margaret Scott (1998), write about a third-grade unit on China they developed called "Building Bridges to China."

▶ Material on the "Schools of California Online Resources for Education" (SCORE) Web site *(http://www.rims.k12.ca.us/score/)* is organized by California's curriculum framework. Excellent resources and activities on China can be found by clicking on "Grade 6."

▶ In addition to the reproductions of Chinese writing produced by masters from the 10th century to the present, the "China the Beautiful" site *(http://chinapage.com/china-rm.html)* has a good essay that provides the background information a teacher would need to know.

Chapter 3

The Transformed Curriculum: Infusing Multicultural Perspectives

Sara's letter read:
November 22, 1778

Dear Patricia,
My dear cousin, I can't believe your last letter. I don't know how to tell you this, but you are a traitor. Your brother Andrew has made a big mistake by joining Washington's army. When Andrew is caught, he will be hanged. My father has gone to join the British army, and they will win! God save our wonderful King George III.

Your loving cousin,
Sara

P.S. Is it cold in Virginia? It is freezing in South Carolina.

Sara and Patricia were fifth-grade classmates. They were studying the American Revolution, and during one of the unit's projects, they participated in a writing simulation. The class divided into pairs; Sara pretended to be a Colonial child whose family remained loyal to British King George, and Patricia pretended to be her cousin from Virginia whose family fought for the Rebel cause. The girls exchanged letters after participating in multiple lessons that identified the political differences between Loyalists and Rebels. The letter exchange in Sara and Patricia's classroom was an activity designed to make American history more personally relevant for students.

Getting students to become more actively engaged in social studies lessons "transforms" learning for them. And, because the planning takes students' cultural backgrounds and interests into account, social studies becomes more multiculturally focused. Thus, the social studies curriculum of a truly multicultural classroom is transformed when students are made aware that historical events affect more than those people who are traditionally identified. Social studies comes alive in classrooms where activities illustrate that there is no single view of any social phenomenon (a historical event, a current issue). Sara and Patricia's teacher included the letter exchange activity as part of an American Revolution unit developed to include objectives for learning about the roles of Colonial women and children, Native Americans, African Americans, common soldiers, and the Loyalists, in addition to content about events leading to and during the Revolutionary War (see Gay & Banks, 1975, and the discussion at the end of this chapter). The objectives and activities were designed to capture the interests of students and their various, diverse backgrounds.

▲   ▲   ▲

In this chapter, you will read about:

▶ James Banks's perspectives on how to transform the teaching of social studies to incorporate more pluralistic concepts and generalizations
▶ Three considerations for transforming social studies units of study, including scope, geographic boundaries, and people

▶ Available resources that help present multicultural perspectives
▶ Teaching students to use oral histories to appreciate significant events and to connect more personally to family and community history

The Dimensions of Multicultural Education

Multicultural education is probably a familiar topic to you. I would guess that you have either taken a course titled "Multicultural Education" or have discussed multi-culturalism in several of your college courses. Our concern here is how to transform the elementary social studies curriculum so that it may be accurately described as multicultural. James Banks, perhaps the most influential scholar in the field, has written that multicultural education is "an idea or concept, an educational reform movement, and a process" (1997b, p. 3). As so often is the case with school-related words and phrases, *multicultural education* has many definitions. Multicultural ed-ucation really consists of two interrelated dimensions:

1. *The Curricular Dimension*. In a multicultural education, students learn about many cultural groups, both those that compose the pluralistic society in the United States and those that live in other countries. A multicultural social studies provides students with opportunities to learn about other cul-tures as they learn about themselves. Students should study both the current status of cultural groups and the history that led to the present. The personal experiences of each student should be considered valuable and worthy of inclusion in the social studies curriculum. A multicultural cur-riculum does not limit itself to presenting information about a wide range of people; it provides the perspectives of people who frequently have been silenced or relegated to the margins in traditional social studies programs.
2. *The Equity Dimension*. Multicultural education is the reform process that creates classrooms where all students have equal educational opportunity. This means that teachers take positive steps to ensure that students of both genders, of every ethnicity, with non-English native languages, with chal-lenging conditions, and from all social classes reach their full potential (J. A. Banks & Banks, 1997; Garcia, 1994).

Levels of Curricular Integration

James Banks (1997a) has described four levels of integration for incorporating mul-ticultural perspectives into the curriculum:

The Contributions Approach. The contributions approach is sometimes called the "heroes and holidays" approach. The social studies curriculum remains the same because the only things added are a few lessons on Martin Luther King, Jr., during January; a dance festival for Cinco de Mayo; and a Multicultural Day on which parents bring to school the "foods of their homelands." The key element missing is depth: No comprehensive study of other cultural groups is undertaken, nor is any attempt made to look at topics from a full range of perspectives.

The Additive Approach. In an additive approach, the units of study change only in that content is added to include multicultural perspectives. For example, in a fifth-grade social studies curriculum on the United States, two units of study are added: "The Civil Rights Movement" and "The Immigrant Experience." The additive approach is an improvement over the contributions approach, but the problem is that experiences and perspectives of minority groups in the United States and people in foreign countries appear as an afterthought.

The Transformation Approach. In the transformation approach, the social studies curriculum has undergone a significant revision. According to James Banks, the key element of a transformed social studies curriculum is "to enable students to view concepts and issues from more than one perspective" (1997a, p. 237). Each unit of study therefore needs to be "infused" with various "perspectives, frames, references, and content" (p. 237). For example, a third-grade class studying their community learns about an important event in their city—the construction of an airport with major airline passenger service. As the children participate in a variety of activities focusing on the airport, some should present the controversy surrounding the decision to build the facility. The decision to build the airport was not unanimously supported; in fact, bitter opposition was expressed by homeowner groups representing people living in the proposed flight paths.

Another excellent example of a curriculum that provides multiple perspectives is "Land and Landscape: Views of America's History and Culture," which was developed by the National Museum of American Art of the Smithsonian Institution (Powe, 1998). Students view a series of historic photographs and then compare and contrast the Native American and European American ideas of the ownership of land. A transformed curriculum is essential in a society that values diversity and is part of the foundation on which effective social studies teaching is built.

The Social Action Approach. The social action approach includes all the elements of the transformation approach but goes further and asks students to make decisions and to take action. This action is often in the form of community service. Proctor and Haas (1993) state that community-oriented projects should be a "part of formal education beginning in the primary grades" (p. 381). For example, if a class of elementary students were to study their city, they would learn about problems the city faces. If the teacher had adopted the social action approach, then students would not only talk about issues but also would prepare a simple "position paper" and present it to the city council. Not all units present the possibility for social action, and some actions are appropriate only for middle school and high school students. In this chapter, our discussion covers the how-to process of transforming the curriculum. A more complete examination of social studies service and social action projects is discussed in chapter 11, on citizenship education.

The Transformation Process

Transforming social studies curriculum to make it multicultural is an evolutionary process and includes the following steps:

1. *Reconsider the scope of the social studies curriculum.* This task, in most cases, should be undertaken by a committee of teachers. Units of study should be analyzed for their content. Do they reflect only the perspectives of the mainstream, European American majority? Should some units be eliminated? Should new ones be created? For example, most fourth graders study their state; Virginians study Virginia, Californians study California, and so on. The curriculum is almost always chronological. In the study of Virginia, for example, the units would be "The Natives," "Colonial Virginia," "Virginia in the New Republic," "Virginia in the Civil War," "Reconstruction in Virginia," and "Virginia in the 20th Century." The transformed curriculum would include information on African Americans, Native Americans, immigrants to Virginia, women, and children. Units need not be based on historical periods; instead, issues or themes could be used as the focus:

- "People and the Natural Resources of Virginia." What are the resources of Virginia? How have Natives, Colonists, and subsequent inhabitants of the state used these resources? What must be done to preserve natural resources of the state? Throughout the history of the state, why have different groups taken opposing positions on the use of the state's resources? Are the resources that are recognized to be important to Virginians today the same as those recognized to be important in Colonial times? How have the resources of Virginia shaped the economy and jobs of the people of Virginia? What natural resources in Virginia are threatened today, and what can be done to save them?
- "The Struggle to Be Free." At the same time that prominent Virginians led the American Revolution, what was the status of Native Americans, African Americans, women, and poor European Americans? How did laws in Virginia maintain a system of slavery and indentured servitude? How might a slave, an indentured servant, a shopkeeper, and a plantation owner have reacted differently to the Declaration of Independence and to the adoption of the U.S. Constitution? During the period of segregation (1876–1965), what was life like for African Americans living in Virginia? How did people gain civil rights in Virginia? What else should be done to create a just society? (Often, in fourth grade, the study of state history stops shortly after the Civil

War. In a transformed curriculum, the civil rights movement of the 20th
century receives the same attention as the Colonial period.)

- "Technology and Life in Virginia." How have the tools and machines used
  by Virginians changed over the years? How did the Industrial Revolution of
  the 19th century change the way people lived in Virginia? What does the information age mean for the citizens of Virginia? Will technology close the
  gaps between the rich and the poor or exacerbate the differences?
- "Production, Distribution, and Consumption." What have Virginians produced? How have goods and services been distributed? What has been im-
  ported and exported? How did a slave-based economy function? How did
  the economy of Virginia change after the Civil War? How do Virginians earn
  their livings today?

2. *Expand the geographic boundaries of units of study.* Take a global perspective and look for cross-cultural comparisons. For example, first graders should not
only study their school and neighborhood but also compare them with schools and
neighborhoods in other states or countries. If third graders are learning about what
characterizes a city, they could explore how their city compares with other cities.

3. *Introduce students to a rich mosaic of people.* This is the *who* of the transformed curriculum. Whatever the topic, consider the contributions of, and the
impact on, African Americans, Asian Americans, Native Americans, Hispanic Americans, women, and children. This should be a process of inclusion, not exclusion.
For example, the addition of Revolutionary War hero Sybil Ludington, who warned
the residents of Danbury, Connecticut, of an impending British raid, does not mean
eliminating coverage of William Dawes or Paul Revere. The transformed curriculum
should continue to present information that has traditionally been a part of social
studies. The issue of expanding the scope of the social studies curriculum can be
controversial. The national history standards (National Center for History in the
Schools, 1996) tried to do just that, but coverage of women and people of color
made this set of standards *(National Standards for History for Grades K–4: Expanding Children's World in Time and Space; National Standards for United States
History: Exploring the American Experience;* and *National Standards for World
History: Exploring Paths to the Present)* highly controversial. Critics claimed that the
standards failed to mention important historical figures who are White males in
order to make room for women and people of color (Nash & Dunn, 1995).

In Their Own Words: Children's Books

To transform the curriculum, children must hear the voices of a wide range of people. It
is one thing to read secondhand descriptions of the experiences of other people; it is
another to read firsthand accounts, written or dictated by people who were participants

in the events. After many years of neglect, currently many books share the perspectives of African Americans, Asian Americans, Hispanic Americans, Native Americans, members of religious minorities, children, and people from outside the United States. Some accounts are autobiographical; others are anthologies of oral histories.

For example, in *Voices From the Fields: Children of Migrant Farmworkers Tell Their Stories,* editor Beth Atkin (1993) interviewed and photographed nine children of migrant workers. Perspectives of children usually are overlooked in elementary social studies, so Atkin's book is an important addition to our reservoir of instructional resources. Other edited books can provide students with the words of slaves (*To Be a Slave,* Lester, 1968), teenage civil rights activists (*Freedom's Children: Young Civil Rights Activists Tell Their Own Stories,* Levine, 1993), African Americans throughout U.S. history (*The Black Americans: A History in Their Own Words,* Meltzer, 1984; and *The Black Americans in U.S. History,* Toppin, 1973), and Native Americans who came in contact with European Americans (*Native American Testimony: An Anthology of Indian and White Relations,* Nabakov, 1978).

Autobiographical accounts provide an essential level of authenticity to social studies teaching. This transforms the curriculum. For example, students can expand their knowledge of Asian Americans by reading about the following topics:

Conditions in North Korea during the 1940s and 1950s (*The Year of Impossible Goodbyes,* Choi, 1991)

A childhood in Vietnam (*The Land I Lost: Adventures of a Boy in Vietnam,* Huynh, 1982)

A Chinese girl's immigration to Brooklyn (*In the Year of the Boar and Jackie Robinson,* Lord, 1984)

Life in Japan immediately after World War II (*The Bicycle Man,* Say, 1988)

The internment of Japanese Americans during World War II (*Journey to Topaz,* Uchida, 1971)

Figure 3.1 lists some children's books that are first-person accounts.

LESSON PLAN

Grade 5: From *To Be a Slave*

Overview: This lesson is a part of a fifth-grade unit on the Southern Colonies and uses a book, *To Be a Slave,* to identify first-person accounts of life as a slave. Working with a modification of Jigsaw (a cooperative group structure discussed in chap. 5), all 30 students will take part in reading and responding to narratives dictated by enslaved people in the 19th century.

Resources and Materials: (a) copy of the book *To Be a Slave;* (b) copies of the following narratives from that book: Moses Grandy (p. 43), Anonymous (pp. 44–45), Josiah Henson (pp. 48–49), Charles Ball (p. 54), Sis Shackelford (p. 56); (c) timeline

Figure 3.1 Books for Children: First-Person Accounts

Atkin, S. Beth (editor). *Voices From the Fields: Children of Migrant Farmworkers Tell Their Stories.* Atkin interviewed and photographed nine children.

Choi, Sook Nyul. *The Year of Impossible Goodbyes.* The author tells of her childhood in North Korea during the 1940s, the Japanese occupation, and escape to South Korea.

Crews, Donald. *Bigmama's.* African American author-illustrator Crews reminisces about summer trips to his grandparents' farm. Easy-to-read picture book.

Frank, Anne. *The Diary of a Young Girl.* More able fifth and sixth graders can read this well-known diary of a Dutch Jewish girl in World War II.

Garza, Carmen Lomas. *Family Pictures.* Mexican American painter Garza tells of growing up in a small town in Texas. Easy-to-read picture book; the text is in Spanish and English.

Hautzig, Esther. *The Endless Steppe.* The author, who was born to wealthy Jewish parents in Poland, provides an account of growing up in a slave labor camp in Siberia.

Huynh, Quang Nhuoug. *The Land I Lost: Adventures of a Boy in Vietnam.* The author remembers incidents from his childhood in Vietnam.

Lester, Julius (editor). *To Be a Slave.* This book is an anthology of autobiographical narratives told by several former slaves.

Levine, Ellen (editor). *Freedom's Children: Young Civil Rights Activists Tell Their Own Stories.* Thirty African Americans who were children or teenagers during the 1950s and 1960s describe their experiences.

Lord, Bette Bao. *In the Year of the Boar and Jackie Robinson.* This book is a fictionalized account of the author's immigration from China to Brooklyn in 1947.

Meltzer, Milton (editor). *The Black Americans: A History in Their Own Words.* This book is testimony of African Americans from the early 1600s to the 1970s.

Nabakov, Peter (editor). *Native American Testimony: An Anthology of Indian and White Relations.* This books contains 200 years of Native American commentary and is an excellent teaching resource. Almost all entries can be read by fourth- or fifth-grade students.

Reiss, Johanna. *The Upstairs Room.* The author describes her experience when she and her sister were hidden by a farm family during World War II.

Say, Allen. *The Bicycle Man.* Author-illustrator Say, who grew up in Japan, tells the story of the day when two American soldiers visited his school.

Uchida, Yoshiko. *Journey to Topaz.* This is a fictionalized account of the evacuation and internment of the author's family during World War II. The sequel is *Journey Home* (1978), in which Uchida and her family are released from the camp in Topaz, Utah, and return to California.

for the unit; (d) map of the United States of 1859. Note: This lesson can be conducted with any collection of narratives from enslaved people. For example, portions of Charles Ball's narrative are included in the Web site "Excerpts From Slave Narratives" *(http://vi/uh.edu/pages.mintz/primary.htm)*

Content Objectives: Students will understand the history and economics of slavery. They should reach the generalization that African American slaves in the United States were bought and sold like other "goods." Facts presented in the lesson will include that (a) slaves were transported from Africa in inhumane conditions; (b) slaves were bought and sold without regard to the status of other members of their families; (c) some slaves were sold privately, from neighbor to neighbor; (d) many slaves were auctioned; and (e) slaveholders would give extra food to slaves about to be auctioned.

Process Objectives: Students will (a) *listen* to their teacher read the background information, (b) work in groups to *analyze* one slave narrative, (d) *answer* three questions about the narrative, and (d) *compare and contrast* their answers with those of groups who analyzed different narratives. A member of each group will report to the whole group.

Values Objectives: Your students should believe that all people have fundamental human rights, such as liberty. In this lesson, students will learn more about a period in U.S. history when human rights were denied to enslaved African Americans.

Teaching Sequence

1. Be sure all teaching resources are in place. You will need six copies of each of the five narratives.
2. A few days before the lesson, select one student from each group to be a "reader." The reader will read the narrative to the rest of the group. Readers should have 2 or 3 days to rehearse their oral readings. If you prefer, readers can record their readings of the narratives on audiotape.
3. Start the lesson by referring to the timeline and the map. This lesson should be preceded by others on (a) the cultures of West African tribal groups and (b) the "middle passage" from Africa to Colonial America. Subsequent lessons would cover the working and living conditions of enslaved people in the American South.
4. Tell the class that today they will learn about how slaves were bought and sold. Read to the whole class Lester's explanatory comments from chapter 2. It is not necessary to read all of his commentary, but be sure to include the text on pages 39, 40, 43, 44, and 46. Some slave narratives include the defamatory "n" word. Discuss the historical context of this word and emphasize that it is insulting and should not be used today.
5. Write the following questions on the chalkboard:
   1. Who dictated the narrative you read? Was the slave a man or a woman, a grown-up or a child?

2. In your narrative, what happened to the slaves?
3. If a slavemaster is mentioned in your narrative, what did he or she do?

Explain that each group is to answer these three questions for the narrative each has read. Distribute copies of the narratives to the groups. Allow time for the readers to read the narratives to the other members of their groups. Then have each group select a reporter to share their answers with the class.

6. For each of the five narratives, first have the reader read the narrative to the whole class. Then, have the reporter share the group's answers to the three questions.

Evaluation: Take notes as you circulate among the groups, recording the names of students who do a good job of answering the questions. This type of anecdotal record keeping will provide useful information if you gather data on an ongoing basis over the course of the year.

Effective Teaching in Today's Diverse Classroom: Small-group work is essential in a diverse classroom. Research shows that regular experiences in cooperative learning improve intercultural relations. Students from different cultural groups will get along better if they work together to accomplish common goals (see chap. 5 for a review of the research). Also, group work will help many students enter a ZPD (Vygotsky's zone of proximal development). One other note: If your class is homogeneous in reading ability, then you can have each student read the narratives on his or her own, rather than use group readers.

In Their Own Words: Oral History

All people have interesting stories to tell. Children should never consider social studies a dry subject that only tells the stories of other people living in other places. Our families and communities can be rich sources of information. Oral histories collected by our students will help us transform the curriculum. *Oral history* is a method of gathering spoken, first-person accounts of past events (Neuenschwander, 1976; Ritchie, 1995). Oral histories collected by adult historians are tape-recorded, carefully indexed, and placed in accessible archives. Several authors have written about how students can collect and use oral histories (Downs, 1993; Hickey, 1991; Hirshfield, 1991; Mehaffy, Sitton, & Davis, 1979; Olmedo, 1993, 1996; Zimmerman, 1992).

The Benefits of Oral History

The process of collecting, analyzing, and reporting oral histories is a wonderful experience for our students for many reasons:

- Oral history allows students to become historians; they will learn how historians work and will have firsthand knowledge of one important source of historical evidence.
- Oral history transforms the curriculum in that it inevitably increases the sources of information available to our students. If we limit social studies to print sources, then we ignore the history that is most immediate, relevant, and comprehensible to our students: their history, the history of their families, and the history of their immediate communities.
- Oral history is an excellent language arts activity. In the process of gathering, analyzing, and reporting oral histories, students listen, speak, read, and write. Olmedo (1996) notes that oral history is a good activity for English language learners. Oral histories may be collected in any language, so we can encourage our bilingual students to gather oral histories in their native languages.
- Olmedo (1996) explains why oral history projects work well with English language learners: These projects are relevant to their experiences, they teach social science inquiry processes, and they allow English language learners to use both of their languages.
- Oral history makes any subject more interesting. Hirshfield (1991) notes, "Oral history attaches emotion to events that can be provided only by the person who has lived through them, the young interviewer inevitably develops a deeper understanding of the recent past" (p. 111).

Guidelines for Oral History Projects

Oral history projects require thorough planning. The following guidelines will help us prepare for the use of oral histories and help us prepare our students:

1. *Determine the focus of the oral history project.* Choose one or two possibilities for the project focus. First, oral histories can *supplement* other resources. For example, a group of fourth graders studying the recent history of their state will read about recent immigrants in their textbooks and in children's books. Add oral histories to the print and other media resources. Second, oral histories can be the *sole source* of information for a lesson. A fifth-grade class did a project on how their grandparents met. In this project, the only source of data for a book the students wrote was the oral histories they gathered.

2. *Engage students in doing some background work.* The more students know about the time, places, people, and events that are the substance of the inter-

view the better. They will need this knowledge to make sense of what they hear and to ask follow-up questions. This is easier in some projects than in others.

3. *Direct students to plan their interviews*. After the topic has been defined and students have acquired background knowledge, ask the class to make a list of people whom they could interview. Discuss with students why thinking carefully about how the person(s) they choose to interview will inform their own knowledge base and contribute to their oral history project. Explain how being a good communicator can help them better reach their goal. Determine as a group that the value of any interview is directly related to the quality of the questions asked.

4. *Create a list of questions to be asked during the interview*. In some projects, a standardized set of questions should be asked of all interviewees. In other projects, each interviewee should have a different set of questions. Questions should be open ended; questions that can be answered with one word or a short phrase should be avoided. For example, a group of sixth graders compiled an oral history of playground games as part of the large project "Kids at Play: A History From Ancient Egypt to Today." Rather than ask senior citizens, "Did you play with jump ropes when you were in elementary school?" students should say to them, "Tell me about the games you remember playing at recess when you were in elementary school." Generate with your class samples of open-ended questions, such as the following:

- What do you remember about . . . ?
- How old were you when . . . happened? How do you know that the event happened when you were . . . ?
- How did this event affect (change) your life?

Effective teachers work with their students in a variety of instructional settings. All children benefit from individualized instruction.

- What did you do when . . . ?
- What else was going on during the same time?
- Who was the person who most influenced you, and in what way?
- What sequence of events caused . . . to happen?
- How did the sequence of events make a difference in the history of . . . ?

5. *Help students understand how to "go beyond" previously determined questions.* As Hickey (1991) states, predetermined questions should be "a guide rather than a strict script" (p. 217). We might even have our students interview us. Interviewing is difficult for students to master, but the ability to ask a good follow-up question is essential for the oral historian. When students hear something unusual, they should ask additional questions even though it means deviating from the standardized list of questions. Remember, too, our students should be interested in interviewing people who have *firsthand* knowledge. It is inevitable that some interviewees will repeat things they have heard. Family stories that have been passed down for generations will be told and are interesting to hear. From a historical sense, the real value of oral history is in recording eyewitness accounts.

6. *Hold the interviews in a controlled setting.* A significant challenge in an oral history project is the logistics of the interviews. In many cases, the teacher will contact informants and arrange for them to come to school for their interviews. In other projects, students make contacts with letters and follow-up telephone calls. If interviews take place outside school, students must be accompanied by their parents. Hirshfield (1991) lists two essential features of the interview setting. First, the interview should be one-on-one. Second, the interview should be in a quiet place with no distractions. Be sure that interviews are conducted only after appointments for them have been made and confirmed.

7. *Help students be good interviewers.* Students should ask one question at a time. If students use a tape recorder, they should know how to operate it. If students write down the answers provided by the interviewee, they should be trained to write fast and accurately. My experience has been that the vast majority of students cannot write fast enough to record what the interviewee is saying. Tape recorders are a much better tool for the interviewer to use. Students should be sure they have the correct spelling of names and places. They should ask follow-up questions to be sure that dates, places, and names are stated (and recorded) clearly. It's a good idea to role-play oral history interviews beforehand so that students become comfortable with the process and efficient in getting information (one student of a pair plays the informant, the other the interviewer). To help students while they role-play the act of interviewing or to help them feel more confident when they conduct their interviews, consider providing some kind of planning form such as displayed in Figure 3.2. Students can use this form to think critically before they conduct any interviews and to hold them accountable for getting their interview plans in motion.

Figure 3.2 **Planning the Interview**

Interviewer _____ Date _____
Whom will you interview?
_____

What is the purpose of your interview? _____
_____
_____

When will you conduct the interview? _____
_____
Date   Time

What questions do you intend to ask and in what order?

1. _____
   _____

2. _____
   _____

3. _____
   _____

4. _____
   _____

5. _____
   _____

Remember, answers you hear to your questions may change any follow-up questions you may ask. Be flexible!

8. *Request that interviewees sign a release form.* A release form authorizes the interviewer to share what he or she has heard from the interviewee. The form can be simple (a sample is shown in Figure 3.3) and should be approved by the school principal. The important thing is that people who are interviewed know that other people will hear or read what they have said and that their comments "belong" to the school (in the unlikely event that they are published, the copyright and any money generated by the publication they appear in belongs to the school).

9. *Support interviews with documents and artifacts.* Many times, an interview will lead a person to "dig out" old clothing, photographs, letters, souvenirs, gifts, or other items. Usually, these are too valuable to take to class. Under some circumstances, they can be borrowed, photographed, or photocopied. These documents and other artifacts are important historical sources and can provide illustration for the text of a report based on interviews.

10. *Analyze interviews.* After students have completed their oral interviews, their work has just begun. First, students should do what real historians do: make an index (list) of the interviews. Second, they should meet in groups and attempt to make sense of what they heard. The simplest form of analysis is to edit out irrelevant

Figure 3.3　Permission Form for Oral History Interviews

Please complete the following before or after your interview. Thank you.

I agree to be interviewed by _____

I understand that what I say will be shared as part of a classroom project. I
also understand that my comments may be published for school use and that if
the school decides this interview project is important enough to be shared

beyond the use of _____ that I will be
School name

contacted for further permission.

_____
Signature of Interviewee　　　　　　　　　　　　　　　　Date

---

comments and to compile an anthology of the interviews. This would work if all interviewees responded to one broadly stated question (e.g., "What do you remember
about the teachers' strike in 1980?"). Students will learn more if they compare and
contrast interviews. Some projects lend themselves to a chronological review; events
described in several interviews can be arranged in the order they took place. Typically, though, analysis will look for similarities and differences.

**GROUP
PROJECT**

Grade 3: An Oral History Project— "The History of Our School"

Project Description: A third-grade teacher decided to have her class write a history
of their school, Theodore Roosevelt Elementary School. The children used old photographs, school records, and newspaper articles as sources, but they needed more
information than those items could provide. Oral history seemed essential to provide
a more complete story. The class made a list of people who might provide oral histories. When two children showed the list to the principal, she steered them toward specific people with whom they would want to talk. The roster of interviewees included the
following:

- The superintendent of schools at the time the school was built (1965). Although in his 80s, the former superintendent still lived in the community.
- Three teachers who were on the first faculty. These teachers could share the
  memories of the first year of Roosevelt School.

- A teacher who had taught at the school from 1970 to 1992. Her longevity would make her an important source for "longitudinal" data on changes over time at the school.
- A school board member at the time the school was built. In his 80s, he would be a valuable source because a heated debate surrounded the naming of the school. One faction wanted to name the school after a former mayor who had just died; another faction wanted to name the school after a famous baseball player who had grown up in the community. Roosevelt was chosen as a compromise.
- Two principals in the school district—one at a junior high and the other at the local high school. Both had gone to Roosevelt School as children and could offer a "child's-eye view" of Roosevelt in previous decades.
- A member of the school board and her brother, the city attorney. These two prominent members of the community were among the first African American students to attend Roosevelt in 1974.
- A group of current sixth graders. These students at Roosevelt could provide information on the more recent history of the school.
- Five current faculty members, each who has taught at the school for at least 10 years. Like the sixth graders, members of the current faculty could comment on recent events at the school, and the interviews would be convenient to arrange.

Project Activities

1. The children developed questions for the interviews. Each person was asked a very broad opening question: "What is the first thing that comes to your mind about Roosevelt Elementary School?" Then, more specific questions were written for each interviewee.
2. The interviews were scheduled. Some had to take place outside school. These had to be approved by the principal, and each child doing an outside interview was accompanied by a parent.
3. The interviews revealed fascinating details. For example, the African American former students and the teachers who were at the school at the time remembered acts of both kindness and resentment when the African American students first attended. The superintendent told how difficult it was to decide on the design of the school. The teacher who had taught at Roosevelt for 22 years commented on how different the students have dressed over the years.
4. In addition to personal interviews, some children researched old newspaper articles, which provided more specific historical details. School records revealed the number of students who had attended the school at various times and the number of classrooms.
5. The children gathered all this information and wrote a book about their school, illustrated with copies of old photographs. The oral histories brought the book to life through the stories that people told.

Effective Teaching in Today's Diverse Classroom: This project is a good example of a transformed social studies curriculum. In learning about their school, the children learned a great deal about the social history of their city and our nation, and they learned it by listening to voices that would never be included in a textbook. Although some members of the community would have preferred to ignore the racism that greeted the first African American residents of this city, the book written by this group of children tackled the issue "head-on."

Incorporating the Personal Experiences of Your Students

Firsthand accounts of events, including both those found children's books and those recorded as oral history, can transform the curriculum. Equally essential is using the personal experiences of students as a basis for social studies teaching and learning (Alleman & Brophy, 1994a). Virtually everyone who writes about social studies and minority students stresses the importance of incorporating the personal experiences of students into the curriculum (e.g., J. A. Banks & Banks, 1997; Garcia, 1994; Short, 1994). This is a venerable idea, advocated in the late 1800s by Francis Parker, John Dewey, and other Progressive educators (Cremin, 1961). By "personal experience," I mean the daily existence of students outside school. Alleman and Brophy call these "out-of-school opportunities." Following are some ways to connect social studies to the personal experiences of students.

Cultural Universals. All people share basic needs (food, clothing, transportation). Units and lessons can begin by having students consider their own existence, proceed to a middle section where information is presented about people living in other places or in other times, and conclude with cross-cultural comparisons. For example, a unit on the Pilgrims might include an activity such as "Lunch With the Pilgrims, Plimoth, 1622." First, students in the class would answer these questions:

- When do we eat lunch at school?
- Does your family have a "lunch" at home on the weekends? (Many cultural groups eat their main meal at midday.)
- What types of foods do we eat for lunch at school? How are they different from foods eaten at breakfast and dinner?
- Whom do you eat lunch with at school? (Do adults eat with children?) Whom do you eat lunch with at home?
- How does lunch begin at home? (Some students might begin with a prayer or other ritual.)
- What beverages do we drink with lunch at school? What do you drink with meals at home?

Students would learn that the first Pilgrims ate with their fingers, drank a low-alcohol beer with their midday meal, and consumed incredible amounts of food each day (a half pound of butter, a half pound of meat, and a pound of bread). Several children's books would serve as resources: *Colonial Living* (Tunis, 1957), *Meet the Real Pilgrims: Everyday Life on Plimoth Plantation in 1627* (Loeb, 1979), *Eating the Plates: A Pilgrim Book of Food and Manners* (Penner, 1991), and *Sarah Morton's Day: A Day in the Life of a Pilgrim Girl* (Waters, 1989). Students could then make comparisons and identify the similarities and differences between the lunch of today's students and the midday meal of the Pilgrims. Finally, they could examine how the coming of European Americans changed the food sources and meal customs of the Native Americans living in Massachusetts during the 17th century; a small group of students could prepare a presentation for their classmates.

The Experiences of Childhood. When we are teaching about another cultural group or about people who lived in the past, one effective way to link that subject matter to the personal experiences of our students is to focus on the experiences of children. All too often in social studies, the curriculum seems to ignore the existence of children. I think the status of children is highly relevant and an interesting avenue to understanding other cultural groups. Today, almost all children go to school and participate in some form of recreational activity. School and play are perfect topics to include in any study of another group of people, whether they lived long ago or are living today. Comparisons based on school and play will provide information about many other topics we wish to cover, such as roles of men, women, and children; values of the group; and technology of the group of people being studied.

For example, consider the second-grade unit "Our Grandparents." The teacher calculated an "average age" for her second graders' grandparents. (The year was 1997, so most of her second graders had been born in 1990. She figured that their parents were 25 when the children had been born: 1990 − 25 = 1965. She then figured that the grandparents were 25 years old when the parents had been born: 1965 − 25 = 1940. Thus, the grandparents, on the average, had been born in 1940 and turned 7 in 1947.) What games did the grandparents play when they were in second grade? What books did their teachers read aloud to them in 1947? How did their grandparents dress when they went to second grade? The unit provided answers to all these questions as the class looked at what it was like to be a second grader in 1947.

A Child's Life History. The life histories of our students can be used in a variety of ways in a social studies program:

- Some of our students may have participated in events our class is studying. For example, in California, the experiences of immigrants are part of the social studies curriculum in Grades 2, 3, 4, and 5. Students in our rooms who are immigrants can tell about their immigration; these oral histories can supplement other resources. (One important note: Some students may have fled their native countries under horrible conditions; if these students do not want to recount their experiences, then that wish should be respected.)

- Students can learn how historians work by writing *documented* autobiographies. There is value in having students write from memory. Memories can be combined with a historical record, however; old photographs, report cards, and birth certificates should be consulted and referenced. Students should interview their parents, siblings, former teachers, and other people who have known them. The addition of documentation will show students how historians gather data to support their texts.

- In third grade, when students learn about their communities, they should be provided with many opportunities to incorporate previous experiences. Our students have a history of living in our city. It is important that our curriculum incorporate the people and places they know well. For example, students walk and ride past many buildings with historical significance everyday. Students can take "walking field trips" to visit these buildings and learn when each building was built and who has occupied it.

Current Events. Events of the day can also be used to provide a link between personal experiences and social studies. Three general strategies come to mind:

- Of greatest value are events our students experience firsthand. Although the content may not fit with the curriculum guide or the textbook we are following, it makes sense to break away and explore significant events. For example, some students in Los Angeles County have lived through a traumatic civil disturbance and a powerful earthquake. Both events generate possibilities for social study.

- Primarily through television, but also through the Internet, other media, and daily conversation, our students experience vicariously important events as they happen. For example, a class of third graders followed the 1996 presidential election from September, when school began, until January, when President Clinton was inaugurated. In 1999, a sixth-grade class used events in Kosovo to learn more about the people of the Balkans when stories about the region frequently were in the newspaper and on television.

- Students could look through newspapers to find articles about events that parallel those they are studying. For example, Short, Mahrer, Elfin, Liten-Tejada, and Montone (1994), in their junior high school unit on the American Revolution, ask students to search newspapers for articles about current political unrest in a lesson about Colonial protests to British policies.

Consumer Goods. Articles of clothing, toys, canned food, and other consumer goods can be the starting point for lessons in geography and economics. Students will see that the goods they use everyday come from many countries. For example, several children in a second-grade classroom had shirts made in Sri Lanka (they found this information on the labels sewn into the collars). This led to a mini-unit on that nation. Where is Sri Lanka? What resources does it have? What is life like for workers who made the shirts? How do the shirts arrive in the United States? Why is it less expensive to make the shirts in Sri Lanka than in the United States?

Adapting a Traditional Unit of Study

Almost all fifth graders study the history of the United States. An important unit of study during the year is the American Revolution. How could a standard unit on the American Revolution be transformed so that the scope of the unit, its geographic boundaries, and the people discussed become more multiculturally focused?

First, all the activities in a transformed unit should go beyond those suggested in a traditional teacher's edition of a basal social studies textbook series. For example, Houghton Mifflin's fifth-grade social studies textbook, *America Will Be* (Armento, Nash, Salter, & Wixson, 1991), does a commendable job of presenting information about ordinary, working people, women and children, and people of color. Yet, more can be done to further transform the unit. As teachers, it is our responsibility to gather information from other sources, such as a middle school unit on the American Revolution prepared at the Center for Applied Linguistics (Short et al., 1994). Designed for English language learners, this material is a good example of a curriculum that relates to today's diverse classrooms. This material and others can help fifth graders see the perspectives of people often left out of traditional units of study, such as children and teenagers, women, Native Americans, African Americans, and Loyalists. Review the following examples.

Expand Material Found in Traditional Units. Additional materials can be added to a traditional unit to enhance information and descriptions of people, events, and ideas. For example, earlier in this chapter I noted that a lesson on Paul Revere could be expanded to introduce Sybil Ludington. In 1777, 14-year-old Sybil warned the militia in Danbury, Connecticut, of the movements of a British raiding party. Three good sources of information about Sybil Ludington are (a) an old children's book, *Sybil Ludington's Ride,* by Erik Berry (1952); (b) *America Will Be,* in which a 9-page excerpt describes Sybil and the significance of her warning; and (c) a poem about Ludington by Cindy Mahrer, located in a unit published by the Center for Applied Linguistics (Short et al., 1994). Students who need a simpler version may find Drollene Brown's (1985) picture book, *Sybil Rides for Independence,* easier to follow.

Include Perspectives of Common Foot Soldiers. Most units on the Revolution fail to present the perspectives of the common, ordinary foot soldiers in the Colonial army. Some of these soldiers, however, were not much older than today's fifth graders. To provide a sense of the youth who served as foot soldiers, use Milton Meltzer's *The American Revolutionaries: A History in Their Own Words, 1750–1800* (1987). Two passages that I suggest including for young people to read are those written by 16-year-old Colonial soldiers James Collins and Thomas Young. They describe the bloody battle of Kings Mountain, where a Rebel army defeated an army of Colonial Loyalists. A good activity is to have students participate in a readers' theater project, with students reading aloud in dramatic fashion excerpts from the passages dictated by Collins and Young. A more elaborate readers' theater presentation could use a script taken from many of the oral histories and documents preserved in Meltzer's book.

Present a Wider Spectrum of Biographies. It is worth our students' time and will perhaps create more personal relevance to include the review of a wider spectrum of Revolutionary personalities: Deborah Sampson, who fought in the Revolutionary War disguised as a soldier (see the children's books *I'm Deborah Sampson: A Soldier in the War of Revolution* by Clapp, 1977; *The Secret Soldier: The Story of Deborah Sampson* by McGovern, 1975; and *Deborah Sampson Goes to War* by Stephens, 1984); prominent Colonial women such as Abigail Adams and Mercy Otis Warren; Margaret Corbin and Molly Pitcher, who participated in extraordinary war efforts; African Americans James Armistead, Austin Dabney, Saul Matthews, and Salem Poor, who all served in the Colonial army; British military leaders, such as John Burgoyne, Lord Cornwallis, and Banastre Tarleton; and Native American leader Thayendanegea (Joseph Brant), who fought for the British. Students could create biographical posters (portraits with 5–10 interesting facts) or "video" features as a Group Project.

Reveal a Wider Range of Events. Traditional social studies units on the American Revolution are, for the most part, limited to political and military events. Again, no good unit can ignore the signing of the Declaration of Independence or the battle of Yorktown. A unit on the American Revolution could also include information that most adults, much less elementary children, don't know. How many of us, for example, are aware that the central problem for those who remained at home during the war was runaway inflation or knew that women at home assumed new roles such as running the businesses their husbands left behind when they went to war? To embellish textbook coverage of the home front, I suggest two excellent children's books: John Loeper's *Going to School in 1776* (1973) and Barbara Brenner's *If You Were There in 1776* (1994).

In addition, a transformed curriculum can help students understand a wider range of a perspectives. Several activities could accomplish this goal. For example, students could use a Venn diagram to compare and contrast the political views of the Colonists who remained loyal to the British king (Loyalists) with those of the Rebels. Students will see that although these two groups differed fundamentally on some issues, they did agree on other issues (e.g., both groups in the South

The transformed curriculum enables students to view history from more than one perspective. As part of this field trip, children will learn about the roles of women, children, and enslaved people in Colonial America.

supported slavery). Otherwise, the class can divide into two groups of equal number—one group being Loyalists, the other group being Rebels—and each Loyalist pair up with a Rebel. Throughout the unit, the "two cousins" of each pair can write to one another—the Loyalist urging fidelity to the Crown, and the Rebel advocating revolution, denouncing the king. Sara's letter at the beginning of this chapter was completed as part of this unit.

Encourage the Reading of Fictional Novels. Students should be encouraged to read fiction with characters who are young people, Loyalists, or African Americans. For example, James Lincoln Collier and Christopher Collier have written a trilogy that tells of the wartime and postwar experiences of African Americans in the North (*Jump Ship to Freedom, War Comes to Willy Freeman,* and *Who Is Carrie?*). Another book by the same authors, *My Brother Sam Is Dead,* tells the story of Sam, the only Rebel in a family led by a Loyalist father. Two juvenile novels written by well-known authors also focus on the tension between Loyalists and Rebels (*Early Thunder,* by Jean Fritz, and *Johnny Treegate's Musket,* by Leonard Wibberly).

Use the Internet. The Internet continues to grow as a significant resource for a transformed social studies. The best source of information on the experiences of African Americans during the Revolutionary War is "Revolution," a Web site created by the Public Broadcasting System (PBS) as part of the *Africans in America* television series *(http://www.pbs.org/wgbh/aia/tguide)*. Many fifth graders can read the text on this Web site, which also includes reproductions of historical documents. Students could read about Prince Hall and Colonel Tye, African Americans who fought on opposing sites during the war.

Even people, events, and ideas traditionally covered in a unit on the American Revolution can be transformed by offering a different perspective. George Washington, for example, is usually presented as a political and military leader. To many children, I suspect, he seems as lifeless as his image on a dollar bill. I suggest two children's books to help students see the "human" side of Washington: Miriam Anne Bourne's *Uncle George Washington and Harriet's Guitar* (1983) is based on Washington family letters written from 1790 to 1795; we see Washington from the perspective of his nieces and nephews. Jean Fritz's *George Washington's Breakfast* (1969) brings the daily routines of his life to the classroom. Finally, although any unit should emphasize Washington's unique contributions to U.S. history and his rightful status as "father of our country," students should also examine Washington's economic interests as a slaveholder and the consistent criticism of his leadership of the Continental Army (see the children's book *George Washington and the Birth of Our Nation* by Meltzer, 1986).

SUMMARY OF KEY POINTS

▶ James Banks described four levels of integration of multicultural content: contributions, additive, transformation, and social action.

▶ To transform the curriculum, we should reconsider the scope of what we teach; introduce our students to a wide variety of people, their experiences and perspectives; and expand the geographic boundaries of our instructional units.

▶ To have a curriculum that is truly multicultural, we should be sure our students are exposed to firsthand accounts of events written by African Americans, Asian Americans, Hispanic Americans, Native Americans, members of religious minorities, women, children, and people living outside the United States.

▶ Another way to transform the curriculum is to have students collect oral histories. Oral histories expand the social studies curriculum by incorporating the histories of the students themselves, their families, and their communities.

▶ The transformed curriculum incorporates the personal experiences of our students.

FOR FURTHER READING

▶ Many journal articles provide examples of how a topic can be transformed so that a wide variety of perspectives and experiences are incorporated. For example, Kornfeld (1994) discusses children's books on World War II. His goal is to incorporate multicultural and global perspectives. Drew's (1992) review of African American literature for young people is a good resource for curriculum planners. A special issue of *Social Studies and the Young Learner* (Murphy, 1993) is devoted to teaching about holidays in elementary classrooms. Articles look at how we as teachers can avoid superficiality and which holidays should be covered. D. Banks (1997) shows how children's books can enhance a unit on immigration to the United States. *With History-Social Science for All: Access for Every Student* (California Department of Education, 1992c) has a chapter on connecting history to the personal experiences of students.

▶ I mentioned interviewing grandparents as part of an oral history project. Hittleman and Hittleman (1998) provide the unit "Bringing Grandparents Into Social Studies." On the American Revolution as a topic for elementary social studies, see also Drake and Drake (1990) for a discussion of relevant children's literature and Hatcher and Olsen (1984) for a description of an American Revolution fair at a local mall that involved stories, songs, and filmstrips. DePauw's (1994) article on the roles of women in the American Revolution and the Civil War is good background reading for teachers.

Part II

The Fundamentals of
Social Studies Teaching

Chapter 4

Lesson Plans: Organizing Instruction

The students in Donna Richard's fifth grade took part in a 6-week instructional unit on Native Americans. They studied the cultures of five tribes—the Mohawk, the Seminole, the Oglala Sioux, the Tlingit, and the Navajo—before the arrival of Europeans to North America. Mrs. Richard decided to do this unit so that her students could learn about the diversity and history of Native Americans and to see for themselves the problems of stereotyping a cultural group when knowledge is limited. By allowing students to compare the historical diversity of multiple Native American groups, they would find out that not all Native Americans lived in tipis, hunted buffalo, wore feathers, or committed savage acts of violence. Further, students would learn where and how "Indians" live in the United States today.

To initiate this unit of study, Mrs. Richard started with a study of the Sioux of the mid-19th century. Using an LCD (liquid crystal display) overhead projector, Mrs. Richard projected an image of a painting by George Catlin—*Buffalo Chase, Upper Missouri*—onto a movie screen positioned at the front of the classroom. The painting, also called *Buffalo Chase, Bulls Making Battle With Men and Horses,* is part of a collection stored at the Smithsonian Institution (it's also on the Smithsonian's Web site, *http://www.si.edu/*). Providing black-and-white copies of the painting to student groups, Mrs. Richard asked students to study the painting and to answer a series of eight guided-response directives. The next-to-last query was "Pretend you are one of the Sioux. Write down what you are thinking, feeling, hearing, or seeing." Answers to this request led to several lively discussions. In one group, Darlene started off by saying that if she were a Sioux in the painting, she would be scared. She wanted to know why one Sioux was jumping on a buffalo. In response, Jerome speculated that the Sioux wanted to pull one of his arrows out of the buffalo and use it again. Mrs. Richard noted that Jerome's guess was a good one because the book *Buffalo Hunt,* by Russell Freedman, related how some arrows were shot with such force that the arrows went all the way through the buffalo. She further shared from the book that sometimes arrows would barely penetrate the buffalo's hide and the Natives would try to pull them out to use again.

Dontray said that he was going to write about shooting the buffalo with arrows. Before she left the group to allow them to start writing, Mrs. Richard asked about things the Sioux might have heard during the hunt. Andrew stated that it was loud because that's the way it was in the buffalo hunt in the film *Dances With Wolves.* Darlene added that one thing the Sioux would have heard was the horse screaming. Mrs. Richard asked whether anybody had anything else to say in response to directive number seven. No hands went up, so the five students started writing their responses. After about 10 minutes, members of each group shared their work.

The final query in the study guide led to the second half of the lesson. That directive was "Think back to what we learned about the Mohawk. Think what the Mohawk ate and how they got their food. Think about what we have learned about the Sioux. All people need some way of getting food. What is the same and what is different about these two tribes?" Mrs. Richard encouraged each group to make a simple comparison chart by folding a sheet of paper in half lengthwise and on one side writing details they remembered about the Mohawk, and on the other side writing what they learned about the Sioux. Mrs. Richard had information books and encyclopedias ready as help for students who couldn't recall information about the Mohawk. Fortunately, though, at least one member of each group noted that the Mohawk had fields and raised crops of squash, corn, and beans. After all the groups reconvened, Darlene stated an accurate conclusion: "The Mohawk had a lot more ways of getting food. They farmed, they fished, they gathered berries. The Sioux just hunted and gathered." Matt added that both groups hunted but that they hunted different things: The Sioux hunted buffalo, whereas the Mohawk hunted deer and turkeys and other birds. Jerome made another comparison: The Sioux hunted while riding horses, whereas the Mohawk hunted on foot. Mrs. Richard then asked the class why the food-getting practices of the two groups were different. Students first considered this question in their groups. All the groups quickly stated that the Mohawk couldn't hunt buffalo because no buffalo lived where the Mohawk lived and that the Sioux couldn't fish because the Plains did not have enough rivers and streams. By the time the lesson ended, most students could not come up with a good explanation of why the Mohawk farmed and the Sioux did not, so Mrs. Richard decided to plan a lesson on that topic.

This lesson is noteworthy for two reasons. First, the lesson was an important component in Mrs. Richard's attempt to help her students take a comprehensive look at Native Americans. The final directive, comparing the food-getting practices of the Sioux and the Mohawk, helped students understand that, before the coming of European Americans, there were significant cultural differences among the Native American tribes of North America. The diversity among Native American tribes, unfortunately, is rarely taught in elementary schools (Brophy, 1999). Second, the success of this lesson, like almost all lessons that go well, was the product of Mrs. Richard's thoughtful and thorough planning. This chapter is about planning lessons and will introduce a variety of formats for preparing exciting, challenging, and effective social studies lessons.

▲   ▲   ▲

In this chapter, you will read about:

- ▶ Simple guidelines to help in planning effective social studies lessons
- ▶ Instructions on writing instructional objectives
- ▶ Perspectives on using two kinds of lesson sequences—Hunter's seven-step model and Joyce and Weil's concept attainment model

General Guidelines for Planning Social Studies Lessons

The concept of lesson should be broad and include each of the following:

- • Lessons that are teacher directed and involve the entire class (often called "whole-group" lessons)

- Lessons that are designed for small groups or individuals
- Lessons that place the teacher in a less central role as the teacher serves as facilitator, tutor, and provider of resources

Regardless of the specific lesson format we use, we should follow two guidelines when planning an effective lesson:

1. *First, decide precisely what we expect students to do.* This guideline seems obvious. I have seen hundreds of people teach; some were student teachers I supervised, others were veteran teachers participating in research projects. When a lesson "crashes and burns," more times than not it does so because the teacher does not have a clear idea of what the students are supposed to do *from the beginning of the activity to the end*. Some lessons go poorly because the teacher knows exactly what the students are to do at the *end* of the lesson but hasn't really thought about what they should do before then. This does not mean that we should choreograph every step so that all our students behave like members of a chorus line. Many lessons will have some students do one thing while their classmates do another. Other lessons will have time for students to be creative. Still other lessons should have times when students can choose what activity they pursue. The point is that we should plan for each of these situations. Before we teach a lesson to the whole class, before we work with a small group, before we hold a conference with one student, we should be sure we know what we expect the student(s) to do. I suggest that, before we write a lesson plan, we should make a simple list. For example, for her lesson on *Buffalo Chase, Upper Missouri,* Mrs. Richard wrote:

1. I want the students to look closely at the painting.
2. I want them to answer questions about the painting while working in small groups.
3. I want them to compare and contrast the food-getting practices of the Sioux and the Mohawk.

2. *Second, decide what we, the teachers, must do in order for our students to achieve what we expect of them.* After we have a clear idea of what we expect our students to do during the lesson, we must think of ourselves. If our students are to be successful, what must we do? We have much to consider here: What materials must we gather? Will the classroom furniture need to be rearranged? What visual aids will we need? What must we say and when? What problems should we anticipate? Again, I suggest that before we make a formal lesson plan, we should jot down a list of things we must do. Mrs. Richard wrote:

1. Get the LCD projector.
2. Write the study guide and run 32 copies.
3. Make sure the timeline and the map are ready.

Lesson Plan Formats

I distinguish two general formats for lesson planning: the *comprehensive* lesson plan and the *abbreviated* lesson plan. Comprehensive lesson plans are detailed and quite time-consuming to prepare. The lesson plan at the end of chapter 1 was a comprehensive lesson plan (for *A Chair for My Mother*). Abbreviated lesson plans are much less detailed, take less time to prepare, but still require care and thought in their preparation.

The Comprehensive Lesson Plan

The comprehensive type of thorough lesson planning has several forms. As you have no doubt discovered, it seems as if each person who teaches a methods course has a preferred form. Relatively few times during our careers do we prepare comprehensive plans: We write them during our methods courses and field experience (internship or student teaching) as part of learning to teach. We write them during our teaching years mainly for two reasons: (a) When we are being evaluated by a principal, the process usually includes the preparation of comprehensive lesson plans; and (b) when we are doing a complex or innovative activity, it's a good idea to write a comprehensive plan. It would be impossible for us to write a comprehensive plan for each instructional activity we teach because there simply isn't enough time to do so. These lengthy, detailed plans are important because their preparation is part of learning to teach. They require attention to each aspect of a lesson and ensure that lessons are logically sequenced. Figure 4.1 is an outline of the comprehensive lesson plan format I use throughout this book.

Now let's take a closer look at each part of this format.

1. *Overview.* The overview places the lesson in context. In this section, state the grade level and number of students who will participate in the activity. Provide the title of the instructional unit the lesson is from.

Figure 4.1 Comprehensive Lesson Plan Format

1. Overview
2. Resources and Materials
3. Content Objectives
4. Process Objectives
5. Values Objectives
6. Teaching Sequence
7. Evaluation

2. *Resources and Materials.* Instructional resources are things like Web sites on the Internet, textbooks, CD-ROMs, children's books, and audiovisual items. Materials are things like paint, glue, and construction paper.

3. *Content Objectives.* I prefer a simple form for writing objectives. This section is a list of the content, the subject matter we expect our students to learn in our lesson.

4. *Process Objectives.* This is a list of what we expect our students to accomplish during the lesson. Whereas content objectives list the "what" of the lesson, process objectives focus on the activity of students, both mental and physical.

5. *Values Objectives.* Not all lessons will include this section. Here, we list any values the lesson will help our students acquire.

6. *Teaching Sequence.* At this point in preparing a comprehensive lesson plan, we shift our focus and make a list of things that we ourselves will do. Considerable controversy surrounds the topic of teaching sequences. Many authorities have advocated sets of teaching steps that are usually called teaching "models" (B. R. Joyce & Weil, 1980). Some teaching models are discussed in a subsequent section of this chapter. My approach is pragmatic and situation specific because the things we as teachers do and the order in which we do them depends on what we expect our students to do. We should tailor our teaching sequence to fit the needs of our students, the resources we use, and the objectives of our lesson. Our teaching sequence should start with the things we will do before we begin teaching, such as preparing materials and gathering resources.

7. *Evaluation.* You can collect several types of data to help you determine whether or not students achieved the lesson's objectives. In chapter 8, you will read about the many ways you can evaluate your students.

Let's look at an example of a comprehensive plan, this one for Mrs. Richard's lesson with *Buffalo Chase, Upper Missouri.* Mrs. Richard decided to use what historians call a *primary source,* something produced during the historical period being studied. For example, a letter written *by* Martin Luther King, Jr., is a primary source; a biography *about* King is not. In this case, the primary source was a painting by the American artist George Catlin completed in 1833. Catlin traveled West and observed the tribes who lived on the Plains. The painting *Buffalo Chase, Upper Missouri* hangs in the Smithsonian Institution. Mrs. Richard wanted students to look closely at the painting to learn as much as possible about how the Natives hunted buffalo. She wanted her students to compare the food-getting practices of the Sioux and the Mohawk. Following is a comprehensive lesson plan for this activity.

Grade 5: *Buffalo Chase, Upper Missouri*

Overview: For a lesson in a mini-unit on the Oglala Sioux, a part of a unit on 19th-century Native Americans, students will work in groups to discuss a historical painting depicting a buffalo hunt, an important aspect of Sioux life.

Resources and Materials: (a) study guide, one per student (see Figure 4.2); (b) timeline for the unit; (c) map of the United States; (d) children's books: *Buffalo Hunt* (Freedman, 1988), *Buffalo Woman* (Goble, 1984), *Indians of the Plains* (Rachlis, 1960), and *Where the Buffaloes Begin* (Baker, 1981); (e) sources to help students recall what they learned about the Mohawk (e.g., information books, encyclopedias, charts the students completed).

The essential resource for the lesson is a copy of George Catlin's painting *Buffalo Chase, Upper Missouri* (also called *Buffalo Chase, Bulls Making Battle With Men and Horses*). You could use either of two formats:

1. *With a Computer.* A copy of the painting is available on the Smithsonian Institution's Web site, *http://www.si.edu/*. The painting is part of the collection of the National Museum of American Art in the Smithsonian. You could displayed it for the class with a liquid crystal display projector or with a liquid crystal display panel mounted on an overhead projector.
2. *Without a Computer.* A copy of the painting can be found in most books on the work of George Catlin, such as *George Catlin and the Old Frontier* (Mc-Cracken, 1959, p. 146). Use an opaque projector to display the painting. A much-reduced copy of the painting is shown in Figure 4.3.

Content Objectives: Students will grasp the concept of human-environment interaction as they see an example of how resources influence the food-getting practices of a cultural group. They will learn that the buffalo (American bison) was the essential resource of the Sioux and other Natives of the Plains. Specifically, the lesson teaches that the Sioux used bows, arrows, and lances to hunt buffalo; the Sioux hunted in groups; the use of horses increased the Sioux's efficiency; and the buffalo hunt was dangerous to both the Sioux and their horses. The comparison of the Sioux and the Mohawk will help students understand two concepts: (a) there were great differences in how Native Americans lived prior to the coming of Europeans, and (b) the resources of a region play a central role in determining how groups of people obtain food.

Process Objectives: Students will (a) *observe* the painting, (b) *respond* to the teacher's open-ended question, (c) *describe* the physical setting and the action taking place in the setting, (d) *speculate* on why one hunter is not riding a horse, (e) *compare* hunting buffalo with and without horses, (f) *speculate* on what the hunters thought, felt, heard, and saw, (g) *compare and contrast* the food-getting practices of the Sioux and the Mohawk, and (h) *state* why the practices of the two groups differed.

Values Objectives: Students will acquire the values of cultural understanding and respect as they learn more about the Sioux.

Teaching Sequence

1. Prepare the resources for the lesson: Web site, projector, books, study guide, timeline, map, materials for review of the Mohawk.
2. Ask the students to look at the painting. Show it for a brief time and identify your expectations for the lesson: You will ask students to examine the painting to learn more about how the Sioux hunted buffalo.
3. Point to the relevant dates on the timeline: (a) 1680, the earliest probable date that Natives of the southern Plains had horses; (b) 1730, the date that the Blackfoot, a northern Plains tribe, had horses; and (c) 1885, the approximate date by which buffalo had virtually disappeared from the Plains.
4. Use the map to show the region of the United States where Natives hunted buffalo.
5. Again, show the slide. Ask an open-ended question: "Would anyone like to say anything about this painting?" Use students' responses as a basis for discussion.
6. Divide the class into groups of four to work on the study guide. Distribute the study guides. Tell students that before they write, they should discuss each question. Circulate among the groups and help students share ideas.
7. Call the groups together and have the students return to their seats. Ask for volunteers to share their answers.
8. Use the last query in the study guide to stimulate a comparison of the food-getting practices of the Sioux and the Mohawk. Have students answer the query in groups and then share conclusions with the whole group. Finally, ask each group to explain what factors caused the two tribes to use different ways to get food.
9. Introduce related books to the class. Discuss each one and encourage the students to read them.

Evaluation: Collect the study guides. This would be a good source of information to place in the students' portfolios. You could also take notes as you circulate among the groups.

Effective Teaching in Today's Diverse Classroom: In the 21st century, all our students will need to know how to use resources on the Internet. This lesson could be extended so that students use the Internet. The National Museum of American Art in the Smithsonian Institution has an extensive collection of George Catlin's paintings, including 10 depicting Natives of the Great Plains hunting buffalo. A small group of students could complete a project using the Smithsonian's Web site as an instructional resource *(http://www.si.edu/)*. The quality of the color and the specificity of the detail in the paintings will depend on the quality of your hardware (computer, monitor, and liquid crystal display). I was particularly interested in his two paintings of Natives

Figure 4.2 Study Guide: *Buffalo Chase, Upper Missouri*

Name _____

Date _____

Look closely at the painting. Talk about each question with the members of your group. Then write your answer. You do not have to write the same answer as the other members of your group.

1. How would you describe the land where the action takes place?

2. How many Sioux can you see?

3. What weapons are the Sioux using to kill the buffalo?

4. What is happening to the horses in the painting?

5. In the middle of the painting, we see one hunter who is not on a horse. Why?

6. Imagine hunting buffalo without horses. Why would it be more difficult?

7. Pretend you are one of the Sioux. Write down what you are thinking, feeling, hearing, and seeing.

8. Think back to what we learned about the Mohawk. Think what the Mohawk ate and how they got their food. Think what we have learned about the Sioux. All people need some way of getting food. What is the same and what is different about these two tribes?

Figure 4.3 George Catlin toured the American Great Plains in the 1830s. He painted what he saw. This painting, completed in 1833, is known by two descriptive titles: *Buffalo Chase—Upper Missouri,* and *Buffalo Chase, Bulls Making Battle with Men and Horses. (Source: Smithsonian Institution's Web site, http://www.si.edu/.)*

hunting buffalo in deep snow. An ambitious project would be for a group of students to create a multimedia scrapbook on Catlin's paintings. The scrapbook could comprise text information provided by the students and images taken from the Smithsonian Web site. The text and the images could then be "pasted" into a program on a CD-ROM that could be viewed by their classmates. One other point: As I noted in the description of the lesson, it is important that students learn about the great diversity among Native American tribes. That's why lessons about the Natives of the Great Plains must be part of a broader study of other tribes. It is also important to have students learn about how Native Americans live today.

Figure 4.2 is the study guide Mrs. Richard developed for the lesson; Figure 4.3 shows the painting *Buffalo Chase, Upper Missouri.*

The Abbreviated Lesson Plan

When we assume responsibility for teaching all day, either as student teachers or when we get our first job, we will not have time to prepare comprehensive lesson plans for each activity that takes place. We will use an *abbreviated* form and save comprehensive planning for those lessons that require extra attention. We should, of course, continue to think about all the elements that are part of a good lesson.

The Plan Book Grid. The most common form of abbreviated planning is done in a planning book. Several companies produce these plan books, although each is in a unique format. Almost all, however, are spiral bound. A week is spread across two pages; along the left side are the days of the week, and along the top are blocks of time. In each square, about 2 inches on each side, we write what we will do that day in that block of time (the blocks usually represent 1 hour). Figure 4.4 shows what Donna Richard wrote in her plan book for the lesson with the painting *Buffalo Chase, Upper Missouri*.

Three-Column, Single Sheet. Another form of abbreviated plan is completed on a sheet of paper with three columns. The useful outline format requires a separate sheet of paper for each lesson. Table 4.1 provides an example of this format, again with the *Buffalo Chase* lesson.

Writing Lesson Objectives

An essential element of lesson planning is the writing of instructional objectives. These objectives delineate the expectations we have for our students in any given lesson. I shared with you in chapter 2 that social studies lessons can be reliably broken down into considerations for content, process, and values objectives. The

Figure 4.4 Teacher's Plan Book: *Buffalo Chase, Upper Missouri*

12:45 to 1:50

SOCIAL STUDIES
    Day 3 of mini-unit on Sioux

▶ View *Buffalo Chase, Upper Missouri*
▶ Complete study guide in groups
▶ Introduce follow-up projects

Resources: Smithsonian Web site, LCD projector, timeline, map, 32 copies of study guide, related books, books on Mohawk

Table 4.1 Three-Column, Single-Sheet Lesson Plan
Lesson: *Painting—Buffalo Chase, Upper Missouri*
Date: Tuesday, October 11
Time: 12:45-1:50

Objectives	Teaching Sequence	Materials/Resources
CONCEPT: Human-environment interaction GENERALIZATIONS— (1) The buffalo was the essential resource for the Sioux (2) The Sioux and the Mohawk had different food-getting practices FACTS— (1) Use of bows, arrows, lances to hunt (2) Sioux hunted in groups (3) Horses increased efficiency (4) Danger	(1) Use L.C.D. projector to show the painting (2) Timeline, map (3) Show painting again, students comment (4) Work in groups on study guide, questions 1–7 (5) Reconvene as a whole group, discuss 1–7 (6) In groups, discuss question 8 (Mohawk-Sioux comparison) (7) Reconvene as a whole group—question 8 (8) Introduce related projects and books	(1) Smithsonian Web site, *www.si.edu* (2) L.C.D. projector (3) 32 copies of study guide (4) Timeline (5) Map (6) Related books

standards documents (discussed in chap. 1) and our curriculum course guides (provided by local school districts) will help us in determining our needs for content objectives. To establish how to write more meaningful process and values objectives, I want to introduce you to considerations that curriculum developers often make.

Making Objectives More Meaningful

One key to making objectives more meaningful is to write objectives that identify specific and observable performances by students. According to Ralph Mager, author of *Preparing Instructional Objectives* (1984), effectively written objectives identify "what a student is expected to do and demonstrates how he does it" (p. 4). Using Mager's standards, we can differentiate a poor objective from richer ones with these examples. "To be able to develop an appreciation of music" is an inadequate statement of performance. It does not tell what the student is to do, and it is not observable. However, "To build a model of the Parthenon" or "To list three reasons why the American Colonists declared independence from Great Britain" both can provide more meaningful structure to lesson planning. Instructional objectives that provide focus and direction for both teachers and learners are essential to planning more effective lessons.

One simple component of objectives that can help focus expectations for students is the verb that describes the desired performance. Action verbs, as discreet as possible, can better pinpoint what we want students to do. For example, if, after watching a film on the economy of Mexico, students are expected to identify the correct answers to questions on a worksheet, then the instructional objective could be "Students will circle each product that is exported from the Republic of Mexico."

Raising the Levels of Performance

Social studies lessons provide students with opportunities to engage in higher level thinking. In chapter 7, I go into more detail about how to get students to think more critically, but, for the purposes of our discussions on lesson planning, consider that when writing objectives, we want to raise the levels of student performance and expectations. In his *Taxomony of Educational Objectives* (Bloom, 1956; Gronlund, 1991), Benjamin Bloom created a framework for writing objectives at many cognitive levels. Bloom's taxonomy remains a useful tool for teachers, especially because it provides a basis for planning activities that require complex, critical thinking. In his taxonomy, Bloom categorizes mental activities into six sequential levels: knowledge, comprehension, application, analysis, synthesis, and evaluation. The knowledge level of cognition may ask students to recall knowledge or to define terms and is considered the least thoughtful. Students who are required to synthesize information they have learned or to evaluate it to make an informed decision are asked to think more critically and to reach a higher level of cognition. Instructional objectives should be written to move students to use higher level thinking processes.

1. *Knowledge.* Bloom (1956) stated the following definition for the knowledge category: "Knowledge involves the recall of specifics and universals, the recall of methods and processes, or the recall of a pattern, structure, or setting" (p. 201). This is the mental process of remembering. As conceived by Bloom and his associates, this is a broad category involving knowledge of facts, terminology, sequences, categories, processes, principles, and theories.
2. *Comprehension.* To Bloom (1956), comprehension "refers to a type of understanding . . . such that the individual knows what is being communicated and can make use of the material . . . without necessarily relating to other material or seeing its fullest implications" (p. 204). The ability to restate or summarize is evidence of comprehension, as is the ability to state the main idea in something.
3. *Application.* At the application level, the student begins to use what he or she knows and understands. Application is "the use of abstractions in particular and concrete situations" (p. 205). An objective in this category would

ask a student to apply a law or theory. Another example is the ability to apply a process learned in one context to another context.

4. *Analysis.* The analysis category refers to the ability to identify the component parts of something and to describe their relationship. It includes distinguishing one thing that is closely related to another and comparing and contrasting things. Bloom noted that distinguishing fact from hypothesis is an analytic operation.

5. *Synthesis.* In the synthesis category, the learner creates something new as the parts of something are rearranged into an original configuration. This category includes the activities of speculating and hypothesizing. Students who develop a plan to solve a current social problem are engaged in this category of cognitive activity.

6. *Evaluation.* The last category of the cognitive domain involves "making judgements" (Bloom, 1956, p. 207). This includes rating a list of things in priority order or judging things according to a set of criteria.

Performance Objectives: An Appraisal. Performance objectives are popular for several reasons. They focus on student performance, and this should be the main concern of every teacher. To many of us, they are essential for the preparation of lesson plans because performance objectives provide clear and concise statements of what we expect of our students. Administrators and policymakers like them because they are useful for demonstrating precisely what students have achieved.

Objectives for the lesson with *Buffalo Chase, Upper Missouri* could be written using Bloom's taxonomy. Notice that, to have objectives in each of the six categories of the cognitive domain, some activities would have to be added to the lesson:

1. *Knowledge:* List the weapons the Sioux used to kill buffalo.
2. *Comprehension:* Describe the dangers to the Natives' horses during a buffalo hunt.
3. *Application:* Dramatize the buffalo hunt by pretending you are a hunter who is telling his children about the day's hunt.
4. *Analysis:* Compare the food-getting practices of the Sioux and the Mohawk.
5. *Synthesis:* Speculate on the sounds of the buffalo hunt and write about what the Sioux would have heard.
6. *Evaluation:* Make a list ranking the most important qualities and characteristics of an effective buffalo hunter.

Figure 4.5 provides a list of verbs, arranged by category within the cognitive domain, that could be used in writing objectives.

Figure 4.5 **Taxonomy of Educational Objectives: Cognitive Domain. Suggested Verbs to Use When Writing Objectives**

1. Knowledge	3. Application	5. Synthesis
define	demonstrate	compose
identify	dramatize	design
list	illustrate	hypothesize
match	sequence	invent
recall	show how to	speculate
2. Comprehension	4. Analysis	6. Evaluation
describe	compare	criticize
explain	classify	judge
paraphrase	diagram	justify
restate	distinguish	prioritize
summarize	verify	rate

In addition to writing objectives that attend to cognition, Krathwohl, Bloom, and Masia (1964) developed instructional objectives that address an affective, taxonomic domain. This domain provides a structure for writing objectives to develop student character and values. Look at the following list. When writing value objectives, especially in relationship to valuing cultural differences, consider how the levels of affective instructional outcomes might be implemented to move students from one level to a higher one.

1. *Receiving:* Students are willing to listen with an open mind.
2. *Responding:* At this level, students demonstrate new behaviors and volunteer to become involved.
3. *Valuing:* Students who value what they have learned make a commitment to an issue or cultural group and maintain their involvement in an ongoing way.
4. *Organizing:* A level above getting regularly involved is to commit to organizing an event or a group of people to lead others and see change implemented.
5. *Characterizing by value:* Beyond the classroom and perhaps as a career move, students can be characterized by their values, model behaviors, and attitudes that are ingrained into who they are and what they do.

Perspectives on the Teaching Sequence

As I noted earlier, many authorities have developed step-by-step teaching sequences. In this section, I describe two of these teaching models.

Hunter's Seven-Step Model

Madeline Hunter, former principal of the University Elementary School at UCLA, developed a generic, seven-step teaching sequence that she believes can be applied to any subject at any grade level (Hunter, 1984). The Hunter model, including the training that goes with it, is called *instructional theory into practice (ITIP)*. It is safe to say that this model of teaching is better known than any other because it has been officially adopted by hundreds of school districts, and 16 state departments of education have endorsed or mandated it (Kirp, 1990). I chose to discuss the Hunter model because of its popularity, although research indicates questions about its effectiveness in boosting student achievement (Mandeville & Rivers, 1988/1989; Slavin, 1989 / 1990; Stallings & Krasavage, 1986). The Hunter model is a teaching sequence of seven steps:

1. *Anticipatory Set*. During the first step, the teacher directs student attention to the lesson. The goal here is to get students who will participate in the activity to stop thinking about other things and start thinking about the lesson. For example, Mrs. Richard began by asking students to look at the projected image of the painting. This focused students' attention on the task at hand.
2. *Objective and Purpose*. Next, the teacher states the purpose of the lesson. Hunter (1984) suggests that this include "what will be learned and how it will be useful" (p. 175). For example, "Today we are going to look at a painting of the buffalo hunt, an important aspect in the lives of the Plains tribes. This will help us better understand how these Native Americans lived."
3. *Input*. Hunter (1984) states that "students must acquire new information about the knowledge, process, or skill they are to achieve . . . from discovery, discussion, reading, listening, observing, or being told" (p. 176). This can be a selection from a textbook, a demonstration, a film, or a lecture.
4. *Modeling*. In the fourth step, the teacher, another adult, an older student, or a member of the class demonstrates what all the students will be expected to do. This may involve showing a range of options and then having students choose one to complete.

5. *Check for Understanding.* Before allowing students to work independently, Hunter suggests, teachers should find out whether the students know what they are supposed to do. This can be determined by asking questions or by taking a quick look at the initial efforts of a few of the students.

6. *Guided Practice.* The students work, the teacher circulates. The teacher gives help on request and looks for students who are having difficulty.

7. *Independent Practice.* The final step does not appear in every lesson. This is a time when students complete tasks without help from the teacher.

Following is an example of how the lesson on *Buffalo Chase, Upper Missouri* could be written using the Hunter format.

LESSON PLAN ▶

Grade 5: The Hunter Format:
Buffalo Chase, Upper Missouri

1. *Anticipatory Set:* Show the painting. Ask students to look closely at it.

2. *Objective and Purpose:* Say, "Today, we are going to learn about how the Sioux and other Native Americans who lived on the Great Plains hunted buffalo. We will look closely at this painting, and then you will work in groups to answer some questions about the painting. Then, I will ask you to think about the similarities and differences between the Sioux and the Mohawk."

3. *Input:* Use a timeline to show students the historical period when Natives hunted buffalo on horseback. Use a map to show them the region of the United States where buffalo roamed and the location where the artist George Catlin observed the buffalo hunt depicted in the painting. Then, ask the class to break into groups. Distribute the study guides and explain how the students are to work in groups. Turn the projector on again so that all students can see the painting.

4. *Modeling:* Read aloud the first query and work with one group on the response. Stress the importance of listening to what each member of the group has to say before writing a response. Also point out that the students should talk just loudly enough so that other members of the group can hear them but not so loudly that other groups can hear.

5. *Check for Understanding:* Ask each student to write a response for the first query and then to work on the second query. Move from group to group to be sure that students write responses in the appropriate places and that each group discusses before writing.

6. *Guided Practice:* As the groups work on queries 3, 4, 5, 6, and 7, circulate among the groups. Try to maximize the number of students who talk in each group. Help groups fully explore queries 6 and 7. After discussing the first seven queries, have each group respond to the last query, which asks students to compare the Sioux and the Mohawk.

Lessons often begin with a whole class activity to motivate learning or provide procedural directions.

Some lessons require planning for small-group work, guiding concept development or teaching students how to review what they have learned.

Daily lessons should include time for students to become engaged in critical thinking activities or independent practice. Teachers can then answer individual questions about a project or assignment

7. *Independent Practice:* Ask for volunteers for projects. One group of students could use the Smithsonian Web site to create a CD-ROM scrapbook on George Catlin's paintings. Another group could look at other books, especially *Buffalo Hunt* (Freedman, 1988) and *Indians of the Plains* (Rachlis, 1960), for pictures showing other techniques used to hunt buffalo; then that group can write their own book, *How to Hunt a Buffalo.* A third group could make a large chart comparing the cultures of the Sioux and the Mohawk.

The Hunter Model: An Appraisal. I take the perspective that no one teaching sequence can be applied to every teaching situation. *How* we teach should depend on *what* we teach and *whom* we teach. One problem with the Hunter model is that some educators think it *does* work for all subjects and at all grades. This, despite what Madeline Hunter (1984) wrote: "Because making a basic lesson design explicit was 'welcome news' to so many educators, it has unfortunately become a rigid measuring stick of 'correctness' in teaching. That was never its intent" (p. 175).

Nonetheless, Hunter believes that one of the seven steps should be eliminated only if the teacher has a good reason. The Hunter model is one of many models that can be used for social studies. It should never be the only teaching sequence we follow, but it should be one we consider.

The Concept Attainment Model

Authorities recommend other teaching sequences, and I use many of them in this book (e.g., in chap. 5, the Three-Step Interview and Jigsaw). These teaching sequences are designed for specific purposes, not as generic models (like the Hunter model). To provide one example for comparison, here I describe the teaching sequence developed by B. R. Joyce and Weil (1980) to help children acquire concepts. It is based on the research of Jerome Bruner and his colleagues (Bruner, Goodnow, & Austin, 1956). It is called the *concept attainment model,* and it is frequently used in social studies. I have found that it works better with older children than with younger ones and that it should be used at the end of an instructional unit. The concept attainment model has three variations. I describe the reception form, which has the greatest level of teacher direction. It has three phases, each with three parts:

1. *Presentation of Data and Identification of Concept*

1.1. The concept attainment model is like a game. It begins with the teacher explaining the purpose of the activity, which is to help students better understand a concept. The first phase starts with the teacher presenting students with examples and nonexamples of a concept. The examples and nonexamples can be the names of people or places, things, or events. The teacher tells the students whether each item is an example or a nonexample of the concept.

1.2. Next, the teacher encourages students to compare the examples and nonexamples: What makes them different? What do all the examples have in common?

1.3. At this point, students should be ready to state a definition for the concept. The definition is a hypothesis that will be refined in the second and third phases.

2. *Testing Attainment of Concept*

2.1. In the second phase, the teacher presents items that are *not* labeled as "examples" or "nonexamples." Students state whether or not each item is an example of the concept. The definition may be revised because of the characteristics of the items.

2.2. The teacher now comments on the definition the students have developed. If necessary, the teacher may restate the definition of the concept.

2.3. The final part of this phase is a challenge. Now, the teacher asks students to generate examples of the concept. This will test whether or not they can apply the definition they have learned.

3. *Analysis of Thinking Strategy.* The third phase need not be included each time the concept attainment model is used. This phase asks students to reflect on the first two phases of the model.

3.1. Students describe how they reached their conclusions about the status of each item. What were they thinking when they decided that something was or was not an example?

3.2. Students then talk about how they changed their definitions. Why did they have to change their early definitions?

3.3. Finally, students talk about the characteristics of the concept and consider the process of hypothesis testing.

Following is an example of how the concept attainment model could be used at the conclusion of the unit "19th-Century Native Americans."

Grade 5: The Concept Attainment Model: The Sioux of the Plains

LESSON PLAN

Concept: The Sioux (Dakota); more specifically, the culture of this tribal group of Native Americans who lived on the Great Plains (sometimes called the "Western Sioux")

1.1. Explain to students that you will present some sentences to them. Each sentence will be either an example of something or a nonexample. (You might have to use other words to explain this distinction, like "this fits but this does not fit.") Here, each sentence will be labeled as a "Yes" or a "No." Write the following sentences on sentence strips, number them, and display them on a pocket chart:

1. No: They made boats out of driftwood and tar.
2. Yes: They hunted buffalo for food, clothing, and shelter.
3. Yes: They lived in tipis.
4. No: They lived in long houses in villages surrounded by a fence.
5. Yes: The most important ceremony was the Sun Dance.
6. No: They trapped beaver.
7. Yes: The men wore their hair long.
8. Yes: Men paid for desirable things with horses.
9. No: They farmed corn.
10. No: For the most part, they lived peacefully and did not fight with other tribes.

1.2. Ask students to compare the two groups of sentences. What do the "Yes" sentences have in common? What makes the "No" sentences different from the "Yes" sentences?

1.3. Ask students to write a definition or description for all the "Yes" sentences. They should come up with something like "Things we know about the Sioux."

2.1. Now you present five more sentences to the students (see numbered list below). This time, the sentences are not labeled "Yes" or "No." The students must decide whether each is a "Yes" or a "No":

1. They communicated with a written language.
2. Women owned property; daughters inherited it.
3. The goal of a warrior was to "count coup" by touching an enemy.
4. The wealthy were expected to give feasts and offer presents to the poor.
5. They made beautiful clay pottery.

2.2. Comment on the definition the students have developed. If necessary, restate the definition of the concept.

2.3. Finally, ask the students whether they can generate examples of the concept. Ask, "Who can say something else about the Sioux that would be a 'Yes' sentence?"

SUMMARY OF KEY POINTS

▶ Lesson plans are of two general types. Comprehensive lesson plans are detailed and lengthy. Abbreviated plans are written in outline form.

▶ All planning comes down to do two things: First, we must decide precisely what we expect our students to do; second, we must decide what we, the teacher, must do for our students to achieve what we expect of them.

▶ Instructional objectives focus the direction and expectations of teachers and students. When they are well-written, these objectives provide specific and observable expectations of student performance.

▶ Bloom's taxonomy of cognitive objectives describe levels of thinking processes. Instructional objectives can be written to require students to use higher level mental activities. The affective taxonomy can be used in writing values objectives, helping students be more responsive to cultural diversity.

▶ Madeline Hunter's generic, seven-step lesson plan model has gained considerable popularity. The concept attainment model is less well known.

FOR FURTHER READING

Lesson Plans

▶ The books by Eggen and Kauchak (1988); Gunter, Estes, and Schwab (1995); and B. R. Joyce and Weil (1980) are the best sources for models of teaching. I think the clearest statement of Madeline Hunter's teaching model is her chapter in *Using What We Know About Teaching,* the 1984 publication from the Association for Supervision and Curriculum Development. Books by Mager (1984) and Gronlund (1991) are a must for anyone who has to write behavioral objectives.

▶ You probably have had your fill of lesson models and formats. This chapter, of course, has only scratched the surface. For example, Engle and Ochoa (1988) defined a model for reflective teaching in issues-centered social studies programs; their model has five steps. Felton and Allen (1990) developed an eight-step lesson format for using visual materials, such as photographs and paintings, in social studies. Of particular interest is a fine article by D. E. Freeman and Freeman (1991) on how social studies lessons would be constructed under the whole language philosophy of teaching and learning.

Native Americans

▶ The Internet, the ERIC system, and social studies journals have too many good resources on teaching about Native Americans to list all of them here. I think that Donna Richard's unit is appropriately named ("19th-Century Native Americans"). It is important that children realize that Native Americans do not live today as they did in the past. In her article, Harvey (1993) addresses the issue of the past and present in the study of Native Americans. The January 1999 issue (Vol. 63, No. 1) of *Social Education* has several good articles on teaching about Native Americans and includes a list of tribal Web sites. One topic often overlooked in lessons and units about Native Americans is the governmental systems created by the Iroquois League, the Lakota Nation, the Muskogee Nation, and the Pueblo (Sahr, 1997). The article I mentioned by Powe (1998) in the previous chapter presents a curriculum that uses other paintings by George Catlin.

▶ By all means, look at the children's books that Donna Richard brought to class for her lesson. *Buffalo Hunt* (Freedman, 1988) is the best book on the topic for children. It is illustrated with paintings by Catlin and Karl Bodmer, another artist who visited the Plains before the Civil War. *Buffalo Woman* (Goble, 1984) is a folktale, told in similar versions by several tribes. *Indians of the Plains* (Rachlis, 1960) is an older book but a good one and is part of the American Heritage Junior Library. It contains a chapter ("Indian Cattle") on buffalo hunting. *Where the Buffaloes Begin* (Baker, 1981) is a story collected and retold by Olaf Baker. Baker was an Englishman who came to the United States in 1902. He traveled West and lived among the Blackfoot. This folktale is about a lake where the buffalo were created. An excellent essay on a related topic was written by Jennifer Turan Rothwell (1997). She discusses how a variety of visual images can be used to teach about the Plains Indians.

▶ Many Web sites are available about the Sioux. One good one is part of the site for the Glenbow Museum in Calgary, Canada *(http://www.glenbow.org/srobe.htm)*. The Glenbow Museum has a buffalo robe with pictographs that tell the story of a group of Sioux warriors. For each section of the robe, a narrative describes the meaning of the pictographs.

Chapter 5

Cooperative Learning: Enhancing Skills and Knowledge Through Group Activities

This was the last day of Rosa Navarro's third-grade social studies unit on boats. For 13 days, the children had participated in a variety of activities. The third-grade teachers at Ms. Navarro's school chose Transportation as an organizing theme for the first of the school year (the second half would be devoted to the history of their community). After the unit on boats, Ms. Navarro planned on teaching a unit on airplanes. Today, the final lesson on boats would be a "segue" activity, one that led the class to the unit on airplanes. This simple activity would use a cooperative learning structure called *Think-Pair-Share*.

On a sheet of chart paper, Ms. Navarro had written the following questions:

- How are boats and airplanes alike?
- How are they different?

In the first phase of the activity, she asked the children to think quietly about each question. She encouraged them to write down any answers they had to either question. She then asked the children to sit next to their "buddies." (Ms. Navarro assigned each child a different buddy each week so that, during the year, every child in the room would get a chance to work with every other child.) After each set of buddies was "paired up" and ready to share their answers, Ms. Navarro asked one member of each duo to give an answer, and then the other. She allowed time for partners to chat casually about the similarities and differences of their responses. Finally, Ms. Navarro called the class back to their seats. It was time to share responses with the whole class. Tiffany and Maria volunteered to go first. Tiffany stated that they made a list of the many ways boats and airplanes were alike ("They carry people around," "They go faster than walking," "They come in many sizes"). Roger noted two differences: Boats only travel on water but airplanes travel in the air, and the fastest airplanes were "a lot faster than the fastest boats." The sharing continued for another 10 minutes.

This was a good social studies activity for two reasons. First, it accomplished the goal of forming a bridge from one unit of study to another as Ms. Navarro's class started thinking about the content of their next unit—airplanes. Second, every child in the room had the opportunity to express his or her ideas. In most class discussions, only a few children talk; most children spend their time listening. In Think-Pair-Share, all 28 children in the room had an opportunity to express their perspectives.

▲   ▲   ▲

In this chapter, you will read about:

- ▶ The fundamental reasons why cooperative learning is a powerful instructional tool for teaching social studies
- ▶ Several cooperative learning structures, including Group Projects, Jigsaw, Think-Pair-Share, Three-Step Interview, and Student Teams-Achievement Divisions (STAD)
- ▶ Factors that affect the success of cooperative group learning; the development of group goals, individual accountability, social skills, and effective planning

▶ Decisions we as teachers make to organize cooperative groups; how to place students in groups, when to use ability and interclass grouping, how long members of groups should work together, and when to change group dynamics

Introduction to Cooperative Learning

Collaboration and cooperation among students have been essential parts of social studies for more than 100 years. During the Progressive era (about 1890–1940), students in elementary schools frequently worked on projects with their classmates. One of the greatest Progressive thinkers, William H. Kilpatrick (1918, 1925), proposed that social studies consist almost entirely of students working on projects they selected and planned. This was the ultimate "child-centered" approach: Children would study what they found interesting. Although students could work on projects individually, Kilpatrick encouraged group work. His three characteristics of a successful project are worth remembering in the broader context of cooperative learning: Children should be involved in "purposeful activity" conducted in a "hearty fashion" in a "social surrounding" (1918, p. 321). Recently, educators have shown intense interest in instructional formats that require students to work together in groups. New models for group work have been developed, and hundreds of studies have been conducted. Today, when educators talk about cooperative learning, they usually refer to one of the models advocated by the "big four of cooperative learning": Spencer Kagan, Robert Slavin, David Johnson, and Roger Johnson.

Let's look at two definitions of cooperative learning that epitomize these models:

It involves students working together as equals to accomplish something of importance to all of them. (Slavin, 1990b, p. 34)

Cooperative learning means instructionally using small groups so that students work together to maximize their own and each other's learning. (Johnson & Johnson, 1992a, p. 45)

Spencer Kagan (1985, 1989, 1989 / 1990) has popularized over a dozen cooperative learning *structures*. These structures are "content-free ways of organizing social interaction in the classroom" (1989 / 1990, p. 12). Kagan distinguishes cooperative "structures" and "activities":

Teachers can design many excellent cooperative *activities,* such as making a team mural or a quilt. . . . In contrast *structures* may be used repeatedly with almost any subject matter, at a wide range of grade levels, and at various points in a lesson plan. (1989/1990, p. 12)

Robert Slavin (1990b) prefers to call these structures "systematic and practical cooperative learning methods" (p. 21). I refer to them as either "models" or "structures" and describe five models of cooperative learning. First, though, let's take a look at the research that supports the use of cooperative learning.

A Research-Based Rationale for Cooperative Learning

Research on cooperative learning shows that it can have positive results (Johnson, Maruyama, Johnson, Nelson, & Skon, 1981; Slavin, 1980, 1990a). Cooperative learning can boost student achievement, but we must keep two things in mind. First, almost all the studies have focused on learning basic skills in reading and mathematics. Second, to be effective, cooperative learning must involve *group goals* and *individual accountability* (Slavin, 1992). Group goals exist when students work toward some reward for their group. Individual accountability means that each member of the group must demonstrate what she or he has accomplished. After reviewing 46 studies, Qin, Johnson, and Johnson (1995) concluded that cooperative effort produces higher quality problem solving than does individual effort. This is an important finding because problem solving is an essential part of social studies. When confronted with a problem, students working in groups are able to exchange information, share insights, and compare the worth of various solutions.

Virtually none of the best research on cooperative learning has looked at elementary social studies. Slavin's (1990a) analysis considered the 60 studies that met his "best evidence" criteria. Only six dealt with social studies content. Only one involved students in Grades K–6 (Yager, Johnson, Johnson, & Snider, 1986). The other major study on cooperative learning and social studies was also conducted under the guidance of David and Roger Johnson (K. A. Smith, Johnson, & Johnson, 1981). The Yager et al. (1986) study is problematic because of the narrow view of social studies teaching and learning taken by the researchers. Third graders participated in a 25-day unit on transportation. What did the children do? They completed a worksheet each day. "Learning" was limited to the recall of information. The results did show that children who learned the material while working in small groups *and* who were trained to work together knew more than other third graders who were in groups but received no training in working together. Classmates who completed the worksheets individually learned less than the children who worked in groups.

The K. A. Smith et al. (1981) study is of more interest because it looked at higher level thinking. Sixth graders considered the expansion of logging and mining in wilderness areas of Minnesota. The results showed that a process called *constructive controversy* can help students learn social studies content (Johnson & Johnson, 1992b). In constructive controversy, students are placed in four-member groups. Two members argue the pro side of an issue, and two members argue the con side. The four members together write a single report. The study did assess learning at several levels of Bloom's taxonomy, but the problem with the study lies in the limited way material was presented to students: Each student was given a packet of information and was asked to read it.

Research involving the mix of cooperative learning, social studies, and elementary students is lacking. It seems safe to say, though, that on the basis of research on cooperative learning in other areas of the curriculum and with older students, cooperative learning should be a part of our social studies program. Remember, too, the social studies curriculum is concerned with more than content. We also teach processes and values. Among the values we want students to adopt are a respect for diversity and a reverence for democracy. A good K–6 social studies program emphasizes social processes, which include working cooperatively toward a common goal.

A classroom of diverse students should have many opportunities for cooperative learning because research does show that the use of cooperative learning improves intergroup relations. Cooperative learning helps students of different cultural groups respect each other. It promotes positive feelings toward students with disabilities. Slavin (1989/1990) summarized the results of several studies:

> When students of different racial or ethnic backgrounds work together toward a common goal, they gain in liking and respect for one another. Cooperative learning also improves the social acceptance of mainstreamed academically handicapped students by their classmates . . . as well as increasing friendships among students in general. (pp. 53–54)

In addition to the research base, a theoretical argument can be made for using cooperative learning. Our common sense would tell us that "two heads are better than one." Interaction with other people exposes us to different perspectives and helps us clarify what we know. A compelling theoretical argument for cooperative learning was presented by the Russian psychologist Lev Vygotsky (his ideas are discussed in chap. 2). Recall that he believed a gap exists between what children can learn and do independently and what they *could* learn and do if they had help. This assistance could be collaboration with an adult or peers (Vygotsky considered the best situation to be one where a child works with more capable peers). Vygotsky's ideas place great emphasis on the social aspects of learning. Fifty years before cooperative learning became part of the conventional wisdom, Vygotsky had explained why it helps children learn.

As with any instructional technique or resource, moderation in cooperative learning seems like a reasonable attitude. We as teachers would be making a mistake if we never used cooperative learning; and we would be making a mistake if we used only it and excluded whole-group and individual activity. Now let's take a look at five cooperative learning structures (a sixth structure, Group Investigation, is one of the models of inquiry presented in chap. 6).

Group Projects

In the Group Projects cooperative learning structure, two or more students work together to produce something. In social studies, Group Projects fall into five categories:

1. *Inquiry projects,* in which students work together to solve a problem (they "produce" an answer)
2. *Written projects,* in which students work together to produce a written product, like a book or a script
3. *Visual arts projects,* in which students work together as they paint, draw, sculpt, or use another media to produce a work of art
4. *Performing arts projects,* in which students work together to act, dance, or sing in a performance
5. *"Combination" projects,* in which students are asked to use more than one format (e.g., some projects require students to do things in both the visual and performing arts); a written product often results from an inquiry

Group Projects work best if students volunteer to participate. Once students volunteer, these become "interest" groups because the members have expressed an interest in the project. Sometimes, though, we as their teachers assign students to work on a project. We might want to create a group that is heterogeneous and has a mixture of genders, ability levels, and ethnicities. Or, we might decide that some students need to participate in a project because they have not chosen previously to do so. Some students, for example, never choose to participate in a performing arts project unless it is a requirement.

The big issue in planning a Group Project is what role each student will play in the common task of finishing the project. In some cases, the students themselves will decide what each member of the group will do. In others, we will assign the tasks. On some projects, students work together throughout the project, whereas on others, group members complete tasks individually and their efforts are reassembled at some later point.

Here is an outline of the steps in a Group Project in the social studies. They are written from the teacher's point of view, but notice how, in each step, student autonomy can be increased:

1. *Form the group.* For greater student autonomy, we should ask for volunteers.
2. *Provide an overview of the project.* In some situations, students themselves will define precisely what they will produce. In every case, we as teachers should listen to the interests, ideas, and needs of the group members and make adjustments accordingly.

3. *Decide what each student will do.* In performing arts projects, this means assigning roles. In writing projects, it means listing what will be written and by whom. If we wish to increase the level of student control over the project, then we should allow students to decide what roles they will play.
4. *Make a list of materials and resources.* We should be sure that all materials and resources will be available when they are needed.
5. *Establish a timetable.* The timetable for completing the project should include times when the entire group will meet again. In some projects, it may be best to let members of the student group establish the timetable.
6. *Work with individuals, subgroups, and the full group.* We should have a schedule indicating when we will provide guidance and assistance to members of the group. To increase student autonomy, we should encourage them to help each other before they turn to us.

Following is a description of a Group Project that produced a chronological mural.

Grade 3: "Chronological Mural"

Al Braccio's third graders spent the second half of the school year studying their city. Now, Mr. Braccio thought it might be worthwhile to have a group of children create a *chronological mural* of the history of their city. A chronological mural shows several scenes in the order they took place. Earlier, I listed the six steps in completing a Group Project like this one:

Step 1: Form the Group
Mr. Braccio asked for volunteers. Privately, he encouraged his two English language learners (Sara and Ben) and his two lowest achieving students (Cliff and Dan) to take part. All four said they would like to work on the mural. Six other children volunteered. It was a diverse group in gender, ethnicity, and ability (the group included high-achieving students too).

Step 2: Provide an Overview of the Project
The next day, Mr. Braccio met with the group. He showed the children photographs of a mural fifth graders had completed depicting scenes from U.S. history. Mr. Braccio told the group their mural would be similar and suggested eight possible scenes from their city's past:

- Morning at a Gabrielino village (the Gabrielino were the Native tribe that lived where their city now stood)
- Mission San Fernando Rey de España (actually a few miles from their city, but very important)

- A wedding at the rancho that covered most of the land the city now occupied
- The house of the dentist who founded the city
- The teacher and her students at the first public school
- Workers entering the aircraft plant, which was the city's largest employer
- Actors, camera operators, and a director making a movie, another of the city's important industries
- Airplanes at the city's regional airport, which opened for commercial passenger service in 1975

The group discussed these scenes. Someone suggested they add a drawing of city hall. The other children agreed; this was not surprising because the old city hall was one of the places the children visited on their field trip of the city. Mr. Braccio suggested they add some buildings damaged in the earthquake of 1994. All agreed this would be a dramatic addition to the mural.

The group decided that, for each of the 10 scenes, they would provide an illustration, title, and a brief caption. The illustrations would be on large sheets of construction paper. When finished, the illustrations would be stapled to a large bulletin board. For example, for the earthquake scene, the title was "1994: Earthquake!" The caption read, "On January 17, 1994, a big earthquake shook our city; 750 buildings were damaged, and 47 people were hurt. All of us felt it, that's for sure!"

Step 3: Decide What Each Student Will Do

When the group met again, Mr. Braccio made a chart identifying the 10 scenes in their mural. He suggested that the group divide into five subgroups of two children each. Each pair would draw and describe two scenes. Mr. Braccio wanted to be sure Sara and Ben did not work together; he also wanted to separate Cliff and Dan. He made a list of the five subgroups and presented it to the group. Then, each subgroup selected the scenes they would depict. Mr. Braccio made a chart showing the assignments:

Scene 1: A Gabrielino village—Sara, Debbie
Scene 2: Mission San Fernando—Ben, Denise
Scene 3: The rancho adobe—Sara, Debbie
Scene 4: The dentist's house—Brad, Claudia
Scene 5: The first school—Brad, Claudia
Scene 6: Old city hall—Cliff, Tina
Scene 7: Aircraft plant—Ben, Denise
Scene 8: Making a movie—Cliff, Tina
Scene 9: New airport—Dan, Amber
Scene 10: Earthquake—Dan, Amber

Step 4: Make a List of Materials and Resources

Mr. Braccio and the group decided they would need the following materials:

Colored marking pens and crayons
Large white construction paper (18 × 24 inches)

Study prints (large photo reproductions) of the history of their city
10 copies of the soft-cover social studies textbook on the history of their city,
    which included other photographs
Photographs Mr. Braccio took while he and the class were on their field trip (He
    had good photographs of city hall, the mission, the dentist's house, the
    first school, the airport, the aircraft plant, and buildings damaged by the
    earthquake.)

Step 5: Establish a Timetable

Mr. Braccio and the group met the next day to begin work. The 10 children agreed on the following timetable:

May 10: Pencil drawings finished for each scene
May 16: Final illustrations
May 17: Rough drafts for titles and captions completed
May 18: Titles and captions completed
May 19: Bulletin board "backed" with powder blue paper, title of mural stapled
    to board, illustrations and captions stapled to the board

Step 6: Work With Individuals, Subgroups, and the Full Group

This project was completed during the final social studies unit of the year, "Our City Today and Tomorrow." Of the 10 children who worked on the mural, only one set of partners had some problems communicating. Dan and Amber had some trouble working together; Dan wanted to draw both scenes, which gave Amber nothing to do but the captions. Mr. Braccio helped them resolve their differences by leading them to discuss their scenes and agree on the composition of each one. Then, they were directed to draw and color both scenes together.

The students did a good job adhering to the timetable, although one group fell behind because they had trouble getting started. Once Mr. Braccio helped them "block out" their drawings, they moved along fine. After the mural was finished and displayed for all to see, each student was proud of what he or she had created.

NOTE: While these 10 students were working on the chronological mural, other students were engaged in different projects in groups or independently. One class group looked at what the city might look like in the year 2100 and illustrated a book to share their ideas. Another group conducted a Group Investigation to determine why people might immigrate to their city.

Effective Teaching in Today's Diverse Classroom: Group Projects like this one and all other forms of cooperative learning will enrich the educational experience of minority children. Kagan's research shows how consistent use of cooperative learning can improve intergroup relations. Cooperative learning has great appeal to students who thrive in instructional formats requiring social learning (see chap. 2). Cooperative learning is also essential for English language learners (E. G. Cohen, 1986).

Children have the ability to provide comprehensible input to their classmates who are English language learners. A student often can explain a difficult idea to

For over 100 years, groups of elementary school students have worked together on social studies projects. One member of a group puts the final touches on a mural.

someone his or her own age with more clarity than an adult. Cooperative learning, if done properly, creates an environment free of anxiety because students relax when working with their classmates. Sometimes you will want your English language learners to work together under your guidance (so it's easier for you to provide comprehensible input). Usually, though, you should disperse your English language learners so that they gain the benefits from working with their English-only classmates.

Student Teams–Achievement Divisions (STAD)

Robert Slavin (1989, 1990a, 1992) has been an effective advocate of cooperative learning. He and his colleagues at Johns Hopkins University developed several cooperative learning structures. One of the most popular is Student Teams–Achievement Divisions (STAD; Slavin, 1978, 1986, 1990a). According to Slavin, STAD is "most appropriate for teaching well-defined objectives with single right answers, such as specific locational characteristics in geography and some map skills, knowledge of events in history, and principles of economics or government" (1992, p. 21). Thus, STAD should be limited to teaching students basic information. STAD is not a method of teaching; it is an *alternative* to independent seat work (during which, at the conclusion of a lesson, students work alone on follow-up assignments).

The teacher places students in four-member heterogeneous teams that are a cross section of the whole class—boys and girls, a mix of ethnicities, and high-achieving, mid-achieving, and low-achieving students. The teacher presents a lesson or group of lessons to the whole group, and then the students work together to learn the material. This "team study" may take from a half hour to several days. Slavin recommends that the teacher prepare worksheets the students complete together. STAD works only if all members of the team accept that it is their responsibility to help their teammates learn all the material the teacher presents. The teacher then gives a quiz, which students take individually. The teacher compares each student's quiz score with that student's performance on earlier social studies quizzes and gives each student a score that reflects how much that student exceeded her or his average previous performance. The four scores for each team are added to create a team score, and the teams with the highest scores are given points, certificates, or some other reward. Following are some examples of instructional objectives that would lend themselves to units using STAD:

- *Grade 2:* Explain what role each of the following plays in keeping our community safe: firefighters, police officers, public health inspectors, public works crews, school crossing guards.
- *Grade 3:* Identify the following places on a map of our city: Miller Elementary School, City Hall, Olive Park, Verdugo Park, McCambridge Park, St. Joseph's Hospital, Burbank-Pasadena-Glendale Airport, Media City Mall, NBC Studios, Warner Brothers Studios, Golden State Freeway, Ventura Freeway.
- *Grade 5:* List and describe three examples of "checks and balances" in the U.S. Constitution.
- *Grade 6:* Compare and contrast the Aztec and Inca systems of government, economic production and distribution, religion, and social organization.

Jigsaw

Jigsaw was developed by Elliott Aronson and his colleagues (Aronson, Blaney, Stephen, Sikes, & Knapp, 1978). Here is how it works: The teacher places students in six-member groups (a class of 30 students would have five groups). The teacher then breaks down a topic or unit into six subtopics. For example, if a class of students were to do a unit titled "City Workers," the six subtopics might be (a) police officers, (b) firefighters, (c) recreation leaders, (d) sanitation workers, (e) librarians, and (f) animal control officers. Each member of a team is assigned a subtopic and is expected to become an expert on that subtopic.

Students then learn about their subtopics. Aronson describes Jigsaws in which students would be able to read a section of a text to find out what they needed to know. (I think Jigsaw works well when students learn from a variety of sources, including videos, computer-based resources, audiotapes, and lessons taught by the teacher.) Once students learn information about their topics, they then meet in "expert groups." For example, the six students who all had learned about firefighters would meet together, the six who had learned about recreation leaders would meet, and so on. In these expert group meetings, students can compare what they found out and decide on how they wish to present what they learned to the other members of their group. Students then return to their original groups. Each student is an expert who has information to share. The students take turns teaching the other members of their groups all they have learned.

Think–Pair–Share

Think-Pair-Share is a simple cooperative learning structure that works well in social studies (F. T. Lyman, 1992; L. Lyman, Foyle, & Azwell, 1993). Think-Pair-Share greatly increases the number of students who actually say something during a class discussion. If a teacher leads a discussion in front of the whole class, few students actually make contributions. Rarely do more than a quarter of the class do anything but listen; it is not unusual for three or four students to dominate. In Think-Pair-Share, every student in the class will have an opportunity to express her or his perspective. This cooperative learning structure has three phases:

1. *Think*. The teacher poses a question that should stimulate a discussion. The question cannot be too difficult or too simple. If the question is too difficult, then students will have nothing to say. If the question in too simple, then all that can be said will be over quickly. I think the question should be written either on the chalkboard or a sheet of chart paper. All students then think about possible answers. Depending on the complexity of the question, the teacher might want students to write their answers on paper. For a third-grade unit on the future of their city, a teacher could ask her students to answer any of the following questions through Think-Pair-Share:

   - What challenges would our city face if its population increased significantly in the next 20 years?
   - Which of the city's businesses will grow in the next 20 years? Which of the city's businesses might have a difficult time?
   - What will the schools in our city be like in the next 20 years? How might they be different from the way they are today?

2. *Pair*. Each student then works with a partner. The partners explain the rationale that led to their answers. During this phase, each student in the class will have an opportunity to talk.

3. *Share.* Now, the whole class reconvenes. The floor is open; students may share their answers with their classmates. If partners have arrived at a shared answer, then each partner may talk a bit about how the duo arrived at their answer.

Three-Step Interview

Like Think-Pair-Share, Three-Step Interview is a cooperative learning structure that maximizes student participation (Kagan, 1985, 1989, 1989/1990). Three-Step Interview is simple and can be used repeatedly during a social studies unit:

1. During the first step, the teacher asks a question (or questions). Again, the questions should be written on the board or chart paper, and they should be thought-provoking. The class then separates into groups of four. Within each group, each student works with a partner. One partner is the interviewer and the other is the interviewee. For example, Ahmed, Ashah, Keiko, and Hideo are the members of a group. During this first step, Ahmed asks Ashah questions; Keiko asks Hideo to give his answers to the questions.
2. In the second step, students reverse roles. This time, Ashah interviews Ahmed while Hideo interviews Keiko. Three-Step Interview works best when students learn how to ask "follow-up" questions, much like a good newspaper reporter: "Why do you think that is the answer?" "What makes you think that?" Follow-up questions should be asked with respect, but they can be challenging: "Are you sure? What about _____ (some fact or idea the interviewee had not considered)?"
3. In the third and final step, the group of four reconvenes. In round-robin fashion, each student shares her or his answer.

Making Cooperative Learning Work

Robert Slavin concluded that two features must be present for cooperative learning to be effective: (a) group goals and (b) individual accountability. Johnson and Johnson provide a third feature: (c) social skills. My review of the literature on cooperative learning and my experience as a teacher lead me to argue for a fourth feature: (d) effective planning.

Group Goals

As Johnson and Johnson (1992a) note, "Students must believe that they sink or swim together" (p. 47). The Johnsons call this *positive interdependence.* The group must have a clear sense of what they are supposed to accomplish, and this goal must be shared and understood by all members of the group. Sometimes, the group goal is simple. For example, in Think-Pair-Share, the partners have the goal of listening to each other and exchanging ideas. In a Group Project, the goal is to produce something. The Johnsons and Slavin believe that there must be tangible rewards for groups that accomplish their goals. I'm not sure. I have seen many groups work together beautifully and their only reward was their joy in creating something they were proud of. Tangible rewards include points (which can be redeemed for rewards) and certificates. I have seen rewards as diverse as Popsicles and the opportunity to be first in line for lunch. If tangible rewards are given, then they must be given to each member of the group.

Individual Accountability

As Johnson and Johnson (1992a) explain, "Students learn together so that they can subsequently perform better as individuals. To ensure that each member is strengthened, teachers hold students individually accountable to do their share of the work" (p. 48). It is essential that each student's performance be evaluated. This does not necessarily mean assigning a score or grade to each student. It does mean keeping some sort of record that describes two things: (a) the student's performance in the *process* of working in a group and (b) the student's level of achievement in the *product* the group created. I describe ways of keeping evaluative records in chapter 8, including an example from the chronological mural project described earlier in this chapter.

Social Skills

Johnson and Johnson (1989/1990) have discussed at great length the social skills students must master to be successful in cooperative learning. Students must "get to know and trust one another, communicate accurately and unambiguously, accept and support one another, and resolve conflicts constructively" (p. 30). Here are the four steps in teaching these social skills:

1. *Students must see the need for the skill.* For example, we can explain to our students how resolving conflicts quickly and fairly will help a group finish their assignment.
2. *Students must understand the skill.* Unfortunately, this book does not have enough space to describe fully the social skills of trust, communication, support, and resolution. I recommend the books the Johnsons and their colleagues have written (Johnson & Johnson, 1986; Johnson, Johnson, & Holubec, 1984). One simple method is to describe the words that are used in the social skill. For example, to support the other members of their group, students can say things like, "That looks great!" "Tell me more about

where you found that out," "Let's be sure that idea is in our report," and, "I haven't thought about that; thanks for bringing it up."

3. *Students must have many opportunities to practice these social skills.* Students must have frequent chances to work in groups, *and* we as their teachers must monitor and support those students who work well together.

4. *Students must evaluate how well they are doing.* The Johnsons call this *group processing.* The group needs to talk about their successes and frustrations. Rather than focus on individual behavior, the group processing should bring clarity to the behaviors that make group work easy and pleasant.

Effective Planning

Some cooperative learning structures require minimal planning (Think-Pair-Share, Three-Step Interview). Other structures will only work if they have been thoroughly planned (Jigsaw, Group Project, Group Investigation, STAD). For all cooperative activities, each of the following must be accomplished:

- *Be sure the goal is clear.* If a group is to perform a play, then the members of the group must know what the play will look like when it is performed. Will costumes be worn? How long will the play be? Where will the performances take place?
- *Be sure the goal is attainable.* That is, given the best of circumstances, will the group achieve the goal? If a group is given a task that is beyond their level of ability, expect lots of problems.
- *Be sure that roles are clearly and reasonably defined.* Each student must know what he or she is expected to do. If some students have to do a great deal of work, and others little, this must be decided at the beginning of the activity and accepted by the members of the group.
- *Be sure the group has adequate materials and resources to finish their task.* Nothing will stop a group from being effective faster than a lack of books, paper, maps, or other essential resources.
- *Be sure that timelines are set and that members of the group adhere to them.*

Other Issues in Grouping

What Is the Proper Place of Cooperative Learning in Social Studies?

In their overview of cooperative learning in social studies, R. J. Stahl and VanSickle (1992a) state that "cooperative learning strategies should not replace all other teaching strategies in the social studies classroom" (p. 4). Some activities will involve the whole class. Individual work has its place as children go about exploring topics of personal interest. Cooperative learning, however, helps make social studies *social*. It provides children with the opportunity to "learn and practice the knowledge, abilities, and attitudes necessary to function effectively within the social group and as part of the social community" (p. 4).

What Criteria Should Be Used to Place Students in Groups?

Most groups should be formed on the basis of either *interest* or *proximity*. Group Projects and Group Investigations work best when students volunteer to take part (thus, the basis for forming the group is interest in the topic or project). Simple cooperative learning structures, like Think-Pair-Share, lend themselves to proximity grouping; students work with whoever is seated near them. Almost all groups should be *heterogeneous:* Each group should be a microcosm of the class, with boys and girls from all ethnic groups. Each group should have students at a range of abilities. This is not to say that occasionally a group of girls (or boys) might be the only volunteers for a project. The point is that if segregation gets to be a pattern, then we should intervene and modify the composition of the group. For some cooperative learning structures, like Three-Step Interview, Jigsaw, and STAD, we will assign students to groups.

Ability Grouping. The National Council for the Social Studies (NCSS) has issued a policy statement on ability grouping (NCSS Ad Hoc Committee on Ability Grouping, 1992). *Ability grouping* is the practice of placing students in groups on the basis of their level of academic achievement. It tends to happen more in elementary language arts and mathematics than in social studies. The research on ability grouping is voluminous and contradictory (Kerckhoff, 1986; Lou et al., 1996; Oakes, 1985; Slavin, 1987, 1989/1990). Although grouping students by ability can work in some subject areas if done properly (mathematics, reading), educators agree that students should not be placed in "permanent" ability-based groups. Ability grouping, unfortunately, often leads to the segregation of the least able, the challenged, the poor, and the linguistically different. Some activities during the year we plan just for our most able or least able students, but for the most part we should design our units so that students work in several different groups and with classmates of every ability.

Interclass Grouping. Some schools use a form of interclass grouping for social studies, although this is more prevalent in language arts and mathematics. In a *departmentalized* elementary school, a fifth-grade teacher might teach three 2-hour social studies/language arts blocks each day. Other teachers would teach a mathematics/science block and the arts/PE block.

Team teaching has many forms. For example, two third-grade teachers may decide to rotate their students each day from 12:45 to 3:05 p.m. From 12:45 to 1:50, Teacher A teaches social studies while Teacher B teaches art. Then students change rooms, and from 2:00 to 3:05 p.m., Teacher A repeats her social studies lesson and Teacher B repeats her art lesson. In a purer form of team teaching, three second-grade teachers may work together and share responsibility for the 90 second graders in their school. Together, they plan the week's activities for all the second graders. At different times during the year, each teacher would take the lead in planning a social studies unit. The other teachers would play a supporting role, helping fulfill the planning teacher's ideas.

How Long Should Students Stay in a Group?

The amount of time students should spend working in the same group varies. For some models of team learning, the teams should be kept together for several months (Vermette, 1998). Most other groups, however, will not exist for that long. Most groups should be ad hoc; they should exist until they achieve their goal, which may take from a few minutes to 4 or 5 weeks. A Group Project, for example, may take a month to complete, whereas a Think-Pair-Share group activity may last only a few minutes. Ideally, each student in a class should work with every other student in that class in a cooperative group sometime during the school year.

SUMMARY OF KEY POINTS

- ▶ Group work has a long history in social studies. For more than 100 years, elementary school children have worked together as part of social studies.
- ▶ Recently, cooperative learning structures have been used widely in elementary classrooms. Structures are models for organizing group work.
- ▶ Research shows that the use of cooperative learning improves intergroup relations.
- ▶ Cooperative learning structures include Group Projects, Jigsaw, Think-Pair-Share, Three-Step Interview, and Student Teams-Achievement Divisions.
- ▶ The following features increase the chances that cooperative learning experiences will be positive: group goals, individual accountability, social skills, and effective planning.

FOR FURTHER READING

- ▶ Much has been written about cooperative learning, and it is difficult to know where to start. Most relevant to social studies is the fine little book *Cooperative Learning in the Social Studies: An Introduction to Social Study*

(R. J. Stahl & VanSickle, 1992b). An excellent place to start your reading is the special edition of *Educational Leadership* devoted to cooperative learning (December 1989/January 1990, Vol. 47, No. 4). It has articles by Kagan, Slavin, the Sharans, and the Johnsons. Probably close to 100 books are available on cooperative learning. I like Slavin's (1990a) *Cooperative Learning: Theory, Research, and Practice* and Vermette's (1998) *Making Cooperative Learning Work: Student Teams in K–12 Classrooms*. If you want to know how to teach students the social skills necessary for successful group work, then read the books and articles by David and Roger Johnson cited in the text. For more on cooperative learning structures, try Kagan's book.

▶ As I have stated repeatedly, group work and cooperation have always been a part of social studies. The work of Alice Miel, a true giant in the field of social studies, has a great deal to say to all teachers, no matter where, when, or who we teach. I recommend her book *Cooperative Procedures in Learning* (1952). Another old book I like is Ruth Strang's (1958) *Group Work in Education*.

▶ Also of interest: Edward De Avila, Sharon Duncan, and Cecelia Navarrete developed a curriculum based on cooperative learning to teach science to bilingual students. It is called Finding Out/Descubrimiento (De Avila, Duncan, & Navarrete, 1987a, 1987b). It is one of the few attempts to apply cooperative learning specifically to teaching content to English language learners. An excellent research review on grouping and social studies written by Nancy Winitzkey (1991) is found in *Handbook of Research on Social Studies Teaching and Learning*.

▶ Two good classroom examples of Jigsaw, though written for teachers of older students, are in journal articles by Ferguson (1988) and Palmer (1988). Sullivan (1996) discusses how a form of Group Investigation was used in a middle school unit on the Civil War. Taylor and Larson (1998) explain the advantages of using cooperative learning with students who have attention deficit learning disorder.

Chapter 6

Inquiry: Challenging Students With Discovery Learning and Problem Solving

Let me begin this chapter with a memory from my own teaching experience. An important part of the fourth-grade curriculum in Burbank, California, was the study of California history. Each year, my fourth graders viewed a filmstrip on the California missions, which were built under the direction of Franciscan missionaries between 1769 and 1823. I remember this filmstrip because it featured excellent photographs of the missions (today, filmstrips have been replaced by computer-based delivery systems). I preferred showing filmstrips without their accompanying narration because then the class and I could linger on interesting images and discuss them.

In the middle of this filmstrip was an old drawing of a group of Natives attacking a mission padre. The padre was bound with ropes, and the Natives were beating him with clubs. In previous years, when my classes viewed the same filmstrip, this image did not generate any interest. This time, Susan, one of the students in my class, raised her hand and asked, "Mr. Zarrillo, did that really happen? I don't think anybody would attack a priest." Instead of answering the question, which would have been impossible because I didn't know the answer, I decided that the question would make an excellent inquiry. I responded by saying I didn't know the answer but that a small group of students could work with me to find an answer. We worked for a month to answer Susan's question. It was an exciting and challenging experience for the students who participated. This inquiry project provided all the students in my class with a better understanding of how California's Natives suffered during the Mission Era. In this chapter, I describe how to design inquiry activities, and you will learn more about how my students found an answer to Susan's question.

▲   ▲   ▲

In this chapter, you will read about:

- ▶ Social studies instruction that is structured around inquiry-based activities
- ▶ A general teaching sequence for inquiry activities that requires teachers and students to play roles different from those they traditionally play in social studies lessons
- ▶ The Group Investigation and Suchman inquiry models
- ▶ Teaching students to access references from both traditional and computer-based resources
- ▶ Factors that will enable all students to participate successfully in fun and challenging inquiry activities

Inquiry: An Overview

Inquiry is a process that begins when a problem is identified, either by students or by the teacher. Students then consider the problem, offer possible solutions in the form of hypotheses, gather information, and analyze what they have learned to determine whether or not a hypothesis is a reasonable solution to the problem. Finally, the initial hypothesis (or hypotheses) is accepted, revised, or rejected in favor of a different solution (Massialas & Cox, 1966; Wilen & White, 1991). Some social studies educators use the term *problem solving* to describe the inquiry process. The goal of inquiry activities is to help students acquire the ability to resolve problems in a rational and systematic fashion.

Inquiry, or problem solving, has a long history in elementary social studies. John Dewey, as you will recall from chapter 1, was the greatest thinker of the Progressive era of American education, which began in the late 1800s. Dewey (1910/1933) used the term *reflective thinking* to describe the type of inquiry-based activity he thought should be at the center of Progressive schools. To Dewey, an activity requiring reflective thinking presented children with "a forked-road situation, a situation that is ambiguous, that presents a dilemma that proposes alternatives" (p. 14). Dewey thought that the social studies curriculum should give children opportunities to engage in reflective thinking and to become "versed in the methods of experimental inquiry and proof" (p. 217). In Dewey's view, inquiry should be child centered as children define problems and develop plans to gather data and reach solutions. Dewey's ideas continue to serve as the basis for many models of inquiry teaching.

The 1960s saw the introduction of the "New Social Studies" programs. Many of these programs were "inquiry based" because most lessons in a unit of study were based on problem-solving activities. These inquiry-based programs were greatly influenced by Jerome Bruner (1960, 1961). Bruner used the term *discovery learning* to describe inquiry activities. He wanted children to acquire "an attitude toward learning and inquiry, toward guessing and hunches, toward the possibility of solving problems on one's own" (1960, p. 97). Bruner thought that children should solve problems the same way as real-life social scientists and become child versions of anthropologists, sociologists, economists, and historians. Many New Social Studies inquiry-based curricula were exciting and challenging for both students and teachers.

Brophy (1990), however, noted several difficulties with these innovative programs. Many problems were too difficult for children. Some activities were based on hypothetical communities or countries, and children did not spend enough time studying real ones. Too often inquiries were entirely teacher centered. Teachers or the textbook defined the problem and dictated how to solve it. These "problem-solving" activities were really exercises with predetermined answers. Keep these criticisms in mind as we look at how to design inquiry activities.

A Teaching Sequence for an Inquiry

Researchers do not agree on the exact steps an inquiry should follow. For example, Eggen and Kauchak (1995), Massialas and Cox (1966), the Sharans (S. Sharan & Sharan, 1976; Y. Sharan & Sharan, 1989 / 1990), and Suchman (1962, 1966) each developed a unique sequence for an inquiry. A synthesis of their methodologies would be as follows:

1. Define the problem
2. Speculate on possible answers
3. Gather information
4. Analyze the information and test hypotheses
5. Reach a conclusion

Let's now take a closer look at each step.

1. *Define the problem.* The social studies textbook may provide the problem, we may pose the problem, or students may generate the problem. A certain excitement accompanies questions that come from students. Recall the opening vignette to this chapter; Susan's question was a good example of the motivational power of a student-generated question. When she questioned the authenticity of the drawing, several other students agreed with her, and they were determined to find an answer! Depending on the series, textbooks can be a source of good questions for inquiries. These questions are often at the end of the chapters under subtitles like "On Your Own" or "For Further Research." When we plan a unit of study, we should be sure to look at the suggested inquiries in our textbook series.

Inquiry questions can be placed on a continuum. The worst are those that have simple answers that can be found in a single source. A question like "What agricultural products are raised in South Africa?" is only an inquiry if the definition of that term is broad. To answer such a question, students do not need to go through the entire sequence of steps to find the answer; such questions are merely exercises in using reference materials. Better, but not perfect, are inquiry questions that have complex answers and require data from more than one source. An example is "Why do people live in our community?" Students can speculate on answers, gather data through a survey, and then reach conclusions. Another example is "How was elementary school in Colonial times different from elementary school today?" This question would require students to consult several sources of information and make comparisons with their own classroom and school. The best inquiries have no single correct answers, usually because authorities in the field disagree. Examples are "What happened to the lost colony of Roanoke?" and "Who built the Easter Island monuments and for what purpose?" Questions like these require data from many sources. Because even authorities do not agree on an answer to such a question, students will reach a solution solely on the merits of the data, rather than by finding verification of their hypothesis in a book. Figure 6.1 illustrates the range of inquiry questions.

2. *Speculate on possible answers.* After the inquiry question is refined and agreed on, we need to help students make *educated* guesses on possible answers. The discussion will reveal how much students know about the problem. In this

Figure 6.1 Range of Inquiry Questions

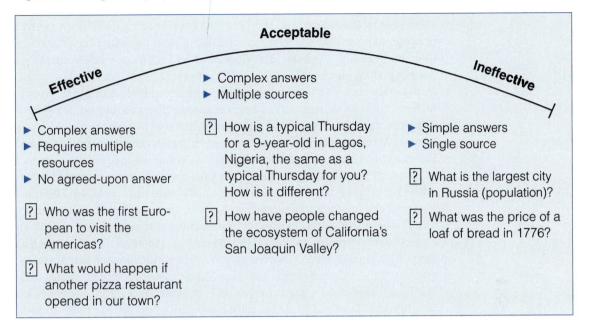

Acceptable

Effective

Ineffective

▶ Complex answers
▶ Multiple sources

▶ Complex answers
▶ Requires multiple resources
▶ No agreed-upon answer

? Who was the first European to visit the Americas?

? What would happen if another pizza restaurant opened in our town?

? How is a typical Thursday for a 9-year-old in Lagos, Nigeria, the same as a typical Thursday for you? How is it different?

? How have people changed the ecosystem of California's San Joaquin Valley?

▶ Simple answers
▶ Single source

? What is the largest city in Russia (population)?

? What was the price of a loaf of bread in 1776?

sense, the hypothesis-generating discussion will help us assist students in finding information. Some inquiries are done individually, but most involve small groups of students. It is not necessary that all students agree on one possible answer; they may have several hypotheses. Sometimes students may not be able to make a realistic guess, and then we need to broaden their background knowledge before they look for answers. Hypotheses should be recorded, and as the inquiry progresses, they may be revised.

In my class's inquiry into the attack by California Natives against a mission priest, a group of five students agreed to resolve the question. Two competing hypotheses were advanced: One member of the group speculated that the picture was accurate, that the Natives had killed a priest; the other students hypothesized that, for some unknown reason, the picture was a fake.

3. *Gather information.* After students have speculated on possible solutions to the problem, it is time for them to gather information. We can break down our question into subtopics and assign students to look for answers in different sources (e.g., Aimee scans the Internet, Fred checks the encyclopedia, Li looks at information books). It is best if students play a leading role in developing the "research" plan. Our role will vary, depending on the complexity of the question, the abilities of our students, and the difficulty of the sources of data. In some situations, we may only need to point students in the right direction. In others, we may need to locate materials and help students read them.

Many sources of information can become a part of research plan:

- *Bibliographic and electronic information.* Inquiry activities provide perfect opportunities for students to master the use of both computer-based sources (e.g., the Internet, CD-ROM encyclopedias) and hard-copy references (e.g., encyclopedias, almanacs).
- *Primary sources.* The best inquiries ask students to look at original, historic material such as diaries and old newspapers. When an inquiry leads to a primary source, students are doing history like real historians.
- *Surveys.* Many inquiry-based activities can be based on contemporary issues. For example, one group of third graders was commissioned by the principal to investigate what all the school's students thought about a revised lunch schedule. Should the school move the lunch period up an hour? The third graders surveyed their schoolmates to find out the answer to this question.
- *Miscellaneous resources.* Just about any teaching resource can be used in an inquiry. For example, an inquiry to determine the links between ancient Egypt and ancient Greece would require an examination of maps, charts, graphs, films, videocassettes, filmstrips, audiocassettes, prints, realia, CD-ROM and hard-copy encyclopedias, the Internet, and information books. We shouldn't limit our students; rather, we should encourage them to seek information from all appropriate sources.
- *Direct observation.* Although this data source is essential in the natural and physical sciences, it is more difficult to use in the social sciences, especially in the elementary grades. Many inquiries, however, can be answered through direct observation. A visit to a harbor, for example, helps students answer the inquiry "What different jobs do people perform at the harbor?"

In my class's inquiry into the attack on the mission priest, students searched through old fourth-grade textbooks, information books in the library, and encyclopedias. In addition, at my suggestion, one student wrote to three professors of California history, each at a different campus of the California State University system. This inquiry activity took place before widespread use of the Internet; today, we could have checked many Web sites. My favorite is "Spanish Missions of California" *(http://tqd.advanced.org/3615)*. This site was developed by two high school students in Southern California, is full of useful information, and is written at a level that most fourth graders can understand.

4. *Analyze the data to test the hypothesis.* Analysis of the information students gather is fairly simple in an inquiry: How do the data support or challenge our hypotheses? As students gather information, they will do one of three things with each of their initial hypotheses: (a) Reject it as being too far from the data to be supported, (b) revise it because the information gathered supports some aspect of the hypothesis but not all of it, or (c) accept it because the information indicates that the proposed answer was accurate.

In my class's inquiry, students found that a few Native uprisings took place, but not many. Interestingly enough, each professor written to wrote back, and *each gave us a different answer.* This was an eye-opener for my students, who at that point seemed stunned that "authorities" wouldn't all give the same answer. Despite the disagreements, all the professors did support the answer the information books had given—that isolated incidents of Native rebellion against mission priests did take place.

5. *Reach a conclusion.* In the final step of the inquiry, students state an answer and share it with the class. Although most inquiries will result in definitive answers, some will be left "dangling." In some instances, the best that can be done is to state a few possible solutions and admit that the data do not warrant a final answer. In other instances, the concluding statements may lead to a new inquiry and the process can begin again. Whatever the results, students should share what they have learned with their classmates. Following are several possibilities for doing this:

- *Computer-based multimedia.* Several computer-based possibilities are suitable for "reports." Perhaps the most exciting is to use a CD-ROM and a software program like Hyperstudio to create a report that has photographs, diagrams, maps, written text, and audio. Another possibility is a "virtual museum" (Ricchiuti, 1998) that becomes part of a school Web site.
- *Written material.* Students can write a book or issue a short summary of their inquiry.
- *Illustrations.* Sometimes the answer to an inquiry can be presented visually by using illustrations or photographs displayed on a bulletin board, an overhead projector, or via computer-based technology.
- *Charts and graphs.* The best way to share numerical data is to communicate the results with charts or graphs.
- *Oral reports.* Oral reports are more successful if students rehearse, if the report is brief, and if the report summarizes the process students followed to find the answer.

My fourth graders' inquiry concluded when the group made an oral presentation to their classmates. To support their presentation, they compared the three answers the professors offered.

Inquiry as Cooperative Learning: Group Investigation

Group Investigation is an instructional model that combines inquiry teaching with the principles of cooperative learning. A group of students choose a question to investigate and attempt to find possible answers. To answer the question, some group members explore subquestions. Finally, the group makes a presentation to their classmates that summarizes the findings. Group Investigation has its roots in the Progressive ideas of John Dewey and has been defined by the Israeli scholars Yael Sharan and Shlomo Sharan (1989/1990; S. Sharan & Sharan, 1976). The Sharans developed their model from earlier work done by Miel (1952), Thelan (1960), and B. R. Joyce and Weil (1980). Sharan and Sharan recommend that Group Investigation follow six consecutive stages:

1. *Stage 1: Identify the question to be investigated and organize the group.* Again, the best questions are asked by our students. For each unit we teach, we should develop a list of questions that could serve as the focus of a Group Investigation. Once a topic is chosen, it should be phrased as a question. The question should have more than a single simple answer or else the Group Investigation model won't work. In this first stage, we and our students must decide whether or not the topic in question can be better answered by dividing the investigation into subtopics.

2. *Stage 2: Plan the investigation.* In this stage, students decide what each member of the group will do. For example, two members of the group will read

A problem, usually stated as a question, will motivate students to gather the information they need to find an answer. In this classroom, the search for answers takes place in a social studies center, complete with costumes, models of historical objects, and information books.

nonfiction books, another will use CD-ROM encyclopedias, a fourth will surf the Internet, and a fifth member of the group will write a final report. The group decides what resources they will need. Sharan and Sharan suggest that the group write a plan describing how and when the investigation will be completed.

3. *Stage 3: Carry out the investigation*. Group members gather information, take notes, compare their findings with those other members of the group, and state possible answers to their question.

4. *Stage 4: Prepare the final report*. Quite appropriately, Sharan and Sharan have a liberal definition of *report*. Some groups will report via computer, others will construct bulletin board displays, and some will perform skits. The key, of course, is that the final presentation answer the question the group has investigated.

5. *Stage 5: Present the final report*. We should work with our students to be sure the prepared presentation is comprehensible. Because it will be presented publicly, written material should be edited and the final draft should be in a easy-to-read display format. If the final report is oral, then students should rehearse.

6. *Stage 6: Evaluate*. Each member of the group evaluates her or his experience. Simple questions can focus this evaluation: What went well for our group? When did we have difficulty? If we were to do another investigation, what would we do differently?

Suchman's Inquiry Model

The first two models of inquiry teaching I presented in this chapter are quite similar. Richard Suchman, however, developed a unique teaching sequence for an inquiry activity (Eggen & Kauchak, 1995; B. R. Joyce & Weil, 1980; Suchman, 1962, 1966). Suchman developed his model of inquiry teaching for the process of investigating and explaining atypical natural phenomena. Although he based his model on the work of physical scientists, Suchman's procedures have been used successfully in social studies. The Suchman teaching sequence is concise, and an activity following the model can be completed in less than an hour because we provide all the information our students require. Another advantage of this model is that it encourages students to work together toward resolving the question.

A Suchman inquiry has five phases:

1. *The teacher presents a puzzling situation to students*. It is essential that the situation confuse the students and lack an obvious explanation. We then might display pictures, diagrams, or maps that visually reveal the problem. Alternatively, we might use eyewitness accounts, newspaper reports, or diary entries. We can also provide students with a "fact sheet," a list of information that cannot be presented visually. Whatever the resources, we should present the problem dramatically.

2. *Students ask yes/no questions to verify data*. This is the unique aspect of the Suchman model. After we present the problem, students ask us questions that can

be answered only yes or no. If a student asks a question that cannot be answered yes or no, then the question must be restated. At this point, the questions must relate to the information that has been presented and not attempt to answer the inquiry.

3. *Students ask yes/no questions to formulate hypotheses.* Again, students may only ask questions that can be answered yes or no. This third phase is different from the second in that students should introduce possible solutions in their questions. Their questions should seek to support those solutions.

4. *Students state their explanations and discuss them.* Each explanation should be fully discussed in the light of the data that have been revealed. Students should acknowledge the strengths and reveal the weaknesses of each hypothesis. During this phase, we have a decision to make: Should we tell our students "the answer"? This depends. If our students have come up with an answer that is close to the correct one, then we probably should acknowledge and reward them for their success. If our students appear frustrated because their answers don't seem adequate, then we might want to explain the answer to the problem. If students appear to be interested in gathering more data on the problem, however, then we shouldn't give an answer; instead, we should encourage them to continue to investigate.

5. *Students analyze the inquiry process.* One purpose of the Suchman model is to help students become more proficient at solving problems. After the activity is over, we should lead a discussion about the first four phases: What questions were most effective? How must members of the group work together? What questions might have been asked that would have led to a quicker or more definitive answer?

Following is a description of a lesson using the Suchman inquiry model.

Description of a LESSON

Grade 5: A Suchman Inquiry—"Samoset Greets the Pilgrims"

Mrs. Kim's fifth graders were working on a 3-week unit on the Pilgrims. The class learned about the suppression of Separatist religious groups in England, how a group of Separatists first emigrated to Holland, the voyage of the Separatists and others to New England aboard the *Mayflower,* and the establishment of the Plimoth colony during January and February of 1621. Her students had taken a "virtual field trip" to the wonderful living history museum of Plimoth Plantation, which is an exact replica of the Plimoth colony of 1627 (the tour is available on the Plimoth Plantation Web site, *http://media3.com/plymouth/vtour*). She used the Suchman inquiry model for a lesson about the appearance of Samoset, a member of the Abenaki tribe, in Plymouth on March 16, 1621.

Step 1: The Teacher Presents a Puzzling Situation to Students

Mrs. Kim started the lesson by reviewing what the students had learned so far. After looking at several sources on the Pilgrims, including the superb Web site "Mayflower on the Web" *(http://members.aol.com/caleb.mayflower.html)*, she found the best description of Samoset's visit in an old book from the wonderful American Heritage Junior Library, *The Pilgrims and Plymouth Colony* (Ziner, 1961). She wrote and read aloud the following account of an event that occurred on March 16, 1621:

> March 16 was a cool morning in Plimoth. Most of the men had gathered in the Common House for a meeting. The women and children were busy with their chores. A small number of men with guns stood guard. Many of the Pilgrims were ill from the "General Sickness" that had killed over half the people who had sailed on the *Mayflower.* So far, the Pilgrims had only seen a few Natives. Each time, the Natives ran away and hid. But on the morning of March 16, one of the guards looked up and saw a Native brave walking toward the village. He was tall, with feathers in his hair. He was smiling and waving at the Pilgrims! The guards shouldered their rifles and were about to demand that he stop. Then the Native shouted at them, "Welcome, Englishmen! My name is Samoset!" Samoset talked to the Pilgrims in English for quite some time. He told them about the region near the settlement. He talked with them well into the night. The Pilgrims were astonished that Samoset could speak English.

Mrs. Kim then said, "It was amazing that Samoset could speak English. How did he learn English?"

Step 2: Students Ask Yes/No Questions to Verify Data

Mrs. Kim explained that the class was to figure out how Samoset learned to speak English. She explained that the students could ask her any questions they wanted, but there were two rules: (a) She could only answer yes or no, and (b) their questions should try to get more facts. Most questions the students asked were appropriate:

> "Had Samoset ever been to England?" (No.)
> "Was Samoset really a Native?" (Yes. Students thought Samoset might be an Englishman in disguise.)

Eventually, students asked questions that served as the basis for two possible answers to this historic riddle:

> "We learned about Jamestown, in Virginia. Wasn't that before Plimoth?" (Yes. Here, Mrs. Kim went beyond the Suchman format to locate Jamestown and Plimoth on the map. She wrote the year 1607, when Jamestown was founded, on the board.)
> "Were the Pilgrims the first English people to visit New England?" (No.)

Step 3: Students Ask Yes/No Questions to Formulate Hypotheses

Mrs. Kim now moved to the third step, where students asked questions that would support possible answers. One group of students thought that Samoset had lived for a time in Jamestown. This answer worked until one girl asked, "Had Samoset ever lived at Jamestown?" (No.)

"Had he ever visited the English at Jamestown?" (No.)

Now, three students focused on the English who had visited New England prior to the coming of the Pilgrims. They asked: "Did Samoset ever talk to the English who visited New England before the Pilgrims?" (Yes.)

"Did he work for them?" (The answer to this isn't clear because Samoset had sailed with English captains along the Maine and Newfoundland coasts. He may have served as a guide, or he may have just been along for the ride. Again, Mrs. Kim deviated from the Suchman model by replying that Samoset had sailed with English captains who had explored the New England and Canadian coasts.)

Step 4: Students State Their Explanations and Discuss Them

At this point, it was easy for students to state an explanation: Samoset had learned to speak English when he sailed along the coast with the English explorers.

Step 5: Students Analyze the Inquiry Process

Most students said they enjoyed this activity and wanted to do more like it. Some students complained that their classmates didn't ask good questions. Mrs. Kim was satisfied with the activity, although she was disappointed that more students didn't participate. Next time, she decided, she would modify the teaching sequence so that students discussed the puzzling event in small groups before they started asking questions.

Mrs. Kim planned the Samoset inquiry for two reasons: (a) She wanted her students to practice the critical thinking that is part of the Suchman model, and (b) she wanted to help her students understand a historical generalization: The English had considerable contact with New England and Canada before the coming of the Pilgrims. After the Samoset inquiry, she used a timeline and a map to show the following events:

1497: John Cabot landed at Cape Breton Island in Canada.
1583: Sir Humphrey Gilbert sailed to St. John's, Newfoundland, and established a temporary English settlement.
1602: Bartholomew Gosnold explored the Maine coast and sailed to Cape Cod (he named it).
1605: Sir Ferdinando Gorges and George Waymouth landed on Monhegan Island off Maine. They supposedly took another Native, Tisqauntum (Squanto), back to England.

1607: Gorges and Sir George Popham established a colony at Sagadahoc (or Popham), Maine. The colony, which was to serve as a base for fishing, failed in 1608.

1614: Captain John Smith, one of the settlers of Jamestown, sailed along the New England coast from Maine to Cape Cod. He made a map and wrote a book, *A Description of New England,* that the Pilgrims took with them on the *Mayflower.*

Effective Teaching in Today's Diverse Classroom: One important component of effective instruction for English language learners is "primary language support." Primary language support for English language learners can be provided by a bilingual teacher, an instructional aide fluent in the students' first language, or bilingual classmates. The support can be oral, as the teacher explains an activity in the primary language, or it can be written. In this lesson, the description of Samoset's visit could be translated into the primary language(s) of the English language learners in the class. The English language learners could read the translation, or the translation could be read to them.

Inquiry Using Computer-Based Resources. Regardless of which model of inquiry teaching we use, our students will have to be able to gather information from both computer-based resources and traditional, hard-copy references sources. The microcomputer, along with supporting software and hardware, is changing the face of social studies instruction (Alter, 1995a; Simpson, 1997, 1998). Microcomputers (or "personal computers") can be found in virtually every elementary school in the United States. Unfortunately, most surveys reveal that teachers do not use computer-based resources in teaching social studies (Ehman & Glenn, 1991; Hoge & Saye, 1994; Honey, 1994; Northrup & Rooze, 1990). In this chapter, our discussion of computers will look at resources that elementary students could use in gathering information. The technology changes rapidly, and by the time you read this book, new and improved technology may well be in place.

Computers with *modems,* devices that connect computers through telephone lines, have the potential to be linked with vast mainframe computers and with individual users all over the world. A computer user is "on-line" when her or his computer has been linked with other computers. Once on-line, a computer in a classroom becomes part of the "information superhighway" (Wilson, 1995). The most extensive on-line system is the *Internet* (Boldt, Gustafson, & Johnson, 1995; Cowan, 1997; Monahan & Dharm, 1995; Risinger, 1996b, 1998; E. K. Wilson & Marsh, 1995). The Internet is actually a collection of networks (a *network* is a collection, or system, of computer resources and users). Nobody owns the Internet, and your access to it can be free if the school district is connected. Commercial on-line services that can be used for Internet access charge a fee; these include America Online, Prodigy, and CompuServe. Commercial on-line services designed for teachers and students include Classroom Prodigy, Scholastic Network, and the AT&T Network.

As I write this chapter, it is difficult to gauge the ultimate impact of the Internet on social studies teaching. It is conceivable that the next generation of elementary school students will know *only* the Internet and that hard-copy reference books will become obsolete. Certainly, the Internet has the potential to be the ultimate source of information for teachers and students. The World Wide Web (WWW) has greatly facilitated the challenge of finding relevant information on the Internet. Users are able to search (or "surf") for information on the Web through software programs, the most popular being Netscape. Each Web site has a unique address (e.g., *http:/www.ncss.org* is the address for the NCSS). When we connect with a Web site, we first look at the "home page," which shows what is available. With a click of the computer mouse, it is possible to see text, video, and graphics and to hear sound. A University of Texas site, *http://volvo.gslis.utexas.edu/-kidnet/*, includes a useful set of "Internet do's and don'ts."

Here are two examples of the Internet's potential: Risinger (1996b) reviewed several Web sites on the U.S. Civil War, including *http://lcweb.loc.gov.exhibits/G.Address/ga.html*. This Library of Congress Web site has versions of the Gettysburg Address, which students could compare and contrast. Hattler and Ledford (1996) describe Web sites that have information on the federal government and federal elections. These include "Welcome to the White House," with a special "White House Kids" section *(http://www:whitehouse.gov/WH.Welcome-plain.html)*; "The Jefferson Project," which has Web pages for all members of Congress *(http://ww.voxpop.org.jefferson)*; and "Thomas," an accessible service created for members of Congress, with the texts of all bills enacted into law *(http://thomas.loc.gov)*.

Risinger (1998) notes that of all the possible problems with using the Internet, including the possibility that children will find pornographic material, "the real problem is information evaluation and validation" (p. 148). We as teachers and our students should not assume that everything we read on the Internet is accurate, timely, clear, and important. We should help our students evaluate Internet sources in the light of who provided the information and for what purpose, on the basis of how old the information is, and for the validity of the information when compared with other sources. This issue makes the "Schools of California Online Resource for Educators" (SCORE) social studies Web site so valuable for all teachers; all Web sites and links listed there have been reviewed by classroom teachers *(http://www.rims.k12.ca.us/score/)*.

CD-ROM (**c**ompact **d**isc-**r**ead **o**nly **m**emory) is one of the most promising computer-based formats. CD-ROMs have incredible storage capacity and can hold still photographs, videos, charts, graphs, text, and narration and other sounds. The CD-ROM is replacing the diskette as a format for educational software (Mitchell-Powell, 1995). Many new social studies textbook series now come with supporting material on CD-ROM. An entire encyclopedia can be stored on a single disc. The most popular CD-ROM encyclopedia has no hard-copy equivalent—*En Carta* (Microsoft). IBM acquired the electronic rights to the largest selling hard-copy children's encyclopedia, *World Book,* and has produced a CD-ROM version. As

CD-ROMs take more and more of the encyclopedia market away from hard-copy versions, an increasing number of CD-ROM encyclopedias will become available. Besides encyclopedias, other reference sources are becoming available on CD-ROM. For example, *3D Atlas 97* is a CD-ROM atlas designed for upper elementary students (Bennett & Dawson, 1998).

Using a CD-ROM encyclopedia is similar to, yet different from, using a traditional, hard-copy encyclopedia. For example, if a student wanted to find information on Molly Pitcher, a hero of the American Revolution, using *En Carta,* here is what the student would do:

1. Assuming that *En Carta* is properly loaded, the student would review an opening menu and "click" (with a mouse) the choice of "Contents."
2. The student could "scroll" on an alphabetic list, but it would be faster to type in "Pitcher, Molly."
3. Then, after a brief time, an entry of 65 words and an illustration of Molly Pitcher from the National Archives would appear.
4. Unlike with hard-copy encyclopedias, the student would then have several options, such as (a) printing the illustration, (b) printing the text of the entry, (c) enlarging the text for easier reading, or (d) looking at related information by simply putting the mouse on the related entry word (or words) and clicking the mouse. None of these options, of course, would be available with a hard-copy encyclopedia.

Semrau and Boyer (1995) describe an instructional experience using CD-ROM. First, students examined murals in their own neighborhoods (e.g., on the outsides of buildings, in bank lobbies). Then, the teacher placed the students in groups and each group selected one mural and investigated it. Then, the students learned about murals in the ancient world by interacting with *Ancient Lands,* a CD-ROM by Microsoft. *Ancient Lands* has information on several ancient cultural groups. The students could compare murals in their community with those created by the ancient Minoans, Egyptians, and Romans.

Grade 2: Tamika Sees and Hears Dr. Martin Luther King, Jr.

Description of a STUDENT USING A CD-ROM ENCYCLO-PEDIA

In Tom Sinna's second-grade classroom, children were participating in a unit titled "People Who Made a Difference." Tamika was learning more about Dr. Martin Luther King, Jr., and she had read several picture biographies of him. Mr. Sinna, however, was looking for a way to give Tamika a multimedia experience. During a visit to the school's computer lab, he decided to work with Tamika on the CD-ROM encyclopedia *En Carta* (Microsoft, 1994 version).

Together, Mr. Sinna and Tamika sat down at a Macintosh Centris 650 computer. Mr. Sinna clicked on "En Carta" and went to a menu and selected "Historical Audio." With Tamika operating the mouse, they scrolled a list of names, and sure enough, there was Martin Luther King, Jr. Tamika recognized his name and said, "There he is!" They were in luck. *En Carta* had an audio recording of Dr. King. They clicked "Martin Luther King, Jr." and on the monitor appeared a picture of Dr. King delivering his "I Have a Dream" speech in Washington, DC, in 1963. As the picture came into view, the recording began, and Mr. Sinna and Tamika listened. After the speech, Tamika said, "I read about this speech in some picture books I read, but this is the first time I heard it. Can I listen to it again?" This was not a problem; the "tape" was easily "rewound" with a click of the mouse, and Tamika listened to the speech one more time.

Effective Teaching in Today's Diverse Classroom: The information age has the potential to improve the educational experiences of every child. Lack of access to computer-based resources, however, could exacerbate the gap between the affluent and the impoverished in our society. It is important that we as teachers ensure that all our students, especially those with challenging conditions and those who are English language learners spend as much time working with computer-based resources as their classmates.

Traditional, Hard-Copy Reference Books. Even with the power of computer-based resources, our students should continue to search for information in traditional, hard-copy reference books such as encyclopedias, almanacs, and atlases. Several children's encyclopedias are available for elementary-age students, such as the *World Book* and *Children's Brittanica*. Unfortunately, many encyclopedias, though written for children, are beyond the ability of many of our students. Almanacs have mountains of statistical information. Older elementary students can learn to use adult almanacs, such as the *Information Please Almanac* or the *New York Times Almanac*. Each of these is updated and published annually. An *atlas* is a book of maps. Many social studies textbooks have a mini-atlas and a "gazeteer" (a dictionary of geographic terms). Two children's atlases I suggest are the *Rand McNally Children's World Atlas* and the *National Geographic Picture Atlas of Our World*. A good source for teaching ideas with reference books is the column "Into the Curriculum," which appears regularly in the *School Library Media Activities Monthly*.

Teaching Students to Use Reference Books. Our students will learn how to use reference books as they use them to complete inquiry projects. We should plan some well-designed lessons that will help our students be more proficient when they use reference books. Too often, our reference skills lessons can become boring and meaningless. We should keep these lessons simple, and those students who have demonstrated their proficiency with reference books should be excluded from activities aimed at teaching them what they already know. Here are some types of lessons that will help our students:

- Lessons on the organization of an encyclopedia. Students must understand that information is arranged by topics (called "entries"), that entries are placed in alphabetical order, and that most encyclopedias have multiple volumes.
- Lessons on how to use a table of contents, an index, page guide words, and cross-references.
- Lesson on how to scan for specific information.

Once students have received this basic instruction, give them a chance to practice what they have learned. Here are some activities:

- *For practice with encyclopedias.* Provide the class with access to a full set of an encyclopedia. Give students topics and have them figure out which specific volume has an entry for each topic. A good way to do this is to write each topic on a separate index card (e.g., "wheat," "barley," "corn," "rye"). Have students place each card in front of the appropriate volume.
- *For practice with a volume of an encyclopedia.* Give each student several topics and have her or him find the page where each topic begins. Encourage students to use the guide words.
- *For practice using cross-references in the entries.* Give each student the name of an entry and have the class write the cross-references that appear in their given entries. In some encyclopedias, the additional references are boldfaced. In others, they appear at the end of the entry.
- *For practice with a single entry.* Provide each student with a copy of the same entry. Challenge students to scan the entry to find a specific date or bit of information (e.g., for "gold," find the three countries that mine the most gold annually).
- *For practice with an atlas.* Ask students to use the table of contents and the index to find maps of continents, nations, states of the United States, cities, rivers, lakes, oceans, mountain ranges, and deserts.
- *For practice with almanacs.* Give students topics and have them use the index to find the appropriate page number of each topic. In an almanac, the index usually appears at the beginning of the book.

Inquiry for All Students

Every student in our classrooms can be successful and enjoy the challenge of inquiry activities. Our students with disabilities and our English language learners, however, may experience difficulty with inquiry. For most English language learners, inquiry activities can be difficult because the language associated with them is

To solve inquiries, students must use a variety of resources, including maps with very small print!

not comprehensible. Problems arise because of the students' level of English proficiency. With students with disabilities, the issue is not second language acquisition, but rather the complexity of the task that makes things tricky. For English language learners who also have disabilities, both level of English proficiency and task complexity make inquiries difficult. Notice that I have tried to use "conditional language" throughout this paragraph because it is a mistake to underestimate our students; they will succeed at times when we may not expect it. We can help our students with inquiry and critical-thinking activities:

- *Use step-by-step guidance.* Students with disabilities will need help at each step of an inquiry. Whereas students with less severe disabilities may breeze through an inquiry, some students will need considerable help during each step of the inquiry process. Explicit instructions, delivered with patience, will be necessary.
- *Present information through charts, graphs, and pictures.* Many students with reading difficulties will be unable to participate in an inquiry if all the data are written at a level they cannot read. The alternatives are obvious: Use charts, graphs, photographs, illustrations, or films to provide the information needed to resolve the problem. In this regard, the Suchman inquiry

model has particular promise because it works well when the problem and the supporting information are presented visually.

- *Allow students to work together.* According to Vygotsky's zone of proximal development, any child will be able to do more with help. This help can come from us, or it can also be provided by the child's more competent classmates. Thus, inquiry activities that may seem to be beyond some students are "doable" if the students work with their fellow students.

For English language learners, we should also consider the following:

- *Use the primary language.* Those of us who are bilingual and those with bilingual aides should allow our English language learners to complete inquiries in their native language. Cummins (1979, 1986a, 1992) has made a convincing case that students who learn how to gather data and solve problems in one language will easily transfer those abilities to their second language. Because some important sources of information will be available in languages other than English, the ability to use non-English resources will be an advantage for our English language learners. For example, if an inquiry project requires interviews of people living in the community, our bilingual students will be able to gather information from people who speak little or no English.
- *Remember that comprehensible input is the key.* We should be sure that the English we use when leading an inquiry is understandable. We may need to slow down, repeat things, and carefully consider our choice of words. It is important, when working with our English language learners, to stop from time to time and ask questions to check whether students are following our presentation.

SUMMARY OF KEY POINTS

- ▶ Inquiry is a process during which a problem is identified. Then, students speculate on possible solutions, gather data, analyze the data, and reach a conclusion.
- ▶ Inquiry activities have long been a part of social studies instruction.
- ▶ Two specific models for inquiry activities are the cooperative learning structure called Group Investigation and the Suchman inquiry model.
- ▶ During inquiries, students will gather information through computer-based resources, especially the Internet and CD-ROM encyclopedias.
- ▶ We as teachers should continue to teach students to use reference books (encyclopedias, almanacs, and atlases).
- ▶ With a skillful teacher, all students can participate successfully in inquiry activities.

FOR FURTHER READING

▶ On the topic of inquiry, I suggest the books by Massialas and Cox (1966) and Clements, Fielder, and Tabachnick (1966). Although these books are more than 30 years old, the ideas they contain are still valid.

▶ The journals *Social Education, The Social Studies,* and *Social Studies and the Young Learner* frequently have articles about the instructional use of computer-based resources. The March 1998 issue of *Social Education* is a themed issue on teaching in the information age (Simpson, 1998). In February 1996, *Social Education* began a regular section on uses of the Internet and the World Wide Web. For software, you may want to check the following newsletters and guides: *Children's Software Revue* (313–480–0040), *Children's Software* (713–467–8686), the *High/Scope Buyer's Guide to Children's Software* (annual editions, High Scope Press, Ypsilanti, MI), and *The Latest and Best of TESS* (The Educational Software Selector, 516–728–9100). Also, you may want to look through the following computer-oriented journals: *Electronic Learning: The Magazine for Technology and School Change, Multimedia Schools, Technology and Learning, The Computing Teacher,* and the more scholarly *Computers in the Schools.* For those of you unfamiliar with the Internet, I suggest the little book *Education on the Internet: A Student's Guide* (Stull & Ryder, 1999). Of the many journal articles published in the last few years on computers and social studies, one of the most useful is "Using Technology for Powerful Social Studies Learning" by Stephen Rose and Phyllis Maxey Fernlund (1997).

Chapter 7

Critical Thinking: Confronting Students with the Complex and the Controversial

Neither slogans nor the more careful arguments for the teaching of thinking seem to have influenced practice on a wide scale. Studies continue to show that most instruction in social studies as well as in other subjects follows a pattern of teachers transmitting information to students who are then asked to reproduce it. (Newmann, 1991, p. 324)

Our social studies lessons should help our students become proficient in complex, analytic thinking. Each set of national standards in the social studies requires students to think critically. For example, the *National Standards for History* ask students to compare and contrast ideas, distinguish fact and fiction, analyze data sources, consider multiple perspectives, challenge historical arguments, and hypothesize on the influence of the past (National Center for History in the Schools, 1996, p. 21). Yet, almost all authorities would agree with Fred Newmann's conclusion in the quote above: Few teachers actually plan and implement lessons that allow children to develop the ability to think critically. I hope this chapter will play a role in reversing the pattern.

In this chapter, you will read about:

▶ *Critical thinking,* also referred to as *complex thinking* or *higher order thinking*
▶ A taxonomy provided by the National Council for the Social Studies (NCSS) that can be a useful source to order the development of critical-thinking skills
▶ Four instructional approaches that can be used to teach critical thinking skills to elementary school children
▶ The use of multimedia resources to teach critical thinking

Critical Thinking: An Overview

In social studies, the desire to move students beyond rote memorization to more complex modes of thinking has been a consistent goal for educators since the early 1900s (W. C. Parker, 1991). Writing in 1985, Barry Beyer noted that "social studies teachers have been bombarded with competing definitions of critical thinking" (p. 276). Beyer defined critical thinking as "the assessing of the authenticity, accuracy and/or worth of knowledge claims and arguments" (p. 271). Other definitions, though using different words, stress that critical thinking involves raising questions about statements of fact and opinion and making judgments about the validity of those statements (Brophy, 1990). Other authorities sometimes use the terms *complex thinking* or *higher order thinking* to refer to critical thinking.

Educators cannot agree, however, on what critical thinking is or how we can help our students become proficient at it (Wilen & Phillips, 1995). The variety of perspectives on critical thinking is reflected in the number of books that have been written about the topic (e.g., Baron & Sternberg, 1987; Beyer, 1987; McPeck, 1981, 1990; Ruggiero, 1988; Schiever, 1991). Beyond the question of just what types of thinking are "critical thinking" are several viewpoints on the relationship of critical thinking to content. Wright (1995) describes three ways of conceptualizing critical thinking. First, some authorities believe in a set of generic critical-thinking skills. Once we learn them, we can use them to think about any topic. Second, critical thinking is different from subject to subject; that is, critical thinking in economics is different from critical thinking in history. Wright prefers a third view, that some critical-thinking skills are transferable from subject to subject and some are not. On a related issue, Olsen (1995) summarizes the arguments in favor of the position that, for our students to develop critical thinking, we as teachers must cover a topic in depth. This means that we should cover fewer topics each year because it seems that in-depth coverage presents more opportunities for our students to engage in critical thinking.

What Are Critical-Thinking Skills?

Beyer's (1987) definition is that critical thinking involves assessing and judging statements. Within this definition are two parts to critical thinking: (a) an analysis of the data or evidence used to support a statement and (b) an evaluation of whether or not the data or evidence meets some standard of sufficiency. For example, young children could think critically about the following statement: "Our city has enough parks; we don't need any more." Thus, their teacher would lead the children to gather and analyze data relevant to the statement—data that look for answers to questions such as, How many parks does the city currently have? What are they used for? How many people use them each week? Are any people and groups unable to use the parks because of insufficient time or space? Then, the teacher would show the children how to analyze the data by using agreed-on criteria. Finally, the children would have to make an evaluation—verbally, in writing, or with charts and graphs, indicating whether or not the current park system meets the needs of the community.

Other definitions of critical thinking are broader than the one offered by Beyer. Indeed, which thinking skills are "critical" seems to be a somewhat arbitrary decision. Perhaps it would be a good idea to look at one taxonomy, or classification, of social studies thinking skills. Of particular interest is a taxonomy developed by the NCSS Task Force on Scope and Sequence (1989) that mirrors Bloom's cognitive taxonomy (see chap. 5). The NCSS Task Force delineated activities that identify

To think critically, students must have something to think about. Hands-on learning experiences will stimulate critical thinking.

lower level to higher level critical-thinking processes. The six categories where these skills are ordered are listed below:

1. *Classify information*

   Identify relevant information
   Group information in categories
   Place information in sequence

2. *Interpret information*

   State relationships among sets of information
   Identify cause-and-effect relationships
   Draw inferences

3. *Analyze information*

   Divide a topic into subtopics
   Detect bias in information
   Compare and contrast the credibility of different
       accounts of the same event

4. *Summarize information*

> State the significant ideas supported by the information
> State conclusions based on the information
> State hypotheses for future research

5. *Synthesize information*

> Propose a plan based on the information
> Speculate on what might happen if the information were different
> Propose a solution to the problem related to the information

6. *Evaluate information*

> Judge the source of the information to determine objectivity
> Examine the technical accuracy of the information
> Determine the currency of the information

The sixth category of thinking skills lists criteria students will find useful in examining and evaluating sources of information. For example, when we admonish our students to "consider the source," we are requesting that they determine whether the information is appropriate for judging data. Several factors are crucial to considering whether sources are appropriate or not. One of the most obvious factors is if the data that are used to support a statement come from an unreliable or, in some cases, unprofessional source. If the answer is yes, then the validity of the data would be in question. *Objectivity* is another essential factor if we are to rely on information. Information provided by sources with a bias should be questioned. Modeling for students statements that indicate an author may be biased would alert them to look for a prejudiced opinion or study. Students should also consider the *technical correctness* of what they read. If, in the critical-thinking exercise about the number of parks in the city, information on the level of park use was taken from a survey that improperly defined a sample (e.g., the first week of every month), then the information may provide an inaccurate portrait. Finally, *currency* is essential in social studies. Unless we are examining historical data, the older our information is, the less likely it is to be accurate.

Developing Critical-Thinking Skills

Several specific instructional strategies have been promoted as essential for developing critical thinking (see books cited earlier in the chapter). Here, I discuss (a) a metacognitive approach to teaching thinking skills, (b) the application of Fred Newmann's research on critical thinking in high school to elementary social studies, (c) Hilda Taba's instructional strategies for concept formation, (d) the integrative model of teaching reasoning and content developed by Paul Eggen and Donald

Kauchak, and (e) a lesson plan model for teaching critical thinking while using visual and auditory resources.

A Metacognitive Approach to Teaching Critical Thinking

William Wilen and John Phillips (1995) provide a useful description of the metacognitive approach to teaching critical thinking. *Metacognition* is thinking about thinking. The approach described by Wilen and Phillips involves teaching critical thinking while teaching social studies. The key component is the teacher's modeling of a critical-thinking process. The approach is metacognitive because it attempts to help students think about the task before them, monitor their level of understanding, and select an appropriate way of thinking to complete the task successfully. The approach has three steps: (a) explanation by the teacher, (b) modeling by the teacher, and (c) modeling by the learner.

1. *Explanation by the teacher.* In the first step, the teacher explains one critical-thinking skill. The skill could be almost any of those listed in the NCSS list, such as distinguishing fact from opinion, detecting bias, challenging the credibility of a statement, noting cause and effect, or comparing and contrasting conflicting accounts of the same events. Then, the teacher explains what is involved in the thinking skill. This can be accomplished by showing examples and nonexamples or by using thinking exercises. For example, the teacher could present the thinking skill of predicting likely outcomes on the basis of factual information. The teacher would explain how, on the basis of a set of data, it is possible to make good guesses about the future. He or she could show students graphs and charts depicting purchases in the United States of foreign-manufactured automobiles over a 50-year period. Then, the teacher could use these data to predict how many people in the United States will purchase foreign cars over the next 20 years and speculate on what will happen to people in the United States who work for domestic auto manufacturers and to people who work for foreign auto manufacturers. In contrast to this type of informed speculation, the teacher could make wild guesses about the winner of next year's Kentucky Derby on the basis of the horses' names.

2. *Modeling by the teacher.* In the second step, the teacher models the thinking process. Let's continue our discussion with the skill of predicting likely outcomes on the basis of factual information. The teacher could select the following question to model this thinking skill: Which cities in the United States will most likely show population growth in the next 10-year census, and which cities will most likely show a decrease? The teacher would first identify relevant data sources. In this case, they would be census data from 1950, 1960, 1970, 1980, and 1990. Then, the teacher would model the process of noting trends, most likely in graphs and tables. Finally, the teacher would show how a prediction based on the data can

be made—in this case, explaining why it appears that cities in the West and in the Sunbelt will show significant growth, whereas cities in the Northeast will not keep pace with places like Orlando, San Antonio, Phoenix, and Las Vegas.

3. *Modeling by the student.* In the third step, students have the opportunity to practice the thinking skill. This is best done in small groups. A very useful strategy for assessing students' level of competence is "think alouds." The teacher asks students to describe their thinking processes and then listens as the students do so. For example, the teacher could ask students to predict the average family income for the year 2025. The teacher would supply the relevant data, and the students would work in small groups to make informed guesses.

Newmann's Research on Critical Thinking in Social Studies

Fred Newmann (1990a, 1990b, 1991) has conducted interesting research on the teaching of critical thinking in high school social studies classes. His findings should help us elementary teachers become more effective in developing our students' ability to think critically. Newmann (1991) concluded:

> At best, much classroom activity fails to challenge students to use their minds in any valuable way; at worst, much classroom activity is nonsensical or mindless. The more serious problem, therefore, is not the failure to teach some specific aspect of thinking, but the profound absence of thoughtfulness in classrooms. (p. 330)

Newmann (1991) identified six dimensions that are fundamental for a classroom where critical thinking can be developed:

1. *Sustained examination of a few topics is better than superficial coverage of a few.* Newmann noted that "sustained concentration" on a topic is essential for in-depth thinking (p. 330). If we are in a position to shape the social studies curriculum for the grade levels we teach, then we should limit the number of topics that are covered. When it comes to the development of critical thinking, less is more.

2. *Lessons must present content in a coherent, continuous manner.* Newmann reached this conclusion after observing secondary teachers, but this dimension is also crucial to elementary teaching. The content we present to our students should be logically sequenced and well organized. In other words, the concepts we teach should build upon one another and be presented in a clear, predictable manner. For example, if a teacher is introducing third-grade students to some principles of economics, then she probably would conduct activities to help students understand the difference between producers and consumers before she explains the law of supply and demand.

3. *Students should be given an appropriate amount of time to think and prepare answers to questions.* As Newmann noted, "thinking takes time" (p. 332). I have found in my observations that teachers are uncomfortable with the silence that should follow a provocative question (it is as if they were engineers of a radio program and had been trained to avoid silent times, which are called "dead air"). Critical thinking takes time, and one test of whether a question will stimulate complex thought is that it cannot be answered quickly.

4. *Teachers must ask challenging questions or present challenging tasks.* This dimension, of course, should go without saying. Newmann calls for questions and tasks that "demand analysis, interpretation, or manipulation of information" (p. 332). It takes courage to prepare lessons that are challenging because some students will find the experience frustrating. The frustration that some students feel when they are confronted with complex tasks is essential for their development as critical thinkers.

5. *Teachers should be models of thoughtfulness.* We should show interest in our students' ideas, explore alternative approaches to problems, show how to think through a problem, and acknowledge the difficulty in answering some questions. A good way to do this is to work through a problem with students and to "think aloud" so that students can see a model of critical thinking.

6. *Students should offer explanations and reasons for their conclusions.* Newmann noted that answers to "higher order challenges are rarely self-evident" (p. 333). Students must be encouraged to explain and support their conclusions. This can be a challenge for elementary teachers, but even our youngest students can be asked to explain why they have adopted a certain perspective.

Newmann's six dimensions are important because they provide a set of fundamental characteristics for creating a classroom environment where children can grow as critical thinkers.

Taba's Strategies for Concept Formation

Hilda Taba, whose ideas on the classification of content in the social studies curriculum were discussed in chapter 1, developed a set of instructional strategies for teaching critical thinking through social studies. In fact, Taba may have been the first to use the term *instructional strategy*. Taba developed three instructional strategies to help children reason inductively. Each instructional strategy is actually a three-step teaching sequence. The three sets are used for concept formation, interpretation of data, and application of principles (B. R. Joyce & Weil, 1980; Taba, 1967).

All three strategies are important. Here, I describe the strategy for concept formation because it is simple, applicable to all the elementary grades, and particularly useful for social studies. Taba (1967) thought the strategy for concept formation should be used at the beginning of a unit. I have found, however, that it works better as a concluding activity. The three steps of the Taba strategy for concept formation are as follows:

1. *Enumeration and listing.* In the first step, we begin the activity by asking students to compile a list—for example, "What are some items we can buy at the market?" "Who were some inventors we learned about this week?" "What are some facts we have learned about Mexico?"

2. *Grouping.* In the second step, we ask students, "Do you see some things that belong together?" (Taba, 1967, p. 93). Students may be right or wrong in their groupings; the important thing is that we encourage them to think about what characteristics the items in the list share and what distinguishes the items. We should help students see many possible ways the items can be grouped. For example, students might place the things they learned about Mexico into the following categories: (a) famous Mexican men and women, (b) names of Mexican cities, (c) things that Mexico produces, (d) Mexican songs and dances, (e) Mexican folktales, and (f) life in a Mexican city.

3. *Labeling and categorizing.* In the third and final step, we help students attach labels to the groups they have created. It may be necessary to rearrange lists or to create new categories.

The concept formation teaching sequence has many possible modifications. To make the exercise easier, we can provide the list of items. It's a good idea to put each item on a separate card so that it can be moved around as students define groups. We can also tell the students how many groups they should form (e.g., "The places we have listed can be placed into five groups"). If students find this type of activity very difficult, then we can also provide the titles for each group. Each of the adjustments, however, should serve as "training wheels." They should be discarded as students become more sophisticated in the process.

An Integrative Model for Teaching Reasoning with Content

Eggen and Kauchak (1995) developed an integrative model to teach reasoning while teaching content. This model is a teaching sequence designed for content teaching, especially social studies. The sequence has five phases: (a) describe, (b) compare, (c) explain, (d) hypothesize, and (e) generalize:

1. *Describe.* We present our students with information. The information can be presented through charts, graphs, illustrations, or written text. One strength of this model is that it lends itself to data presented through charts and graphs. Thus, the integrative model will provide all students, even those who are not good readers, a chance to practice critical thinking. In this first phase, we ask very

Table 7.1 Chart for a Lesson Using the Integrative Model for Teaching Reasoning with Content: Grade 5—Where Will Americans Live in the 21st Century? *(Source: U.S. Department of Commerce, Bureau of the Census.)*

State	State Population by Year in Millions of People			
	1900	1950	1990	2010
New York	7.27	14.83	17.99	?
Pennsylvania	6.30	10.49	11.88	?
Ohio	4.16	7.95	10.84	?
Texas	3.05	7.71	16.97	?
California	1.48	10.57	29.76	?
Florida	0.53	2.77	12.93	?

specific, literal questions about the information. The students are expected to "observe and describe" the information (p. 180). For example, the last unit of the year for a fifth-grade class was "The United States in the 21st Century." Their teacher had prepared a lesson using the integrative model and used Table 7.1 as the basis for the lesson.

2. *Compare.* Then, we ask students to compare different parts of the data. With elementary students, the logical place to start is with the most obvious similarities and differences between two sets of data. For example, if a group of students were looking at photographs of an ocean liner and a passenger jet, then we might direct students' attention to shape and exterior design. Charts facilitate making comparisons because two sets of data can be placed side-by-side.

3. *Explain.* So far, students have been asked to perform relatively easy thinking skills. Now, as Eggen and Kauchak note, "the processing becomes deductive" (p. 181). We ask students *why* some parts of the data are the same and other parts are different. Students must speculate, and we must ask "why" questions that students have a reasonable chance of answering. Almost any set of data will suggest questions that require too much of the students, questions they simply cannot answer. Obviously, we should avoid those questions and instead develop "why" questions that will generate reasonable speculations based on the data.

4. *Hypothesize.* This phase is closely linked to the one before and the one after. Here, we ask students to extend the explanations they offered in Phase 3. We do this by presenting a hypothetical situation as the students are forced to apply what they have learned. For example, if we asked the students to think about travel by ship and by airplane, then we could present them with a variety of travel scenarios and the task of identifying which mode of transportation they would choose

(e.g., "You need to get to Cairo as soon as possible," "You want to relax while you travel").

5. *Generalize.* The fifth and final phase of the integrative model is a chance to summarize. The expectation is that students will state generalizations they have learned during the activity. Many students find this a difficult chore, and primary-grade teachers may have to provide considerable assistance. For example, we could provide the first half of a generalization and ask the students to write the second half (e.g., "If you want to get someplace in a hurry, then you should _____.").

Following is a lesson plan a first-grade teacher wrote for an activity based on Eggen and Kauchak's integrative model for teaching reasoning with content.

Grade 1: Using an Integrative Model—"Summer and Winter"

LESSON
PLAN

Overview: To allow for more participation, the lesson was taught three times, each time to a group of seven children. The lesson was part of the thematic unit "The Seasons," which integrated social studies, science, language arts, visual arts, and performing arts.

Resources and Materials: The lesson uses a single resource—a large chart prepared by the teacher. The chart is divided in half, one side labeled "Summer," and the other labeled "Winter." Along the left side of the chart are three categories— "Special Things to Do," "Food," and "Clothing." Each "cell" is illustrated with photographs cut from magazines. For example, under "Summer," in the "Special Things to Do" cell are photographs of people at the beach, children playing baseball, and a family having a picnic in a park. Under "Winter" in the "Special Things to Do" cell are photographs of people making a snowman, children ice skating, and a family gathered indoors around a fireplace. (A large area of the United States does not have snowy, low-temperature winters; if you are located in this area, adjust your discussions of "Winter" cells with the children accordingly.) Under "Summer" in the "Clothing" cell are photographs of people in shorts, sandals, and T-shirts. Under "Winter" in the "Clothing" cell are photographs of people in winter clothing—show heavy jackets, mufflers, knit hats, and gloves. Under "Winter" in the "Food" cell are photographs of a man placing a stuffed turkey into an oven and of a steaming cup of hot chocolate. In contrast, "Summer" "Food" depicts an outdoor barbecue and a pitcher of iced lemonade.

Content Objectives: Children will learn that weather is one factor that determines how people live. Regarding recreational activity, food, and clothing, children will understand the differences caused by winter and summer weather.

Process Objectives: Children will *describe* the recreational activities, food, and clothing that are typical of winter and of summer; *compare and contrast* photographs of summer and winter; *explain* why people participate in different recreational activities, eat different foods, and wear different clothing during summer and winter; *speculate* on which businesses do better in the winter and which do better in the summer; and *state* a generalization summarizing the relationship of weather to the way people live.

Teaching Sequence

1. Before the lesson, prepare the chart and make a list of the key questions to be asked during each phase.
2. Divide the class into groups of seven children. Have each group sit on the rug, with the chart displayed nearby on an easel. Follow the five-step sequence of the integrative model:

3a. *Describe.* Introduce the lesson by saying, "Today, we are going to look at photographs of things we do, things we eat, and how we dress during the summer and the winter." Direct the children to each of the six "cells" in the chart (Summer/Special Things to Do, Summer/Food, Summer/Clothing, Winter/Things to Do, Winter/Food, Winter/Clothing). For each cell, the key question is "What do you see in this photograph?" Be sure all significant details are noted. It is best to start with the clothing cells, and you may want to pantomime the differences between summer and winter (for winter, you might have the children shiver, rub their hands together, and say things like, "It's freezing out here!").

3b. *Compare.* Help the children make comparisons between each set of photographs. Start with clothing, where the differences are most noticeable. Ask the children to look first at the clothing cell for summer and then to look at the clothing cell for winter. Then ask, "How are the clothes we wear different in summer from the ones we wear in winter?" The children should note that winter clothes cover more of our bodies, they are larger, and they are thicker. Then ask the children to note differences between summer and winter food, and between special things to do in the summer and in the winter.

3c. *Explain.* Ask the first graders *why* we need to wear different clothes in the summer and the winter, why we eat different foods, and why we do different things. The simple answer, of course, is that it is hot in the summer and cold in the winter. Probe further by asking questions like, "Why wouldn't hot chocolate be good at the beach?" "Why is it possible to barbecue in the summer and not in the winter?"

3d. *Hypothesize.* This will be the most difficult part of the lesson for the first graders. On the chalkboard, write the following: "You sell beach umbrellas," "You sell mittens," and other commercial activities that have a busy season. Ask the children to identify which businesses would do better in the summer and which would probably do better in the winter. Help them offer justifications for their answers.

3e. *Generalize.* Finally, help the children understand the concept the information presented in the lesson supports: that the weather is one factor that determines how people live. With first graders, the exact wording is not important. The opening question for this step should be something like, "What have we learned today?" A more specific prompt is, "Why do people do different activities, eat different foods, and wear different clothes during the summer and the winter?" The lesson on summer and winter should lead children to a simple conclusion: that weather is one factor that determines what they do, what they eat, and how they dress.

Effective Teaching in Today's Diverse Classroom: This activity would work well with any group of children experiencing difficulty reading grade-level textbooks. Although most social studies activities require students to read, and in fact, social studies should be an area of the curriculum that helps children become better readers, it is important that not all lessons be based on a text. The goal of this lesson is to promote critical thinking. That goal can be accomplished without the use of written material. The medium used to stimulate thinking was photographs; thus, the lesson would be effective with English language learners, especially those whose level of English proficiency allows them to participate in discussions but who lack the ability to read grade-level texts.

Using Multimedia to Develop Critical Thinking

Critical-thinking activities can use any type of instructional resource. Visual media, auditory media, and realia, however, present excellent opportunities for elementary students to engage in interpretation and analysis. As students are taught to view and listen critically, they will become more proficient in their ability to engage in complex thinking. In this section, I discuss a teaching model for critical viewing (or listening).

Audio and Visual Resources

We as teachers have a wide variety of auditory (or listening) media to use in our classrooms. Sound can be recorded on audiotape or compact discs. The vinyl discs, or "records," that so many of us are accustomed to using are rapidly disappearing. Compact discs have tremendous potential as an instructional resource. Listeners are able to choose an appropriate selection easily by entering a number in the disc player. Compare the ease of choosing a specific selection on a disc with the frustration of rewinding and fast-forwarding tape or, even worse, of attempting to set a phonograph needle on a specific "cut" on a vinyl record! Whatever formats are available, recordings of music, interviews, and other sounds can be a valuable social studies resource (Cooper, 1989; Turner & Hickey, 1991).

Computer technology has given us a variety of ways to present pictures. Videodiscs (or "optical disks") are a type of laser disc that can store thousands of pictures. A single videodisc can store about 50,000 still images. For use with a computer, all a student has to do is insert the videodisc into the computer's videodisc drive (not all computers have videodisc drives, though); type in a request for a picture of a certain person, place, or thing; and if such an image is on the videodisc, it will appear on the computer screen. (Videodiscs can also be used with videodisc players with a separate monitor.) For use with an entire class of students, videodisc images can be projected onto a screen with an LCD (liquid crystal display) placed on an overhead projector. Videodiscs are an improved technology over the more traditional study prints or the illustrations found in textbooks or reference books. I think you can see the advantage of videodiscs; you would need access to hundreds of books, filmstrips, and prints to match the resources of a single videodisc. It is possible to select a series of images and then store them on a standard computer diskette. This requires special hardware, but the potential is wonderful. The stored images can then be accessed as easily as any other file. Visual images can also be presented through CD-ROMs and Hypermedia, but these formats typically combine visual images with auditory images and text. Many Web sites on the Internet present excellent visual images for social studies lessons.

Among traditional visual media, *filmstrips* are rapidly becoming a thing of the past. Filmstrips present a sequence of visual images called frames, typically with a synchronized audiotape narration. *Prints* include photographs and reproductions of paintings. When a print is enlarged for educational use, it is typically called a *study print*. There are other ways to share visual images with students. An image can be photographed, printed on a slide, and projected on a screen. Opaque projectors can be used to display images directly from books or magazines, although they are difficult to find now that schools are using their limited resources to purchase computer hardware.

Realia refers to real things (Braun & Cook, 1985; Lankiewicz, 1987; Rule & Sunal, 1994). The use of realia in social studies is essential because it provides three-dimensional objects for students to see *and touch* (the visual media, whether print or video, are, of course, flat). Realia can be either the real thing or human-made models. The best lessons make use of *artifacts,* real things used by people. Some school districts have collections of items they lend to other schools (e.g., a branding iron, old coins, a butter churn): We just have to send a request, the other district ships what we need to our classrooms for use during a unit, and we ship it back after we're finished with it. Other artifacts can only be viewed at museums (e.g., Native American baskets, an ancient Egyptian mummy). When we use realia in a lesson, we can follow the same teaching sequence we would use with visual media and auditory media. The goals of the lesson are the same: We want students to look closely, to notice all the relevant details, and then to engage in critical thinking

Almost any lesson can become an opportunity for critical thinking. The key, of course, is for the teacher to challenge children to go beyond the simple to the complex.

based on what they have seen (or heard). For this discussion, let's assume that students are viewing a photographic slide projected onto a large screen:

1. First, we *link* the slide to what we previously covered in the unit of study. We need to do this before we show the image (or play the tape or let students examine the artifact). We can establish in several ways the connection between the slide and what students have been learning: discussion, a review of information on a chart, or rereading parts of textbook.
2. Next, we place the slide in *context* by establishing time and place. This usually involves using a map and a timeline. For some inquiry and critical-thinking activities, however, we may want to eliminate this step because the challenge for students will be to determine the time and place of the slide.
3. Then, we ask students to take a *first look (or listen)*. We ask them what catches their attention. What about the image on the slide would they like to learn more about? What questions do they have after a first look? We can do this by having small-group discussions or by having students record their responses in writing. For discussion, the cooperative learning structures of Think-Pair-Share and Three-Step Interview work well. Although this should go without saying, we must be sure the visual image can be seen by all

students participating in the activity (and if students are listening to a tape or a disc, be sure everyone can hear it). If our equipment limits how large an image can be displayed, then we should have students view it in small groups. If we are using an artifact that students can touch, we should arrange a format that permits each students some time with the object.

4. Now, we lead students to a *focused examination* of the slide. We do this by asking them either to look for specific things or to narrow their focus to a certain part of the image (or tape or artifact). This is difficult to do with an audio recording because the recording will have to be replayed.

5. Last, we help students *interpret and analyze* the slide. Here are the types of questions we could ask:

- Challenge students to find *relationships* between the image on the slide and other things. For historic images, recordings, and artifacts, we can help students see the connection between the old and the contemporary. If students were viewing photographs of a fifth-grade classroom of 1900, then we could ask them to compare what they see with their own experiences.

- Help students use the visual image to make broader *inferences* about the people, the place, and the times that produced it. Photographs of the classroom of 1900, for example, would tell us about the relationship between students and their teachers.

- Work with students to help them detect *bias*. In many paintings, for example, the perspective of the artist leads to distortions of reality. It is important that we share with our students biographic information about the artist so that they can critically analyze a painting or piece of sculpture for evidence of bias.

Following is a lesson plan written by a sixth-grade teacher for an activity that requires the critical analysis of photographs of a Roman coin.

LESSON PLAN ►

Grade 6: A Roman Coin

Overview: This lesson would take place during a unit on ancient Rome. It is planned for a group of approximately 25 students. An excellent source of information on Roman coins is the Web site "Dead Romans" *(http://www.iei.net/~tryan/deadroma. htm).* A good source for other Web sites on ancient Rome is the "Schools of California Online Resources for Teachers" (SCORE) site *(http://www.rims.k12.ca.us/score)*

Resources and Materials: (a) wall map of the Roman Empire; (b) piece of construction paper; (c) the timeline created for the unit on ancient Rome; (d) a sheet of chart paper on which are written three facts about Marcus Aurelius; (e) two photographic transparencies (slides) of a Roman coin bearing the likeness of Emperor Marcus Aurelius, one for each side of the coin; (f) slide projector; (g) a sheet of chart paper on which are written focused examination questions (see the list in the section "Focused Examination" below); (h) copies of a photograph of Abraham Lincoln from *Lincoln: A Photobiography* (Freedman, 1987) and copies of a photograph of Franklin Roosevelt from *Franklin Delano Roosevelt* (Freedman, 1990); (i) several U.S. pennies and dimes.

Content Objectives: Students will learn introductory biographical information about Marcus Aurelius, the characteristics of Roman coins, the relationship between economic activity and the need for money, and a shared characteristic of Roman and contemporary U.S. coins (the idealized images of leaders on the coins).

Process Objectives: Students will *identify* the reign of Marcus Aurelius (C.E. 161–180) on the timeline, *recall* information they learned about the geography and economic activity in the Roman Empire, *examine* slides of the coin, *list* three things that caught their eye about the coin, *speculate* on the reasons why economic trade and the amassing of capital requires the use of money, *compare and contrast* the photographs of Lincoln and Roosevelt with their images on coins, and *speculate* on the purposes of idealized portraits that are placed on coins.

Teaching Sequence
1. *Link.* Using a wall map, review the geographic boundaries of the Roman Empire in the second century of the common era. Then, help students recall what they have learned about economic activity during the height of the empire.
2. *Contexts.* Ask a group of students to help you place a piece of construction paper underneath the reign of Marcus Aurelius on the timeline. Share the information about Marcus Aurelius you wrote on a sheet of chart paper (e.g., he lived from C.E. 121 to 180). I would note that Marcus Aurelius was both a political leader and a philosopher. I think students would find it interesting to discuss his stoic philosophy that emphasized forgiveness, the absence of selfishness, and the common good. That, though, would require another lesson.
3. *First Look.* For most of the activity, students will work in groups of four. Project the slides and ask the students to "look at these photographs of the front and back of a Roman coin and write down three things that catch your eye." Then use the cooperative learning structure Three-Step Interview to allow each student to share his or her response. Reconvene the group and listen to three or four students present what they wrote.
4. *Focused Examination.* Now ask each group to take another look at the slides and, working as a group, to answer the following questions, which you listed beforehand on a sheet of chart paper:

- What general shape is the coin?
- What do you think the coin is made of?
- Do you see any writing on the coin?
- Are there any numbers on the coin? Write them down.
- What part of Marcus Aurelius can you see?

Reconvene the whole group and share answers to the questions.

5. *Interpret and Analyze.* Working with the whole group, see whether you can help students discern the relationship between economic activity and the need for money. (Complex trade, the division of labor, many workers engaged in "service" jobs, and the amassing of capital require money; all were present in the Roman Empire. Notice that this lesson helps students acquire Standard 11 of the *National Content Standards in Economics* [National Council on Economic Education, 1997], which reads, "Students will understand that money makes it easier to trade, borrow, save, invest, and compare the value of goods and services.") You might ask them to imagine what would happen if we did not have money. Be sure students see the connection between the complex, international system of trade and exchange used by the Romans and the need for money.

   Next, have students once again work in their groups. Distribute the copies of the photographs of Lincoln and Roosevelt, the pennies, and the dimes. Ask each group to look closely and compare and contrast the photographs and the images on the coins. How are the portraits similar, and how are they different? Students should see that the images on the coins make Lincoln and Roosevelt look very good (to make the comparison obvious, choose photographs of Lincoln and Roosevelt near the end of their days as president). Why? Why might an artist change the way a person looked when designing a coin?

Evaluation: Collect the written responses of each student. These will provide useful information on whether or not individuals were able to notice details on the Roman coin. You may want to tape-record the whole-group discussions. The tape will help you identify who is talking and whether or not students have engaged in the type of analytic, speculative thinking the lesson requires. You certainly should take notes while the students work in small groups.

The "Dead Romans" Web site mentioned in the "Overview" section of this lesson can be read by more able sixth graders. Some students could use the site as a source of information to learn more about Roman coins (e.g., how they were made, what the inscriptions on these coins mean, when the coins were minted, how to collect them).

 Effective Teaching in Today's Diverse Classroom: The lesson was planned for the entire class (assuming approximately 25 students). For much of the activity, however, students worked in small groups of four. How would you assign your English language learners to these groups? You have three choices:

1. If your English language learners have an advanced level of oral English pro-ficiency, then it would make sense to "spread them out" and place them with students who are fully proficient in English (e.g., one English language learner with three fully proficient students). Because the data for the lesson are visual and require no reading, this arrangement should work. The English language learners will benefit from the comprehensible input provided by their peers who are proficient in English.

2. If you have a group of English language learners with limited oral English skills, so limited that they will not be able to converse with students who are fully proficient in English, then the English language learners should be grouped together and work with you (the teacher) or an instructional aide. If you were working with a group of English language learners on this lesson, then you would need to modify your vocal register. You would speak slowly, repeat things, and limit your vocabulary so that the English language learners can understand the questions written on the chart paper.

3. Finally, if you have English language learners who are in the first stages of ac-quiring English and who would not understand you even if you used a modi-fied vocal register, then these students can benefit from the lesson only if they are allowed to complete it in their first language. It is, unfortunately, not always possible to find the resources (materials, personnel) to allow students to use their first language. If, for example, you have in your class an Urdu-speaking student who recently emigrated from Pakistan, my guess is that you will not have materials written in Urdu nor Urdu-speaking teachers or aides to help you. If you cannot provide a setting where the lesson can be completed in languages other than English, then you must do your best to help your stu-dents who speak little English understand the lesson.

SUMMARY OF KEY POINTS

- ▶ *Critical thinking* has many definitions. This type of thinking requires stu-dents to go beyond rote memorization to analyze, synthesize, speculate, challenge, verify, and generalize.
- ▶ A metacognitive approach to teaching critical thinking requires the teacher to model a critical-thinking skill.
- ▶ Fred Newmann identified six dimensions that are fundamental for a class-room where critical thinking can be developed.
- ▶ Hilda Taba developed instructional strategies to help children reason induc-tively.
- ▶ An integrative model for teaching reasoning with content provides a format for building content knowledge while students think critically.
- ▶ Visual media, auditory media, and realia are excellent resources to use for critical-thinking activities.

FOR FURTHER READING

▶ Dozens of books and hundreds of articles have been written on critical thinking. A good place to start is the March 1995 edition of *Social Education,* which focuses on teaching students to think. W. C. Parker's (1991) chapter in *Handbook of Research on Social Studies Teaching and Learning* is very good, with an emphasis on critical thinking and decision making. I also like Clarke's (1990) *Patterns of Thinking: Integrating Learning Skills in Content Teaching.* If you want to challenge yourself, try the book of readings edited by Robert Sternberg (1994), *Thinking and Problem Solving.* Other good books are by Beyer (1987), McPeck (1981, 1990), Ruggiero (1988), and Schiever (1991). O'Reilly (1998) describes some good activities for developing critical thinking among high school students. Some ideas presented in his article would work with elementary school students.

▶ The Internet provides access to Web sites that allow you to take virtual tours of museums and, thus, to have access to photographs of artifacts that otherwise would be inaccessible. Ricchiuti (1998) describes how students can create a virtual museum that their classmates could visit.

Chapter 8

Assessment: Acquiring and Analyzing Data on Student Achievement

I n chapter 5, you read a description of a Group Project. While one group of students worked on the chronological mural of the city, third-grade teacher Al Braccio entered data on a "Group Project Evaluation Form." The form is a kind of rating scale that enabled Mr. Braccio to document his observations of each child's performance during Group Projects. It also allowed him to make anecdotal notes for future group work planning. For example, Brad wrote an excellent caption for his part of the mural but did not complete tasks in a timely manner. Next time, Mr. Braccio will be sure that Brad works with someone who can help keep him on task. Sara, an English language learner, continued to show excellent work habits and social skills. Mr. Braccio noted that the cooperative nature of the project gave her an opportunity to use her improving English skills, an excellent reason to continue to plan Group Projects for the children. All in all, the evaluation form (see Figure 8.1) proved to be a useful device for recording important data about the progress of each child working on the project.

▲   ▲   ▲

In this chapter, you will read about:

► The purposes and goals of both formative and summative assessment, which provide information on how much progress each student has made toward acquiring content knowledge, mastering processes, and adopting values
► Authentic assessment, an ongoing process that uses multiple sources of data—written products, nonwritten products, multiple-form products—to evaluate student performance
► Creating and using teacher-made tests, anecdotal records, evaluation rubrics, rating scales, and checklists to evaluate students in developmentally appropriate ways
► Guidelines for analyzing data and synthesizing the contents of students' portfolios
► Sharing assessment data with students and parents

▲   ▲   ▲

Purposes and Goals of Assessment

Assessment is the process of gathering, analyzing, and sharing information on the ability and achievement of students. Although some educators have distinct definitions for *assessment* and *evaluation,* in this book the terms are synonymous. In educational settings, assessments are made for two purposes: *Formative assessment* is the process of helping students achieve more (think of a ball of clay being "formed" into a finished work of art). *Summative assessment* is the process of making judgments. In elementary social studies, summative assessment usually means completing a report

Figure 8.1 Group Project Evaluation Form

Title of Project: *Chronological mural of our city*
Dates: *May 6–19*
Participants: *Sara, Debbie, Ben, Denise, Cliff, Tina, Dan, Amber, Brad, Claudia*

	Social Skills	Illustration	Caption	Timetable
Sara	1	1	2	1
Debbie	1	2	1	1
Ben	2	1	2	1
Denise	1	1	1	1
Cliff	1	2	2	1
Tina	1	2	2	2
Dan	3	2	2	1
Amber	2	2	1	1
Brad	2	2	1	3
Claudia	1	2	1	3

1: Excellent   2: Good   3: Needs improvement   4: Unacceptable

Notes:
5-11   Good to see Sara & Debbie work together. Sara is making so much progress in her English.
5-12   Had to intervene with Dan and Amber. They argued. Dan has difficulty sharing. He wanted to do all the artwork.
5-13   The drawings look great. Sara and Ben are exceptional artists. Brad and Claudia needed help with their drawings.
5-15   Brad and Claudia haven't used their time wisely. They will finish a couple of days late.
5-16   I am pleased with the way Tina and Cliff helped each other.

card of some sort (think of "summing" things up). We as teachers must be able to fulfill both purposes of assessment. Our assessment plans for social studies must provide the data we need to make instructional decisions and thus increase the achievement of our students. We also need data to summarize the progress of our students and in categorizing their performance. The goal of the assessment process is to tell us how much progress each student has made toward (a) acquiring content,

(b) mastering processes, and (e) adopting values. In the language of educational standards, we must know what our students know, what they can do, and what they consider important. More specifically, assessment should tell us to what extent students have met the objectives for a lesson or a unit and to what extent they have achieved grade-level goals or standards.

Authentic Assessment

Educational assessment has undergone a revolution in the last two decades (Brandt, 1992; Newmann, Secada, & Wehlage, 1995; Nickell, 1992). Twenty years ago, almost all judgments about student achievement were based on tests. For the most part, assessment was the process of developing, implementing, and interpreting tests. Well-designed, developmentally appropriate tests can provide useful information and should be a part of social studies assessment, but even the best tests do not provide a complete picture of what our students know, are able to do, and value. Tests capture student performance at one point in time, limit ways of expressing knowledge, and require performance in artificial situations divorced from typical social studies activities.

The alternative to tests is generally referred to as *authentic assessment* or *performance assessment,* a process with the following characteristics:

- Data are gathered from tasks that require complex, higher level thinking, often through inquiry and problem solving.
- The ultimate goal is to assess students' performance on tasks that correspond to the types of things people do in the "real" world, rather than to make judgments based on tests that people take only in school.
- Data used for evaluation can come from the everyday assignments students complete, assuming that the teacher plans a wide range of challenging social studies activities.
- The process is ongoing and longitudinal, with data gathered, analyzed, and shared throughout the school year.
- The products students create, or records of them, are stored in portfolios.
- Students show what they know and can do in a variety of ways—through writing, speaking, art, and drama.
- The process places greater responsibility on the student in gathering and analyzing data (Alleman & Brophy, 1998; Darling-Hammond, Ancess, & Falk, 1995; Jones, 1993; Wiggins, 1993).

This process centers on the development of the portfolio, and sometimes the descriptor "portfolio assessment" is used instead of "authentic assessment" (Adams & Hamm, 1992). A *portfolio* is a place of storage, one for each student, and may be as simple as a manila folder. For social studies, however, the portfolio should be a larger container, something like a small box or basket. Some teachers I've known use a single portfolio for all school subjects; others have two or more portfolios for each student. Given the space in most elementary classrooms, my suggestion is that a single portfolio be kept for each student, with dividers for language arts, mathematics, social studies, science, and the arts. In elementary school, development of the portfolio should be a joint venture as teacher and student both insert items (Stiggins, 1994). That students have some control over the sources of information used for evaluation is a significant change from "traditional" assessment, wherein the teacher was in complete control of the entire process. We need to be sure that each of our students understands the concept of the portfolio and the student's role in selecting items for inclusion. Many of us have begun to compile "computer-based portfolios" on each of our students. This is a relatively simple task. Just keep a separate diskette for each student, and store on the diskette copies of material written or created on the computer. Several items can be saved on the diskettes, including essays written on the computer, charts and graphs compiled with computer software, and e-mail messages from students to representatives of organizations.

Too often, "testing" and "authentic assessment" are portrayed as a dichotomy. In fact, both forms of assessment have influenced each other. "Tests" have become more authentic; in fact, some teachers use a writing or arts project as a test (Wiggins, 1989, 1992). For example, a teacher decides that each of her students will produce an illustrated timeline of the history of South Carolina. This is a test in that all students will be required to complete the task and the teacher will use the results to evaluate what students have learned about their state. This assignment is more authentic than most tests, however. First, the task is familiar; students have made several timelines during the year. Tests often measure student performance on tasks that are novel. Second, the task, unlike most tests, does not require students to write. Finally, the task has different "correct" versions. Although successful timelines will share common information, they will not be exactly alike. These projects used for assessment are actually a form of test and are also called *exemplary tasks* (California Department of Education, 1992c) or *performance assessment* (Brandt, 1992). To assess the performance of our students in social studies, we should use both tests and the sources of data provided by authentic assessment (Terwilliger, 1997).

Our assessment plans for social studies, then, should have the following characteristics: (a) Data will be gathered from multiple sources, including tests; (b) the assessment process will be ongoing, recognizing that each day has the potential to generate useful information; (c) student work, or records of it, will be stored in portfolios; and (d) students will play a role in assessing their performance.

Gathering Data

Perhaps the most useful way to go about assessment is to have the process parallel social science research, which has three components: (a) gathering data, (b) analyzing data, and (c) sharing data. Data that are gathered will be placed in students'

Teachers analyze work completed by students to determine what extent each student has learned the content presented in the social studies program. Effective teachers use the results of this analysis to plan instruction.

portfolios. Analysis of these data, perhaps the most difficult part of assessment, is the process of deciding what the contents of the portfolio mean. What the portfolio reveals must be shared among the teacher, the student, and the student's parents. The components are not sequential; items will be placed in the portfolio throughout the year. Likewise, analyzing the contents of the portfolio must occur regularly. Rather than only at required parent conferences or on end-of-term report cards, the sharing of information should take place on an ongoing basis.

Each student's portfolio should contain a wide variety of items. The multiple-source approach uses the following categories of student work: (a) written products, (b) other, nonwritten products (charts, visual arts, performing arts), (c) multiple-form products (e.g., projects that require writing, drawing, and an oral presentation), and (d) tests in a variety of formats. Whereas tests and projects completed by the whole group will be common elements in each portfolio, individual and small-group activities will yield the material that will make each portfolio unique.

Written Products. Because most written products are an appropriate size for placement in portfolios, many end up there. (In this section of the chapter, I use examples from the national curriculum standards for social studies, *Expectations of Excellence,* NCSS, 1994.)

Stories. Stories written by students can be used as a means of evaluating what they learned. *Expectations of Excellence* (NCSS, 1994) provides the following example (p. 57): A teacher wanted her class to understand the concept of an "artifact" and how family artifacts can help people learn about how their relatives lived in the past. The teacher asked her second graders to bring something to class that their parents or grandparents owned when they were young. The children gathered things like waffle irons, newspapers, old photographs, and kitchen tools. Each child then wrote a story about her or his artifact.

Captions. To accompany simple illustrations and as a part of bulletin board displays, students write captions. The captions can be used for assessment.

Editorials. The editorial form of journalistic essay requires the writer to organize facts to persuade the reader and is a good project for older elementary students. Here's another example from the national social studies standards (p. 83): An eighth-grade class examined different perspectives on the American Revolution (Patriot, Loyalist, indifferent). To assess students' understanding of multiple perspectives, the teacher had students work in groups to gather information on contemporary policy issues (e.g., welfare reform). Each student then wrote a newspaper editorial advocating a position on that issue.

   This example would be a good one to explore in terms of defining criteria and a scoring rubric for analysis. Although the essay could be evaluated by several criteria, let's assume the teacher decided on only one: the ability to provide factual support for the position adopted in the editorial. The teacher could develop an evaluation chart with the scoring rubric displayed in Figure 8.2. In this example, the teacher decided on three components of providing factual support in the editorial: (a) number of facts, (b) their relevance to the writer's position, and (c) the degree to which their presentation strengthened the writer's position.

Answers to Questions. When students read from their social studies textbooks, many lessons will require them to answer questions. For assessment, the key is to ask a variety of questions, including those with answers explicitly stated in the text, those that require students to synthesize information from different parts of the text, and those that require interpretation (more on this in chap. 13).

Journals. Many of us have our students write in journals. Some journals are ongoing summaries of what students think they have learned; others are change-of-perspective journals written as if the students were in a different time and place. For example, *Expectations of Excellence* (NCSS, 1994, p. 60) describes a second-grade classroom where the teacher asked the children to select a way they could make their community a better place to live. Working in groups, the children selected an organization in their city that could make their idea happen. The children then sent a proposal to that

Figure 8.2 Evaluation Rubric for Newspaper Editorial

Unit: "The American Revolution"

Assignment: Newspaper editorial on contemporary policy issue

Student's name _____

Date _____

Criterion: Ability to provide factual support for the editorial position

_____ 1. Essay cites several facts, each relevant to the topic, presented in a manner that strengthens the writer's position.

_____ 2. Essay cites few facts, each is relevant to the topic, and they are presented in a manner that strengthens the writer's position.

_____ 3. Essay cites few facts, and they are not relevant to the topic *or* they are not presented in a manner that strengthens the writer's position.

_____ 4. Essay failed to cite facts to support the writer's position.

organization. The teacher required the children to keep journals during this activity. The teacher evaluated the journals for clarity, thoroughness, and accuracy.

Scripts. When our students write scripts for performing arts presentations, we can save these and place them in the students' portfolios.

Summary Reports. After our students participate in a project, we can ask them to write reports summarizing what they did and learned. *Expectations of Excellence* (NCSS, 1994, p. 65) provides an example of how this form of writing can be used for evaluation: A primary class participated in a unit on economic specialization during production. The class was divided into two groups: One group made their cookies with an assembly line; the other group made their cookies as individuals. Afterward, the class compared the two approaches in terms of productivity, pride, creativity, and quality control. Students prepared written summaries about the production process. Their teacher evaluated the summaries in terms of accuracy of description and extent to which each student used economic concepts to describe what happened.

Notes. As students gather information from reference materials, we can ask them to take notes. Although notes usually are used as a tool to create something else (e.g., an oral presentation, a bulletin board display), the notes themselves provide evidence of the extent of each student's mastery of the process of gathering information.

Letters. Students should write letters as part of social studies. The letters can be "real" correspondence and be mailed to other students, to local newspapers, or to government officials. Other letters can be hypothetical, written to imaginary or historical people. In *Expectations of Excellence* (NCSS, 1994, p. 104), an eighth-grade teacher was concerned about the stereotypes his students held about the Islamic world. The teacher had collected letters-to-the-editor published in the local newspaper that showed a lack of respect toward women, social groups, and cultural groups. Students in his class pretended they were members of a slighted group and responded to the published letters. The teacher evaluated the letters according to clarity of purpose, accuracy of information about the target group, and effectiveness of presentation.

E-Mail. E-mail is rapidly replacing "hard-copy" letters. (How many letters have you written in the last year? How many e-mails?) Just as we would save letters our students have written, we can save their e-mail transmissions. In terms of storage space, it is much more economical to save e-mails electronically on a diskette than to save letters written on sheets of paper.

Essays. We should have older students write essays that take a position and support that position with evidence. These essays are the written project most closely resembling a "traditional" test. For essays used for assessment at the elementary level, however, we should require students to work together to gather information, provide opportunities for discussion on what they are going to write, and create a format so that we can give our students feedback on preliminary drafts of their essays.

Nonwritten Products. Social studies should never consist solely of paper-and-pencil tasks. Throughout this book, I present many activities in which students create things that are not "written." The collection and analysis of these products is essential as an alternative to written assessments, especially in a classroom with a diverse student population, because many students find it easier to express what they know through speaking, making charts and graphs, or producing art.

Charts. A great deal of social science data is best presented in charts and graphs. The national social studies standards provides these examples of how charts and graphs can be placed in a portfolio and used for assessment: In one classroom, students interviewed recent immigrants to the United States. Working in three groups, the students made three charts: one summarizing reasons for coming to the United States, the second summarizing problems encountered during immigration, and the third the feelings of immigrants about leaving one place for another. Each group had to respond to questions from their classmates, using the charts as a data source (NCSS, 1994, p. 53). In another classroom, students compiled charts on Native American tribes by using the following categories: geographic region, life before European contact, life after European contact, and contemporary status (p. 81). Charts are a good evaluative tool if we want to assess our students' ability to both identify and categorize relevant information.

Maps. We can assess our students' knowledge of geographic information by asking them to make maps. We should use "mental maps," those drawn from memory, to assess our students' knowledge of geographic features (Wise & Kon, 1990). An example is offered in the national social studies standards: A second-grade class was studying their city, including the locations of major places. The children used a variety of maps to increase their knowledge and made pop-up maps of different areas. To evaluate what they had learned, their teacher asked them to make mental maps of the city and to include features from the area they studied while making their pop-up maps. The mental (or "sketch") maps were evaluated for accuracy (NCSS, 1994, p. 56).

Visual Arts. We can use a variety of visual arts products for assessment. The visual arts are important because they separate knowledge from the ability to express that knowledge through writing or speaking. Murals, posters, cartoons, constructions, and any other visual art form can be used to determine what students have learned. A good example is provided in *Expectations of Excellence* (NCSS, 1994, p. 52): In a unit on their community, primary-age children each selected a topic from this list: transportation, land use, schools, people, stores, residences. Each child then drew two illustrations: one depicting the topic as it appears today, and the other as it appeared long ago. The teacher used the drawings to assess the children's understanding of the broad concept of change and their specific knowledge of how their city had changed. The checklist in Figure 8.3 could be used to analyze the illustrations.

Oral Activities. We can use a variety of speaking activities to assess our students in social studies, especially mastery of the process of civil discourse. By listening to our students, we can also judge their ability to work productively in groups. Whereas we can assess more formal oral reports in the same fashion as an written essay, discussions require us to use one of the following analytic techniques:

  • *Listen to a group and assess only one objective.* For example, we could observe three students discussing a topic and record information on the sole

Figure 8.3 Evaluation Checklist for Now and Then Illustrations

Unit: "Our Community: Yesterday and Today"

Assignment: Now and then illustrations

Student's Name _____

Date _____

Check all that apply:

_____ Illustrations depict the same topic or place.

_____ "Now" illustration provides three or more clearly distinguishable

features.

_____ "Then" illustration provides three or more clearly distinguishable

features.

_____ "Then" illustration is historically accurate.

_____ Illustrations were completed on time.

objective "takes turns and allows others to speak." We would assess each
student in the group on her or his achievement of the objective.

- *Listen to a group and record in anecdotal form a few observations.* We could
take notes and record only those observed phenomena that "stand out"
("Heidi was able to support her position with evidence," "Vijay was patient
and waited politely to speak," "Shannon wanted to dominate and inter-
rupted others").

For example, in a fourth-grade classroom, students took part in a simulation
on international trade and the relative wealth of nations. Some groups were given
considerable resources (school supplies such as glue and tape), whereas other
groups were not and were considered "impoverished." After the simulation, the
whole class met to discuss the experience in relation to the international economic
concepts they were studying. The discussion helped the teacher assess the extent to
which the students could apply those concepts to a specific situation (the simulation) (NCSS, 1994, p. 66).

Performing Arts. If we are skilled, we can use drama, dance, and song to learn about
our students. Students will provide us with much useful information for assessment in
social studies prior to their performance—in the writing of the script, the creation of

the setting, and the design of the costumes. Each of these components will reveal the depth of a student's knowledge of other people, places, and times. In a class studying the American Revolution, for example, children were placed in groups. Each group selected a person from the period (e.g., Mercy Otis Warren, George Washington, Elizabeth Freeman, Patrick Henry). The group then produced a scene depicting that person's contributions before, during, or after the war. The scene had to include dialogue and a setting (backdrops and/or props). The teacher evaluated each group for the accuracy and importance of the information they presented in their scene. The teacher asked the class to place the scenes in chronological order. The teacher used this for evaluation as well (NCSS, 1994, p. 53).

Multiple-Form Products. Many social studies activities challenge students to produce something that requires a combination of writing, the arts, charts, and speaking. In many classrooms, these multimedia products are completed with computer-based resources as students create high-tech reports on CD-ROMs with software like Hyperstudio or add links to a class Web site. In both cases, the finished products will feature written text, visual images (photographs taken with a digital camera or a video), and charts or graphs. Although it is possible for us to look at just one aspect of the product for evaluation (e.g., just the written part), many products should be evaluated as a whole. For example, a third-grade class was learning how humans change the environment. The children decided to undertake a whole-class project on the effects of the Styrofoam cups used in the school cafeteria. The children gathered data on the number of cups used annually and the amount of fluorocarbons released by the cups. They summarized information on the topic they found in hard-copy and computer-based reference materials. They learned about the cost of replacing the Styrofoam cups with paper cups. The class prepared a videotaped proposal for their schoolmates and, eventually, the school board.

The teacher asked each child to compile a portfolio during the project, which contained all the child's work during the project, a record of daily activities, and summaries of what he or she learned. The teacher then evaluated each portfolio (NCSS, 1994, p. 68). Although no one item in a portfolio told the teacher all she needed to know, all the pieces gave her a clear picture of each child's achievement during the project. In this example, the teacher could assess each child on her or his ability to (a) understand the scientific basis for replacing the Styrofoam cups, (b) acquire mathematical data and summarize it on a chart, (c) gather and summarize data from reference sources, (d) participate productively in small-group work, (e) meet required deadlines, and (f) write a script for a videotaped presentation. Because not all children participated at the same level in each activity, the teacher will have to use the portfolio along with other data to reach a summative conclusion about each child in the class.

In another example, a seventh-grade class studied international economic interdependence. Teacher and students together constructed a survey to determine the global connections of local businesses. Members of the class used the survey to interview representatives of those businesses. Each student then prepared a poster illustrating the international aspects of the business. Each student was to prepare a short statement, similar to a news story, to use with the poster in a presentation. The teacher evaluated each student, using both the poster and the written statement, in terms of thoroughness, depth of information, and accuracy (NCSS, 1994, p. 102).

Authentic Tests. Well-designed and developmentally appropriate tests should also be a part of our assessment plans. They will provide us with information that cannot be found in the other items in the portfolio. Tests will also provide information we can use to support conclusions we have made after we have reviewed the other items in the portfolios. As I noted earlier, "tests" are becoming more and more authentic to the extent that some tests seem no different from a project typically undertaken as a part of a social studies unit. You are undoubtedly familiar with "traditional" tests in the formats of multiple choice, fill in the blank, essays, or true/false.

Perhaps we should begin with a brief review of some key words and concepts relating to tests. A test should be *reliable,* which means the results of the test will be consistent when given in similar situations. A test must be *valid,* which means it measures what it is claimed to measure. With our English language learners, test validity is a big issue because some tests do not measure the test taker's knowledge of social studies; rather, they measure the test taker's ability to read and write in English. A *standardized test* has a testing procedure that must be identical each time the test is given. Standardized tests given to a national sample of students can provide *norm-referenced* results, which report student scores in comparative numbers (e.g., grade-level equivalents, percentiles). A *criterion-referenced test* establishes a criterion for each part of the test (e.g., 8 of 10 answers correct).

How do we as teachers transform our social studies tests so that they are more authentic? Here are some ways the tests have been modified:

Time. The more traditional tests have strict, uniform time limits. Some projects used for assessment, however, should have flexible time limits; students need to be given ample time to finish the task.

Location. Traditional tests are taken in school, at the student's seat. Many of us, however, are developing tests for students to complete at home, on field trips, or in the library.

Collaboration. In a traditional test, students work on their own. Many social studies activities, however, require students to work in groups, and some tests require group work too. Sometimes the group work is a prelude to the performance that will be assessed. For example, each second grader must draw a picture of his or her favorite place in the community and write a brief rationale for this decision. Prior to beginning, small groups of children talk about what they will draw. The drawings and accompanying essays will be used for evaluation.

Alternatives to Reading and Writing. Most traditional tests demand a high level of literacy: The test taker reads questions and then writes answers. Some tests, however, ask students to draw, to make maps, or to talk.

When compared with language arts and mathematics, far fewer commercially prepared, standardized tests are used in social studies. For one thing, these tests are developed for a national market, and they may not fit every curriculum. Textbooks usually come with tests, and like all other aspects of a textbook package, we should use some of these tests, adapt others, and ignore the rest. The United States now has national tests in history and in geography (Risinger & Garcia, 1995). The National Assessment of Educational Progress (NAEP) assesses 4th, 8th, and 12th graders (a national sample of about 20,000 students). Results of the 1994 assessments in geography and history make interesting reading (geography: Williams, Reese, Lazer & Shakrani, 1995a; history: Williams et al., 1995b).

We should create tests that are aligned with the units of study we have prepared. Again, no teacher should rely solely on tests for social studies assessment. When used with other sources of information and more authentic tests, more traditional tests can provide useful information. *Essay tests* are particularly helpful when they ask students to compare and contrast (remember, though, we should only use essay tests when our students have well-developed writing skills). *Multiple-choice tests* have the advantage of being easy to correct and, if properly constructed, can cover a wide range of content. This type of test, along with *true/false tests,* typically fail to assess more than knowledge of facts and reveal little about students' grasp of concepts and generalizations. It takes time to prepare a good multiple-choice test. An item has a "stem" ("The city with the most people in our state is . . .") and then three or more "options" (a. Los Angeles, b. San Francisco, c. San Diego). The options should be plausible, but only one of them should be a correct answer. Other forms of tests include *matching* (students link items in one column with items in another) and *completion* (students "fill in the blank(s)" of a partial sentence). Those of us who use these traditional forms of tests should follow the guidelines listed below:

- Plan activities that help students become familiar with the test format (practice tests, tests completed in groups).
- Be absolutely sure that the form of the test matches the developmental level of the students who will take it. Be sure that tests used with primary-age children are simple and short.
- Teach older students, especially those who will go to a middle school or junior year in the subsequent year, how to study for tests.

Contents of Student Portfolios

The four sources of data described in the previous section will provide us with a large amount of information. The problem is that some student-produced projects will not fit into a portfolio. For example, what do we do with a mural? Other items, like a journal, however, are easy to save. Here's what goes into a portfolio:

- *The products themselves*. Many items that students produce can be saved "as they are" because they are small enough to fit into a portfolio (e.g., an essay, a small chart, an illustration done on 8 1/2 × 11-inch paper).
- *Media versions of products*. Large visual arts projects are a problem in terms of storage. One solution is to take *photographs* and place these into the portfolios of the students who created the project. *Audiotapes* can be used to record performing arts projects such as readers' theater, and they can be used to record discussions. *Videotapes* should be used for oral presentations and performing arts projects. Because most projects are group efforts, some photographs, audiotapes, and videotapes will have to be stored separately, rather than in any one student's portfolio. Multimedia projects can be saved on a *CD-ROM*.
- *Computer diskettes*. Many of us are beginning a process that undoubtedly will become routine in the future: the storage of student work on computer diskettes. For example, a teacher may have a variety of written projects by one student all saved on a diskette. Checklists, rating scales, and anecdotal notations can all be stored on diskette.
- *Teacher records*. We teachers gather a great deal of information over a period of time for each of our students. It makes sense to store anecdotal records, rubrics, checklists, and a copy of a group evaluation form or other rating scale in individual student portfolios. Keeping these records where they are easily accessed allows us and our students to better evaluate progress or lack thereof when reviewing new or ongoing projects.

Records Teachers Should Keep

In addition to the products created by students, or media versions of them, we need to keep several types of records that provide data on the performance of our students.

Anecdotal Records. Anecdotal records can be written on sheets of paper, on Post-it Notes, or in computer files (it is not difficult to imagine a time when most teachers will use laptop computers to record their classroom observations). "Kid watching" is an essential part of evaluation, and these anecdotal notes will provide us with a great deal of important information. As we watch our students participate in social studies activities, we should write brief descriptions of noteworthy events. We should include the date, time, and context of the activity. Obviously, we will **not be** able to write something about each student every day, but over the course of time, our anecdotal records will show patterns. Below are two examples:

DECEMBER 1, 1998

Shontae is reading an encyclopedia entry on the production of sugar. He is using the data retrieval chart and is recording important information.

FEBRUARY 14, 2000

Diana is having difficulty working with her group during their discussion of what to include in their mural. She is not listening and will not let others speak unless I intervene.

Evaluation Rubrics and Rating Scales. An example of a rubric was shown in Figure 8.2. A *rubric* provides a scale with written descriptors to categorize student performance. A rubric should have three or more categories, and the descriptor for each category should be written with enough detail to distinguish it from the others. Reliable and valid rubrics are difficult to develop, and the best ones require a group effort and are tested in several classrooms so that the descriptors are refined. Other forms of *rating scales* may use single-word descriptors (e.g., "outstanding," "above average"). Figure 8.4 shows an example of a rating scale for assessing a Group Project. After studying the Seven Wonders of the Ancient World, students were placed in groups and given the challenge of constructing a model of an Eighth Wonder (see NCSS, 1994, p. 100).

Checklists. Checklists allow us to record information about our students (Figure 8.3 and 8.6 are examples). Unlike rubrics or rating scales, checklists do not provide a continuum so that we can capture gradations of student performance. They are simple and typically require a yes/no judgment.

Analyzing and Sharing Assessment Data

We analyze the items in our students' portfolios to determine to what extent each student has learned the content we presented in the social studies program. We can reach separate conclusions for lessons, for units, and for the school year. It is easy for those of us who work in elementary schools to reach broad conclusions because we work with the same group of children for the school year (e.g., "Caitlin knows a great deal about our city; learning social studies information is easy for her."). We should, however, be able to make more specific judgments and to base these conclusions on our objectives for lessons and units.

Figure 8.4   Rating Scale for Assessing an Eighth-Wonder Project

Unit: Europe and the Middle East in ancient days *Assignment:* Group project—Construct an Eighth Wonder					
	Names of Students				
	Roberto	Zelia	Ned	Jiri	Winona
Criteria					
1. Helped group reach agreement	4	1	3	2	4
2. Supported other members of the group	4	1	3	2	4
3. Showed knowledge of characteristics of seven ancient wonders	1	1	4	1	4
4. Assisted in the design of the Eighth Wonder	4	1	1	1	4
5. Used art skills to contruct Eighth Wonder	4	1	1	1	4
6. Provided a cultural context for defining Eighth Wonder	1	1	4	1	4

1: Excellent   2: Very good   3: Acceptable   4: Area of difficulty

Verifying Acquisition of Content

For all social studies lessons, we must have some means to assess the extent to which our students achieved the objectives for the lesson. As students talk, write, draw, and act, they are providing the evidence necessary for us to judge their level of achievement. For example, chapter 13 contains a plan for a lesson that took place during a sixth-grade unit on careers. Students completed a variety of tasks based on advertisements for jobs in the local newspaper. The content objective was that students "understand the specialized nature of jobs, how each job has unique responsibilities and requirements." Groups of students selected ads and answered questions the teacher wrote on a sheet of chart paper. The written responses indicated to what degree each group could identify the unique responsibilities and requirements of the job described in the ad they selected. The teacher also kept notes as she observed each group working.

We as teachers must have evidence so that we can judge to what extent our students have achieved the content objectives established for a unit. Chapter 10

Figure 8.5 Teacher's Assessment Plan for Unit "Boats"

BOATS

Objective 1: What are the different types of boats, and why are they different?

Unit activities used for assessment of this objective:
Field trip to harbor
Concept attainment lesson
Unit test

Objective 2: Where in our state, country, and world would you find people using boats?

Unit activities used for assessment of this objective:
Map reading activity
Inquiry — The Voyage to Hawaii
Unit test

Objective 3: What types of jobs do people perform on boats, and how have those jobs changed over time?

Unit activities used for assessment of this objective:
Bulletin board display
Videocassette, *Ships*
Unit test

Objective 4: How have boats changed over time?

Unit activities used for assessment of this objective:
Bulletin board display
History of boats lesson
Unit test

contains an example of a third-grade social studies unit on boats. The unit is organized around four questions, which serve as the unit's content objectives. Although every lesson in the unit will produce either behaviors or products that can be assessed, some activities are particularly important from an assessment standpoint. The unit assessment plan in Figure 8.5 shows how the unit's activities will be used for assessment purposes.

Measuring the Understanding of Processes

Either checklists or rating scales can be used to record student progress toward mastering the processes of social studies. Here, our concern is with what students can

Figure 8.6 Checklist for Assessing Use of Print Encyclopedia

Student's Name _____

School _____

Teacher _____

Date Achieved	Project or Assignment	Objective
_____	_____	1. Uses information in encyclopedia to answer questions
_____	_____	2. Compares information in encyclopedia with other source
_____	_____	3. Uses index to locate an entry
_____	_____	4. Given a topic, locates appropriate entry(ies)
_____	_____	5. Scans for relevant details
_____	_____	6. Records information in a format that facilitates future use

do (content objectives establish what we want students to *know*). We need to observe our students, keep good records, and refer frequently to the portfolios to reach conclusions about each student's abilities. Here's an example of use of a checklist: A school district wrote objectives for the use of print encyclopedias in fourth grade. Teachers used the checklist in Figure 8.6 for assessment.

Good checklists can be used effectively, but the achievement of process objectives is a matter of degree, and checklists do not allow us to record different levels of achievement. Rating scales do, though, and are a better tool for recording each student's level of success. For example, if one third-grade social studies

Figure 8.7 Class Profile: Geographic Skills, Grade 4

Names	1.1 Ask geographic questions	1.2 Distinguish geographic/non-geographic	2.1 Locate information	2.2 Record observations	3.1 Prepare maps	3.2 Construct graphs	4.1 Use maps	4.2 Use tables and graphs	4.3 Use texts and photos	4.4 Use simple math	5.1 Present geographic information	5.2 Use geographic inquiry	5.3 Apply geographic generalizations

− Achieves objective partially and only with assistance.
+ Achieves objective partially without assistance.
⋆ Achieves objective.
★ Achieves objective at high levels of proficiency.

objective for the year is that each student "adjust his or her behavior to fit the dynamic of various groups and various situations," then it is unlikely that any students will fail to demonstrate this behavior on at least some occasions. Let's look at an example of a rating scale for achievement of process objectives.

The national geography standards established geographic skills to be learned by the end of the fourth grade (Geography Education Standards Project, 1994). These are process objectives, describing what students should be able to do and organized in five sets of skills. Figure 8.7 shows a rating scale, in the form of a class profile, for these geographic skills (for the complete wording of each objective, see Geography Education Standards Project, 1994, pp. 46–49).

Evaluating Development of Values

Values are standards or criteria by which behaviors, beliefs, and attitudes are judged. For example, Justice is a value. Those accused of crimes are entitled to a fair trial is a belief, keeping an open mind while serving on a jury is an attitude, and speaking in favor of due process rights of people in totalitarian regimes is a behavior; each is consistent with the value of Justice. This aspect of social studies is difficult to evaluate. We can only make judgments about a person's values, beliefs, and attitudes by observing her or his behavior. As teachers, we can take essentially two approaches. In the first approach, we can ask our students to express their attitudes and beliefs through discussion and writing. The content of these discussions and written statements can be judged for consistency with the values of our social studies program. For example, the *National Standards for Civics and Government* (Center for Civic Education, 1994) lists Equality of Opportunity as a fundamental value of American democracy. We could ask our students to establish criteria for classroom officers, and then we could assess those criteria in terms of how inclusive they are.

In the second approach, we can observe our students' behavior to see to what extent they have adopted the values we are trying to teach. This is somewhat trickier than it might seem because of cultural differences. For example, a teacher wants his students to adopt the value of Equality of Opportunity. He thinks that a behavior demonstrating this value is when his students listen quietly and let others take turns during group discussions. This behavior, however, will be easier for children from some cultural groups than from others. Korean American children, especially those whose parents were born in Korea, have learned at home a set of rules for taking part in a discussion: Be quiet and don't talk unless the leader of the group asks you a question. Native Hawaiian children, in contrast, who have participated in traditional "talk story" events, are accustomed to jumping into conversations in a way that many European Americans would consider inappropriate and Korean Americans would find shocking (Au, 1993). It is important to consider cultural influences on behavior before we make a judgment about whether or not a behavior was the result of a commitment to a value.

Sharing What Has Been Learned

We have gathered data from a variety of sources. We have analyzed those data to determine to what extent each student has acquired content, mastered processes, and adopted values. The final component of assessment is sharing the results of our analysis. This will take place in a variety of formats:

Informal Conferences With Students. Conversations with our students about their progress is an essential part of good teaching. These should be private and can address any aspect of the social studies program. For example, "Fred, your drawing of the Iroquois village is very good. I always look forward to your artwork, but this isn't what long houses looked like. Where could you find more information about them?" In this case, we have commented on Fred's failure to achieve a content objective—the ability to describe accurately Native American dwellings. Our comments could focus on process: "Carmela, I looked at your map of the city, and it really shows you know how to create your own symbols." Here, we are informing her that she has achieved a process objective—the ability to construct an accurate map with original symbols. Finally, the purpose of a conference could be to address a need in terms of values and beliefs: "Kenny, I noticed today at recess that you called Orlando out when it was clear to everyone else he was safe. Why is it important for all of us to follow the rules when we play softball? How would you feel if you had been Orlando?"

Parent Conferences. We should communicate with parents in a variety of formats. Schools may schedule formal conferences once or twice a year. In terms of social studies, we should be able to state our conclusions to parents *and support them with items from their child's portfolio.* I recommend that we say something about content, process, and values. I think it is good practice not to wait until the formal conferences to talk with parents about how their child is doing in social studies. When our students do something great, we should take the time to call their parents. All too often, we only contact parents when something wrong happens.

Report Cards. All schools have some form for reporting student progress. These summative reports vary widely in format. "Social Studies" usually appears as a topic on the report card. Some school districts use *letter grades* (e.g., A, B, C). Strong arguments can be made against using letter grades in elementary school, especially with our youngest students. If we are in a situation where we give grades, then we should be sure our students understand our criteria for making judgments. We must tell students what activities will be used to determine grades. Many school districts have report cards with *categories* or *scales.* Categories, for example, might be "area of need," "making progress," or "area of strength." Some districts have constructed summative rubrics with categories described in several sentences. Each student then is placed in the appropriate category. Finally, some report cards ask us to make *written comments*. Usually, this format is combined with either grades or a scale. Providing written comments for each student is time-consuming, and rarely is there enough space to write all that we want. Whatever the format, we must be able to support our judgments with evidence from our students' portfolios.

Assessment and Diversity: Final Thoughts

Our theme of Diversity dictates that we use a variety of data sources to help us determine what our students know and are able to do. Diverse sources allow us to reach accurate conclusions about the achievement of our students. For too long, paper-and-pencil tests were the only assessment tool used in social studies. Both cultural and personal characteristics make it difficult for some students to show what they know on this type of test. When we shift to authentic assessment, especially when we use discussion, the visual arts, and the performing arts, we create a more equitable and accurate system for evaluation.

For our English language learners, it is important that assessment be decoupled from English literacy tasks. We are on the wrong path if our assessment reveals the student's level of English proficiency, rather than what he or she has learned in social studies. Quite simply, we frequently don't know whether low achievement among our English language learners is the result of their not knowing social studies content or their not knowing English. To make the distinction, English language learners must have the opportunity to show what they know through the performing arts and the visual arts. When possible, assessment should be done in the student's primary language. For example, if one of our content objectives is that students accurately describe the dwellings of four 15th-century Native American tribal groups, it doesn't matter if the descriptions are written in English or Spanish (note, too, that the descriptions could be drawn rather than written). Primary language assessment requires a bilingual teacher or a bilingual instructional aide and, of course, may not be possible in all schools for all children.

SUMMARY OF KEY POINTS

▶ The process of assessing students has undergone great changes in the last 20 years. A shift has occurred toward authentic assessment, an ongoing process in which data are gathered from everyday social studies assignments and placed in student portfolios.

▶ Assessment has three parts: gathering, analyzing, and sharing data.

▶ Assessment plans should gather data from multiple sources, including written assignments, discussions, charts and graphs, maps, the performing arts, and the visual arts.

▶ In addition to saving student work, we as teachers should use anecdotal records, evaluation rubrics, ratings scales, and checklists.

▶ We should analyze the items in the portfolio to determine to what extent each student has acquired content, mastered processes, and adopted values. Our conclusions should be made in reference to our stated objectives for lessons, units, and the year.

▶ We should share our conclusions with students and parents in a variety of formats. Informal discussions, formal conferences, and report cards should be used.

▶ For a diverse classroom, it is essential that students be allowed to show what they know and can do through discussion and the arts.

FOR FURTHER READING

▶ The most valuable further reading you can do is to look at the documents used for social studies assessment in a local school district. Start by looking at the report card form and the guidelines for completing it. Ask whether the district has guidelines for student portfolios. Any tests, checklists, rubrics, or rating scales would be worthwhile items to examine.

▶ For an introduction to authentic assessment in social studies, take a look at the 1992 special issue of *Social Education* (Nickell, 1992). To learn more about the basic ideas of authentic assessment, read the work of Fred Newmann (Archbald & Newmann, 1988; Newmann & Associates, 1996; Newmann et al., 1995) and Grant Wiggins (1989, 1993, 1998). Terwilliger's (1997) article criticizes the use of the word *authentic* and argues that "alternative assessment procedures should be adopted in combination with more traditional forms of assessment" (p. 24). Kon and Martin-Kniep's (1992) article on performance assessment of geographic knowledge is excellent. Alleman and Brophy (1998) provide guidelines for assessment consistent with constructivist learning theory; their article has examples of rating scales and checklists.

Chapter 9

The Integrated Curriculum: Incorporating the Language Arts, the Performing Arts, and the Visual Arts

ugenia Potenza was excited about the unit she was planning for her second graders: "People Who Made A Difference." This unit was suggested by California's *History-Social Science Framework* (California Department of Education, 1997). Ms. Potenza wanted to add some activities to the sample unit written by her school district's curriculum committee. One project in the unit would be a bulletin board display titled "Inventors Who Made a Difference." The district's media center had good materials on Thomas Edison, George Washington Carver, and three other well-known inventors. Ms. Potenza was looking for inventors who were not as well known.

While teaching, Ms. Potenza was taking courses toward her master's degree. One course she had completed the previous summer was on multicultural children's literature. A light bulb went on! She remembered the perfect children's book to share with her class when they studied inventors: *Shoes for Everyone: A Story About Jan Matzeliger* (Mitchell, 1986). Jan Matzeliger, an African American, invented the "lasting machine," the device that made it possible to manufacture shoes in a factory. Ms. Potenza wanted to be sure she included minority inventors, and she wanted to share information about inventions that had affected the lives of the children, so *Shoes for Everyone* would be ideal.

Ms. Potenza also came up with a clever idea for a bulletin board. The day before the unit began, she backed the bulletin board with powder blue paper and then attached several sentences onto the board. Each sentence described a current condition. For example: "There are thousands of shoes to choose from in stores" (for Jan Matzeliger) and "I like peanut butter and jelly sandwiches" (for George Washington Carver). As children discovered the names of the inventors and their inventions, they would write the names of the inventors on strips of paper and connect them to the appropriate sentences with colored yarn. Additional captions and illustrations would be added to complete the bulletin board. Ms. Potenza's bulletin board project is an example of how language arts can be integrated with social studies, one topic covered in this chapter.

▲　▲　▲

In this chapter, you will read about:

- ▶ The benefits of integrating the social studies curriculum with concepts from other academic disciplines
- ▶ The advantages and disadvantages of using social studies textbooks as an instructional resource
- ▶ Instructional strategies to help students when reading textbooks or fictional and nonfictional trade books
- ▶ Planning challenging writing activities especially suited to the social studies curriculum
- ▶ Guidelines for developing a classroom climate that promotes civil discourse
- ▶ Performing arts and visual arts activities that can be used to enhance students' social studies experiences

The Integrated Curriculum

Social studies should link several areas of the curriculum. Those of us who plan and implement this type of instruction describe our teaching as "cross-curricular," "thematic," or "integrated." Although these descriptors are often used as synonyms, I use the term *integrated* in this book. Our social studies curriculum becomes integrated when we go beyond history and geography to include concepts from the other social sciences (political science, anthropology, economics, psychology, and sociology), mathematics, science, physical education, literature, and the arts. The focus of this chapter is on how to integrate the language arts, the performing arts, and the visual arts with social studies. Chapter 11 shows how significant ideas from political science can be a part of elementary social studies, and chapter 13 discusses the importance of teaching students concepts from anthropology, economics, psychology, and sociology.

The Language Arts

The social studies curriculum should provide students with many opportunities to support literacy and become more proficient in the language arts (Camperell & Knight, 1991; Gilstrap, 1991; Irvin, Lunstrum, Lynch-Brown, & Shepard, 1995; Natoli, 1992; Selwyn, 1995). The development of literacy includes teaching children to listen, read, speak, and write. Many of us, therefore, have organized our curriculum so that language arts and social studies are integrated as social studies provides many opportunities for students to develop as readers, writers, speakers, and listeners (Roberts, 1996). The reading material most accessible for teaching social studies is the social studies basal textbook. This can be problematic, however, as I soon explain.

Social Studies Textbooks

Almost every school district in the United States purchases social studies textbooks. Textbooks are part of a classroom package that usually includes a teacher's edition, student texts, worksheets, and supplemental items like videodiscs, CD-ROMs, audiotapes, maps, and charts. Each publisher produces a series of textbooks, one for each grade level, although publishers produce different products for elementary and secondary markets. (Note: I distinguish *textbook* from *text*. To me, *text* has a broader meaning and includes anything that is written.)

For many of us, the social studies textbook is at the center of social studies instruction. Far too often, it is the only resource we use (Finkelstein et al., 1993). Despite their widespread use and popularity, social studies textbooks have been criticized (Beck & McKeown, 1991b; Wade, 1993; White, 1988). Most authors of journal research articles reach the conclusion that textbooks are "generally inadequate" (Beck & McKeown, 1991b, p. 496). The criticisms of textbooks can be summarized as follows:

- *Social studies textbooks tend to avoid controversy and fail to present conflicting points of view.* Textbooks are marketed nationally, with particular attention to California and Texas, where state committees decide which texts will be approved for purchase for the entire state. Publishers try to produce textbooks with wide acceptability; thus, the presentation of conflicting perspectives is avoided because of the potential for alienating prospective buyers.

- *Social studies textbooks can be dull.* The writing is bland, and many textbooks ignore interesting historical incidents and people. Textbook coverage is broad, and topics are not covered in detail; they ignore the fact that the detail is what makes things come to life. Isabel Beck and Margaret McKeown have conducted several important studies on elementary social studies textbooks. In one, they discovered that if they gave a "voice" to a social studies textbook, students would learn more material (Beck, McKeown, & Worthy, 1995). A passage on British taxation of the American Colonists was rewritten so that it read more like fiction. The "voiced" version had more action, included quotations, and made connections to the readers' emotions.

- *Many textbooks do not always present content that is coherent.* Beck and McKeown (1988, 1991a, 1991b) studied the coherence of elementary social studies textbooks. They concluded that, in many textbooks, the main point is not emphasized, authors stray from their central point with meaningless digressions, examples and comparisons are often inadequate, the reader is given no sense of time, and many passages fail to state clearly the consequences of an event.

- *Social studies textbooks are written for a generic student.* Even if social studies textbooks were written with more panache and greater clarity, using them would still involve significant problems. Quite simply, many students cannot read their grade-level textbooks. Also, textbook-centered instruction will not be compatible with the learning styles of all students. In chapter 2, I discussed the different styles of learning, communication, and participation among African American, Asian American, Hispanic American, and Native American children. Most textbook lessons assume passive behavior among students, yet many students in our classrooms will prefer more active learning experiences. Finally, many of our students learn better from visual images other than text (e.g., charts, photographs) and through hands-on activities.

Fortunately, recent elementary social studies textbooks are an improvement over their predecessors. The illustrations and the graphics in almost all textbooks published after 1995 are excellent. Old paintings, cartoons, and drawings enrich chapters covering historical material. Timelines, several types of maps, bar graphs, and summary charts present material in a form that students readily understand. Textbooks for the primary grades (K–3), in contrast, are still filled with cartoon-like, stylized illustrations that do not present accurate images of people, places, and things. Recent textbooks have broadened their coverage to include more information about minorities, women, and children. Racist accounts and inaccurate stereotypes that plagued textbooks in the first half of the 20th century have been eliminated. Finally, the most recent textbooks have increased the amount of primary source material they contain. Along with the chapter narrative, readers will find transcripts of oral histories, journal entries, songs, and newspaper articles.

Even with these improvements, textbooks should never be the only resource we use to teach social studies. The role of the textbook will depend on what we are teaching. For some topics, the textbook will be a good resource; for others, it will be of little or no value. Also, it is important to be selective once we decide to use the textbook. It would be impossible to implement all the activities suggested in the teacher's edition. We should read the teacher's edition carefully and choose only those portions of a chapter and those instructional activities that we think will be useful.

Instructional Strategies: Reading the Textbook

Effective use of instructional strategies can help our students read their textbooks (Tierney, Readance, & Dishner, 1995). Our discussion looks at the following:

> Strategies that will help students recall what they know about a topic before they read
> Strategies that can be used to teach new vocabulary
> Strategies that facilitate comprehension and can be used while students read and after they have finished
> A teaching sequence that can be used with a textbook-centered lesson

Activating Background Knowledge Before Students Read

K-W-L Chart. The K–W–L chart (Ogle, 1986) has become a popular instructional strategy to help children recall what they know about a topic. Let's assume that a group of second graders will read a selection in their textbooks about the Pledge of Allegiance. The teacher divides a sheet of chart paper into three parts: one with the heading "What We **K**now About the Pledge of Allegiance," the second column with "What We **W**ant to Learn About the Pledge of Allegiance," and the third with "What We **L**earned About the Pledge of Allegiance." The first two columns are completed during the prereading phase of the reading lesson. The third column can be completed either as the material is read or after the reading is completed. If the children do not come up with all the topics the teacher had planned to cover under the "W" portion of the chart, he or she should add them. If children in our classes show a special interest in a topic we had not planned to cover, we should modify our plans so that it is covered.

PreReading Plan (PReP). The PreReading Plan (PReP) is another technique that will help readers recall what they know about a topic before they start reading (Langer, 1981). For example, a sixth-grade class will read about ancient Egypt. In the first phase of PReP, the teacher asks the students to express their initial associations with the topic: "What comes to mind when I say, 'Egypt'?" or "What do you think of when I say, 'Egypt'?" Next, the teacher asks the students to reflect on their initial responses: "What made you think of (whatever the students said)?" This should lead to a discussion during which students explain the sources of their knowledge. Finally, the teacher asks whether the students have any new ideas about the topic or whether they changed their perceptions: "Do any of you have new or different ideas or thoughts about Egypt?" While using PReP, the teacher will analyze the student responses. Langer (1981) suggests that individual responses can be characterized as (a) showing very little knowledge, (b) showing some prior knowledge, or (c) showing much prior knowledge. If we use PReP with a group of students, then we should adjust our plans according to student responses. Those students who have very little prior knowledge about a topic should not be asked to read the selection. Rather, they need to acquire enough background knowledge about a topic so that they can be successful.

Graphic Organizer. An older technique that can be used in the prereading phase is the graphic organizer (Barron, 1969). A graphic organizer is a diagram that shows the structure of something—in this case, a chapter or selection in a social studies textbook or a block of text from another source. For example, first the teacher looks at the chapter and identifies the important concepts. The teacher then selects key words to represent those concepts and prepares a diagram that shows the structure of the chapter. The diagram may be placed on a chart or on an overhead transparency and is used in leading a discussion with the students before they read. The discussion may lead students to offer annotations, questions, or comments, which are placed on the graphic organizer. The whole discussion shouldn't take a long time, just 5 to 10 minutes. Figure 9.1 is an example of a graphic organizer prepared for a class of fourth graders who will read a textbook chapter about the physical geography of their state, Connecticut.

Vocabulary. Students will learn little if they are asked to perform the task of looking up the meanings of words in a dictionary or glossary. Other instructional strategies should prove more effective. One guideline to keep in mind is that any word selected for a lesson should meet two criteria: (a) It should be a word that students cannot define and (b) it should be a word that is important in that a student who does not know what it means will have a difficult time understanding the text.

Figure 9.1 Graphic Organizer

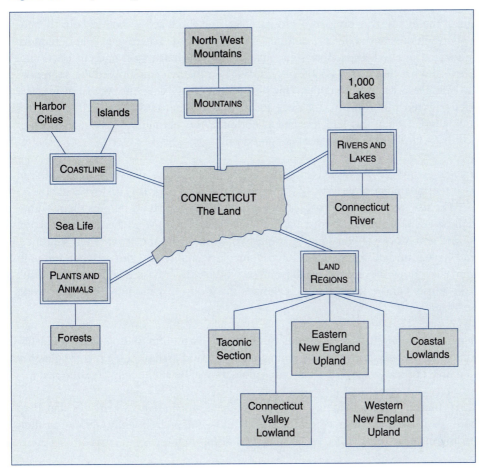

Contextual Redefinition. For our older students, *contextual redefinition* (Cunning-ham, Cunningham, & Arthur, 1981) is a strategy to consider. For example, fourth graders will read the portion of a chapter on the California Gold Rush that discusses the absence of law in the mining camps. The teacher identified the following words for contextual redefinition: *bribe* and *vigilante.* Then, the teacher found the first sentence in the text where each word appeared. Before the lesson, he wrote these sentences (in some cases, the sentence immediately before or after the sentence must be included) on a sheet of chart paper. For our example, these were the sentences:

1. Not all elected leaders were honest. Some took <u>bribes</u>.
2. In some mining camps there was so much crime that the citizens did not feel safe. They became <u>vigilantes</u> and punished people who had broken the law.

To begin the lesson, the teacher asked his class to come up with definitions for the words *bribe* and *vigilante* before they saw the chart with the sentences. This part of the lesson was done as a group effort, and the teacher tried to help the students reach consensus on one definition for each word. To arrive at one definition, students compared and contrasted what their classmates said and, in so doing, added to what they knew about the words. Then the teacher showed the sentences and read them with the students. This step was to clarify what the words meant. The teacher asked the group to try once again to reach consensus on a definition for each word. Finally, he had the group compare the definitions in a dictionary or glossary with the ones the students agreed on.

Possible Sentences. Possible sentences is another process that will help children learn the meanings of new words (Moore & Moore, 1986). It is relatively simple to use: The teacher selects the vocabulary words from the text and writes them on the chalkboard. Then, she asks that each child write a sentence containing each word. (Moore and Moore [1986] suggest using two words from the list in each sentence, but I have found this quite difficult for elementary children.) Then, teacher and children talk about the sentences they have written and revise sentences that don't make sense. Finally, the teacher challenges the group to write new sentences using the words.

Picture Glossaries. Picture glossaries can be made by finding photographs or illustrations of key words, copying or clipping them out, and assembling a picture glossary for a unit. For many words, a look at this glossary will be all the help children need.

Word Analysis. Older students may benefit from word analysis activities that help them learn the meanings of prefixes and suffixes that frequently appear in their reading material (e.g., *anti-, co-, inter-; -ette, -ism, -logy*).

Captioned Bulletin Boards. Labeled bulletin board displays will help children acquire vocabulary.

Lessons on How to Use a Glossary. At the right time, all students will benefit from lessons on how to use the glossary in their social studies textbook. A glossary is simply a mini-dictionary. To use the glossary, students must be able to alphabetize words; older students will need to be able to rank words with the same first two letters.

Comprehension. The ultimate goal of all reading, of course, is to understand the text. Many resources are available for those of us who want to learn more about "comprehension building" strategies (Camperell & Knight, 1991; Martorella, 1991a, 1991b; Pearson & Fielding, 1994; Vacca & Vacca, 1998).

Reciprocal Teaching. Reciprocal teaching is a comprehension-building process that has proved effective in several studies (Palinscar & Brown, 1984; Rosenshine & Meister, 1994). In reciprocal teaching, teachers and students work together to understand a text. The goal is to teach students to use a set of metacognitive strategies independently while they read (*metacognitive* means thinking about our own thinking). The strategies are (a) generating questions before they read, (b) clarifying unclear portions of a text, and (c) predicting what might appear next. The teacher models these processes until students become proficient. The text is read in sub-parts, usually one paragraph in upper grade texts or one page in primary texts. Reciprocal teaching should be implemented with small groups of students. The process goes like this:

1. The teacher asks the students to predict what they are going to read, usually by asking questions they think the block of text will answer. At first, the teacher models this strategy and explains why she or he thinks the text will answer each question (e.g., because of an illustration or a subtitle).
2. Teacher and students read the block of text silently.
3. The teacher models the process of clarifying unclear portions of the text by asking questions (e.g., "I am not sure how the Stamp Act worked. Why were the Colonists so bothered with it?").
4. The teacher then shows students how to summarize the content of the block of text. Many students have difficulty identifying the main idea or most significant facts in a block of text. The teacher may have to "think aloud" and explain why one bit of information in the text is more important than the rest of the text.

After the process is completed, the teacher and the students move on to the next block of text (the subsequent paragraph or page). The teacher's role gradually diminishes as students take over more and more responsibility in the group lesson.

Question-Answer Relationships (QARs). Question-answer-relationships (QARs) will help students answer questions more efficiently and accurately (Ouzts, 1998; Raphael, 1982, 1986). Questions and their answers can be placed into four categories according to the relationship between the question and the location of the answer:

1. *Right There*. The answer to this type of question is explicitly stated in the text and is easy to find. Example: How long did the San Francisco earthquake of April 18, 1906, last?
2. *Think and Search*. The answer is stated in the text, but the required information is in more than one place. The reader has to "put together" two or more parts of the text to come up with the answer. Example: What three

factors led to the "population boom" in Southern California in the early 1900s?

3. *Author and You*. The answer is not in the text. The reader synthesizes information in the text with his or her personal knowledge or perspective. Example: We read about the first automobiles driven in California. How are they different from today's automobiles?

4. *On My Own*. This type of question is related to information in the text, but the reader could answer it without having the text. Example: We read about how John Muir and other conservationists worked to create national parks in California. Have you visited a national park in California? Tell us about your visit.

The purpose of QARs is to teach students to recognize questions from each category. Once they can categorize a question, they will know what is involved in finding the answer. As social studies teachers, we can start by using QARs to write questions for a chapter in the social studies textbook. Students answer each type of question until they become proficient. Later, when students have difficulty finding an answer, we ask them to decide whether it is a "right there," "think and search," "author and you," or "on my own" question.

Illustrations and Text Features. Students can sometimes understand a text better if they first learn to preview the material. A simple way to preview is to look at the subtitles, italicized words, and illustrations in the text.

Text Structures. Social studies texts frequently follow one of two patterns: (a) chronological or (b) cause and effect. As students read their textbooks, we can help them better understand these structures by using timelines and flowcharts.

Who-What-When-Where Charts. These simple charts can help students keep track of the important people, events, dates, and places in the text. Such a chart has four columns, and students record information in the proper column as they read.

Student-Generated Questions. We can ask a small group of students to write questions after they have read a text. Then, we have the group play a friendly quiz-show game. The students who wrote the questions ask their classmates to provide the answers. We should be careful to avoid situations that become too competitive or that embarrass individual students.

Ordering. After students have read several chapters in their textbooks, we can ask them to place people, places, or things in order. Three of the many possible ways to categorize are chronologically, by size, or by importance.

Teaching Sequence for a Textbook-Centered Lesson. For lessons using the textbook as a teaching resource, I suggest the following teaching sequence:

1. *Link* the content of the day's lesson to what we covered previously. To do this, we could look again at an important illustration in the preceding pages of the textbook, reread a chart that lists the key information students have learned, or ask questions about the topics previously presented.
2. Place the material that students are about to read in historical and geographical *context*. The best way to do this is with timelines and maps.
3. Choose a strategy that will help students activate their *background knowledge* (K-W-L, PReP, graphic organizer).
4. Teach essential *vocabulary* (see suggestions in the previous section).
5. Set a *purpose* for reading, either orally or in writing. I suggest writing the purpose on the chalkboard or on a chart paper (e.g., "Today, we are going to read pages 11 to 14 to learn more about firefighters.") Another way to do this is to write three or four questions on the chalkboard that students should be able to answer after they have done the reading.
6. *Read the material.* We have quite a few options here. We can read aloud, students can read aloud, students can read silently, or students can listen to an audiotape. We should let students who are going to read aloud practice their reading the day before. Also, we should never have students read aloud material that is beyond their level of ability. Our goal should be to allow all students in the room hear a fluent reading of the text.
7. *Focus on essential information.* We may want to use reciprocal teaching or the QARs to help students understand the important information in the text. To be effective, we must highlight the essential information in the block of text the students read. It is usually a good idea to summarize the important information on chart paper.
8. The reading experience often serves as a *springboard to other activities.* These follow-up activities can be for the whole group, small groups, or interested individuals.

Children's Literature: Information Books and Biography

Information books are an essential resource for the social studies teacher (Alter, 1995c; Cullinan, 1993; E. B. Freeman & Person, 1992; T. M. McGowan, 1996; Tunnell, 1993; Zarnowski & Gallagher, 1993). The descriptor "information book" is now more widely used than "nonfiction." Books about people, places, things, ideas, and events are all information books. The best books are a blend of art and science, a combination of a vivid text, inspired illustration, and uncompromising accuracy. Why are information books so valuable for social studies teaching?

- Books are available on almost any topic. Need a book on chairs? Try James Cross Giblin's *Be Seated: A Book About Chairs* (1993). How about the Iditarod Dogsled Race? No problem. Students could read *Racing the Iditarod Trail* by Ruth Crisman (1993). Do you know who Ruth Law was? Students who read *Ruth Law Thrills A Nation* (D. Brown, 1993) will find out that she flew solo from Chicago to New York in 1916.

- Information books are available at all reading levels, from simple picture books to books for our oldest, ablest students. Either as a supplement or as an alternative to the textbook, information books will provide every student in your room with material that he or she can read. For example, among the many juvenile biographies on Dr. Martin Luther King, Jr., are simple picture books like David Adler's *A Picture Book of Martin Luther King, Jr.* (1989) and *Martin Luther King Day* by Linda Lowery (1987). Readers with more advanced abilities could read challenging biographies by Lillie Patterson— *Martin Luther King, Jr. and the Freedom Movement* (1989)—and by Diane Patrick—*Martin Luther King, Jr.* (1990).

Selection of Information Books. The local public library should have a good collection of information books for young readers. Most children's libraries allow teachers to check out 10 to 20 books at a time. The libraries at our elementary schools will have some information books, although the quality of a collection will depend on several factors (e.g., resources, expertise of whoever selects books). The real problem, of course, is finding books on the topics we plan to cover. In the ideal situation, a school district has a committee of teachers, administrators, and librarians who periodically review information books and consider which ones support the social studies curriculum. The district social studies curriculum guide is then updated so that teachers have a current list of books that fit their units of study. Fortunately, the task of identifying the best information books is easy. Many sources make suggestions:

- Each year, a joint committee of the National Council for the Social Studies (NCSS) and the Children's Book Council selects a list of books; the list is titled "Notable Children's Books in the Field of Social Studies." Books are selected in several categories: biography; contemporary issues; geography, people, places; social interactions and relationships; and United States history, culture, and life. The annotated list of notable books is published annually in the journal *Social Education* (usually in the April/May issue). Each book is assigned a reading level: *P* for primary grades (K–3), *I* for intermediate (4–6), and *A* for advanced (approximately 7–8). The NCSS also selects the Carter G. Woodson Book Awards annually. Awards go to outstanding books for young readers that treat topics related to ethnic minorities and race relations sensitively and accurately. Winning books are reviewed in the September issue of *Social Education.*

- Articles in professional journals discuss books, usually in the context of a specific topic or category of books. For example, Brown, Malepe, and Sullivan (1996) discuss children's books about Africa; Spagnoli (1995) critiques Asian trickster tales; Hicks (1996) shows how children's books can help develop civic competence in primary-grade children; and Hofbauer and Prenn (1996) review children's books on homelessness. Reviews of books are an excellent resource and are regularly published in the following journals: *Booklist, Children's Literature Association Quarterly, Hornbook, Interracial Books for Children Bulletin, Language Arts, School Library Journal, Social Studies and the Young Learner, The Reading Teacher, Top of the News,* and *Wilson Library Bulletin.* Although some reviews focus only on fiction, many excellent information books are discussed each year.

- Almost all the large, college-level textbooks on children's literature have good discussions of information books. Among the best are *Children's Literature in the Elementary School* (Huck, Hepler, Hickman, & Kiefer, 1997) and *Through the Eyes of a Child: An Introduction to Children's Literature* (D. E. Norton, 1999). A book written specifically for elementary teachers is *Transcultural Children's Literature* (Pratt & Beaty, 1999).

- School and local libraries may have indexes and booklists. Some of the most useful are *American History for Children and Young Adults: An Annotated Bibliographic Index* (Van Meter, 1990), *Index to Collective Biographies for Young Readers* (Breen, 1988), and *World History for Children and Young Adults* (Van Meter, 1991).

- DeAn Krey (1998) identifies excellent children's books published between 1990 and 1997 that can be used for teaching each of the 10 themes in the national social studies standards (NCSS, 1994).

Quality. Recommendations from the sources listed above will give us some assurance of quality. This is an important issue because not all information books are worthy of inclusion in our classrooms. Fortunately, the level of quality has improved in the last 20 years. We can use two general criteria in evaluating information books.

The first general criterion is that *the content presented in the book should be accurate.* Many authors of information books now include a list of sources. For example, Diane Stanley's (1994) picture book biography of Cleopatra includes a "Note on Ancient Sources." Readers learn that there are no existing portraits or statues of Cleopatra and that illustrator Peter Vennema therefore based his pictures on Cleopatra's image on Egyptian coins. Stanley also notes that the main source of information on Cleopatra, the Greek historian Plutarch, wrote 100 years after her death and was influenced by Augustus Caesar's propaganda. Stanley's other picture book biographies are excellent, each easy to read and the product of thorough background work; they include *The Last Princess: The Story of Princess Ka'iulani of Hawai'i* (Stanley, 1991), *Shaka: King of the Zulus* (Stanley & Vennema, 1988), *Peter the Great* (Stanley, 1986), *Bard of Avon* (Stanley & Vennema, 1992), and *Good Queen Bess: The Story of Elizabeth I of England* (Stanley & Vennema, 1990).

Accuracy, especially in biography, has been a problem in children's information books (A. W. Moore, 1985; Wilton, 1993; Zarnowski, 1990). Critics have cited two areas of concern. The first area of concern is that authors frequently painted heroic, mythic images of some of their subjects, ignoring or minimizing their faults and failures (see Katt, 1992, for a criticism of biographies on Lincoln; Bigelow, 1992, on Columbus; M. E. James, 1985, on Washington). Times certainly have changed, however, and recent biographies for upper elementary readers reveal things that had been taboo. Freedman's (1993) biography of Eleanor Roosevelt has a full discussion of FDR's adulterous affair with Lucy Mercer (*Eleanor Roosevelt: A Life of Discovery*). *Thomas Jefferson: The Revolutionary Aristocrat*, by Milton Meltzer (1991), acknowledges Jefferson's romance with a married woman while he was in France. Meltzer also discusses Jefferson's relationship to one of his slaves, Sally Hemings. (It will be interesting to see how future juvenile biographers treat this issue now that DNA evidence has proved a link between Jefferson's and Hemings's descendants.)

The second area of concern is that people of color often were presented in a biased or racist manner. To provide one example, look at two picture book biographies of Pocahontas. A more recent one, written by William Accrosi (1992), is quite good (*My Name Is Pocahontas*). The book has a realistic portrayal of Pocahontas's tribal life, and no "Eurocentric" bias is evident. Compare it with an older biography written and illustrated by two of the best-known authors/illustrators of children's books, Ingri and Edgar Parin d'Aulaire (*Pocahontas,* published in 1946). In this book, Powhatan, Pocahontas's father, is described as a "stern old Indian chief" who "was ugly and cruel." Englishman John Smith, however, "was the handsomest man Pocahontas had ever seen" and was "hardy" and "shrewd." This type of biased, historically unsubstantiated presentation was common in books published during that period.

The second general criterion to use in evaluating information books is that *the writing and illustration should be very good*. As with fiction, a wide range of artistic quality can be found among information books. Of particular merit are the biographies written by Jean Fritz, Diane Stanley, and Russell Freedman. Fritz has shown that biography can be accurate, easy to read, and funny. Freedman won the prestigious Newbery Medal for *Lincoln: A Photobiography* (1987), and his books *Eleanor Roosevelt: A Life of Discovery* (1993) and *The Wright Brothers: How They Invented the Airplane* (1991) were Newbery Honor Books. (The Newbery Medal is awarded annually by the American Library Association to the most distinguished contribution to American literature published for children; the Honor Books are meritorious "runners-up" for the medal.) As I noted earlier, Stanley has brought a new level of quality to the picture book biography. The information books written and illustrated by David Macauley also deserve mention. His detailed drawings and descriptions make *Castle* (1977), *Cathedral* (1973), and *Ship* (1993) unique and highly informative books. Milton Meltzer has elevated the quality of historical writing for children, both through information books and biography. He has also written about the need for social responsibility among authors of children's history (Meltzer, 1994).

How to Use Information Books. Information books can be used as part of the social studies program in many ways. An information book can be read in four ways:

1. *Read independently.* We should introduce our students to information books through classroom displays, lists of books in the local public library, and book talks. A *book talk* is a short presentation that tries to "sell" students on a book. We can read aloud a portion of the book and show a few of the illustrations. Our overall goal is for students to select an information book to read independently. It is probably best to make this a matter of free choice because some students will want to read several books about a topic, whereas others will want to read other things. As part of language arts, many of us budget 10 to 25 minutes each day for students to read silently. This time is called *sustained silent reading (SSR)* or *drop everything and read (DEAR)*. Everybody, including the teacher, reads whatever she or he wants: books, magazines, newspapers, or any other printed material. In addition to SSR, on some days our plan for social studies should allow students to read books independently while their classmates work on projects.

Students will amass an amazing amount of content knowledge through independent reading. Think of the parallel situation among adults. All of us know people who have been "reading up" on a topic. Most adults realize how much a person can learn from reading fiction and biography; the potential of information books is as great for our students.

2. *Read to answer an inquiry.* Information books are an essential resource for students who are "hunting down" the answer to an inquiry. They typically provide more depth than an encyclopedia. Also, when the answer to an inquiry is a matter of interpretation, different books may well provide different answers. Reading to answer an inquiry is very different from the more casual, "kick-your-feet-up" reading done during SSR. For one thing, the reader will skip portions of the book because the only parts that matter are those that answer the inquiry. Also, information will have to be recorded, so parts of the text will be read two or three times. As students read, they take notes or write things down on a data retrieval chart.

3. *Read to complete a project.* This is similar to reading to complete an inquiry. As students work in groups to build, draw, paint, or perform, they will need details that information books can provide. Again, students may not read the entire book because they will have a narrow focus. For example, a group of students working on a mural may only be concerned with a book's illustrations. A student writing a biography may only need to fill in a gap left by other sources.

4. *Read as part of a directed lesson*. It is possible to use an information book in the same way as a textbook if enough copies are available. As part of a teacher-directed lesson, information books for young readers can be read aloud to the class. The purpose of such a lesson would be to teach specific content contained in the information book. The teaching sequence would be similar to the one presented previously for use with a textbook (link, context, background knowledge, vocabulary, purpose, read the material, focus on essential information, and springboard to other activities).

Children's Literature: Fiction

Many authorities recommend including juvenile fiction when teaching social studies in the elementary school (Cullinan, 1993; Field, 1998; Laughlin & Kardaleff, 1991; T. M. McGowan, 1996; Zarnowski & Gallagher, 1993). Journal articles cover a range of topics, including the general use of picture books (Harms & Lettow, 1994), fiction and geography (Louie, 1993; Rogers & Bromley, 1995), fiction and anthropology (Barnes, 1991), fiction about slavery and the Civil War (Perez-Stable, 1996), historical fiction (Lamme, 1994; J. A. Smith, Monson, & Dobson, 1992; Zarrillo, 1989), books to teach concepts (M. James & Zarrillo, 1989; Kim & Garcia, 1996), and books that help children achieve the national standards in social studies (Wunder, 1995). The use of fiction in social studies is quite popular; many of the most recent social studies textbooks include excerpts from fiction (Alleman & Brophy, 1994b).

Several types of fiction can enhance social studies units. It is sometimes difficult to draw the line between fiction and nonfiction. Many biographies, for example, are "fictionalized," as historical figures speak to each other. And some historical fiction includes real people interacting with fictional characters. Three types of fiction can be used in social studies instruction:

1. *Historical novels*. Many social studies units can be enhanced with *historical novels*. Some of the finest children's books fall into this genre, such as Scott O'Dell's *Island of the Blue Dolphins* (1960), Laura Ingalls Wilder's "Little House" books (e.g., *Little House on the Prairie*, 1935), Esther Forbes's *Johnny Tremain* (1943), Patricia MacLachlan's *Sarah, Plain and Tall* (1985), Elizabeth George Speare's *The Witch of Blackbird Pond* (1958), and Karen Cushman's *The Midwife's Apprentice* (1995).

2. *Folktales*. Folktales can be used when a unit looks at a specific cultural group. A *folktale* is a story that has been passed down through generations, typically in oral form. Today, culturally authentic, beautifully illustrated, and well-written versions of tales from cultural groups all over the world are available. For example, one type of folktale is a "pourquoi story," a story that explains a natural or social phenomenon. Pourquoi stories are found in each of the following cultural groups: the Cree (of Canada), the Efik-Ibibo (of Nigeria), the Comanche, the Ojibway (of

Canada), the Bini (of Nigeria), the Blackfoot, the Paiute, the Aztec, the Massai (of East Africa), the Ayoreo (of Bolivia), the Tsimshian (of Canada), and many others (Zarrillo, 1994).

One caution is in order when using folktales in social studies. Almost all picture book folktales portray people in preindustrial settings. In folktales, Native Americans and people from Hispanic America, Africa, and Asia all wear traditional costumes and live in villages. It is important to use folktales in combination with information books that show the same group of people as they live today. One author who has written information books with contemporary settings that complement folktales is Diane Hoyt-Goldsmith. For example, in *Arctic Hunter* (1992), Hoyt-Goldsmith describes Reggie, an Inupait boy living in Kotzebue, Alaska. Although much of Reggie's life is that of a traditional Inupait, we also see Reggie riding in a four-wheel-drive truck, living in a modern house with a television and video games, and eating hamburgers and pizza. The book is illustrated with photographs that show the combination of old and new. *Arctic Hunter* is a good book to use with Eskimo folktales such as *Enchanted Caribou* (Cleaver, 1985), *The White Archer* (Houston, 1967), and *Tikta Litak: An Eskimo Legend* (Houston, 1965).

3. *Contemporary realistic fiction.* This is a broad genre of literature incorporating stories that take place during the present or recent past. For many topics in social studies, contemporary stories can be used. For example, Eve Bunting's *A Day's Work* (1994) is a fictional account of a Hispanic day laborer and his grandson. This book not only tells a good story but also will help children better understand the status of immigrants in the United States. *Too Many Tamales,* by Gary Soto (1993), is a charming Christmas story with Hispanic characters. Both books could be used to illustrate the importance of intergenerational relationships among Hispanic cultural groups (see also Cordier & Perez-Stable, 1996; Main, Wilhelm, & Cox, 1996).

Why Use Fiction? Fiction can help children acquire essential social studies content because a story can provide them with a sense of empathy. Books that combine thorough research with vivid writing will make children feel transported to another place. Consider Lois Lowry's *Number the Stars* (1989). Readers will share the terror of Ellen Rosen, a Danish Jew, and her best friend, Annemarie Johansen, when the girls are awakened in the night by Nazi soldiers. A well-written piece of contemporary fiction can help children connect with other children. For example, while reading *Walk Two Moons* (Creech, 1994), sixth and seventh graders will feel the same emotions as the book's protagonist, Salamanca Tree Hiddle, who searches for her lost mother.

Fiction can help students acquire knowledge about many topics. This assumes, of course, that a work of fiction is accurate—free of bias, stereotypes, and outright errors. Whereas most recent books are accurate, older picture books and novels sometimes present distorted images. For example, Arlene Mosel's *Tikki Tikki Tembo* (1968) is a favorite book of many teachers and students. In the story, a

Chinese boy with the name of Rikki-tikki-tembo-no-sa-rembo-charibari-ruchi-pip-pembo falls into a well. It takes so long for his brother to pronounce this name that Tikki-tikki-tembo nearly drowns. Mosel concludes her story by claiming that this is why, to this day, "all Chinese have short names." It simply is not true that all Chinese have "short" names. Even worse, the cultural rules that determine how names are given in China have nothing to do with parental fear of children falling into wells.

Many picture book versions of folktales, in contrast, are culturally authentic. Author-illustrator Paul Goble set a standard more authors should emulate; he cites the sources of his Native American folktales. Among these are *Her Seven Brothers* (1988), *The Girl Who Loved Wild Horses* (1978), *Buffalo Woman* (1984), and *Lone Bull's Horse Raid* (Goble & Goble, 1973). His stories are based on oral testimony gathered by anthropologists during the last part of the 19th century and the first decade of the 20th. Even though authors of historical fiction are not under the same obligation as authors of information books to provide a bibliography, many list the sources of their stories or provide informative essays on the historical context of the books (e.g., Cushman provides a fine note on medieval midwifery at the end of *The Midwife's Apprentice,* 1995). Nonetheless, historical fiction can present biased images of some groups of people. In some cases, this is inexcusable. In others, the bias is part of a perspective held by many people during the time when the story takes place. Use of a book with a biased perspective can help children understand the historical roots and causes of prejudice. For example, Laura Ingalls Wilder, in *Little House on the Prairie* (1935), characterizes Native Americans as cruel, dirty, and ignorant. While reading this book, we should help our students understand the racism most European American settlers felt toward the Native population.

How to Use Fiction. The same categories of activities presented in the previous section on information books can be used with fiction. The books can be read (a) independently, (b) to answer an inquiry, (c) to complete a project, and (d) as part of a directed lesson. Unlike information books, however, fiction is not written to transmit facts and ideas. The goal of the writer of fiction is to tell a story and, in many cases, to shed light on the human condition. Therefore, the best way to use fiction is as an "adjunct" to a unit to encourage students to read the stories independently. When we use fiction as part of a directed lesson, a major caution is in order. Before they move to the social studies content in the book (or chapter of a book), students should first be allowed to respond to the book as a story. We can do this by asking students open-ended questions that encourage them to articulate their personal feelings, interpretations, and opinions about the story. After all, *Island of the Blue Dolphins* was not written to be a fourth-grade social studies text. It is a work of art that *also* has the potential to teach us about Native Americans. Following is a lesson plan that encourages children to appreciate a good book as literature and then learn social studies content from the story.

Grade 3: *Grandfather's Journey*

Overview: A third-grade class has been studying their community, and they are working on a unit called "Our City Today." Their city has many residents who are immigrants to the United States. Allen Say's Caldecott-winning picture book, *Grandfather's Journey* (1993), will help the children understand that many immigrants to their city are bicultural and have strong emotional attachments to both the United States and their homelands. This lesson is for a third-grade class of 25 students.

Resources and Materials: (a) hardcover copy of *Grandfather's Journey,* (b) chart with response options (see below under "Teaching Sequence"), (c) wall map of the world, (d) various information books, encyclopedias, and atlases.

Content Objectives: Children will learn that many immigrants retain close feelings for their native lands. One group will identify geographic similarities and differences between Japan and the United States.

Process Objectives: Children will *write* a response to the story and *identify* reasons why Allen Say's grandfather felt attached to both Japan and the United States, and a small group will *compare and contrast* the physical geography of Japan and the United States.

Values Objective: This lesson will help children become sympathetic, rather than hostile, to the biculturalism of many Americans.

Teaching Sequence
1. Prepare the chart with the response options and gather information books, encyclopedias, and atlases.
2. Identify for the children Japan and the United States on a wall map of the world. Then read aloud *Grandfather's Journey.*
3. Ask whether any of the children have anything they would like to say about the book. Then call attention to the three journal-writing options you wrote beforehand on chart paper:

Select one of the following:
   a. Write anything you want about <u>Grandfather's Journey</u>.
   b. Grandfather was <u>astonished</u> by the ocean, the enormous rocks, the endless fields, and the towering mountains. Write about something you have seen that is <u>astonishing.</u>
   c. Why do you think Allen Say's Grandfather loved both the United States and Japan?
4. Later that day or the next, bring the class together and reread the story. At the end of the story, ask question (c) to the class. Discuss possible reasons why Grandfather felt attached to both places. Help children see that Grandfather

appreciated the great natural beauty, the different kinds of people, and the wide range of sites and sounds in the United States. At the same time, he could not forget his old friends and the beauty of the places he knew as a boy in Japan.

5. You might also want to go back through the story and point out to the class how Grandfather ages and changes (see illustrations on pp. 4, 5, 16, 18, 25, and 29 of *Grandfather's Journey*).

6. Ask for volunteers for a special project on the geographic similarities and differences between Japan and the United States. This group will use the reference sources to compare the two nations on (a) climate, (b) topography, (c) rivers, (d) population density, (e) cultural groups, (f) industry, and (g) agriculture. The group will decide to report to their classmates with either a bulletin board display or an oral presentation.

Evaluation: To determine whether children have achieved the lesson's content and values objectives, (a) read what they wrote in their journals, (b) listen carefully to what they said during the discussion, and (c) assess the bulletin board display or oral presentation of the children participating in the project.

Effective Teaching in Today's Diverse Classroom: This lesson provides an example of what some educators call *an additive cultural approach* to teaching. This approach calls for a curriculum that takes advantage of the cultural identities of children by using aspects of culture as the focus for lessons. Like Allen Say's grandfather, millions of our children are bicultural. Rather than ask a child to abandon his or her native culture, it makes more sense to encourage the child to "add" the "core" American culture to the one he or she has. For example, if you have Korean American children in your classroom, you should plan a unit that will teach all children about the history and culture of Korea. Such a unit not only would allow your Korean American children to succeed as they read and write about familiar topics but also would provide important information to all your children and help them better understand each other.

Criticism of the Use of Fiction in Elementary Social Studies. Alleman and Brophy (1994b) criticize how fiction is used in elementary social studies textbooks. Almost all contemporary social studies textbooks include either complete folktales, stories, and poems, or they feature excerpts from longer fictional works. Alleman and Brophy's suggestions apply to any use of fiction, whether the story appears as an excerpt in a textbook or in books from public or school libraries:

- The book (folktale, novel, poem) should match the content objectives of the unit. Ideally, a committee of teachers and administrators should review children's books and compile a list of them that matches the content of each instructional unit taught in their district. Otherwise, it is essential that each teacher preview the book to make sure it fits what he or she is teaching.

- The book should be of sufficient value as a basis for social studies teaching and learning to justify the time allocated for it. An obvious point, but one that cannot be repeated too often: Not just any book will do; it should be of the highest quality.
- If an excerpt from a story is used, the excerpt should be long enough so that students will get the point being made.
- As noted earlier in the chapter, the book should not trivialize the content presented, the information should be accurate and authentic, and the book should not lead to misconceptions or stereotyping.

Writing in the Social Studies Program

A good elementary school social studies program will require students to write in a variety of formats, many unique to social studies (Beyer & Gilstrap, 1982; Gilstrap, 1991; Quigley & Bahmueller, 1991). A study of writing in elementary social studies conducted in the early 1980s revealed that "research" reports and book reports were the dominant formats (Gilstrap, 1982). As Gallavan (1997) notes, "teachers frequently assign conventional writing activities that stifle their students' newly acquired knowledge and awareness" (p. 14). This is unfortunate because other forms of writing are relatively easy to use and are more challenging than research and book reports. As we enter the 21st century, it should go without saying that all the forms of writing described in this section should be completed by older elementary students on computers. Our focus here is on (a) forms of writing well suited to the social studies and (b) writing as a part of civic education.

Forms of Writing Well-Suited to the Social Studies. As students gather information, they will do a great deal of nonprose writing, primarily in the form of notes written on charts or graphs. Most elementary students need a great deal of help in learning how to take notes. I suggest providing students with *data retrieval charts* to record their data. Data retrieval charts provide an organizational framework for taking notes (see example in Figure 9.2).

Only after students have completed several retrieval charts should they be asked to take notes without any assistance. Taking notes is difficult because it differs from the types of narrative writing students complete during language arts (e.g., journal entries, personal narratives, stories). Students enjoy projects in which they write from the perspective of a person living in the past (Selwyn, 1995). This is a written form of *role play,* wherein students assume another identity. For example, a fifth-grade class will pretend they are soldiers in the Revolutionary War. Their Valley Forge diaries are to reveal their experiences in the summer of 1777. A good way to begin this assignment is to make a chart of the contextual details students will need when they start writing. They should have a good sense of the setting for their journal entries, including the weather, the clothing people wore, and the design of buildings

Figure 9.2 Example of a Data Retrieval Chart

Native Californians: Comparison of Four Tribes

Tribe	Region: Where did they live?	Dwellings: What type of homes did they build?	Food: What did they eat?	Other: In what other ways were they different from other tribes?
Yurok				
Yokuts				
Mohave				
Chumash				

and other human-made objects. They should read and listen to the words and phrases people in that era used so that their written entries "sound" authentic. For another project, students could write the front page of a newspaper the day *after* an important historical event (e.g., July 5, 1776). This type of written project requires students to gather data and incorporate it into the news stories they are writing. Many students enjoy changing their "voice" as they become persons who lived long ago.

Selwyn (1995) suggests two more challenging formats for writing from the perspective of a person who lived in the past. In the first, members of the class assume complementary roles and write to each other (also described by M. D. Evans, 1995). For example, during a unit on the Civil War, one student could pretend to be an abolitionist living in Massachusetts, and a classmate could assume the role of a slave owner living in Georgia. Both could write journal entries responding to Lincoln's election in 1860. If students understand the anachronism, it would be fun for them to pretend to be on different sides of a historical issue and send E-mail to each other. Tunnell and Ammon (1996) show how children's literature can provide multiple perspectives on a historical event and help students avoid inaccurate generalizations.

What are the alternatives to the standard "research" report (Dimmit & Van Cleaf, 1992; Koeller, 1992)? All too often, the assignment to do a report becomes an exercise in pseudowriting as students plagiarize material from the Internet and encyclopedias. Rather than assign a topic that appears as an entry in an encyclopedia (e.g., "The Navajo," "Harriet Tubman," "Russia"), it is better to pose inquiry questions that require students to find information in more than one place. Topics that require students to gather data through surveys or interviews will eliminate the possibility of copying from encyclopedias. Finally, not all reports should be written. After gathering information on a topic or question, students can prepare multimedia presentations with software programs like Hyperstudio, oral presentations, or bulletin board displays.

Writing as a Part of Civic Education. *Civitas,* the curriculum framework for citizenship education developed by the Council for the Advancement for Citizenship and the Center for Civic Education, describes several types of "participatory writing" that should be a part of elementary social studies (Quigley & Bahmueller, 1991):

Writing to Gather Social Science Data. Students can write surveys to be administered to their classmates, families, friends, and neighbors. They can also write to agencies for information (e.g., League of Women Voters, city council, foreign consulates, state and federal agencies). A survey project is an excellent experience for students because they do two types of writing: composing questions on the survey and then writing a summary of their findings.

E-Mailing Public Officials. E-mail has made it much easier for students to send written messages to public officials. They can write to congratulate candidates who win elections, to express support for a policy decision, and to complain. This type of writing will test the ability of students to adjust their writing to fit their target audience. An E-mail or letter to a member of the U.S. Congress, for example, should not sound the same as a message written to a classmate.

Writing Agendas and Minutes. Students should take part in classroom and school meetings to understand democracy and civil discourse. These meetings should be forums for students to express perspectives and reach decisions. Meetings need agendas and minutes. Writing minutes, especially, is a difficult task. Students will have to master taking notes, pausing to clarify when they are unsure of what was said, and condensing the notes for publication.

Writing for Political Campaigns. Political campaigns require a great deal of written material—speeches, copy for radio and television ads, posters, position papers, brochures. Older students can write campaign materials when they run for classroom and school office. Students can also write political texts for state and federal campaigns.

Writing Laws and Rules. The text of a law or rule requires a special type of writing; the author must be succinct and convey a precise meaning. Students can write rules for the playground, classroom, and school. Every word of a classroom rule will be important and subject to interpretation.

Speaking and Listening in the Social Studies Program

Almost every activity described in this book requires students to speak, either to each other or to their teacher. Most talk should be informal and conversational as students work in small-group formats. More formal speaking assignments are appropriate for students in the upper elementary grades. Students should work together to report the results of an inquiry or a project. One of best formats is several students sharing the responsibility for an oral presentation. Several things can be done to ensure that this is a worthwhile experience both for the students delivering the report and for their classmates who are listening. First, each student who is to speak should practice her or his part several times. Next, no student should speak for more than a few minutes. Finally, the oral report should be supported by visual aids such as charts, graphs, maps, and diagrams.

   As noted in chapter 11, an essential part of citizenship education is helping students master the process of "civil discourse." Students should talk about controversial issues and explore multiple perspectives on events in the past. Rossi's (1996a) excellent article provides guidance for those of us who want to help our students learn how to express their opinions and, at the same time, listen to others in an appropriate fashion. Rossi notes that this is a challenge in the age of radio and television talk shows on which the goal is to incite, not educate, and that "these shows demonstrate merely discussing controversial issues is not sufficient to promote civic competence and democratic attitudes" (p. 18). Rossi's five conditions for creating a civil classroom climate can serve as a framework for a description of how to have productive and polite discussions in an elementary classroom:

1. *A cooperative versus a competitive context.* Repeated cooperative learning experiences will help students learn the value of working together toward a common goal, and this value should carry over into their discussions. We should model the attitude that when disagreements arise, the goal is not to "win," but rather to learn. We should praise students when they ask clarifying questions and make efforts to understand why their classmates have reached different conclusions. Students should learn that monopolizing the discussion is inappropriate. Personal attacks, of course, should never be tolerated in any civil discussion.

2. *Relevant information.* Discussions should be based on accurate and pertinent information. The leader of a discussion (teacher or student) should help students question in a respectful manner the accuracy of statements made by classmates. Rather than stating, "You're wrong," students should say something like, "I don't think it is accurate to say that. . . ." We should record these disputes and help students find information that provides accuracy. It is important that students support their views with facts and explain why they believe the way they do.

3. *Perspective taking.* Role play can help students understand and empathize with someone else's perspective. On some issues, both historical and contemporary, students should assume the role of another person and express that person's views. This activity will help increase the amount of information presented in a discussion and will ensure that a range of opinions is presented.

4. *Disagreeing while confirming.* In discussions in which people disagree, it is essential that "somehow, participants need to be able to disagree with each others' ideas while confirming each others' personal competence" (Rossi, 1996a, p. 20). We must model this behavior by listening attentively and acknowledging the value of each student's comments. This needs to become a part of every student's listening behavior. Our youngest students should understand that interrupting others is inappropriate because they learn less when they listen less. As students grow older, they should learn to say things like, "You have done a lot of work and you know your stuff, but I don't agree with what you said," or, "What you have said is making me think," or, "After listening to you, I see that we agree on many things."

5. *Inclusion.* Many students are uncomfortable talking in a group discussion. We must create situations in which many students have a chance to express

themselves. The cooperative learning structures discussed in chapter 5 maximize participation, but they involve very small groups (Think-Pair-Share, Three-Step Interview). Many students who would otherwise remain silent will speak if they have a chance to prepare and practice their comments. We could provide some students with the discussion topic in advance, help them structure their response, allow them a chance to practice, and provide feedback *before* the day of the discussion.

Students will have opportunities to talk during lessons we present. In chapter 2, I presented some of the cultural differences in how our diverse students talk and listen (Au, 1993; Shade & New, 1993; Smitherman, 1977). One lesson format that has proved effective with English language learners is the *instructional conversation,* a combination of direct teaching and discussion (Goldenberg, 1991; 1992/1993). In an instructional conversation, the teacher selects a focus, or topic, for the lesson. As a first step, the teacher provides students with the background information or helps them activate what they know about the topic. Then, during the discussion, the teacher promotes more complex language and expression by asking students questions like, "Tell me more about _____," or, "What do you mean by _____?" Finally, the teacher asks students to explain their answers by providing supporting detail. After this, the discussion continues according to a set of guidelines. The teacher asks few "known-answer" questions, selecting instead prompts that have more than one correct response. The lesson has a focus and clear learning objectives, and the teacher is responsive to what students say. The goal is to have "connected discourse" as students and teacher build on what speakers say. As the conversation progresses, the teacher says less and less and the environment remains friendly and nonthreatening. Eventually, during the instructional conversation, the teacher no longer determines who speaks because the students will know how to converse in an open and productive manner.

The Performing Arts and the Visual Arts

The *performing arts* are music, dance, and drama. The *visual arts* incorporate a variety of media (e.g., crayon, clay, paint, film, video, computer-based multimedia). The role of the arts in social studies is multifaceted (Eisner, 1991; Selwyn, 1995). First, the arts provide alternatives for the presentation of social studies information. Films, paintings, live dramas, and other art forms are particularly important resources for English language learners. Howard Gardner's (1983, 1991) ideas on multiple intelligences provide a strong rationale for using the arts to help students learn about other people because some students find it difficult to learn from written

To meet the needs of our diverse students, units of instruction should encourage children to express what they know through the language arts, the performing arts, and the visual arts. In this classroom, children have learned to use many visual media.

material. The arts are an alternative. As students view the visual arts and view and listen to the performing arts, they use their senses to learn. These can be powerful experiences because "what all of the arts have in common is their capacity to generate emotion, to stimulate and to express the 'feel' for a situation, individual, or object" (Eisner, 1991, p. 554).

Second, as Selwyn (1995) notes, "the study of the arts is part of the study of history. Music, visual arts, dance, theater, crafts, writing, and other arts are both artifacts of and a means by which to study a culture" (p. 9). As many instructional units as possible should present information through the arts. Many current social studies textbooks include illustrations of paintings, statues, ceramics, and other art forms. We can augment these resources by selecting books that display the art of a particular culture. When students view another culture's art, they will see intercultural differences and similarities. Although the specific forms of art will vary from culture to culture, students will see that certain universal themes are present. For example, forms of dance are wonderfully different among cultural groups, yet all dance can be classified as essentially social, ritual, or performance.

Third, the arts should also be used to allow students to express what they have learned. Too often, social studies tasks are limited to reading, writing, and speaking. Our students should have opportunities to display their knowledge through the performing and visual arts. In the next two sections, we look at some specific art forms that can be used with elementary students.

The Performing Arts

In chapter 12, I describe a lesson in which kindergartners assumed the roles of a 19th-century farm family and pantomimed chores after listening to their teacher read *Ox-Cart Man* (Hall, 1979). This informal form of *role play* can be a powerful teaching tool, and it is easy to implement (Shaftel & Shaftel, 1967; Mahood, 1980). We merely ask students to pretend they are someone or something, and then the make-believe begins. A more formal form of role play is the mock trial described in chapter 11. In that activity, students assumed the roles of judge, attorneys, witnesses, and the jury. Each student performed in his or her new identity without a script. This formal role play required students to learn a great deal about their new identities, to "think on their feet," and to improvise.

Readers' theater is simple, effective, and fun (Laughlin, Black, & Loberg, 1991; Sloyer, 1982; T. A. Young & Vardell, 1993). The text of picture books, excerpts from

Participation in dramatic presentations can help children develop a strong sense of empathy with people from other times and places.

fiction, poetry, and parts of information books all can be presented. In readers' theater, students read their lines during the performance. In *choral reading,* parts of the text are read simultaneously by two or more students. With a *nonedited* form of readers' theater, every word of the text is read. Narrators read the words outside quotation marks, and student actors read the dialogue inside quotation marks. In other presentations, the text of the book is modified for the performance. Three things help make readers' theater experiences positive. First, no student should be asked to read aloud a text that is too difficult. Second, it must be very clear to each reader when she or he is supposed to read. While performing, many students become nervous and simple things become difficult. We could make copies of the portion of a book that is being read, provide each reader with a copy, and highlight each student's part with a colored marker. Third, even though readers' theater does not demand that students memorize their parts, students need to rehearse several times before they read in front of an audience.

Almost all children enjoy acting in *plays.* Here, of course, actors must memorize their parts. When compared with readers' theater, the production is more elaborate, with costumes, a set, and props. Plays are particularly valuable in social studies because they help students learn about people in different places and times. This assumes, of course, that the script, set, costumes, and props have a reasonable degree of historical and cultural accuracy. The first step is to write a script, which may be done by the teacher, the students, or teacher and students working together. The easiest way to produce a script is to adapt a picture book or an excerpt from a children's novel. The second step is to select the parts, and this should be done carefully. We should ensure that the same students are not always the leads, and we should guide students to roles they will be able to perform successfully. Plays, of course, require rehearsal. One form of play that has long been a part of social studies is the *historical pageant,* a multiscene play depicting the history of a place, person, idea, or event. For example, *California* could have the following scenes: (a) a vignette from a Yurok village (Native tribal life), (b) the death of Juan Cabrillo, (c) a California fiesta (during Mexican rule of California), (d) the discovery of gold, (e) the San Francisco earthquake of 1906, and (f) a conversation among migrant workers in the 1930s.

Selwyn (1995) suggests an interesting form of *tableau vivante* for social studies lessons—*human statues.* A group of students is given a scene to portray. The group then discusses how they should position themselves, how each person will kneel, sit, stand, or recline. All the group members come to the front of the class and strike their poses, each a human statue, frozen in position. Unlike true tableau, these statues can speak, and the student-statues can explain how they feel emotionally and physically. The class can ask questions, but this must happen quickly because the statues are human (and can only be still for a limited time).

Students can *dance* as a part of social studies. Some forms of pantomime blur the line between theater and dance as students convey meaning purely through body movements. Performing culturally authentic dances can be a worthwhile experience for students, but it is essential that the dances be treated with respect (such dance is typically referred to as *folk dance*). Students should see the dance performed with authenticity, either by members of the cultural group or by dancers who have studied the dance and understand its cultural context. Also, it is best to avoid sacred dances; these dances can become trivialized and their religious significance lost as the purpose of the dance, with children, shifts from ritual to social. Rather than have our students perform ritual dances, it would be better to have them observe the dance respectfully, either through a live performance or through film or video.

The Visual Arts

A group of student teachers I supervised one semester compiled the following list of media that elementary students can use to express themselves through the visual arts: crayon, paint, ink, torn paper, tissue, photography, motion picture film, videotape, clay, chalk, computer graphics, colored pencils, felt and cloth, charcoal, salt and flour, string, potatoes (to make prints), colored sand. After a day to think about it, we were able to double the list!

Many forms of *murals* can be made as part of social studies units. *Mural* comes from the Latin word for "wall" *(murus),* and all murals are large pictures on walls, typically with several images. Because we cannot paint or draw directly on school walls, our murals are usually bulletin board displays. Even though many murals are made on sheets of "butcher paper," I think it is more practical to draw or paint images on separate sheets of paper and then staple them to the bulletin board. Many murals will involve writing, too, as students write captions to accompany their visual images. One suggestion: Don't worry about scale; it will be fine to have drawings of the Sphinx and Tutankhamen be the same size.

A *diorama* is a three-dimensional display. The simplest ones are completed in shoe boxes, which limit the perspective of the viewer. Larger dioramas, though, are more rewarding and look better. I suggest using a piece of plywood as a base. Dioramas depict scenes from the world around us, both past and present, as they incorporate student-made figures from clay and other materials and manufactured items such as toy houses and people.

Collages are combinations of images. In its simplest form, students construct a collage with cut or torn paper. Pictures from magazines and other materials, like natural objects, textiles, and manufactured items, can be used. A collage should have a clearly stated theme or idea.

Finally, we should be careful as we use the visual arts to teach social studies. Some art projects done as part of social studies actually contribute little, if anything, to student learning of the content of an instructional unit. For example, fourth graders who paint a mural of an Iroquois village will learn very little if they merely follow a prescribed process with no attempt to place the subject of their mural in historical context. In fact, many social studies art projects become nothing more than exercises in mass production. (I have seen too many first graders dutifully manufacture paper replicas of the hats the Pilgrims supposedly wore.) When done as part of social studies, visual arts activities should either help students acquire information or allow them to express what they have learned. Visual arts projects can take many forms and may be combined with the language arts. Just such a project is described below.

Grade 5: A Picture History of *Lone Bull's Horse Raid*

GROUP PROJECT

A fifth-grade class was studying Native Americans prior to the coming of the Europeans. They would learn about five tribes. The class had many English language learners and others who found it difficult to read grade-level material. While the class was learning about the Sioux, the teacher asked for volunteers who wanted to complete a project that would "require a lot of artwork." This group of students read the Gobles' (1973) picture book *Lone Bull's Horse Raid.* The story is told from 14-year-old Lone Bull's perspective. Lone Bull is an Oglala Sioux who steals horses from the Crow. Following is a day-by-day plan for the project:

Day 1

After discussing the book, explain the idea of a "picture history." Describe how the Natives of the Great Plains used picture histories, painted on their tipis or on buffalo robes, to record significant events. You can find good illustrations of picture histories painted on buffalo robes on the Web site of the Glenbow Museum in Calgary, Canada *(http://www.glenbow.org/srobe.htm)*. You also might share illustrations of Grecian urns and Roman columns, cross-cultural examples of other forms of picture histories. Help the group make a list of the scenes from the book to illustrate (e.g., Lone Bull and his friend, Charging Bear, riding with Lone Bull's father; stalking the Crow camp; stealing the horses; fighting the Crow; giving away the stolen horses).

Day 2

Have the group decide who will illustrate each scene. Students may work together or individually. Decide on a form for the picture history. If you are ambitious, you could construct a model tipi 4- to 5-ft high. Edwin Tunis's (1979) old book *Indians* has a good set of directions on pages 90 to 94. If you decide to make a tipi, then the scenes should be painted on the outside of the tipi. A simple picture history could be painted on a strip of paper approximately 2 ft × 6 ft. Students should complete a sketch of their scenes.

Days 3 and 4

Bring several copies of Paul Goble's other books to class for group members to examine. They should try to use the same colors and style as Goble. If you can find books with photographs of decorated tipis, by all means bring them to class. Each scene should be blocked out so that each artist knows the space she or he has. If you are making a tipi, then the scenes from the book should be painted before the tipi is assembled.

Days 5 to 8

Once the art is done, have group members decide whether they want to tell or read the story to their classmates. The picture history, rather than the book's illustrations, should be used during the performance. Be sure the group has plenty of time to rehearse.

Effective Teaching in Today's Diverse Classroom: As I noted in chapter 4, it is important that we help our students develop accurate knowledge about Native Americans, rather than reinforce stereotypical images. This lesson supports the stereotype that all Indians lived in tipis, committed acts that European Americans considered criminal, and thrived on violence. Fortunately, this lesson was part of an in-depth study of Native Americans, with separate units of study on diverse tribes. Goble's books are historically and culturally accurate and are excellent teaching resources. The lesson is ideal for a diverse classroom because it allows students to express what they know through *both* the visual and the performing arts.

SUMMARY OF KEY POINTS

▶ Social studies textbooks can be used effectively in elementary classrooms. They should never, however, be the only instructional resource we use.

▶ We should use of a variety of instructional strategies to help students (a) activate their background knowledge before they read, (b) build their vocabularies, and (c) increase their comprehension.

▶ As part of social studies, information books should be read (a) independently, (b) to answer inquiries and complete projects, and (c) as part of teacher-directed lessons.

▶ Fiction can provide students with a strong sense of empathy with people living in other places and times.

▶ Social studies provides students with many opportunities to write, often in formats they seldom use in other areas of the curriculum.

▶ It is essential that students learn the process of civil discourse, to listen and talk in a polite, respectful manner.

▶ Performing arts activities include role play, readers' theater, plays, and pageants.

▶ Of all the forms of the visual arts, murals, dioramas, and collages have been popular choices for social studies projects.

FOR FURTHER READING

Language Arts

▶ An excellent resource for teachers is *Integrating Language Arts and Social Studies for Kindergarten and Primary Children* (Roberts, 1996). Carter (1995) describes how students can write a "grandma book" to discover the past. McBee (1996) describes how we can address controversial topics in the early grades and provides some worthy cautions for us. Magnuson (1996) describes an activity in which students debate what the ideal school would look like. Fry, Phillips, Lobaugh, and Madole (1996) show how Halliday's (1976) seven functions of language could be used as a framework for planning writing activities in social studies. For example, the writing of classroom rules fulfills Halliday's "regulatory" function. O'Day (1994) describes how informal writing can enhance social studies teaching and learning. B. H. Davis, Rooze, and Runnels (1992) describe a study examining the use of journal writing in fourth-grade social studies. Although journal writing did not lead to an increase in student achievement in social studies, it did improve the fourth graders' ability to communicate in writing.

▶ Avery and Graves (1997) propose a good framework for designing lessons with social studies textbooks. Like the model I propose in this chapter, they, too, emphasize the importance of a three-part plan with prereading, during reading, and postreading phases.

▶ Judith Lechner (1997) wrote an excellent article about accuracy in biographies for children, using biographies of Pocahontas as examples (unfortunately, examples of historical inaccuracy!).

The Performing Arts and the Visual Arts

Carole Cox's (1996) book is an excellent source for suggestions on how to implement the performing arts in an elementary classroom. Epstein's (1994) excellent article discusses how high school students could represent history through the arts; although the article is about high school teaching, it expresses many important ideas that we as elementary teachers should consider.

▶ Labbo and Field (1997) describe how picture postcards can be used in elementary social studies. At the end of their article, they describe how children can create postcards of important landmarks in their community.

Chapter 10

Units of Instruction: Putting It All Together to Create a Powerful Social Studies Program

red Sanders, Elena Rivera, Billy Davis, and Rebecca Wong were members of a school district curriculum committee. Fred, Billy, and Rebecca all taught third graders, and Elena was a school principal. Their task during the summer was to write five instructional units for the third-grade social studies curriculum. Earlier, a districtwide committee had decided that the social studies curriculum should be closely linked with the NCSS curriculum standards (NCSS, 1994). A common format for unit design had also been adopted districtwide: Each instructional unit would be organized around questions written in language that students could understand.

The third-grade social studies curriculum in this district covered two major topics: (a) the history of the community and (b) transportation. Fred, Elena, Billy, and Rebecca were working on a unit on boats. The unit would draw from performance expectations from the NCSS thematic strands of (1) Culture; (7) Production, Distribution, & Consumption; and (8) Science, Technology, & Society. They had decided on the unit's organizing questions:

What are the different types of boats, and why are they different?
Where in our state, country, and world would you find people using boats?
What types of jobs do people perform on boats, and how have those jobs changed over time?
How have boats changed over time?

Fred, Elena, Billy, and Rebecca were discussing what activities the unit should include for the first question, "What are the different types of boats, and why are they different?"

Elena: Marjorie Flack's picture book *Boats on the River* would be perfect for this question. It shows all sorts of different boats . . .
Rebecca: That book is 50 years old!
Elena: But it's a classic. It was a Caldecott Honor Book, and every year I read it, the children love it.
Billy: I know that book, and it would be good. The teacher could read it aloud to the class, the different types of boats could be listed on the board, and then the teacher and the children could go back through the book and talk about each type of boat.
Fred: Yeah, you know, yesterday we talked about how we should focus on the function and design of the different boats, how the design of boats depends on what they are used for. We could introduce that idea with the activity.
Rebecca: Sounds good. Elena, would you like to write the lesson plan for that activity? What other activities should we plan for this question?
Fred: We had a workshop last year on cooperative learning, and I tried using Jigsaw with my third graders. It worked! We agreed we would include information about warships—you know, battleships and submarines. If we had the right materials, we could have Jigsaw on that type of ship . . .

Fred, Elena, Billy, and Rebecca continued their discussion, and after 5 weeks of work, they wrote the five units for the third-grade social studies curriculum (yes, they did receive a nice paycheck for their summer curriculum writing!). The units they wrote were excellent and were included in the third-grade curriculum guide. All teachers in the district were expected to teach each unit, but each teacher was encouraged to customize it to fit the needs of her or his students.

In this chapter, I describe how instructional units in social studies can be designed. Later in the chapter, I present a third-grade unit on boats based on the sample unit developed by Fred, Elena, Billy, and Rebecca.

▲   ▲   ▲

In this chapter, you will read about:

▶ Five principles to consider when planning units of study
▶ A third-grade sample unit on boats
▶ Other formats for planning units, including webs and mini-units

Principles for Planning Instructional Units

An *instructional unit* is a set of related activities with a unifying element, something that serves as a focus for the unit. Although some units are brief and include only three or four lessons (I refer to these as "mini-units"), most social studies units are more ambitious and run for several days. The idea of the unit is an old one. In fact, some of the finest instructional units in social studies are almost 100 years old and were developed during the era of Progressive Education at places like the Laboratory School of the University of Chicago and the Lincoln School in New York City (Cremin, 1961; Mayhew & Edwards, 1936). A good place to start our discussion is with five principles for planning instructional units in the social studies:

1. Units should be integrated.
2. The scope of each unit should be clearly defined.
3. Activities in a unit should follow a logical sequence.
4. Units should feature a variety of instructional resources.
5. Units should include whole-group, small-group, and individual activities.

Units Should Be Integrated

Social studies units can be integrated through content or by process. *Content integration* occurs when a unit goes beyond history and geography to include concepts from other social sciences (political science, anthropology, economics, and sociology), the arts (literature, the visual arts, and the performing arts), science, mathematics, and physical education. *Process integration* is the result of planning activities that make a social studies unit a vehicle for teaching the language arts (speaking, reading, listening, and writing), the performing arts, the visual arts, and technology skills (see chapter 9 on the integrated curriculum).

The Scope of Each Unit Should Be Clearly Defined

All units should have a clearly defined scope. In the jargon of curriculum development, *scope* refers to the limits of the content covered in a lesson, unit, or academic year. Generally, most social studies units attempt to cover too much material. The NCSS Task Force on Standards for Teaching and Learning in the Social Studies (1993) noted that "the most effective teachers do not diffuse their efforts by covering too many topics superficially" (p. 216). For example, rather than planning the unit "Ancient Civilizations of the Americas," it would make more sense to plan the unit "The Aztec." During this unit, comparisons could be made with the Inca and Maya, but the focus would be the Aztec.

The unifying element, or topic, of the unit will define the unit's scope, and fortunately there is no shortage of topics that can serve as the unifying elements for social studies units. Following are some possibilities:

- *Historical Focus (When)*. With the current emphasis on history in the social studies curriculum, units that focus on a particular time and place are very popular. Examples are "Life in the Young Republic: The United States From 1790 to 1850," or "The Early Days of Our City," or "Ancient China."
- *Person or People (Who)*. It also possible to develop units that examine a cultural group—for example, "The Navajo: Yesterday and Today." Excellent units can be constructed around one person—for example, "Dr. Martin Luther King, Jr."
- *Location (Where)*. Sometimes called "area studies," location units have as a unifying element a place—for example, "Japan" or "Hawaii." Units that look at places should also be limited by time. For example, the unit on Japan could avoid superficial coverage by being redesigned to become "Modern Japan: 1945 to the Present."
- *Question or Problem*. Some of the most intriguing social studies units have questions as their unifying elements. Activities in a unit help students develop a complete answer to the unit's unifying question. Examples are "How Does a Person Become President of the United States?" or "Why Is Gold Valuable?" or "What Happened to the Roanoke Colony?"
- *Things*. Things, both human-made and natural, can be the focus of a social studies unit. The unit on boats in this chapter is an example of this type of unit. Other examples are "Rivers" or "Calendars." The idea here is to show how different people in different times and places developed or used the object.

- *Concept or Theme.* An example of a unit based on a concept is "Immigration: Coming to the United States." Broad concepts can be the unifying elements of units. I have seen units on "Change," "Conflict," and "Shelter" that were fascinating. One advantage of conceptual and thematic units is that they allow us to take a global perspective and incorporate content covering several times, places, and peoples.

The process of developing units varies from school district to school district. Most elementary teachers work in school districts that supply curriculum guides for social studies. A curriculum guide typically is written by a committee of teachers and administrators and includes a list of units to be taught at each grade level. The best guides have units that are fully developed, complete with clear learning objectives, lists of available resources, and practical lesson plans. With the recent interest in the quality of our public schools, more and more curriculum is being defined at the state level. Most state offices of education issue frameworks in each area of the curriculum. School district curriculum guides frequently echo the scope of the state framework. In fewer and fewer states is the state-approved curriculum framework purely advisory. Working with the guidelines of the curriculum approved for our school districts, we should customize the instructional units to fit the needs of our students. All our units should allow students to pursue related topics of personal interest.

Activities in a Unit Should Follow a Logical Sequence

Planning effective units of instruction in social studies requires us to think about the sequence of activities in each unit. Which lessons should be planned for the first few days of the unit? Which activities should serve as a culmination to the unit? As I explain later in the chapter, a unit should consist of activities that involve all students in the classroom (whole group), activities that are completed by only some students in the room and are cooperative efforts (small group), and activities that are completed individually (individual). As a general rule, the unit should begin with whole-group activities. As the unit progresses, more and more small-group and individual projects get started, and by the last third of the unit, few whole-group activities may take place as the concluding days of the unit are devoted to small-group and individual projects.

We should meet two goals at the start of a unit: (a) Determine what our students know about the topic we will be studying, and (b) find out whether our students would like to investigate anything in particular. Here are some techniques for accomplishing these goals:

- *The K–W–L Chart.* An example of a K-W-L chart (Ogle, 1986) appears later in this chapter, in the unit on boats. K-W-L charts can be used to assess

The best instructional units in social studies provide out-of-class learning experiences, like this field trip to the Statue of Liberty.

student knowledge of a topic and to discover special areas of student interest (see chap. 9 for a description of this instructional strategy).

- *Open-Ended Journal Prompts.* A simple way to find out what students know about a topic is to have them write a response to "Write what you know about _____." A simple way to learn what is of special interest to them is to say to them, "Write any questions you have about _____." The advantage of open-ended prompts is that they provide information from each student in the classroom. Many of us have our students write responses in journals, which are used throughout the unit.
- *Discussion.* An informal discussion on the first day of the unit can be used to assess student knowledge and interest. We can take notes, or we can record on chart paper what our students say.

It is usually best to start a unit with activities that establish time and place because students need to know the context of what they will be studying. Timelines and chronologies are good ways to establish time, and maps and globes of many kinds can be used to give students a sense of place (see chap. 12). Also, at the beginning of a unit, it is a good idea to use resources that provide an overview of what students will be studying. I suggest starting the unit with videos, films, and the chapter from the textbook. Constructivist learning theory states that it is best to move from the whole to the parts, and I think this is essential in social studies. These initial activities will help students acquire essential "core" understandings, content we expect all students to know.

For the middle of a unit, we should plan a mixture of whole-group, small-group, and individual activities. We should devote the social studies period on some days to small-group and individual work. Students should have begun to study topics of personal interest. Cooperative learning is important as small groups work on projects that involve writing, the visual arts, and the performing arts. The content that students acquire will be more detailed and will vary from student to student.

For the conclusion of a unit, it is a good idea to plan activities that introduce the next unit of study. I call these "segue" activities. A *segue activity* shows students the relationship between one unit and another. These relationships include the following:

- *Chronology.* Time is a frequent source for segue activities. For example, if we were studying the history of our state, then a unit on the Native Americans who inhabited our state would be followed by a unit on the first European settlers. The link between the two units is chronological, of course, in that one set of events follows the other.
- *Geography.* A fifth-grade teacher could teach separate units on the New England colonies, the Middle colonies, and the Southern colonies. The units cover the same period of time. The relationship of one to the others is geographical (in this case, moving from north to south).
- *Culture.* A unit on West African cultural groups (e.g., the Minde) could be followed by a unit on the enslavement of Africans in the Americas. The segue activities examine how some aspects of these cultures survived in the Americas, how others were changed, and how some cultural characteristics were lost.
- *Theme.* Frequently, in the early grades (K–2), the social studies curriculum is linked by theme. For example, first graders might learn about cooperation. A unit on helping each other at school could be followed with a unit on how members of a neighborhood can benefit from working together. Activities should be planned that show how the same spirit of cooperation is embodied by different peoples.

Many units end with culminating activities. Such activities can take many forms, but they usually involve the performing arts. Students act in plays, produce films, and present material they have written. Other culminating activities can be simulations. For example, "A Day With the Ingalls" could be the culminating activity for the unit "The Prairie Pioneers." Several children's books could serve as resources: Wilder's *Little House* books, of course; *The Laura Ingalls Wilder Songbook* (Garson, 1968); *Frontier Living* (Tunis, 1961); *My Prairie Year: Based on the Diary of Elinor Plaisted* (Harvey, 1986); and *Hunter's Stew and Hangtown Fry: What Pioneer America Ate and Why* (Perl, 1977). Students would sing, play, eat, study, and work in historically authentic ways. Part of the day could be devoted to a simulation of the one-room schoolhouse of the late 19th century. In any case, the culminating activity should be a project that students have worked on for some time.

Figure 10.1 presents a summary of the principles for the sequence of activities in a unit.

Units Should Feature a Variety of Instructional Resources

There are two good reasons for using a variety of instructional resources in each social studies unit we teach: (a) The units will be enriched and more appealing to students in our classrooms, and (b) we will have a better chance of meeting the needs of our highly diverse students. Although many students do quite well with units that rely on the social studies textbook, other students will need films, photographs, and other visual media to learn the content we present. In addition to the social studies textbook, we can choose from both hard-copy and CD-ROM reference materials (encyclopedias, atlases, almanacs); children's literature (fiction and information books); charts, graphs, and maps; videos and films; filmstrips, study prints, and listening media (audiotapes and compact discs); realia (real things); community resources (people who visit our classes, places we visit); and computer-based resources (software programs, hypermedia, the Internet).

Figure 10.1 **Sequence of Activities in a Social Studies Unit**

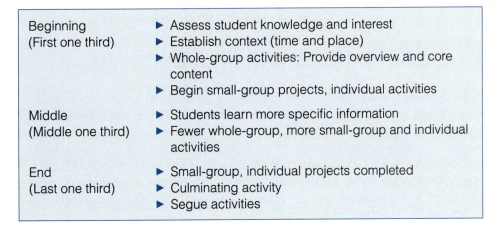

Beginning (First one third)	▶ Assess student knowledge and interest ▶ Establish context (time and place) ▶ Whole-group activities: Provide overview and core content ▶ Begin small-group projects, individual activities
Middle (Middle one third)	▶ Students learn more specific information ▶ Fewer whole-group, more small-group and individual activities
End (Last one third)	▶ Small-group, individual projects completed ▶ Culminating activity ▶ Segue activities

Units Should Include Whole-Group, Small-Group, and Individual Activities

Good social studies units of instruction include activities that require students to work in several grouping formats. All three types of grouping should be a part of a social studies unit. A unit that relies heavily on lessons during which all students are expected to do the same thing at the same time will not meet the needs of a diverse student population. Differences in ability, language status, and cultural identity require frequent use of small-group work and individualized activities.

I distinguish whole-group, small-group, and individual activities:

- *Whole group.* A whole-group activity is an activity that involves participation by all students in the classroom. During some whole-group activities, such as watching a film or listening to a guest speaker, all students participate in the activity at the same time and in the same place. Other whole-group activities include a teacher making a presentation and then students completing an assignment while working in small groups. In others, the teacher may pose a question, and then the students break into groups to discuss the question. Another format for a whole-group activity is a learning center. Students might visit the center in groups of six, one group a day. Again, from my perspective, a whole-group activity is assigned to all students in the room.
- *Small group.* A small-group activity has two characteristics: (a) Only a part of the class takes part, and (b) the participants work together. Small-group activities are projects, usually in writing, the visual arts, or the performing arts. Many of these small-group activities use a cooperative learning structure.
- *Individual.* Individual activities may be voluntary or assigned. Like small-group activities, they do not involve the whole class; rather, a student works independently, typically on a project of personal interest.

Example of an Instructional Unit

Many different formats can be used in planning instructional units in social studies. In this book, I share two with you. In this chapter is a unit on boats, designed for a highly diverse group of 25 to 30 third graders. This unit is organized by performance standards taken from the NCSS *Expectations of Excellence* (for the early grades; 1994). Four unit questions, written in language third graders will understand, serve as the focus for the unit. The unit takes about 3 weeks to complete. Elsewhere in the book (chaps. 2, 11, and 12) are examples of shorter "mini-units," which can be completed in less than a week.

Grade 3: "Boats"
Part I: Organizing Framework

UNIT

This unit uses the NCSS curriculum standards as a framework. The unit covers four of the standards' thematic strands and includes activities that will help children achieve four of the standards' performance expectations. The thematic strands and performance expectations provide useful tools for the adults who are planning social studies units, but you must clearly communicate your expectations to the children. To achieve this purpose, this unit uses a simple format: a set of questions phrased in words that third graders can understand.

NCSS Thematic Strand (1): Culture

Performance Expectation (a): The learner can explore and describe similarities and differences in the ways groups, societies, and cultures address similar human needs and concerns.

In this unit of study, children will learn that all people share certain needs that boats help them meet: finding food, exchanging goods, traveling to achieve personal goals, and defending themselves. The focus in the unit is on the different designs and functions of boats.

Each child is special, wonderfully unique, and capable of thriving under your guidance. As you create instructional units, be sure to include activities that allow each child to be successful.

Unit Question 1: What are the different types of boats, and why are they different?

NCSS Thematic Strand (3): People, Places, & Environments

Performance Expectation (b): The learner can interpret, use, and distinguish various representations of the earth, such as maps, globes, and photographs.

The unit of study on boats will require children to interpret several maps as they learn about the commercial, recreational, and military uses of boats.

Unit Question 2: Where in our state, country, and world would you find people using boats?

NCSS Thematic Strand (7): Production, Distribution, & Consumption

Performance Expectation (e): The learner can describe how we depend upon workers with specialized jobs and the ways in which they contribute to the production and exchange of goods and services.

The division of labor on a boat depends on its purpose and complexity. Children will learn that two factors have increased the number of specialized jobs on boats: size and technical sophistication.

Unit Question 3: What types of jobs do people perform on boats, and how have those jobs changed over time?

NCSS Thematic Strand (8): Science, Technology, & Society

Performance Expectation (a): The learner can identify and describe examples in which science and technology have changed the lives of people, such as homemaking, child care, work, transportation, and communication.

Technology has changed the design of boats, especially in regard to propulsion, to make them more efficient. These changes have modified both the lives of people who work on boats and the lives of people who use them.

Unit Question 4: How have boats changed over time?

Part II: Instructional Activities

(1) Introductory Activities

Unit Introduction: K-W-L Chart

Content Objectives: Children will be presented with the four questions they will be expected to answer during the unit (the unit questions). (Because it is impossible to predict what any group of children will say when asked "What do you know about boats?" other content objectives cannot really be listed.)

Process Objectives: Children will *recall* what they know about boats, *ask* questions they would like to have answered, and *discuss* the unit's four questions.

1. With the children, start a K-W-L chart on boats. Divide a sheet of chart paper into three parts, one with the heading "What We Know About Boats," the second column with the heading "What We Want to Learn About Boats," and the third with "What We Learned About Boats." The first two columns will be completed on the first day of the unit. The third column will be filled as the unit progresses. Items under the "W" column should be written as questions. If the children do not ask questions that cover the subtopics you planned to cover, add them (in this unit, the four unit questions must be written down). If members of the class show an interest in something you weren't planning to include, I suggest you modify your unit plan. Add resources and activities to fit the children's interests.

2. Begin by asking, "What do you know about boats?" Record what the children say under the "K" column. I like to have the four unit questions written on strips of paper so that they can be placed under the "W" column, along with the questions the children ask. Be sure to have a brief discussion about each question so that the children have a clear understanding of what they will be expected to learn. See Figure 10.2 for an example of a K-W-L chart for this unit.

Field Trip to Los Angeles Harbor

Content Objectives: In addition to being motivated to learn more about boats, children will see many different types of boats in the harbor. They will be able to identify the following boats: purse seiners (fishing boats), tugboats, oil tankers, freighters, cruise ships, and the fireboat.

Process Objectives: Children will *observe* the different types of boats, *describe* their design and function, and *synthesize* these data on a classroom chart.

1. Before taking the class on the field trip, show them the slides of the harbor you took the year before. Display a list of the different boats the children will see: purse seiners (fishing boats), tugboats, oil tankers, freighters, cruise ships, and the fireboat. In addition to enjoying the excitement of getting away from school and drinking in the many sights and sounds of a busy harbor, the children will be expected to complete a simple data retrieval chart. Along the chart's vertical axis will be listed the types of boats they will see (e.g., tugboats, tankers). Along the horizontal axis will be columns labeled "Function," "Design," and "Special Features." While visiting each boat, the children will take time to write information on their charts. When the children return to the classroom, they can share their notes as you complete a large, classroom chart to synthesize their observations.

Figure 10.2 **K-W-L Chart for a Unit on Boats: First Day of Unit**

	BOATS	
K *What we Know about boats*	W *What we Want to learn about boats*	L *What we Learned about boats*
• *Lots of us have visited the Queen Mary* • *Some boats have sails, others don't* • *Pedro, Leshana, Juan – their dads work at the harbor, and so does Donna's mom* • *Titanic was a movie about a boat that sank*	*Our questions* A. *How much does it cost to buy a boat?* B. *How fast can boats go?* C. *How can a big boat like the Queen Mary move?* *Unit questions* 1. *What are the different types of boats, and why are they different?* 2. *Where in our state, country, and world would you find people using boats?* 3. *What types of jobs do people perform on boats, and how have those jobs changed over time?* 4. *How have boats changed over time?*	

(2) Unit Question 1: What are the different types of boats, and why are they different?

Teacher Read-Aloud: Boats on the River

Content Objectives: Children will expand their knowledge of the different types of boats and focus on the different designs and functions of the following: ferryboat, paddlewheel, ocean liner, tugboat, motorboat, sailboat, rowboat, freighter, submarine, battleship.

Process Objectives: Children will *listen* to the book being read aloud, *share* their personal responses, *identify* and *differentiate* the design and function of each boat, and *classify* the boats by function.

1. Read aloud the wonderful book *Boats on the River* (Flack, 1946). Afterward, ask the children whether they would like to say anything about the book.
2. Write the following words on the chalkboard: *ferryboat, paddlewheel, ocean liner, tugboat, motorboat, sailboat, rowboat, freighter, submarine, battleship.* Go through the book a second time and discuss with the class Jay Barnum's

paintings of the boats, focusing on what each boat is used for (its function or purpose). Focus on the following principle: that design serves function. Organize the boats under the following categories on the chalkboard: "Used to Move People," "Used to Move Products," "Used for War," "Used for Fishing," and "Used for Fun" (Note: Some boats should be placed under more than one category).

Jigsaw: Modern Warships

Content Objectives: Children will learn about the design and military function of five types of modern warships.

Process Objectives: Children will *identify* five types of warships and then *compare and contrast* their design and function.

1. Break down the topic into five subtopics: (a) aircraft carriers, (b) battleships, (c) submarines, (d) transport ships, and (e) search-and-rescue ships. For each subtopic (type of warship), prepare a datafile, with descriptions and illustrations. Prepare a set of questions about each type of ship, focusing on the design and function of each type of boat.
2. Divide the class into five groups of five children each. Have each member of one group pick a different type of warship; do the same for the other groups so each group ends up with all five warships assigned, a different ship for each group member. As the unit progresses, each group member will become an "expert" on the ship she or he chose. Give each member of each group a copy of the appropriate datafile you prepared on each ship. In the last phase of the lesson, the children will return to their original groups and share the information they have learned.

Bulletin Board Display: "Voyages"

Content Objectives: Children will learn about the different types of boats, both historical and contemporary, used to transport people; contemporary boats include ferries, ocean liners, and recreational craft. They will describe and display Chumash canoes (the Chumash were a tribe of Native Americans in California who built ocean-going canoes). Finally, they will be able to list the common and distinguishing features of two historical boats—the *Mayflower* and the *Titanic*.

Process Objectives: Children will *locate* illustrations and information on boats that are used to transport people, *evaluate* illustrations of the same boat for accuracy, *create* a painting of a boat, *compose* a caption describing the boat, *listen* to a presentation comparing the *Mayflower* and the *Titanic*, *distinguish* the differences between them, and *explain* why one boat sank and the other did not.

1. Children who choose to work on this project will make paintings of boats that are used to transport people. The group will use CD-ROM encyclopedias, Internet resources, hard-copy encyclopedias, and information books as

resources. Each of their paintings will have a caption listing the type of boat and, if the boat has a name, the boat's name. Boats that will be included are contemporary ferries used by commuters, a cruise ship, recreational sail-boats, Chumash canoes, the *Mayflower,* and the *Titanic.*

2. After the bulletin board is finished, the children who painted and wrote about the *Mayflower* and the *Titanic* will make a presentation to their classmates, challenging them to explain why one ship sank and the other successfully completed a transatlantic voyage.

Inquiry: The Voyage to Hawaii

Content Objectives: Children will learn about the migration of people from Tahiti to Hawaii in about C.E. 1200. They will understand that the Polynesians accomplished in-credible feats of navigation, sailing with the resources they possessed. They will locate Tahiti and Hawaii on a world map. The inquiry will ask them to decide what supplies the Tahitians should take on their canoes as they prepare for their voyage to Hawaii.

Process Objectives: Children will *listen* to the historical overview provided by their teacher, *view* pictures of Polynesian catamarans, *locate* Tahiti and Hawaii on a world map, *examine* a list of resources available to the Tahitians, and *identify* the items they would take with them if they were making the voyage.

1. All the information you need for this lesson is available on the Web site of The Polynesian Voyaging Society *(http://leahi.kcc.hawaii.edu/org/pvs.html).* The site has excellent illustrations of the double-hulled canoes the Polynesians used, maps of the journey from Tahiti to Hawaii, and background information on all aspects of Polynesian shipbuilding, navigation, and migration. Present the background information the children will need to complete this inquiry ac-tivity. Explain that historians think a group of people from Tahiti emigrated to Hawaii in C.E. 1200 (an earlier group of Polynesians settled Hawaii many years earlier, but little is known about the original settlers). Display illustra-tions of Polynesian canoes the Tahitians used for the voyage. You may want to take the class onto the playground and draw an outline of Polynesian double-hulled canoes so that the children have some idea of the size of these boats. Share that the catamarans could hold as many as 50 people. Show that storage space would be limited.

2. Use the maps to show the distance from Tahiti to Hawaii. Members of the Polynesian Voyaging Society built a replica of a 13th-century canoe and sailed from Hawaii to Tahiti and back in 1976. The journey from Tahiti to Hawaii took 25 days. Explain the problem the sailors must solve. What should be taken on the voyage? Point out that the Tahitians did not know what they would find when they arrived in Hawaii, so they had to pack for both a long ocean voyage and an uncertain future. Present the children with a list of things the Tahitians could have taken with them: taro, coconuts, breadfruit, pigs, dogs, tools to repair the ship, weapons, extra sails, extra paddles, extra clothes, water, line and hooks for fishing, buckets, shell jewelry. Have each

group of five children generate a prioritized list of the items they would take with them if they were on the first voyage to Hawaii.

(3) Unit Question 2: Where in our state, nation, and world would you find people using boats?

Map-Reading Activity

Content Objectives: Children will learn that where there is water, there will be boats. They will see that, in addition to the port cities on the coasts, many large ports are inland on rivers and lakes. They will identify major ports and waterways in their state and in the United States.

Process Objectives: Children will *examine* state and national maps and *identify* major port cities and inland waterways.

1. Prepare questions ahead of time for the children to answer that should help them see that where there is water, there will be boats.
2. Divide the class into groups of four or five. Give each group two geopolitical maps: one of your state and one of the United States (for our discussion here, the state map will be California). Have them locate major port cities on the ocean, on rivers, and on lakes. If your state has human-made waterways that boats travel, be sure they are clearly marked on the map (you may have to modify the map before you duplicate it). For California, the children should locate the major ports of San Diego, Los Angeles (San Pedro), and San Francisco. Be sure to direct the children to the busy inland port cities of Stockton and Sacramento. Point out inland waterways, like Lake Tahoe and the Colorado River, that are used for recreational boats.
3. Follow the same process for the United States (be sure to emphasize inland ports like Kansas City, Cincinnati, and Duluth).

Teacher Read-Aloud: Freighters

Content Objectives: Children will learn about the design and function of a freighter. They will learn about the different jobs the crew performs. They will learn the location and purpose of the Panama and Suez Canals.

Process Objectives: Children will *listen* to their teacher read aloud, *compare and contrast* the design and function of a freighter with an ocean liner and a fishing boat, *recognize* the purpose of a canal, *identify* the locations of the Suez and Panama Canals, and *examine* a world map to determine the most direct international trade routes between seven port cities.

1. Read parts of the book *Freighters: Cargo Ships and the People Who Work Them* (Ancona, 1985) aloud to the class. Show the photographs. Have the class work in groups to compare a freighter to an ocean liner and a fishing boat.

2. Using a wall map, show the children the locations of the Suez and Panama Canals. Discuss the purpose of a canal.
3. Then, give each group a world map with several international port cities clearly marked (e.g., Athens, Dar es Salaam, Venice, Hong Kong, Los Angeles, New York, Rotterdam). Ask the children to draw the shortest routes that freighters could take between combinations of the cities you have highlighted. Emphasize the importance of the canals in these routes.

(4) Unit Question 3: What types of jobs do people do on boats?

Pantomime: Working on a New England Fishing Boat

Content Objectives: Children will learn the tasks that must be completed by people who live in a New England fishing village.

Process Objectives: Children will *listen* to their teacher read a book aloud, *ask* questions about the content of the book, *identify* the tasks that people in the village must complete, and *dramatize* five of those tasks.

1. Read aloud *Surrounded by Sea: Life on a New England Fishing Island* (Gibbons, 1991). Afterward, ask the children whether they have questions or comments about the book.
2. Then, focus on the different activities that take place on the island from season to season. On the chalkboard, make a list of the work that must be done: mending nets, repairing sails, loading equipment, bringing in the catch, unloading the fish for processing. Have the children pretend to do each job.

Videocassette: Ships

Content Objectives: Children will learn about the different jobs on an ocean liner, focusing on the responsibilities of the cruise director, the engineer, the captain, the stewards, and the radio officer.

Process Objectives: Children will *view* the video, work in groups to *identify* the responsibilities of each position, *assess* the challenges and rewards of each position, and *select* the one they prefer.

1. Show the class the video *Ships*.
2. Afterward, have the children work in groups to complete the following assignment: Tell what responsibilities each of the following people has on an ocean liner: the cruise director, the engineer, the captain, a steward, and the radio officer. After the group work, bring the class together and discuss the challenges and rewards of each position.
3. Then have each child write a paragraph about which of the five positions he or she would prefer to hold.

(5) Unit Question 4: How have boats changed over time?

History of Boats Lesson

Content Objectives: Children will learn that although the functions of boats have remained constant, their design and capacity (e.g., speed, size) have changed radically. They will learn about the design and function of seven famous boats.

Process Objectives: Children will *listen* to information presented by the teacher, *examine* illustrations of each boat, *distinguish* the differences among the boats, and *predict* how boats might be different in the future.
   The lesson will ask the children to examine each of the following boats:

- A Roman trireme
- A Haida canoe (the Haida are a Native tribe living in British Columbia and Alaska)
- The *Constitution* ("Old Ironsides")
- The *Great Eastern* (a ship powered by sail and steam)
- The *Queen Mary (engines)*
- The *Nautilus* (first atomic-powered submarine)

1. Examples of historical boats can be taken from three books with excellent illustrations: *The Book of Fantastic Boats* (Bernard, 1974); *Oars, Sails, and Steam: A Picture Book of Ships* (Tunis, 1952); and *Ships, Sailors, and the Sea* (Humble, 1991). For an illustration of the Haida canoe, use the Web site of the Canadian Heritage Information Network (CHIN; *http://www.chin.gc.ca*).
2. Prepare a timeline that shows when each kind of boat was used; also prepare an illustration of each boat.
3. Display an illustration of each boat and discuss two features: (a) how the boat was powered and (b) how the boat was used. Ask questions that will help children see how each boat is alike and different from the one that preceded it.
4. Finally, have children predict how boats might be different in the future.

Song:"The Erie Canal"

Content Objectives: Children will learn about the barges used on canals in the United States in the first half of the 19th century.

Process Objectives: Children will *sing* the song, *examine* illustrations of the horse- (and mule-) drawn barges, *identify* the location of the canal on a map of the United States, *evaluate* the efficacy of the barges (given the technology of the time), and *propose* possible alternative designs and power sources.

1. Teach the class the American folk song "The Erie Canal." First, read aloud Peter Spier's picture book about the song, *The Erie Canal* (1970). Spier's

illustrations show the horse- and mule-drawn barges that were used on the canal.

2. On the timeline (prepared beforehand by a group of children), find 1825, when the canal opened (see chap. 12 for guidelines on how to construct timelines). Show the location of the canal on a map of the United States.

3. Have the children look closely at selected illustrations of the barges. Discuss why the barges were pulled along by horses and mules. Speculate how the design of the barges could have been improved and what alternative power sources could have been used.

(6) Concluding Activities

Suchman Inquiry: "What Makes Things Float?"

Content Objectives: Children will learn why some things float and others do not. They will see that almost anything will float, regardless of weight, if it is supported by a large enough platform.

Process Objectives: Children will *observe* items of various weights placed in a tank of water, *predict* which items from a second set will float, *ask* questions attempting to resolve the paradox of why some heavy things float and some light things do not, and *propose* a rule that defines why things float.

1. This inquiry activity provides a cross-curricular link to science. Fill an aquarium with water. Then present this puzzler to the class: "Explain why incredibly heavy ships like ocean liners and aircraft carriers float."

2. First, show the class a lightweight item that will float in the tank (a paperclip). Ask the children whether the paperclip will float (they typically think it will). Then place the item into the tank (the item will float if you set it on top of the water horizontally rather than put it in vertically). Next, show a heavier item that will sink (a large nail) and ask the children whether the item will float (they will predict it will sink). Then place the item into the tank (the item will sink). Ask the class whether they can state a rule explaining why some things float and others sink. (Usually, children will conclude that heavy things sink and light things float.) Ask, "How can heavy ships like an ocean liner or an aircraft carrier stay afloat?" Tell the class to ask you yes/no questions as you continue the demonstration. Float plastic plates and trays in the tank as supports under items of differing weights. The children will eventually see that heavy items can float if the surface area of water underneath them is expanded (a heavy wrench will float in the tank if it is placed on a cafeteria-style tray).

Concept Attainment/Assessment

Content Objectives: This activity will assess and reinforce children's understanding of the different functions of boats.

Process Objectives: Children will *classify* 10 boats into four functional categories.

1. This lesson uses a modified form of the concept attainment model for assessment. Make and copy a chart on a sheet of paper divided into four sections labeled "Used to Move People," "Used to Move Things," "Used for Fishing," and "Used for War." Copy illustrations of 10 boats from Web sites, books, and encyclopedias. Provide a descriptor for each boat (e.g., "ferry").
2. Distribute to each child a copy of the chart. Give each child a chance to look at each boat illustration with its descriptor. Have each child work independently to attempt to categorize the illustrations, writing the descriptor under the appropriate label or labels on the chart (e.g., the child would write the descriptor "ferry" under the labels "Used to Move People" and "Used to Move Things").

Unit Test

The third graders will take a simple end-of-unit test. It is important to remember that any test designed for third graders must be brief and should fit the abilities of the children. This test should ask the children to respond to the following: Choose one boat that we have learned about during the past few weeks. Answer each of the following questions:

(A) Which boat did you choose?
(B) What makes the boat go?
(C) What is the boat used for?
(D) Is the boat a modern boat or an old boat?
(E) Where does the boat go?
(F) What jobs do people perform on this boat?

To help children choose, allow them to look at the illustrations of boats you used for the concept attainment lesson. Answer questions the children ask about how to complete the assignment. Give children plenty of time to finish writing their answers. Permit your English language learners to complete the test orally in either English or their first language.

Segue Activity: Think-Pair-Share on Boats and Planes

Content Objectives: Children will learn that despite the obvious differences between airplanes and boats, these serve the same functions (transport people, transport goods, warfare). They will understand the significant differences between airplanes and boats (speed, size, utility).

Process Objectives: Children *compare and contrast* airplanes and boats according to design, capacity, and function; *discuss* their perspectives with a partner, and *listen to* and *critique* the responses of their classmates.

1. Let's suppose the next unit for this class of third graders will be on airplanes. A simple segue activity is for you to pose these questions: "How are ships and airplanes alike? How are they different?"
2. Have each child work with a partner. First, each child thinks about the questions. Then, the partners discuss their responses. Finally, the children share their responses with their classmates.

(7) Enrichment Activities

Every unit should include opportunities for children to explore topics of personal interest. At the same time, enrichment activities will allow you to help children who have special needs. For example, children who are having difficulty using a CD-ROM encyclopedia can be assigned to an activity that will give them an opportunity to become more proficient. Each child in the class should choose (or be assigned to) at least one enrichment activity.

Construction: Paper Boats

Using the directions in *Toy Boats to Make at Home* (Leeming, 1946) or *Let's Make a Toy Sailboat* (Stokes, 1978), show the children how to make one of three types of paper boats.

Oral Presentation on Semaphore

Have a group of children teach their classmates some of the semaphore alphabet (a system of visual signaling by two flags, held one in each hand, and each flag being a square constructed of one white triangle and one black triangle). Suggest that the group use Volume 16 of *Children's Britannica* as a source. The group can construct semaphore flags from black and white construction paper and dowel rods and then teach their classmates the first letters of the semaphore alphabet.

Independent Reading

Children may choose to read one of the unit-related books you have brought to class. Each book should be displayed on a table or in a special bookshelf. Figure 10.5, at the end of this chapter, is a list of books that could be used for this unit.

Design a "Fantastic" Boat

Allow any child who wants to do to draw a picture of a fantastic boat. Encourage children to use their imaginations. Each boat should be different and unusual. *The Book of Fantastic Boats* (Bernard, 1974) could serve as inspiration.

Encyclopedia of Boats

Some children may choose to create a class "encyclopedia" of boats. You will have to provide a booklet that has 10 dittoed pages like the sample in Figure 10.3. Two pieces of 9 × 12-in. construction paper can serve as the cover. Each page has a

Figure 10.3   Form for an Encyclopedia Entry, Grade 3

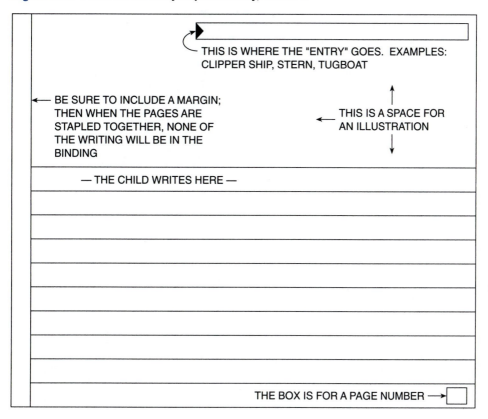

THIS IS WHERE THE "ENTRY" GOES. EXAMPLES:
CLIPPER SHIP, STERN, TUGBOAT

←— BE SURE TO INCLUDE A MARGIN;
THEN WHEN THE PAGES ARE
STAPLED TOGETHER, NONE OF
THE WRITING WILL BE IN THE
BINDING

←— THIS IS A SPACE FOR
AN ILLUSTRATION

— THE CHILD WRITES HERE —

THE BOX IS FOR A PAGE NUMBER —→

place for a title, an illustration, and a brief description. When finished, the children can arrange the entries in alphabetical order and then complete a title page and a table of contents. Help the children bind the booklet together.

Writing: "My Voyage"

Children who have taken a ride or trip on a boat can write simple autobiographical essays about it.

Part III: Unit Support Plans

Outline of Daily Plans: Unit Grid

The easiest way to make an outline of what will happen each day during the unit is with a "unit grid." Figure 10.4 shows a grid for this unit.

Figure 10.4 Unit Grid for "Boats"

DAY 1	DAY 2	DAY 3	DAY 4	DAY 5
1. K–W–L chart 2. Field trip	1. Read aloud *Boats on the River* 2. Introduce independent reading	1. Jigsaw: Modern warships	1. Continue Jigsaw: Modern warships 2. Introduce Encyclopedia of Boats Project	1. Map-reading activity 2. Introduce Semaphore Project
DAY 6	DAY 7	DAY 8	DAY 9	DAY 10
1. Read aloud *Freighters* 2. Song: "The Erie Canal"	1. Video: *Ships* 2. Introduce Bulletin Board Project	1. Life on a New England fishing island 2. Introduce "My Voyage" writing	1. Inquiry: The Voyage to Hawaii	1. History of boats lesson 2. Introduce boat construction and design a fantastic boat
DAY 11	DAY 12	DAY 13	DAY 14	DAY 15
1. Sing "The Erie Canal" again 2. What makes things float?	Individual and small-group work	Student presentations on semaphore and the bulletin board	1. Individual and small-group work 2. Concept attainment lesson	1. Unit test 2. Segue Boats Planes

Assessment Plan for Unit

The assessment plan for this unit was presented as Figure 8.5 in chapter 8. All activities in the unit will generate behaviors and products that can be used for assessment. Certain activities, however, are particularly important for assessment purposes. You need to know to what extent each child has mastered the objectives for the unit. Here, again, is a summary of the assessment plan for the unit:

> *Objective 1:* What are the different types of boats, and why are they different?
> Activities used for assessment: field trip to harbor, concept attainment lesson, unit test
> *Objective 2:* Where in our state, country, and world would you find people using boats?
> Activities used for assessment: map reading, inquiry—"Voyage to Hawaii," unit test
> *Objective 3:* What types of jobs do people perform on boats, and how have those jobs changed over time?
> Activities used for assessment: bulletin board display, videocassette—*Ships,* unit test
> *Objective 4:* How have boats changed over time?
> Activities used for assessment: bulletin board display, history of boats lesson, unit test

Effective Teaching in Today's Diverse Classroom: The unit on boats includes several features that make it appropriate for today's diverse classroom. First, the unit uses a *wide range of resources:* books with excellent illustrations, Web sites, children's books, encyclopedias, a video, a field trip, and maps. Children who are not proficient readers in English can learn the content the unit presents. The K-W-L activity will help children *activate their background knowledge* about boats. As children hear their classmates talk about boats, they will recall things they know. For our English language learners, this unit has a great deal of *"comprehensible input."* The picture books read aloud by the teacher have simple texts and excellent illustrations. Lessons are supported with the use of illustrations. Many activities, like the inquiry on the voyage to Hawaii, feature *cooperative learning.* Group work will push children into their zones of proximal development and provide the *contextual support* English language learners need to succeed. Many children learn best through *the arts.* This unit provides learning experiences in the performing arts (the pantomime and singing of "The Erie Canal") and the visual arts (bulletin board display, design a fantastic boat). *Firsthand experiences* make it easier for all children to learn new things. Many children will see real boats for the first time on the field trip. The mixture of *whole-group, small-group, and individual* activities allows more able children to be challenged and permits children who are particularly interested in boats to satisfy their curiosity. This unit includes information about *non-Western cultural groups* (Chumash, Haida, Polynesians) and the jobs that *"ordinary" people* perform on boats. The autobiographical stories that children write about their rides or trips on boats provide an opportunity to link the content of the unit to their *personal experiences.*

SUMMARY OF KEY POINTS

- ▶ Units should be cross-curricular and integrate the social science disciplines, language arts, the visual arts, the performing arts, science, mathematics, and physical education.
- ▶ Units should have a clearly defined scope. Each unit has a unifying element, which may be a period of history, a person or group of people, a location, a question, a thing, or a concept.
- ▶ Activities in a unit should follow a logical sequence. Activities at the beginning of a unit determine what your students know about the topic you will be covering and establish what subtopics they would like to investigate. Segue activities at the end of a unit introduce the next unit of study.
- ▶ Units should use a variety of instructional resources.
- ▶ Units should have whole-group, small-group, and individual activities.
- ▶ You may use many different formats for planning units, including detailed (comprehensive) unit plans and mini-units.

FOR FURTHER READING

- ▶ Don't reinvent the wheel. Excellent social studies units are available from a variety of sources. Units are available on the Internet. I suggest you start with three Web sites: the site for the National Council for the Social Studies (NCSS), *http://www.ncss.org/online*; the "History/Social Studies Web Site for K–12 Teachers," *http://execpc.com/~dboals/boals.html*; and the "Schools of California Online Resources for Education" (SCORE) Web site, *http://www.rims.k12.ca.us/score/*. The ERIC system includes hundreds of social studies units for elementary students; most were developed under the auspices of state departments of education and school district curriculum committees. Social studies methods textbooks (like this one) are another source of units of instruction. The material in social studies textbooks for children is organized in units. Check the teacher's edition at your grade level and be willing to expand the unit to include resources and activities beyond those provided by the publisher of the textbook. Social studies journals (*Social Education, The Social Studies,* and *Social Studies and the Young Learner*) regularly publish instructional units, although usually in abbreviated form. Here are some units that relate to the two in this chapter:

Boats and Transportation

- ▶ All of these are excellent resources: seven units designed for K–3 on airplanes and flight (Alabama State Department of Education, 1992); a computer-based

Figure 10.5 **Children's Books: Grade 3 Unit "Boats"**

INFORMATION BOOKS

Ancona, George. *Freighters: Cargo Ships and the People Who Work Them.* This book is too difficult for most third graders to read. The photographs, however, are a good source of information.

Barton, Bryon. *Boats.* Illustrated by the author, this is a very easy reading book, within the capabilities of almost every third grader. Barton's illustrations are a problem: They are cartoonlike and lack the realism a good information book requires.

Bernard, Christine. *The Book of Fantastic Boats.* Illustrated by Roy Coombs's brilliant, full-color illustrations of boats through the ages, this book includes novelties such as the first submarine (the *Turtle,* 1776) and the *Popoffka,* a 19th-century Russian warship that was round! More able third-grade readers can understand the text.

Carter, Katherine. *Ships and Seaports.* Illustrated with photographs, this book is very easy reading.

Gibbons, Gail. *Surrounded by Sea: Life on a New England Fishing Island.* This book tells of one year, season by season, on an island off the coast of Maine. Most third graders could read this book.

Hartford, John. *Steamboat in a Cornfield.* Illustrated with historical photographs, this is a picture book about an incident in 1910. The steamboat *Virginia* went aground while traveling on the Ohio River. An excellent book, the period photographs are fascinating. A good choice to read aloud.

Humble, Richard. *Ships, Sailors, and the Sea.* Illustrated by several artists, this book is part of the superb "Timelines" series. Although it is difficult for third graders to read, the detailed, full-color illustrations of historical ships are an excellent resource.

Lasky, Kathryn. *Tall Ships.* Illustrated with Christopher G. Knight's photographs, this book is too difficult for third graders to read, but the photographs are a useful teaching resource.

Lasky, Kathryn. *Tugboats Never Sleep.* Illustrated with Christopher G. Knight's photographs, this book can be read by most third graders.

Macauley, David. *Ship.* This is a fascinating book in two parts. In the first, archaeologists discover a 15th-century caravel. In the second, how the caravel was built is described. As with all his books, Macauley's drawings are great. Third graders will need help with the text.

Olney, Ross R. *Ocean-Going Giants.* Illustrated with photographs, this book can be read by most third graders.

Rosenblum, Richard. *Tugboats.* Illustrated with the author's excellent drawings, this books is for more able readers.

Figure 10.5 **Children's Books: Grade 3 Unit "Boats"** *(Continued)*

Scarry, Huck. *Life on a Barge: A Sketchbook.* Illustrated by the author, this is a wonderful book about the author's trip on a barge in the Netherlands.

Scott, Geoffrey. *Egyptian Boats.* Illustrated by Nancy. L. Carlson, this is a nicely done book that is easy to read.

Tunis, Edwin. *Oars, Sails, and Steam: A Picture Book of Ships.* The text is written for older children, but the author's artwork is one of the best sources on the history of boats.

van Tol, Robert. *Submarines.* Illustrated with photographs, this is a book that most third graders can read.

Wormfield, Hope Herman. *Boatbuilder.* Illustrated with photographs, this is a good book to read aloud. It is about Ralph Stanley, a sailboat maker who lives and works in Maine.

Zeck, Pam and Zeck, Gerry. *Mississippi Steamwheelers.* Some third grade readers can handle this book, which is illustrated by George Overlie.

FICTION

Brown, Marcia. *Henry-Fisherman.* Illustrated by the author, this book was a Caldecott Honor book in 1950. It is within the reading ability of most third graders and tells the story of a boy living in the Virgin Islands.

Fisher, Leonard Everett. *Sailboat Lost.* This is a wordless picture book with wonderful illustrations by the author. In the story, high tide takes a boat out to sea.

Flack, Marjorie. *Boats on the River.* Illustrated by Jay Hyde Barnum, this 1947 Caldecott Honor Book is a perfect book for this unit. Flack's poetry describes a ferryboat, a paddlewheel riverboat, an ocean liner, a tugboat, a motorboat, a sailboat, a rowboat, a freighter, a submarine, and a battleship. The illustrations are bright and accurate, although the book does show its age.

Molloy, Anne Stearns. *Shaun and the Boat: An Irish Story.* Illustrated by Barbara Cooney, this book is for more able third-grade readers.

Spier, Peter. *The Erie Canal.* Illustrator Spier has taken the lyrics to this folk song for his text. His illustrations have accurate historical detail. For the teacher, background on the canal is provided.

Van Allsburg, Chris. *The Wreck of the Zephyr.* Illustrated by the author, this is a picture book fantasy about a sailboat that could fly. Most third graders can read it.

unit that uses transportation as a stimulus for creative writing (Snow, 1990); a cross-curricular unit on flight (Freeland & Smith, 1993).

▶ As for strategies for planning units, Farivar (1993) has a plan for writing cross-curricular units, and Onosko (1992) provides an innovative model for unit design. Every social studies methods textbook I have read includes a format for planning units. If you want a historical perspective that still works, read how social studies units were developed at the Dewey School in the early 1900s (Mayhew & Edwards, 1936). Taba's (1967) thoughtful approach to unit development still makes a great deal of sense.

▶ The children's books listed in Figure 10.5 would make an excellent classroom library during the unit on boats presented in this chapter.

Part III

Sources of Content for Social Studies Teaching

Chapter 11

Democratic Citizenship: Participating in Civic Life

In the primary grades, citizenship can be learned through school service projects. Michiko Murayama, a third-grade teacher, provided her class with an opportunity to welcome new students to their school. Ms. Murayama's school had a significant level of transience among the students, so each year her school service project was "Welcome to Cesar Chavez School." Because each teacher at Cesar Chavez School could expect to lose several students during the year and to gain at least five, the task of welcoming new students was an important one.

The first year Ms. Murayama attempted the "Welcome to Cesar Chavez School" project, she asked her class what could be done to help new students. She had her own ideas, and so did the school principal, but her third graders came up with the following list:

- *Writing and publishing a "Guide to Cesar Chavez School."* Each year, a group of her children worked together to write and illustrate the guide, and she made enough copies for all the new students. The guide, written and illustrated by the children, included information on school rules, holidays, and the recess and lunch schedule. It contained information on special programs at the school, such as an after-school recreation program run by the city. One year, Ms. Murayama's class included a description of their favorite entrees in the school cafeteria.
- *Serving as "First Week Hosts."* Other students took part in this component of the school service project by taking new students on a tour of the school. They ate lunch with the new students and made sure they weren't alone at recess.
- *Serving as translators for non-English-speaking new students at other grade levels.* Several of Ms. Murayama's third graders were bilingual. They spent some days in kindergarten and first-grade classrooms, helping teachers communicate with their new students who spoke little or no English.

School service projects like Ms. Murayama's provide children with opportunities to apply what they have learned about citizenship. Citizenship education is the topic of this chapter.

▲   ▲   ▲

In this chapter, you will read about:

- ▶ Why authorities believe that citizenship education is the primary goal of social studies programs
- ▶ Competing perspectives on citizenship education: to teach students about how government works and to follow the rules, or to teach students how to change society for the better
- ▶ The content of citizenship education as organized around five concerns posed by the *National Standards for Civics and Government* (Center for Civic Education, 1994): (a) what government is, (b) the basic values of

American democracy, (c) the role of the U.S. Constitution, (d) the relationship of the United States to other nations, and (e) the roles and responsibilities of U.S. citizens
- ▶ Engle and Ochoa's teaching sequence for value-based decision making
- ▶ Forms of civic participation appropriate for elementary school students, including school service, community service, and individual service projects
- ▶ How citizenship can be developed as a part of a teacher's plan for classroom management

Democratic Citizenship: The First Goal of Social Studies

Good citizenship is recognized widely as the most important goal of social studies. The definition of *social studies* adopted by the National Council for the Social Studies (NCSS) states that "the primary purpose of social studies is to help young people develop the ability to make informed and reasoned decisions for the public good as citizens of a culturally diverse, democratic society in an interdependent world" (NCSS Task Force on Standards for Teaching and Learning in Social Studies, 1993, p. 213). Why a preeminent place for citizenship education? Knowledgeable and active citizens are essential for the survival of our democratic way of life. Consider the following statement: "Ultimately, a free society must rely on the knowledge, skills, and virtue of its citizens and those they elect to public office. Civic education, therefore, is essential to the preservation and improvement of American constitutional democracy" (Center for Civic Education, 1994, p. 1).

Citizenship education is a topic with many facets (Anderson, Avery, Pederson, Smith, & Sullivan, 1997; J. E. Davis & Fernlund, 1995; Drisko, 1993; Field, 1997; W. Parker & Jarolimek, 1984; W. C. Parker & Kaltsounis, 1991; Patrick & Hoge, 1991; Quigley & Bahmueller, 1991). In 1994, Wade and Everett stated that "there is little consensus about what effective citizenship means" (p. 308). A major study conducted by Anderson and his colleagues (1997) established that teachers have very different perspectives on what citizenship education should accomplish. A good place to start our discussion is with some definitions.

Engle and Ochoa (1988) note that *citizenship* "is conferred on an individual by a state or nation" (p. 16). The type of citizenship we are concerned with is broader than legal status as a citizen, so "whenever individuals make a decision or act in any way that affects others, directly or indirectly, knowingly or unknowingly, they are acting as citizens" (pp. 16–17). Simply put, citizenship is not limited to political activity; it is our public life. The *National Standards for Civics and Government* define this as "civic life," in which individuals are concerned with the "affairs of the community and nation, that is, the public realm" (Center for Civic Education, 1994, p. 7).

Democratic citizenship refers to civic life in a free society, wherein the majority rule while the rights of the minority are respected.

Civics and government are the two social science disciplines at the heart of citizenship education. *Civics* covers "the rights and responsibilities of citizens and their relationship to one another and to the government," whereas instruction in *government* focuses on "political and legal institutions" (Patrick & Hoge, 1991, p. 428). In elementary school, students should learn about how rules are made, enforced, and interpreted in families, at school, in the classroom, and at the local, state, national, and international levels. Instruction that focuses on the functioning of legal systems is called *law-related education* (LRE), and several lessons and units have been produced to accomplish the goals of LRE (Bjorklun, 1995; Hicks & Austin, 1994; J. Norton, 1992; Smagorinsky, 1994; Study Group on Law-Related Education, 1978).

Citizenship Education and Diversity

Citizenship education must at the same time provide for unification and celebrate diversity. The values, principles, and beliefs of a democratic way of life are the unifying elements of the United States. The *National Standards for Civics and Government* (Center for Civic Education, 1994) summarize how the democratic ideal binds us as Americans: "Americans are united by the values, principles and beliefs they share rather than by ethnicity, race, religion, class, language, gender, or national origin" (p. 25). Thus, when students become committed to our democratic system of government, democratic values and beliefs, and democratic civic life, they become Americans.

The NCSS *Curriculum Guidelines for Multicultural Education* make this same point:

> There is, after all, a set of overarching values that all groups within a society or nation endorse to maintain societal cohesion. In our nation, these core values stem from our commitment to human dignity, and include justice, equality, freedom, and due process of law. (NCSS Task Force on Ethnic Studies Curriculum Guidelines, 1992, p. 284)

In your classroom, you may have a half dozen native languages spoken, national identities that encompass all the continents, and religious affiliations of many kinds. All our students need effective citizenship education that leads to a commitment to the democratic ideals of the United States of America.

At the same time, citizenship education is education for diversity. Our units of study in social studies should help students understand the many facets of pluralism in the United States. Our democratic system makes diversity in language, culture, religion, nationality, and political philosophy inevitable. Students should see that diversity is not a threat to our way of life, but rather a part of America that always has existed and will exist in the future. A key component of citizenship education is that students learn that our democratic ideal has not always been realized. Even though the United States was founded on values of justice and equality, public policy and private action have sometimes been unjust and unequal. For example, in California, fourth graders who study the history of their state should learn about the internment of Japanese Americans during World War II. Fifth graders who study the creation of the United States should understand that although the Constitution was enacted by "the people," women, Native Americans, enslaved persons, and men without property could not vote in 18th-century elections.

Research on Citizenship Education

With these definitions in mind, let's take a look at some important research on citizenship education. In their review, Patrick and Hoge (1991) concluded that "the solid findings are too few and unrelated to help practitioners make a powerful difference in how they teach government, civics, and law, and in what their students learn from them" (p. 434).

Some important research has been conducted on what students know and think about government and civics and how these topics are presented in textbooks. Greenstein's (1969) study of political understanding among students in Grades 4 through 8 still makes interesting reading. Greenstein found that fourth graders idealized political leaders, from their mayor to the president. By eighth grade, this reverence had diminished. Of particular interest is Greenstein's finding that elementary students did not base their feelings on political information; they knew very little about the leaders they held in high regard. Patrick and Hoge (1991) reviewed the research on how civics and government are treated in elementary social studies textbooks. They concluded that the research reveals textbooks were "remarkably similar." Textbooks were "designed for passive learning." The goal of textbooks was to present facts and ideas, rather than to provide opportunities "for the active involvement of learners in the pursuit of knowledge." Patrick and Hoge concluded that "textbooks at all levels of schooling tend to be supportive of the status quo" (p. 429).

Wade and Everett (1994) examined how citizenship education was presented in four of the most popular third-grade social studies textbooks. They wanted to find out whether things had changed from the 1960s and 1970s, when textbooks presented an image of a good citizen who was "passive, harmonious, and accepting" (p. 308). All four textbooks devoted several pages to citizenship. Wade and Everett concluded that the textbooks they reviewed were an improvement over earlier ones. A variety of political and social acts were presented as a part of good citizenship. In addition to staying informed, voting, and running for office, good citizens were presented as also taking social action, performing community service, and lobbying public officials. Also, "students were encouraged to see themselves as active participants in their communities now, rather than just as adults in the future" (p. 310). The researchers thought, however, that the books did not provide enough information to help students learn the full range of civic options available to citizens of the United States. Teachers who use those books "will need to go beyond the social studies textbook and challenge students to question prevailing norms and seek out creative ways for improving their classrooms, schools, and communities" (p. 311).

Competing Perspectives on Citizenship Education

Authorities have proffered several perspectives on precisely what citizenship education should try to accomplish. Anderson et al. (1997) conducted an excellent study of how elementary and secondary teachers define citizenship education. They found "four coherent, identifiable, and separate viewpoints on citizenship education" (p. 351). A brief description of each should help us understand why this area of social studies is controversial:

- Some teachers adopt a *critical-thinking* perspective. These teachers believe that citizenship education should help students question the status quo, develop critical-thinking and questioning skills, and encourage open-mindedness and tolerance.
- Other teachers hold a *legalist* perspective. They believe that citizenship education should stress obedience to laws, teach the basic structure of our political system, and inform students of their rights and responsibilities.
- Teachers who have a *cultural pluralism* perspective define citizenship education as the celebration of diversity and pluralism. These teachers believe that rather than teach the basic structure of our political institutions, citizenship education should expose students to a range of ideologies.
- Finally, some teachers adhere to an *assimilationist* perspective, which is similar to the views of the legalists. Assimilationist teachers, however, explicitly reject current ideas of "political correctness" and want to transmit to students the dominant values of our society.

This summary categorizes the perspectives of teachers who belong to the NCSS and reveals the divergent nature of citizenship education. It should be noted, too, that some teachers hold more than one perspective. To simplify things somewhat, another way to look at the competing views on citizenship education is to examine the "transmission versus transformation" debate. This crystallizes one of the more controversial issues in social studies. Simply, should teachers limit citizenship education to how government functions, and should their definition of a good citizen be a person who follows the rules and votes (transmission)? Or should teachers teach students how to analyze social conditions *and* then take action to bring about change (transformation)?

The *transmission model* is adopted by the legalists and assimilationists described by Anderson and his colleagues (1997). Teachers help students understand the structure and function of local, state, and federal government. Students learn about the rights and responsibilities of citizenship and are encouraged to participate in nonthreatening civic activities such as working on political campaigns, staying informed, and voting. As the research of Patrick and Hoge (1991) and Wade and Everett (1994) show, this is the model of citizenship presented in most elementary social studies textbooks.

The *transformation model* is endorsed by many social studies authorities (Engle & Ochoa, 1988; Jennings, Crowell, & Fernlund, 1994), "critical" educational theorists (Apple, 1993; McLaren, 1994), and multicultural educators (J. A. Banks & Banks, 1997). It is the model used by teachers who have both the critical-thinking and the cultural pluralist perspectives described by Anderson and his colleagues. J. A. Banks (1997a) calls for the curriculum to be revised at the "social action" level. In such classrooms, students make decisions and take actions related to the concept, issue, or problem studied in the unit (p. 239). Engle and Ochoa (1988) see citizenship education as a process of both "socialization" and "countersocialization." *Socialization* involves teaching students about existing traditions and values. They argue, though, that social studies programs must also lead to *countersocialization*. This emphasizes "independent thinking and responsible social criticism" (p. 30).

Jennings et al. (1994) provide specific suggestions for how to implement a "transformational social studies." First, we should see our classrooms as places where students can learn about "social relationships, reciprocity, power, and community." This means that we should encourage students to analyze how things work (or don't work) and make suggestions for improvement. Second, the curriculum should present students with historical problem-solving situations that focus on historical "dilemmas of justice," such as those faced by the abolitionists and advocates for child labor laws. Third, we should encourage students to express their own opinions, not just to restate the positions of others. Fourth, the authors argue that we should teach students the dynamic relationship between pluralism and unity in our constitutional system. Finally, we should plan for students to participate in social action projects to convince them of "the power inherent within cooperative efforts against injustice" (pp. 5–6).

You can see how controversial this could become. I think almost everyone would agree that students should be taught to understand and analyze a range of perspectives on important current issues, especially those that are not endorsed by the majority. Students should learn about several forms of civic participation. Those of us who encourage students to take action, however, must be sure that we do not steer our students to any one side of a public policy issue or to a political candidate.

In fact, we should encourage students to define issues, rather than present an agenda to our students. As our students consider social action, we should help them pursue activities appropriate for elementary school children.

Sometimes all of us can underestimate the potential of elementary school children. The most impressive social action project I am aware of took place recently in an *elementary* school classroom. Barbara Vogel, a fifth-grade teacher in Aurora, Colorado, had completed a unit with her students on slavery in American history. Shortly thereafter, Associated Press writer Karin Davies completed a story on the current slave trade in Sudan. The story ran in a local newspaper, and one of Ms. Vogel's students, Kyle Vincent, decided that something should be done to stop slavery in Sudan. (The slave trade in Sudan is the result of civil war as local militias, who fight without pay for the Sudanese government, make captives their slaves. International organizations have been able to purchase the freedom of some of the enslaved people.) Ms. Vogel's class began to raise money, originally collecting coins in jars. This social action project received national media coverage, and eventually large donations began to arrive. By the end of 1998, the project had raised more than $50,000. The money was donated to international organizations and has been used to free more than 1,000 enslaved people in Sudan!

National Projects on Citizenship Education

Two attempts to define the scope of citizenship education are worthy of mention. *Civitas* is a curriculum framework developed by the Council for the Advancement of Citizenship and the Center for Civic Education (Quigley & Bahmueller, 1991). *Civitas* is an essential document for school district committees writing instructional units on citizenship education. The *National Standards for Civics and Government* (Center for Civic Education, 1994) could prove to be very influential. I discuss specific sections of the national standards later in this chapter.

Citizenship Education: Content

Citizenship education has three components: content, values, and processes. The *content* is the knowledge students should acquire in order to be effective citizens. Engle and Ochoa (1988) make an essential point when they note that a citizen in a democracy needs a "broad liberal education" (p. 18). History, geography, anthropology, economics, philosophy, the arts, the humanities, and the sciences are requisite to be an informed citizen. Specifically, though, students need to know a great deal in the fields of civics and government. For most of us, our district curriculum guide and social studies textbooks cover these topics at every grade level. If our district's social studies program follows the expanded horizons format, then kindergartners, first graders, and second graders focus on families, classrooms, and schools; third graders look at civic life in their cities; fourth graders study the government of their state; fifth graders learn about the federal government; and sixth graders examine governments of ancient cultures or foreign nations.

Patrick and Hoge (1991) provide a concise statement of what we must teach our students: "Citizens of a constitutional democracy are expected to know the principles and facts necessary for meaningful participation in government and public affairs" (p. 431). The *National Standards for Civics and Government* (Center for Civic Education, 1994) provides a more specific description of the civic knowledge our students should acquire. The standards organize content under five questions:

1. *What is government, and what should it do?* Our students should be able to provide a basic description of government. For example, students should know how rules are made, how they are enforced, and how they are interpreted. Students should have some understanding of the types of legislatures that exist (e.g., school boards, city councils, state assemblies, U.S. Congress). They should become familiar with courts of law. They should learn about executives such as their principal, the mayor, and the president. It is important that students see why government is necessary and what life would be like without government.

Students should also learn about power and authority. Why does a city council have the power to make laws? Where did it get that power? Students should understand the authority of teachers and principals. They should also recognize examples of "power without authority," such as a robber holding up a bank or a playground bully harassing another student. Young students need to explore the purposes of rules and laws. They should recognize that rules describe the way people must behave. Again, critical analysis is necessary for good social studies lessons because the national standards expect students to evaluate laws according to criteria. Are our classroom rules understandable? Is a playground rule equitable? Is a city ordinance possible to follow and not a demand for the impossible? Finally, under this question, students should begin to understand the concept of limited government. They should see that everyone, including our most powerful elected and appointed officials, must obey the law.

LESSON PLAN

Grade 2: Walking Field Trip—Rules on Signs

A second-grade teacher took her class on a "walking field trip" to the local branch of the city library every month. They looked forward to this event because the children's librarian read aloud a picture book to them, and the children could use their library cards to check out books. The distance from the school to the library was about three

Social studies should teach our students to be good citizens. A key component of good citizenship is participation in community service projects.

quarters of a mile. Two parent volunteers and two sixth graders accompanied the class. The teacher was in the middle of a unit called "Rules and Laws." She decided to use the walk to the library as an opportunity to show her class the many rules that are posted as signs. Here is her lesson plan:

Overview: This lesson is for second graders. It is part of a unit on rules and laws.

Resources and Materials: (a) a 35-mm camera, (b) slide projector, (c) chart paper.

Content Objectives: Children will understand that many rules are posted as signs, that rules describe what people may and may not do, that some rules provide for order and safety, and that other rules protect the rights of people.

Process Objectives: Children will *read* four signs during their walk to the library, *describe* how each rule displayed on a sign limits behavior, and *define* a purpose (safety or protect rights) for each sign.

Values Objectives: This lesson, along with many others, will help children understand and become committed to the democratic value of "the public good," that individual behavior must be limited to achieve an orderly and equitable society.

Teaching Sequence

1. Explain to the children that on this walking trip to the library they will stop to look at rules written on signs. Also review the rules for a walking field trip. (Permission slips from parents have been collected earlier.)

2. Stop at the gate of the fence surrounding the playground and grass field. The sign reads:

   Public welcome to use school grounds when school is not in session. Gates are locked each night at dusk. Use of the following is strictly prohibited:
   Golf clubs
   Alcoholic beverages
   Tobacco products
   Motor vehicles
   Bicycles, skateboards, roller skates, and in-line skates (roller blades)

   Read the sign aloud to the children. Make sure they understand the specific items that may not be used on the playground or grass field. Photograph the sign.

3. Stop along the sidewalk to read to the children the next sign: **No Parking Monday 8–10 a.m.** Photograph the sign.

4. Stop at the speed limit sign and read it aloud: **35 mph.** Photograph the sign.

5. At the library, stop at the sign that reserves parking spaces for people with disabilities. The sign is blue and has a white logo for handicapped parking (a person in a wheelchair). Read it aloud to the children: **Reserved for Handi-capped.** Photograph the sign. Tell the children that after your photographs are developed, you will talk some more about the signs.

6. After the photographs are developed as slides, continue the lesson. Make a chart with three columns: "Rule," "How It Limits Us," and "Why." Show the slide for the first sign (prohibiting the use of certain things on the playground and on the grass field). Read it aloud and discuss it. On the chart, summarize it as "Public use of playground." Help the children understand that this rule limits the items that people can use on the playground. Under the second heading, "How It Limits Us," write down the statement that the children generate; it will probably go something like "Things that can't be used on the playground." The children should understand that many people would like to use the prohibited items on the weekends and early evenings at the school. Don't be surprised if some children have seen this rule being violated. Help the children understand this is a safety rule because the use of golf clubs, alcohol, and skateboards creates many dangers. So, under "Why," write "Makes the playground and grass field safe for everyone."

7. Follow the same procedure for the no parking sign, the speed limit sign, and the handicapped parking sign. The no parking and speed limit signs also are safety signs. The handicapped parking sign is different because it protects the rights of people with disabilities. It is a good example of a rule that reflects a commitment to the common good and respect for minority rights (the majority of the population, who do not have disabilities, give up the chance to

park in the reserved spots so that people with disabilities can more easily use the library).

Effective Teaching in Today's Diverse Classroom: This activity could be difficult for your English language learners. In Cummins's terms, "cognitive demand" is high. Therefore, you need to "embed" the lesson "contextually" (support your English language learners as they tackle a challenging lesson). What could you do? First, your English language learners could have difficulty reading the sign on the playground. You might want to take them aside the day before the lesson and paraphrase the message of the sign in a simplified English they can understand. Fortunately, the other signs are easy to understand (no parking, 35 mph, handicapped logo). Unless your English language learners have a high level of oral English proficiency, they will not be able to participate in completing the chart. After your English language learners listen to the class discussion that leads to completion of the chart, you should work with them in a group and discuss the chart in its final form.

2. *What are the basic values and principles of American democracy?* As a knowledge goal, we want students to describe the important values and principles of our system of government and civic life.

3. *How does the government established by the Constitution embody the purposes, values, and principles of American democracy?* Elementary students should know what the U.S. Constitution is and the important ideas in it. Most social studies programs save most of this material until fifth grade. An important topic that should be explored before fifth grade is how the Constitution and the federal government protect individual rights. Students should begin to understand their First Amendment freedoms. Most fourth graders will learn about their state government and the specifics of their legislature, judiciary, and executive. Third grade has usually been the place where students study municipal government. In any case, by the end of fourth grade, the national standards state that students should know what services their local government provides, how the services are funded, and how people can participate in local government.

4. *What is the relationship of the United States to other nations and to world affairs?* Remember, a valid criticism of the expanded horizons curricular framework is the lack of global education in Grades K–5. The national standards call for students in Grades K–4 to develop knowledge in several international areas. Students should understand the concept of nation. I have found this to be difficult for young students, who frequently cannot understand the difference between a state in the United States, such as Vermont, and a sovereign nation, such as Germany. One concept that students can begin to understand is the interdependence of nations. They should be able to identify cultural exchanges (e.g., music from another nation), trade (products grown or manufactured in other nations), and military linkages (multinational military operations). Students should learn about examples of how nations solve problems peacefully.

5. *What are the roles of the citizen in American democracy?* Students are expected to know the definition of *citizenship,* how people become citizens of the United States, the rights of citizens, the responsibilities of citizens, how we select our leaders, and how U.S. citizens can participate in their government. Following is a mini-unit developed by a fifth-grade teacher with the goal of teaching her students about a basic right afforded us in the U.S. Constitution—a fair trial.

MINI-UNIT

Grade 5: "Fair Trials"

This mini-unit is appropriate for a fifth grade-class engaged in a larger unit on the U.S. Constitution. This mini-unit looks at sections of the Fifth and Sixth Amendments, which guarantee the rights constituting the basis for a "fair trial." Students will participate in a mock trial, *The State v. The Big Bad Wolf,* based on a journal article by Judith Norton (1992). This simulation is an excellent way for students to learn about the U.S. system of criminal trials. Students will analyze a fictional judicial procedure presented in the award-winning historical novel *The Witch of Blackbird Pond* (Speare, 1958). The *National Standards for Civics and Government* (Center for Civic Education, 1994) provides the organizing framework for the mini-unit. The performance expectation is part of the national standards for Grades 5 through 8 (see p. 75 of the standards).

Part I: Organizing Framework

What Are the Roles of the Citizen in American Democracy?

What Are the Rights of Citizens?

(1) Personal Rights. Students should be able to evaluate, take, and defend positions on issues involving personal rights. To achieve this standard, students should be able to identify personal rights and identify the major documentary sources of personal rights (e.g., U.S. Constitution).

This mini-unit will teach students about the specific rights listed in the Fifth and Sixth Amendments, collectively referred to as the right to a fair trial.

This mini-unit answers three questions:

Unit Question 1: What rights in the Fifth and Sixth Amendments to the U.S. Constitution guarantee a fair trial for people accused of crimes?

Unit Question 2: What happens during a trial of someone accused of a crime?

Unit Question 3: Can we identify the rights that are not respected in criminal trials conducted in the United States before the Constitution was written?

Part II: Instructional Activities

Unit Question 1: What rights in the Fifth and Sixth Amendments to the U.S. Constitution guarantee a fair trial for people accused of crimes?

Teacher-Directed Lesson on the Fifth and Sixth Amendments

Content Objectives: Students will learn the specific rights guaranteed by the Fifth and Sixth Amendments.

Process Objectives: Students will *identify* the Fifth and Sixth Amendment rights of people accused of crimes; *define* capital crime, indictment, double jeopardy, self-incrimination, jury, and witness; and speculate on what would happen if the rights did not exist.

1. Provide copies of the Fifth and Sixth Amendments to each student. Show the class transparencies of the amendments on the overhead projector.
2. With the class, create a chart that lists the following rights:

Rights of People Accused of Crimes
From the Fifth Amendment:

1. Can't be tried for capital crime without a grand jury indictment
2. Can't be tried for the same crime twice (no double jeopardy)
3. Can't be made to testify (no self-incrimination)

From the Sixth Amendment:

4. Right to a speedy trial
5. Right to a public trial
6. Right to be judged by a jury
7. Right to be informed of the nature of the crime
8. Right to confront witnesses
9. Right to summon witnesses
10. Right to be represented by a lawyer

Discuss each of these rights with the class. Be sure students understand terms such as *capital crime, indictment, double jeopardy, self-incrimination, jury,* and *witness.* Then, for each right, help students understand what would happen if that right did not exist. For example, ask, "What would happen if we did not have a right to a public trial?" (Help students understand that trials conducted in private could ignore all the rights protected by the amendments—that public trials guarantee the procedure can be evaluated for fairness.)

Unit Question 2: What happens during a trial of someone accused of a crime?

Mock Trial

Content Objectives: Students will learn the definitions of several crimes; the roles of the judge, the clerk, the defendant, attorneys, the jury, and witnesses in a criminal trial; and how the rights in the Fifth and Sixth Amendments are applied in a criminal trial.

Process Objectives: Students will *understand* the definitions of seven crimes; *identify* which crimes the wolf should be charged with; *play the role* of one of the participants in the trial; *gather* and *analyze* physical evidence; *participate* in the mock trial; and *distinguish* which rights were essential parts of the trial.

Note: This activity will take from 4 to 7 days.

1. Read aloud a version of the fairy tale "Little Red Riding Hood." Then present the revised set of facts on page 5 of Judith Norton's article (the wolf beats, not eats, Grandma; the wolf strikes a police officer prior to arrest; the wolf has marijuana in his pocket).
2. Distribute a copy of the "criminal code" from page 5 of Norton's article. The code defines seven crimes: battery, assault, theft, possession of marijuana, resisting arrest, disorderly conduct, and felonious restraint. Help students understand the definition of each. Then ask the class to decide which crimes the wolf should be charge with.
3. Begin work on the mock trial. Norton's simulation has the following roles: judge, court clerk, defendant (the wolf), defense attorneys, prosecuting attorneys, the jury, and witnesses (Little Red Riding Hood, Grandma, arresting officers). Norton suggests that you create some defense witnesses who try to provide the wolf with an alibi or vouch for his character. You can even add "expert witnesses."
4. Gather the physical evidence for the case. This can include a medical report on Grandma's beating, a blood-stained carpet, paw prints, and the police report.
5. Be sure the witnesses know what they are supposed to say. Then, work with the defense attorneys on their case. What questions will they ask? Work with the prosecuting attorneys. How will they present their evidence? What should they ask each witness?
6. Meet with the judge and the clerk and discuss the conduct of the courtroom.
7. Discuss with the entire class the rules of court procedure and proper courtroom conduct (see p. 6 of Norton's article).
8. Today is the trial! Norton provides excellent descriptions of how the case should proceed. The key to a good simulation is working with each student before the trial begins so that everyone is comfortable and confident.
9. After the mock trial is over, take another look at the list of rights you compiled in the first lesson (the teacher-directed lesson on the Fifth and Sixth Amend-

ments). Which rights were evident in the mock trial? (Almost all were: public trial, jury, accused informed of nature of crime, accused able to summon and confront witnesses, accused represented by a lawyer).

Unit Question 3: Can we identify the rights that were not respected in criminal trials conducted before the Constitution was written?

Readers' Theater: The Trial in The Witch of Blackbird Pond

Content Objectives: Students will learn that some trials conducted in Colonial America failed to protect the rights of the accused.

Process Objectives: Students will *dramatize* the trial in chapter 19 of the book *The Witch of Blackbird Pond* and analyze the proceedings to identify which rights were denied the accused during the trial.

1. Before the other activities start and while they are progressing, read aloud to the class *The Witch of Blackbird Pond* (Speare, 1958). This is an excellent piece of historical fiction with an appealing story line. The book fits perfectly with the fifth-grade social studies curriculum in most schools—which usually includes Colonial America. This is the story of 16-year-old Katherine (Kit) Tyler, who is the orphaned daughter of English Royalists. She comes to live with her Puritan relatives in Connecticut in 1687 and is accused of being a witch.

2. About a week prior to the performance, select actors for a readers' theater presentation of chapter 19. Suggest that students rehearse their parts so that this exciting chapter can be presented with appropriate characterization. Present chapter 19 to the class through readers' theater. (In chapter 19, Kit is tried as a witch in a judicial proceeding that is similar to a current-day preliminary hearing. The hearing is conducted by the town magistrate, who serves as judge along with two local clergymen.) After the presentation, have the class analyze the proceeding. One hundred years after this fictional event, the U.S. Constitution granted all Americans fundamental judicial rights. What rights was Kit granted? Students should see that she was informed of the charges against her; witchcraft in Colonial Connecticut was a capital offense. Her hearing meets the requirement of a preliminary proceeding in capital cases (the Fifth Amendment mentions a grand jury indictment). As chapter 19 explains, Kit was not entitled to a jury at this phase because the hearing would determine whether she would be sent to the capital of the colony for a jury trial. Kit was denied certain rights that present-day defendants have in their preliminary hearings. Students should recognize that she did not have an attorney. Also, Kit was forced to testify. Finally, Kit was not allowed to question witnesses, nor was she allowed to call her own witnesses.

3. Although this might be too complicated for fifth graders, you could point out another difference between the proceeding in *The Witch of Blackbird Pond*

and present-day trials: Today, a judge decides at the preliminary hearing whether the accused must stand trial. In *The Witch,* the local judge was joined by two Puritan ministers. The 19th-century New England witch trials were one of the few times in the history of the United States that criminal proceedings were mixed with "ecclesiastical" courts. Ecclesiastical, or religious, courts were common in Europe during the Middle Ages, with full power to convict and punish people. Today, of course, no person can be tried by a religious group unless she or he agrees to participate in the proceeding.

 Effective Teaching in Today's Diverse Classroom: Like the second-grade lesson on rules on signs, this mini-unit will be a challenge for your English language learners. One technique used with English language learners is a form of primary language support called *preview-review.* Before each day's lesson begins, someone who speaks the native language of an English language learner provides that child with a preview of the lesson (this can be you, an instructional aide, or another student). After the lesson has been completed, the English language learner is given a review of the key information and concepts presented in the lesson.

The mock trial will be a real challenge for fifth graders. There will be parts for everybody to play, but try to avoid assigning the most prominent roles only to your most able students. Although no student should be asked to perform publicly at a level beyond his or her ability, you will be surprised how most students can rise to the occasion and exceed your expectations, especially with a little extra help from you!

Citizenship Education: Values

Values are standards we use to judge human behavior. *Civic values* are values relevant to our public life. The *National Standards for Civics and Government* (Center for Civic Education, 1994) are a realistic statement of civic values. The standards call for students to become knowledgeable about the basic values of American democracy. This knowledge "is an essential first step in fostering a reasoned commitment to them" (p. 22). The standards offer this list of fundamental values of American democracy: (a) individual rights to life, liberty, and pursuit of happiness; (b) the public or common good; (c) justice; (d) equality of opportunity; (e) diversity; (f) truth; and (g) patriotism.

The national standards list the following principles of American government: (a) The people are sovereign and are the ultimate source of authority for government, (b) the power of government is limited, (c) the people exercise their authority directly through elections, (d) the people exercise their authority indirectly through elected representatives, and (e) decisions are based on majority rule, but minority rights are respected.

The national standards (Center for Civic Education, 1994) address the relationship of unity and diversity. They state that, by the end of fourth grade, "students

should be able to explain the importance of Americans sharing and supporting certain values, principles, and beliefs" (p. 25). The United States is a place of
many cultural groups, languages, and religions, and the standards correctly state
that "the identity of an American is defined by shared political values, principles, and beliefs" (p. 25). At the same time, "students should be able to describe
diversity in the United States and identify its benefits" (p. 26). A diverse America
provides for new ideas, a range of perspectives on any issue, and choices in all
aspects of life (e.g., the arts, politics). The standards call for students to understand
how diversity can lead to conflict through discrimination and alienation. Social
studies programs should help students see how such conflicts can be avoided and
resolved.

Teaching Democratic Values

Engle and Ochoa (1988) comment that, for teachers, "the temptation is to indoctri-
nate children with the 'right' democratic values" (p. 66). Instead, they call for a study
of values that is analytic. The national standards call for a knowledge of values that
will lead to a "commitment" to them. Thus, for us as teachers, it seems that our first
goal should be to help students understand a value and then to analyze the issues
that can arise when the value guides behavior. Finally, we want students to study
controversial issues and make decisions based on those values.

Grade 6: Solving a School Problem

**Description
of a
PROJECT**

Engle and Ochoa (1988) define a seven-step process for value-based decision
making on public issues. As an example, we will consider this process as it was used
in a sixth-grade classroom. The principal of the school asked that students suggest
how there could be fewer disputes over use of various areas of the playground.
Younger children complained that older children monopolized the more desirable
areas. Engle and Ochoa's seven steps are similar to those for the processes of inquiry
and critical thinking described in chapters 6 and 7:

Step 1: Identify and Define the Problem

In this case, the principal, acting in response to student complaints, defined the
problem: How can the various areas of the playground be used so that there are
fewer arguments about who should be playing where? Some sixth graders did not
think this was a problem. They cited two reasons. First, when they were younger, the
older students "hogged" the good areas. Second, the younger children did not know
how to play some of the games that could only be played in certain areas. At this
point, the teacher turned the discussion toward definitions. Engle and Ochoa note
that this is an important prerequisite to value based decision making. The teacher

wanted agreement on what constituted an "area." After some discussion, the sixth
graders generated the following list of areas:

The sand with the jungle gym
Three diamonds for kickball, one of which has shade for the team that is "up"
Dodgeball circles
Tetherball poles
Two walls for handball games
A small grass field for soccer

Step 2: Identify Value Assumptions

Returning to the issue his sixth graders had raised, that there was no problem regarding the playground areas, the teacher decided to focus on two values: (a) justice
and (b) respect for the rights of others. Engle and Ochoa (1988) wrote that "identifying
value assumptions is not limited to any one phase of the decision-making process"
(p. 74). It is a good idea, though, to clarify and consider values at this stage.

The sixth graders had an extended discussion about justice, equity, and
sharing. The teacher asked for definitions of *justice*. Students responded by saying it
meant that people "were fair" and that "things happened according to fair rules." The
value of justice would seem to require sharing the playground areas. Although all the
students believed in fairness, some had difficulty with the application of this value in
this case. This small group said that justice meant that because they were treated un-
fairly by older students when they were small, it was perfectly fair for them to treat
current fourth graders the same way (fourth, fifth, and sixth graders had recess at the
same time). When coupled with a discussion of the value of respect for others' rights,
this position was difficult to maintain. Other students pointed out that "two wrongs
don't make a right" and that "fourth graders have rights too." The vast majority of the
students agreed that, to respect the rights of all students, the playground areas would
have to be shared.

Step 3: Identify Alternatives

Engle and Ochoa (1988) state that "values, previous knowledge, and experience are all involved in identifying alternatives" (p. 74). At this point, the teacher could
have had his class work in small groups to maximize the number of students who
could participate vigorously. He thought, though, that the whole-group discussion
was progressing well. Students did seem to listen to each other. So far, this was a very
civil discussion. Students had not personalized comments, exchanged threatening
looks, or made rude interruptions. The teacher had two students transcribe ideas as
they were offered. Some ideas were not consistent with the value of justice. One girl
suggested that, for 2 days a week, the areas be assigned to classrooms and that, on
the other 3 days, the current system operate. Another student suggested that each
teacher make a list of students who caused problems and that these students "sit in
the library at recess for the rest of the year."

Two alternatives survived the discussion:

- Because nine classes were at recess together (three classes each in Grades 4, 5, and 6), nine areas should be designated and the classes rotate through them (the "rotation" plan).
- Students could play in any area they wanted, and two sixth-grade monitors would be assigned to each area. The monitors would ensure that all students would have a chance to play the area's game (the "monitor" plan).

Step 4: Predict Consequences

Engle and Ochoa suggest that two questions be considered: (1) What effects will follow from each alternative? and (2) What effect will each alternative have on all parties? Some students noted that the consequence of the rotation plan would be that they would be giving up their prerogative of what to play. Others noted that they wouldn't be able to "play handball everyday, like we want to." Other students interjected the value of justice idea again at this point as they considered the second question. The strength of the rotation plan was its equity; all classes would have the same opportunity to use each area of the playground.

The monitor plan was criticized widely when the sixth graders considered its consequences. First, several sixth graders wouldn't be playing anything; they would be acting as organizers and referees. Although many of the sixth graders would do a good job at these tasks, they would be "giving up" their chance to play. A few noted that the problem might not be solved in the monitor plan. Each area would contain fourth, fifth, and sixth graders. The younger students might continue to be pushed aside. Finally, one student commented that the younger students could not compete with them and that "some of the fourth graders" might get hurt.

Step 5: Reach Decisions

Engle and Ochoa (1988) note that reaching decisions can be filled with tension because, in most cases, no solution satisfies everyone. After considering the consequences, however, this group of sixth graders almost unanimously recommended the rotation plan. The only dissenters were a small group who continued to think that no problem existed and that, as sixth graders, they should claim any area they wanted.

Step 6: Justify Decisions

Once again, the discussion turned to values. When the teacher asked for reasons why the rotation plan was best, several students noted that it was "fair" and would give all classes "the same chance." This was a reliance on justice as a rationale. Other students commented that it seemed to be better than any other plan they could think of. Three students were chosen to present the class's recommendation to the principal (each other class was asked to make a recommendation too).

Step 7: Tentativeness of Decision Making

The teacher wanted his students to understand that their suggested rotation plan seemed like a good one but that it might not work. He prompted his students to remain open-minded and to accept that they may need to revise their perspectives. In this case, it wasn't necessary. The principal adopted the rotation plan. It worked well and has been in place for 4 years now.

 Effective Teaching in Today's Diverse Classroom: Although most comments in this section have dealt with language, culture, and ability, I think the issue here is how to teach children to respect diverse *ideas.* The next section of this chapter explains how we can help our students participate in *civil discourse,* the polite and respectful way citizens in a democracy discuss controversial topics. My 10 years of experience as an elementary school teacher and my 15 years of observation in other teachers' classrooms has convinced me that most children have difficulty respecting perspectives opposite of their own, especially if these are voiced by the least popular members of the class.

Citizenship Education: Processes

The processes of effective citizenship should be practiced at home, in the classroom, on the playground, in the community, and at the state, national, and international levels. Recently, considerable interest has been expressed in expanding *service learning* in the K–12 curriculum (Clark, 1997). Service learning occurs when students participate in community or school activities or projects. A good place to discuss the "doing" of citizenship education is with a set of attitudes, called *dispositions,* that students should adopt. The *National Standards for Civics and Government* (Center for Civic Education, 1994) argues that these dispositions will enhance "citizen effectiveness and promote the healthy functioning of American democracy" (p. 37). These dispositions are beliefs that guide behavior. They include individual responsibility, self-discipline, civility, respect for the rights of other individuals, honesty, respect for the law, open-mindedness, critical-mindedness, negotiation and compromise, persistence, civic-mindedness, compassion, and patriotism. Each of these dispositions involves a process. For example, the process of open-mindedness has many components that can be practiced and developed in the classroom. First, students can learn to listen, without interruption and without preconceived notions, to the opinions of other students. Next, students should learn to question the perspectives of others without personalizing their comments. Finally, students should learn to accept the valid points another person makes, rather than reject all of a message because some parts make little sense.

This open-mindedness is part of civil discourse, the polite way citizens in a democracy discuss public issues. Civil discourse is an essential process for students

As some aspects of social studies change, others remain constant. Computer-based resources are replacing older, traditional resources. At the same time, the development of good citizens remains the most important goal of social studies.

to learn (Rossi, 1996a). In *Civitas,* the curriculum framework developed through the Center for Civic Education, two essential components of civil discourse are defined (Quigley & Bahmueller, 1991, p. 13):

- *Addressing the issue:* Participants in a discussion focus on their contributions to the issues at hand and do not engage in personal attack.
- *Respecting the right of others to be heard:* Civil discourse requires good listening; participants in a discussion should not disrupt other speakers.

W. C. Parker (1995) describes an assessment tool developed in Oakland County, Michigan, to assess student acquisition of civic discourse. Of particular interest is the list of positive and negative behaviors generated by the assessment tool. Positive behaviors during discussions are when the student:

- Acknowledges the statements of others
- Challenges the accuracy, logic relevance, or clarity of statements
- Summarizes points of agreement and disagreement
- Invites contributions of others

Negative behaviors, those not conducive to civil discourse, are when the student:

- Makes irrelevant, distracting statements
- Interrupts, monopolizes the conversation
- Engages in personal attack

We should work with our students so that they consistently demonstrate the positive behaviors and cease to exhibit the negative behaviors. To do this, we will have our work cut out for us because an interesting study conducted by King and King (1998) showed that, in the sixth/seventh combination classroom they studied, students "asserted themselves at the expense of others . . . there was little positive listening" (p. 104).

The national standards go on to define "the means by which citizens can influence the decisions and actions of their government" (Center for Civic Education, 1994, p. 38). These are (a) read about public issues; (b) discuss public issues; (c) communicate with public officials; (d) vote; (e) take an active role in interest groups, political parties, and organizations; and (f) attend meetings of governing agencies, work in campaigns, circulate petitions, take part in peaceful demonstrations, and contribute money to parties, candidates, and causes. Each of these can be implemented in some form in the elementary classroom:

Read About Public Issues. Newsmagazines written for children, like *Weekly Reader,* do an excellent job of presenting national and global issues to children. On-line computer resources are beginning to provide accessible information to elementary students (e.g., the on-line resource KidsNet). Our oldest and most able elementary students can read articles in newspapers, magazines, and on appropriate Web sites on the Internet.

Discuss Public Issues. Children at all elementary levels should discuss issues that relate to their classroom, school, and community. Older elementary children who have read a variety of perspectives should be encouraged to discuss state, national, and global issues.

Communicate with Public Officials. One of the first public officials students should communicate with is their teacher. Students, at the proper time and in a respectful manner, should have the opportunity to talk with us about topics of concern. Students at all levels should learn how to speak and write to their principal on school issues. We should encourage our older students to write to their school board, city council and mayor, state legislature and governor, representatives in Congress, and the president. Our goal as teachers is to present information, to allow a range of perspectives to be heard, and to model written and oral formats of communicating.

Vote. Elementary students should take part in classroom and school elections. These elections should be as close to the real thing as possible. All elections should provide for a secret ballot, even those in the classroom. Many schools are voting places in "real" elections, and it is a good idea to let students experience a voting booth as they vote in mock state and federal elections.

Take an Active Role in Interest Groups, Political Parties, and Organizations. A variety of youth organizations encourage civic life, such as Girl Scouts, Boy Scouts, and youth groups in religious institutions. All elementary schools, however, should have student governments. J. A. Heath and Vik (1994) report how elementary school student councils allow children to exercise leadership, share ideas, resolve problems, and manage projects.

Attend Meetings of Governing Agencies, Work in Campaigns, Circulate Petitions, Take Part in Peaceful Demonstrations, and Contribute Money to Parties, Candidates, and Causes. Students should learn the petitioning process in elementary school. They can petition for changes in classroom and school policies. I know teachers who have encouraged students to consider community issues, to define a position, and to make presentations to the city council. Students can participate in fund-raising drives, but this must be done cautiously. The cause should be noncontroversial and school related, and the process should protect those students who are unable to make a financial contribution. Students should see that they can make contributions in other ways, such as collecting things (e.g., newspapers, cans) or giving one's time.

The real test of the effect of citizenship education is whether or not our students become active citizens when they are older—whether they, in fact, participate when they are not directed to do so by a school assignment. The activities planned as part of the social studies curriculum should show students the range of options available to active citizens in a democratic society.

Participatory Writing

In *Civitas,* Quigley and Bahmueller (1991) provide several examples of a type of civic participation they call *participatory writing.* I discuss this more fully in chapter 9 in the section on language arts and social studies. Examples of participatory writing are listed below:

- *Writing to fellow citizens we do not know.* These citizens could include victims of an earthquake or a person in another state who has done something heroic.
- *Writing to public officials.* For schoolchildren, public officials include their principal. Older students can write to their city councilors, mayor, state legislator, governor, federal representative or senator, or the president.

- *Writing to advocate positions on public issues.* In a schoolwide referendum on a school issue (e.g., how to spend $5,000 of state lottery money awarded to the school), students could write brochures and make posters advocating their position.
- *Writing/Creating public symbols.* Students can create classroom and school mottoes. The United States has *E pluribus unum;* each state has one (e.g., New Mexico's is *Crescit eundo* ["It grows as it goes"]); and a classroom can have a motto too. Or, students could design a flag for their classroom.

Community Service

Proctor and Haas (1993) and Wade (1994) discuss community service as a part of citizenship education for elementary students. Proctor and Haas argue that participation in community service projects should "be a part of formal education beginning in the primary grades and continuing through graduation. The responsibilities and opportunities for community and social behaviors are present and need to begin at an early age" (p. 381). They describe a hierarchy of school-based community service projects:

1. *School service projects.* These include cross-age tutoring, planting trees, raising money to buy computers for the school, and the venerable clean-campus crusade. Many of these projects can be run by the school Parent-Teacher Association. (At the end of this chapter is a description of how a second-grade teacher designed school service projects for her students.)
2. *Community service projects.* These serve the neighborhood and the community. Proctor and Haas suggest that these begin in third grade. Community service projects typically involve cooperation with out-of-school agencies; examples are collecting food for victims of a disaster and converting a vacant lot into a park.
3. *Individual service projects.* Proctor and Haas suggest that these are appropriate for middle school and high school students. These projects involve a commitment of many hours over an extended period of time, such as volunteer work at a preschool or a senior citizen center.

Wade (1994) shows how service projects can integrate the curriculum. Students could prepare a survey asking seniors what services they need (language arts). A school project could require fund-raising, which entails bookkeeping (mathematics). Environmental projects, like a community garden, demand knowledge in botany and ecology (science).

Willison and Ruane (1995) describe how students in each elementary grade of a school they studied provided service to local senior citizens. Kindergartners made holiday cards for residents of a nursing home. First and second graders sang and performed in theatrical programs at the nursing home. Third and fourth graders had senior pen pals and visited seniors who lived on their own. Fifth and sixth graders visited their "adoptive grandparents" at the nursing home, read to them, and played games with them. All the students studied their grandparents and the elderly to break down stereotypical images of old people.

Citizenship and Classroom Management

A discussion of classroom management, the process of promoting and maintaining a productive environment for students, is beyond the scope of a social studies methods textbook. We should realize, however, that citizenship and classroom management are related topics (Brophy, 1985; Goodman, 1992; Hoover & Kindsvatter, 1997; Ross & Bondy, 1993; Schimmel, 1997; Wolfgang & Kelsay, 1995). Although some aspects of classroom management must be exercised by adults, our classrooms should be democratic. Ross and Bondy (1993) note that although teachers and students will never be equals, more teachers should "shift the emphasis away from controlling students' behavior to teaching students how to be responsible members of a community" (p. 328). Students at all grade levels should be allowed to do each of the following:

- *Play some role in the development of classroom and playground rules.* We should establish some rules (e.g., keep your hands and feet to yourself). Many aspects of classroom life, however, lend themselves to a variety of possible rules. Students need the experience of considering possible rules and the consequences of their implementation. Schimmel (1997) makes a persuasive argument that the development of school and classroom rules should involve everyone in the school community—students, parents, and staff.
- *Resolve problems through collaborative effort.* Students should approach us as their teacher with problems they think should be addressed. Likewise, we as teachers should bring some problems to our classroom community for consideration. Some problems have to be resolved only by us with the student(s) directly involved (e.g., problems that reveal private information about students); other issues should be brought before the whole class for an open and democratic discussion. Problem resolution activities will give students a chance to practice civil discourse and value-based decision making.
- *Make decisions about how they allocate their time and about what activities they pursue.* Even though we as teachers plan much of the school day, all our students should have some time when they make choices about what they will do. Likewise, we select most topics covered in class. Our students, though, should be able to choose areas of personal interest to study,

especially in literature, social studies, and science. Democracy requires choices, and the elementary school day should present opportunities for students to learn how to make reasoned and informed decisions.

Schimmel (1997) makes two other important points about classroom rules and citizenship education. First, any list of classroom or school rules should include a list of student rights. Any just legal system is a balance of responsibilities and rights. Too many classroom rule systems are lists of things students may *not* do; there is no corresponding list of what students *may* do. For example, students should have the right to free expression as long as it does not interfere with teaching and learning, the right to a safe classroom environment, the right to participate in classroom activities, and the right to make their grievances known to school authorities.

Second, classroom rules should be taught like any other part of the curriculum. Schimmel (1997) correctly points out that, all too often, classroom rules are presented on the first day of class with little or no explanation. After parents and students have their chance to help create the classroom rules, the rules should be taught through small-group discussion and simulation. Lessons on classroom rules should be a part of a unit on laws in broader jurisdictions, like the school, the city, the state, and the nation. At the very least, students should understand the rationale for each classroom rule. The bottom line is that we cannot expect our students to become effective citizens in a democracy if their classroom experiences are completely undemocratic. Hoover and Kindsvatter (1997) sum it up: "What students learn from our disciplinary activities can significantly shape their future behavior as citizens in our democratic society" (p. 71).

SUMMARY OF KEY POINTS

▶ The development of good citizens is the most important goal of social studies.

▶ Controversy surrounds whether citizenship education should be limited to information on how government works with a definition of a good citizen as a person who follows the rules and votes (transmission), or whether citizenship education should teach students to analyze current issues and to take action for social change (transformation).

▶ The content of citizenship education is government and civics. Students should learn about what government is, what government should do, the basic principles and values of American democracy, the U.S. Constitution, the relationship of the United States to other nations, and the nature of good citizenship.

▶ Social studies programs should make students knowledgeable about basic American civic values. This knowledge should serve as the basis for a commitment to those values.

▶ A process of value-based decision making includes identifying social problems, identifying relevant values, identifying alternative courses of action, predicting consequences of actions, reaching a decision, and justifying a decision.

▶ Good citizens in a democracy are active. Active citizenship requires participation: reading about public issues, discussing public issues, communicating with public officials, voting, taking an active role in political organizations, and attending meetings.

▶ Elementary school children can participate in a variety of school and community service projects.

▶ We cannot expect our students to become effective citizens in a democracy if their classroom experiences are completely undemocratic; students should play some role in developing rules, resolve problems through collaborative effort, and make decisions about how they spend their time.

▶ Citizenship must provide for unification, as all students learn about our common core of democratic values; citizenship education must celebrate diversity as an inevitable and desirable outcome of life in a democratic society.

FOR FURTHER READING

▶ The Web site of the Center for Civic Education has many useful links *(http://www.civiced.org)*.

▶ Grant and Vansledright (1996), in their well-reasoned article, dissent from the view that citizenship education is the heart of social studies. They argue that the relationship between social studies and citizenship is "tangential at best" (p. 57).

▶ The January 1996 issue of *Social Education* has several excellent articles on teaching controversial issues (Rossi, 1996b). The March/April 1996 issue of *Social Studies and the Young Learner* addresses moral, social, and civic issues (Alter, 1996). The September/October 1997 issue of *Social Studies and the Young Learner* has the theme Teaching Young Citizens (Field, 1997); that issue contains many excellent articles, particularly Gloria Alter's (1997) piece on curriculum design.

Values and Moral Education

▶ The teaching of values and the related topic of moral education has generated a great deal of published material. In this chapter, I have focused on civic values. On other approaches to teaching a broader set of values, I like two older works: Kirschenbaum (1977) and Raths, Harmin, and Simon (1978). Another excellent book is by Fine (1995).

▶ If you are interested in moral and character education, be sure to read the classic works by Kohlberg (1981) and Gilligan (1982). See also Benninga

(1991) and Lickona (1991). The Fall/Winter 1997 issue of *Social Studies Review,* the journal of the California Council for the Social Studies, has the theme Character Education (Brooks, 1997).

Law-Related Education

- ▶ Bjorklun (1995) discusses how to teach personal injury law.
- ▶ Hicks and Austin (1994), like J. Norton (1992), show how fairy tales can be used as the basis for mock trials. Hickey (1990), Smagorinsky (1994), and Selwyn (1995) discuss legal simulations.
- ▶ McCall (1996) provides a set of guidelines for teachers who want to integrate social problems and social action in the curriculum. If you want to introduce controversial issues in your classroom and have students take action, then this article is essential reading.

Curriculum Frameworks

- ▶ *Expectations of Excellence: Curriculum Standards for Social Studies* (NCSS, 1994) has two themes that relate to citizenship education. Theme 9, Power, Authority, and Governance, covers the content of civics and government. Theme 10, Civic Ideals and Practices, sets standards for civic values and participation.
- ▶ Although they are lengthy, both *Civitas* (Quigley & Bahmueller, 1991) and the *National Standards for Civics and Government* (Center for Civic Education, 1994) are worthy documents full of important information.

Classroom Management and Citizenship Education

- ▶ I suggest three books, *Teaching Children to Care: Management in the Responsive Classroom* (Charney, 1993), *Preparing for Citizenship* (Mosher, Kenney, & Garrod, 1994), and *Democratic Discipline: Foundation and Practice* (Hoover & Kindsvatter, 1997).

Chapter 12

History and Geography:
Understanding People
of Different Times
and Places

ancy Grant's third graders were working on a unit titled "All About Us." All the children were to complete a project on a history of their families. The choices were (a) complete a family tree, (b) write a biography of one of your grandparents, and (c) make a family timeline. Lourdes Delgado wanted to make a family timeline. Mrs. Grant explained that Lourdes would have to be selective because it would be impossible to put every important event on the timeline. The first step, then, was to compile a list of the dates that were to be charted. After talking with her mother and father, Lourdes decided on the following:

1994: The Delgado family takes a vacation to Yellowstone National Park.
1992: Maria Chacon, Lourdes's great-great-grandmother, dies at the age of 101.
1987: Lourdes Delgado is born.
1978: The first of Lourdes's three brothers is born.
1977: Lourdes's father and mother buy a house in Burbank. The family has lived there ever since.
1974: Hector Delgado and Teresa Chacon marry at Mission San Fernando.
1973: Hector Delgado (her father) and Teresa Chacon (her mother) graduate from California State University, Northridge.
1949: Lourdes's grandfather and grandmother Delgado move from Mexico City to California.
1937: Lourdes's grandfather and grandmother Chacon move from Guadalajara to California.

Next, Mrs. Grant helped Lourdes figure the time span to be covered by the timeline. It would have to cover 58 years (1937 to 1995). Lourdes wanted to make her timeline on a sheet of poster board 2 ft × 3 ft. If she left room for margins, she would have to place 58 years on a line 30 in. long (so each side would have a 3-in. margin). To make it easier, Mrs. Grant suggested that Lourdes have the timeline cover 60 years and that each half inch would represent a year. After Mrs. Grant helped Lourdes figure the proper scale for the timeline, the rest was easy. She left space at the top of the poster for her title ("The History of My Family: Lourdes Delgado"). Lourdes then drew her line and marked the 2-in. intervals. Mrs. Grant suggested that she place larger marks for the years 1940, 1950, 1960, 1970, 1980, and 1990. This confused Lourdes for a moment, before she realized she needed to measure halfway between the mark for 1939 and the mark for 1941 to find the correct location for 1940. She then wrote "1940" in bold numbers below the mark. Then, Lourdes wrote the years below the marks for the designated years on her timeline: 1937, 1949, 1973, 1977, 1978, 1987, 1992, 1994. She found that she had to write small and to stagger the placement of the years. Finally, she wrote brief captions under each year, explaining what happened. With great pride, Lourdes displayed her timeline on a side bulletin board with projects other children completed.

This project was valuable because Lourdes learned a great deal about her family and about the history of her community in Southern California. At the same time, she experienced firsthand the "doing" of history—gathering data, organizing it chronologically, and presenting it in a format that could be understood by other people.

▲   ▲   ▲

In this chapter, you will read about:

- ▶ Research that describes the ability of students to understand historical concepts
- ▶ Using the national history standards to determine the historical content that should be taught in the elementary school
- ▶ The historical processes students should master
- ▶ Guidelines for teaching with primary sources, historical fiction, and timelines
- ▶ Research on geographic teaching and learning
- ▶ Using the national geography standards to determine the geographic content that should be taught in the elementary school
- ▶ How to teach students to use symbols, scales, grids, and direction to read maps
- ▶ How to teach students to make mental maps, relief maps, and thematic maps

History and Social Studies

History has been a part of the elementary school curriculum since the United States became a nation (Downey, 1985; Downey & Levstik, 1988, 1991; Levstik, 1991). Controversy, however, has surrounded the role history should play in the social studies curriculum: Should elementary social studies focus primarily on history? Or should history assume a less central role as time is devoted to the other social sciences (anthropology, economics, political science) and topics of special interest (environmental education, global education)? During the late 1980s, some authorities thought U.S. students knew too little about the past because the study of history had been diminished to make room for content from the other social sciences. These authorities advocated that history once again be the primary focus of social studies (Bradley Commission on History in the Schools, 1988; Finn & Ravitch, 1988; Ravitch & Finn, 1987). This view was reflected in the national educational reform efforts of the early 1990s as the U.S. Department of Education funded the writing of national standards for history. How much history we teach as part of our social studies program will depend on decisions made by our state government and our local school board.

Publication of the national standards for history by the National Center for History in the Schools in 1994 resulted in an unparalleled level of national debate from both educators and those outside education over what students should know and be able to do historically. Critics thought the standards were guilty of "multicultural excess and political correctness," in that they gave too much attention to women and people of color (Nash & Dunn, 1995, p. 5). It is impossible to include everything and everybody in the social studies curriculum, and historical events are subject to interpretation, so whenever some group decides what aspects of history should be taught, questions inevitably arise about "whose history" is being presented. The national standards are in four documents: *National Standards for History for Grades K–4: Expanding Children's World in Time and Space, National Standards for United States History: Exploring the American Experience, National Standards for World History: Exploring Paths to the Present* (National Center for History in the Schools, 1994a, 1994b, 1994c), and an abbreviated version of those documents, published in 1996, *National Standards for History: Basic Edition*. It is difficult to say how influential the standards will be on textbook publishers and local school districts. Political conservatives have viewed national standards as a federal intrusion on the traditional prerogative of local authorities to determine what children are taught, and they have been particularly critical of the history standards (R. Cohen, 1996). Advocates of the national standards note that they broaden the scope of history with increased emphasis on the histories of Africa, Asia, women, people of color, and the "everyday" lives of common people (Nash & Dunn, 1995). Before examining the historical content that children should learn, let's look at what research reveals about the capacity of children to learn historical concepts.

Research on Children's Ability to Understand History

Many elementary school children, especially if their social studies curriculum follows the "expanding environments" model, receive virtually no historical content until fourth grade, when they study their state. A rationale for delaying the study of the past has been that small children (before age 8) are unable to understand historical concepts (Thorton & Vukelich, 1988).

Research has shown, however, that this view is unwarranted (Barton, 1997; Barton & Levstik, 1996; Downey & Levstik, 1991; Levstik, 1991). One reason why educators misunderstood the capacity of children to learn history is that a previous model of the child's cognitive development and historical thinking, called the "Piaget-Peel-Hallam" model, underestimated what children can learn (Downey & Levstik, 1991). British scholars E. A. Peel and Roy Hallam applied Jean Piaget's stage theory of cognitive development to historical thinking. They concluded that children need to be at the "formal level" of cognitive operations to understand the past. History would have to wait until junior high school! This model is flawed because it was based on faulty experimental tasks and does not represent an accurate portrait of the abilities of children.

The most important study of children's understanding of history was completed by Keith Barton and Linda Levstik (1996). Barton and Levstik were critical of previous studies, noting that almost all earlier research on this topic suffered from one of the following flaws: (a) The researchers drew conclusions without evidence, (b) the researchers failed to consider the possibility that children younger than age 8 could understand historical concepts, and (c) the studies reflected a limited view of history, focusing solely on the sequence of dates.

Barton and Levstik (1996) asked children from kindergarten to Grade 6 (a) to place in sequence nine pictures and (b) to explain their rationale for doing so (the pictures, both photographs and drawings, depicted scenes from 1772 to 1993). The results were fascinating and important for elementary teachers. First, the youngest students can make distinctions in historical time. Kindergartners and first graders were able to go beyond a simple split between pictures that belonged either in "long ago" or "close to now" categories. Most kindergartners and first graders and all the second graders identified other categories as they recognized some pictures that were older than the ones they had seen previously, whereas other pictures were identified as being newer, and some were placed between the previous pictures.

Second, for the most part, kindergartners and first and second graders have no sense of what dates signify. Not until third grade do children try to assign dates to the pictures. Beginning in fourth grade, dates are useful to children, although not until fifth or sixth grade did children in the study use dates to identify the pictures accurately. Third, almost all children, regardless of age, seem to think that "a particular time is characterized by only one image" (Barton & Levstik, 1996, p. 440). For example, children in the study did not seem to understand that illustrations continued to be drawn after the invention of photography; thus, they thought that any drawing was automatically older than any photograph. Nor did the children understand that while pioneers were building cabins in the 1880s, large cities were being built in other geographic areas. Their rationale was "first there were pioneers, then there were cities" (p. 440). As with any study, the results of this one may someday be challenged, but it seems safe to say that children at all elementary grades should have a social studies curriculum that includes historical content.

History in the Elementary School: Content

The expanding environments approach to social studies defined a curriculum with little historical content until students reached the fourth grade. Kindergarten and first- and second-grade social studies curricula have focused on social development, the school, the family, and the neighborhood. Third graders studied their community, with a small amount of local history. Not until fourth grade, when students learn about their state, was any significant historical content presented. Fifth-grade social studies, following the expanded environments framework, has always been historical, as students learned about the history of the United States. Sixth grade covered foreign nations—typically Canada, Mexico, Central America, and South America. So, in the traditional scheme, global content has been covered in Grade 6, but virtually not before that grade level.

Although they have generated considerable controversy, the national history standards represent the combined effort of many dedicated historians and educators. Let's take a look at the proposed topics for Grades K through 4 included in the *National Standards for History for Grades K–4* (National Center for History in the Schools, 1994a). The eight content standards will help us understand what students in Grades K through 4 should know:

1. *Students should understand family life now and in the recent past; family life in various places long ago.* This standard represents a shift in several states and school districts. Rather than learn only political and economic history, students should learn about their personal histories and the everyday lives of people in the past.

2. *Students should understand the history of their own local community and how communities in North America varied long ago.* Community history has traditionally been a part of elementary social studies. Students should use a variety of resources to learn about their community, including field trips, old photographs, newspapers, and interviews with senior citizens.

3. *Students should understand the people, events, problems, and ideas that were significant in creating the history of their state.* State history, long the focus of fourth-grade social studies, should cover the Natives who first lived in the state, the early non-Native explorers of their state, and the people who have moved to their state throughout its history.

4. *Students should understand how democratic values came to be and how they have been exemplified by people, events, and symbols.* Many state and local social studies curricula delay this topic until fifth grade. This national standard bridges history and citizenship and calls for students to understand how the United States was formed through a revolution with England and to identify the basic principles in the Declaration of Independence and the U.S. Constitution. Other parts of this standard are familiar topics for the early grades: national holidays, American symbols, the Pledge of Allegiance, and the national anthem.

5. *Students should understand the causes and nature of various movements of large groups of people into the United States now and long ago.* This standard combines history and geography. Included here would be the forced relocation of Native Americans; the stories of immigrant groups who have come to the United States throughout our history; the internal migrations of African Americans, Mexican and Puerto Rican workers, and Dust Bowl families; and the 20th-century migration of Americans from farms to cities.

6. *Students should understand folklore and other cultural contributions from various regions of the United States and how they help form a national heritage.* Students should be able to describe regional folk heroes, stories, and songs; use folk literature to describe the way people lived in various sections of the United States; and describe the national influence of regional art, crafts, music, and language.

7. *Students should understand selected attributes and historical developments of societies in such places as Africa, the Americas, Asia, and Europe.* This standard represents an attempt to internationalize the social studies curriculum and is an important addition to the typical K–3 fare of family, classroom, neighborhood, and city. Students would compare and contrast different structures of family life, retell folktales and legends, describe significant historical achievements of many cultural groups, and analyze the art produced by various cultural groups.

8. *Students should understand discoveries in science and technology, some of their social and economic effects, and the major scientists and inventors responsible for them.* The content in this standard seems like a worthwhile addition to the elementary curriculum, especially as students face technological change at an unprecedented

The challenge of teaching history to children is how to make the past "come alive." This student gets a good sense of what it was like to go to school in the 19th century as she uses a fountain pen and a bottle of ink.

pace. Students would examine changes in transportation and communication and learn about the technological achievements of many cultural groups, such as Chinese paper, Mayan calendars, Egyptian mummies, and English steam engines.

This list just covers the historical content for Grades K through 4! The *National Standards for United States History* (National Center for History in the Schools, 1994b) and the *National Standards for World History* (National Center for History in the Schools, 1994c) set ambitious goals for fifth and sixth graders. These standards, which cover Grades 5 through 12, call for students to learn an incredible amount of information about national and world history. The specific historical content we teach will depend on the curriculum frameworks for our state and the curriculum guide for our school district (which may or may not reflect the national standards).

History in the Elementary School: Processes

In addition to their acquiring historical information, we want our students to become proficient at several historical processes. This is the "doing" of history, as students begin to think and act like historians. The *National Standards for History for Grades K–4* (National Center for History in the Schools, 1994a) provides a useful categorization of the thinking and doing skills of history:

1. *Chronological thinking.* This includes the ability to distinguish past, present, and future time; establish temporal order in constructing their own historical narratives; measure and calculate calendar time; make and interpret timelines; and explain continuity and change over time.
2. *Historical comprehension.* Students should be able to reconstruct the literal meaning of a historical passage, identify important questions in historical narratives, identify historical perspectives, use historical maps, find information in illustrations, and understand data in charts and graphs.
3. *Historical analysis and interpretation.* This is an essential set of skills for the historically literate. It includes the ability to formulate questions for inquiry, compare and contrast different ideas, distinguish fact and fiction, compare different versions of the same event, explain causes in historical events, and hypothesize how the past has influenced the present.
4. *Historical research capabilities.* Students should be able to state historical questions, locate historical data, interpret data, and use their knowledge to write a story, explanation, or narrative.
5. *Historical issues: Analysis and decision making.* These important critical-thinking skills include the ability to identify issues in the past, compare the

interests and values of various people, suggest alternative choices for solving a historical problem, prepare a position on an issue, and evaluate the consequences of a decision.

These historical processes usually are taught through participation in lessons that present historical content. It is possible, however, to design lessons that focus solely on historical processes. For example, consider the following mini-unit.

Grade 6: "The Historian as Detective"

Gavrish (1995) describes a unit titled "The Historian as Detective." Although designed for secondary students, it could be adapted to teach historical methodology in elementary classrooms. The organizing framework for the unit draws on the national history standards (*National Standards for History: Basic Edition,* National Center for History in the Schools, 1996).

Part I: Organizing Framework

Standards in Historical Thinking

Standard 3: Historical Analysis and Interpretation: (D) distinguish fact and fiction and (G) consider multiple perspectives

In this mini-unit, students will be asked to think like historians as they deal with the unreliability of eyewitness accounts, work with primary sources, and challenge the accuracy of a document.

This mini-unit answers three questions:

Unit Question 1: To the historian, how reliable are eyewitness accounts?
Unit Question 2: What are primary sources, and why are they more valuable than secondary sources?
Unit Question 3: How do historians challenge the accuracy of documents they read?

Part II: Instructional Activities

Unit Question 1: To the historian, how reliable are eyewitness accounts?

Activity I

Content Objectives: Students will learn that eyewitness accounts are not always trustworthy and that this causes a problem for the historian.

Description
of a
**MINI-
UNIT**

Process Objectives: Students will *examine* the geographic figures on the board, *draw* what they recall, and *assess* the accuracy of their recollections.

1. Tape three diagrams to the chalkboard. Each should have an outer figure (e.g., circle, square) of one color and an inner figure of another color. Tell the students, "Look at these diagrams." Leave the diagrams on the board for a short time and then remove them. Then ask the students to draw each diagram from memory: What shape is the outer figure? What color? What shape is the inner figure? What color? This task puts students in the same place as the historian, who cannot replay events. Have the students work in small groups to determine the accuracy of their drawings.
2. Help students draw the comparison between this exercise and eyewitness accounts of historical events. Why might historical events be faulty? (With the diagrams, bias is not the issue. Like eyewitnesses to real events, the students (a) may have faulty memory and (b) probably did not look as carefully as they would have had they known they would be asked to recall specific details.

Unit Question 2: What are primary sources, and what is their value to the historian?

Activity 2

Content Objectives: Students will learn the definition of primary sources and understand their value to the historian.

Process Objectives: Students will *list* and *evaluate* the value of the sources they could use to write an accurate autobiography. They will *define* primary source and *state* the value of primary sources to historians.

1. In the second activity, students consider what sources of information they would use to answer questions like the following: Where were you born? How much did you weigh at birth? What age were you when you took your first step? What age were you when you said your first word? Read aloud the questions. Then ask the class what sources of information they would use to answer those questions. Students will probably say they would just ask their parents (or other family members). Ask the students to recall what they learned in the previous lesson about the unreliability of eyewitness accounts. Then ask them what other sources they could use besides parents or other family members. Help students see that several sources would be useful: birth certificates, baby books, photographs. Have documents for one student (or even yourself!) available to use as examples (these should be copies, and the parents and the student must approve of their use). Point out that these are all *primary sources.*

2. Tell the class that if a classmate were to write a biography of you, that biography would be a *secondary source.* Make sure the class understands the distinction between primary and secondary sources. Finally, ask the students why primary sources are so valuable to the historian.

Unit Question 3: How do historians challenge the accuracy of documents they read?

Activity 3

Content Objectives: Students will see that not all written documents are accurate.

Process Objectives: Students will *read* the historical letter prepared by the teacher and *identify* examples of historical inaccuracy.

1. In this third activity, students are told about a letter that was recently "discovered." Actually, you will have to create such a letter or use the one created by Gavrish (1995) in his article. His fake letter was supposedly written by George Washington. You could write your own, so long as the letter is full of historical errors (anachronisms) that make it an obvious fake. The sample letter provided by Gavrish has many errors (it is written to Queen Victoria, it is written in Chicago, and it mentions the use of tanks in battle). Show the students the letter and challenge them to find each error.
2. I would have students work in small groups and share the errors they find. This lesson helps students learn to analyze a document. It shows that historians must view primary sources with a critical eye.

Effective Teaching in Today's Diverse Classroom: The first two activities in this mini-unit have features that would make them appropriate for a diverse student population. In the first, when students are drawing the geometric figures from memory, they do not need to be able to read grade-level texts to be successful. The second activity is based on shared, personal experience of the students—their births! One caution is in order here, though. Some students will have access to more primary source data about their births than their classmates. Whereas some students will have baby books, photographs, and birth certificates, others will not (for any of a number of reasons). Try to obtain birth-related primary source material for four or five students and use it for the lesson. The third activity is a challenging one. To find the errors in the historically inaccurate letter, students will need to know enough historical information to spot the mistakes. Because you will write the fake letter (or use the one from Gavrish, 1995), I suggest you write it so that your students will find it easy to read. Your goal is to help them see that written documents can be inaccurate, and this can be accomplished with an easy-to-read document.

Teaching History in the Elementary School

Perhaps it would be a good idea for us to review here the elements of effective social studies teaching in a classroom with a diverse student population presented in previous chapters. Because so much of teaching social studies is teaching history, the elements are worth repeating:

- For our English language learners, learning history will require a great deal of contextual support (cooperative learning, visual aids, hands-on activities, modification of how the teacher talks, primary-language support).
- A variety of lesson plans and teaching sequences should be used to teach history. For some lessons, Hunter's seven-step plan will work; for others, we may want to use a teaching sequence designed for inquiry, the use of artifacts, or critical thinking.
- Cooperative learning can be used effectively to teach historical content; it is essential for students to practice historical analysis and interpretation.
- Because the events of the past are subject to many interpretations, activities that require critical thinking, like the integrative model for teaching reasoning and content, are important in teaching history. Inquiry activities should be a part of every unit that has historical content.
- History must be taught through a variety of resources: textbooks, children's literature, reference material, charts and graphs, films, realia, and computer-based resources. In the report of their study, Barton and Levstik (1996) make a persuasive case for the importance of visual images in teaching history. Pictures should be used frequently as a teaching tool, and students should be encouraged to show what they know by drawing.
- The history curriculum should be transformed so that our students learn about women, children, immigrants, African Americans, Native Americans, religious minorities, and those who have dissented from the majority. Also, history should be personalized and localized; an effective means is through oral history. Barton and Levstik (1996) argue that "the most accessible knowledge for younger children [is] related to material culture and the patterns of everyday life" (p. 442). The best way to introduce students to another time is through food, clothing, household tools, schools, play, and the other things and experiences children know firsthand.

As with other aspects of social studies, historical teaching in the elementary school has been too dependent on the textbook. Isabel Beck, Margaret McKeown, and their colleagues have published some revealing research about how history is presented in elementary social studies textbooks (Beck et al., 1995; McKeown, Beck, Sinatra, & Loxterman, 1991). Generally, they have found that textbooks do a poor job of presenting historical material and that textbook passages can be rewritten so that they are easier to understand. Children do not understand historical cause and effect and will need clarification and explanation. Also, when historical passages had a "voice" and sounded more like historical fiction, children learned more history. Textbooks should never be the sole resource for teaching historical content; rather, they should be used in concert with other resources.

Let's now look at three resources that are essential for good history teaching history in an elementary classroom: (a) primary sources, (b) children's fiction, and (c) timelines.

Primary Sources

The essential resource for the professional historian is the primary source. A *primary source* is a document, work of art, or artifact produced during the period being studied. To teach history well, we must have our students work with primary sources. Teaching with primary sources has two problems: (a) We must locate sources that are relevant to the time period we are covering, and (b) the sources must be comprehensible to our students. Actually, primary sources can be found in many places. The Internet has become an excellent resource for primary sources. I have found that the "History/Social Studies Web Site for K–12 Teachers" is the best place to begin a search *(http://execpc.com/~dboals/boals.html)*. For example, if we were studying the American Civil War, we could use material on the "Poetry and Music of the War Between the States" Web site *(http://www.erols.com/kfraser)*; this site has poetry written by women on the home front, both North and South. Several sites have the narratives of former slaves. The oral histories collected by WPA researchers from 1936 to 1938 are available at "American Slave Narratives" *(http://xroads.virginia.edu/~HYPER/wpa.wpahome.html)*, a Web site maintained by the University of Virginia. Several narratives include descriptions of life as a slave during the war. The addition of these poems, songs, and narratives, usually omitted from a unit on the Civil War, could transform a curriculum by providing students with access to voices too long ignored in elementary social studies.

Fortunately, the newest elementary school social studies textbooks incorporate more primary source material than textbooks published in the past. Many textbooks now include excerpts from diaries and newspapers and reproductions of old maps and paintings. When it comes to artifacts, a good museum is essential, and many cities have excellent museums of local history. Field trips to museums give students a chance to examine historical artifacts. The Internet has made it possible to take virtual tours of museums (again, I suggest using the "History/Social Studies Web Site for K–12 Teachers" to locate virtual tours). Also, we should not forget that many of our students have old items at home that, with parental cooperation, can become a learning resource.

Although some historical documents can be read by elementary students, most are too difficult. Some of these primary sources can be adapted for young readers, and many fine children's books have done exactly that. For example, the well-known children's author Margaret Wise Brown edited a version of *Mourt's Relation* for children. *Mourt's Relation* is a journal written by several *Mayflower* pilgrims, most likely William Bradford and Edward Winslow. It was first published in 1622 and is the basis for much of what is known about the early days in Plimoth. It is far too difficult for elementary students to read. Brown's adaptation, called *Homes in the Wilderness* (1939 / 1988), is delightful and well within the reading ability of most third and fourth graders. Also noteworthy are the books written by Brett Harvey. Harvey has used the diaries of women who lived in the past as the basis of easy-to-read but historically accurate picture books. His books include *My Prairie Year: Based on the Diary of Elinore Plaisted* (1986), *Cassie's Journey: Going West in the 1860s* (1988), and *Immigrant Girl: Becky of Eldridge Street* (1987).

Songs are primary sources too. Many old ones reveal a great deal about a time or place. Noteworthy is *The Laura Ingalls Wilder Songbook* (Garson, 1968), which includes the words and lyrics to all the songs mentioned in the *Little House* books. Most elementary music texts contain several historical songs. My favorite anthology of American folk songs is *Gonna Sing My Head Off: American Folk Songs for Children* (Krull, 1992).

Teaching Sequence for a Primary Source. Both historical comprehension and historical analysis can be developed through work with primary sources. For lessons using primary sources, I suggest a teaching sequence similar to the one presented for realia, visual media, and auditory media in chapter 9:

1. *First, establish time and place.* Before we share a primary source with our students, we should place it in context. This usually requires using a timeline to establish time and a map to establish location. A good idea is to bring out a summary chart, a data retrieval chart, or a web we made earlier in the unit. The important thing is that students not have the primary source "thrown at them," absent a meaningful context.

2. *Present the primary source.* If a primary source is written, then it should be neatly reproduced or displayed on a large screen through an LCD (liquid crystal display), an overhead projector, or a photographic slide. Even when presented in a reader-friendly fashion, many written primary sources will have to be read aloud to students. Artifacts must be presented in a way that permits every student to see them easily. Sometimes this means letting students look at the artifact in small groups.

3. *Start with open-ended questions.* "Does anyone wish to make a comment?" "Who has a question about the diary entry (or letter, newspaper advertisement, coin, etc.)?"

4. *Then ask very specific questions.* These questions should require students to take a closer look at the primary source. With some written primary sources, it helps to number the lines of the text like a legal document and then ask students about

specific words, phrases, and sentences. If the primary source mentions names, places, or things, students should take notice of them. With artifacts, questions we ask should narrow students' focus, such as, "What do you see in the upper right corner of the painting?" or "What places are mentioned in the diary entry?" The purpose of these questions is to call attention to the specifics we want our students to remember.

5. *Finally, analyze the primary source.* Ask analysis questions. For example, "What new things does it show us?" "What does it tell us about the person(s) who wrote (or made) it?" Place the primary source in the context of larger themes and ideas. Following is a description of an instructional activity using a primary source.

Grade 2: "Old Buttons"

Description of a LESSON

Rule and Sunal (1994) provide an example of an activity that uses primary sources and builds the process skills of history. They describe a lesson in which children analyze a common historical artifact—a collection of old clothing buttons.

First, divide your class into small groups and give each group 8 to 10 buttons. The children should examine each button and write a description (e.g., size, shape, color, number of holes, material, condition). Next, the children should hypothesize about the age of the buttons. Ask each group to arrange their buttons chronologically, forming a button timeline, with the oldest at one end and the newest at the other end. After they have finished this task, ask the children to make inferences from the data (the buttons) in front of them. Then, call the groups together. With the whole class, make a list or web showing the characteristics of buttons. Ask the children to compile a list of factors that indicate age. They might identify material (plastic buttons would be more recent), condition (old buttons should appear worn), and color (old buttons could be faded). Finally, you could use the information in Rule and Sunal's article to provide some "expert" information on buttons. The article includes details of how you can tell old buttons from newer ones. Finally, the children should have the opportunity to revise their timelines.

Effective Teaching in Today's Diverse Classroom: At this point, you probably can identify the characteristics of a lesson that make it appropriate for a diverse student population without my help! Here, we have a hands-on experience and cooperative learning in small groups.

Children's Fiction: History as a Story Well Told

Fiction written for children has excellent potential as a resource for teaching history. Levstik (1986, 1989, 1990) and Beck et al. (1995) have written about the power of presenting history through narrative. Simply put, children learn more through stories than they do with other forms of presentation (most notably, textbook selections).

A great deal has been written about how teachers can use fiction to teach history (M. James & Zarrillo, 1989; Lamme, 1994; M. J. McGowan & Powell, 1996; T. M. McGowan, Erickson, & Neufeld, 1996; Zarnowski & Gallagher, 1993).

Historical fiction written for children is of two forms: (a) novels for older children and (b) picture books aimed at the youngest students. Some of the finest children's books ever written are historical fiction, including Newbery Award winners like Scott O'Dell's *Island of the Blue Dolphins* (1960), Esther Forbes's *Johnny Tremain* (1943), Patricia MacLaughlin's *Sarah, Plain and Tall* (1985), Elizabeth George Speare's *The Witch of Blackbird Pond* (1958) and *The Bronze Bow* (1961), and Karen Cushman's *The Midwife's Apprentice* (1995). Many excellent picture books tell stories that take place in other times, like *Thy Friend, Obadiah* (Turkle, 1969), *The Ox-Cart Man* (Hall, 1979), *How My Parents Learned to Eat* (Friedman, 1987), and *Follow the Drinking Gourd* (Winter, 1988).

Harms and Lettow (1994) provide a useful set of criteria for selecting picture books with historical settings:

1. *Developmental appropriateness.* The book should be written and illustrated at a level that children in your classroom can understand.
2. *Quality.* The book should be a good book, one children will find appealing and that at least some authorities consider to be well illustrated and written.
3. *Authenticity.* Historical accuracy extends to both text and illustration. In more and more historical picture books, authors and illustrators include a list of their sources or bibliographic notes that reveal and/or comment on the sources the author and illustrator used.
4. *Complementary text and illustration.* This is a characteristic all good picture books share. Text and illustrations should work together, rather than appear disjointed. Harms and Lettow note that this is essential in picture books with historical settings because the illustrations can enhance the level of historical understanding the reader acquires.
5. *Three-dimensional central characters.* As noted earlier, children can understand historical concepts when the past is presented as a story well told. Good stories require well-developed characters with whom children can develop a sense of empathy. This is a real challenge for authors and illustrators of picture books because of the limited space in picture books; most have fewer than 40 pages.
6. *Freedom from bias.* As teachers, we should avoid books that present stereotypes or biased views (although older children should read such books for the purpose of detecting bias). We should seek books that show events from the perspectives of all the participants in an event. Harms and Lettow, for example, note that in Jean Fritz's *The Great Adventure of Christopher Columbus* (1992), the Natives who greet Columbus are portrayed as "uncultured and witless," unable to understand Columbus and too willing to

accept trinkets in exchange for valuable information (Harms & Lettow, 1994, p. 153). It would be interesting for older children to compare this book with Jane Yolen's *Encounter* (1992) or Michael Dorris's *Morning Girl* (1992), books that present the perspectives of the Taino Natives. A story well told can provide children with a sense of empathy because fiction that is well researched and well written will make children feel transported to another place. Consider Lois Lowry's *Number the Stars* (1989). Readers will share the terror of Ellen Rosen, a Danish Jew, when she is awakened in the night by Nazi soldiers. Fiction also offers children strong images of the details of living in the past. This assumes, of course, that a work of fiction is accurate, free of bias, stereotypical images, and outright errors. After listening to their teacher read *Thy Friend, Obadiah* (Turkle, 1969), for example, children will have a sense of the clothing, buildings, and means of transportation in 19th-century Nantucket.

Children's fiction can be used in several ways. Children can read books independently. Historical novels and picture books can be read a second time to provide the specific information needed to answer inquiries and to complete projects. Fiction should be used as part of teacher-directed lessons in social studies. A word of caution is in order, however. Fiction is not written with the same purpose as a textbook; rather, the goal of the author is to tell a story. It seems reasonable that we should allow children to respond to the book as a story before they move on to a history lesson. We can do this by asking open-ended questions that encourage children to express their personal feelings, interpretations, and opinions about the story (Zarrillo, 1994). Following is an example of teaching history with a picture book.

Kindergarten: *Ox-Cart Man*

LESSON PLAN

In a journal article, I describe history lessons that can be taught with children's literature (Zarrillo, 1989). An exciting, cross-curricular lesson can be developed with *Ox-Cart Man,* a Caldecott-winning picture book written by Donald Hall (1979) and illustrated by Barbara Cooney. This book tells the story of a New England farmer and his family, apparently in the early 19th century.

Overview: This lesson is for a kindergarten class of 25 children.

Resources and Materials: (a) a copy of the book *Ox-Cart Man* (Hall, 1979) and (b) chart paper and an easel.

Content Objectives: Children will understand that life in times past was different from life today. Specifically, they will see differences in clothing, tools, transportation, and food preparation. They will also learn about the work done on a farm many years ago.

Process Objectives: Children will *listen and watch* as their teacher reads aloud the book and demonstrates the productive activities of the farmer, his wife, son, and daughter; *pantomime* those activities under the teacher's direction; and *distinguish* differences between how the farmer and his family lived and how we live today (clothing, transportation, food preparation).

Teaching Sequence
1. Before the lesson, write the following on a sheet of chart paper: carve a new yoke, saw planks for a new cart, split shingles, embroider clothing, make candles, tap syrup, shear sheep, spin yarn, plant crops.
2. Display the chart on an easel.
3. Ask the children to come to the read-aloud area and to sit cross-legged on the floor.
4. Read aloud *Ox-Cart Man*.
5. Ask the children whether they have any questions or comments about the story.
6. Read aloud each farming activity on the chart and demonstrate, through pantomime, how each would be done.
7. Ask the children to stand and, under your guidance, pantomime each activity.
8. Point to the illustrations in the book that show how the farmer and his family dressed, how they prepared food, the tools they used, and how they transported goods. Allow the children to look at each illustration closely and to talk about what they find interesting. Then, ask, "What is different about how the farmer lived and how we live today?"

Evaluation: You may want to tape-record the children's responses to the question "What is different about how the farmer lived and how we live today?" The comments will reveal to what extent the children understand the lesson's content objective.

 Effective Teaching in Today's Diverse Classroom: Howard Gardner has written about *multiple intelligences* (1983, 1991). This concept defies the older idea that intelligence is a single entity that can be measured and quantified (with an intelligence quotient, IQ). It seems to make sense that some people are gifted (or challenged) in one area, like the arts, but challenged (or gifted) in another, like mathematical thinking. In any case, some children are frustrated with school because they typically have so few opportunities for learning and expression through the arts. This activity will make their day by providing an opportunity to assume the roles of the ox-cart man and his family.

Timelines

Timelines are charts that show the chronological intervals among events. Timelines can be used as an instructional tool to present information to students. Students could also construct timelines as part of instructional units with a historical focus (Hoone, 1989). Students can make many types of timelines:

- Timelines can be either vertical, with the earliest date at the top of the line and the most recent date at the bottom, or horizontal, with the earliest date on the reader's left and the most recent date on the reader's right.
- The standard form of a timeline has a long line with intervals of time designated by short perpendicular marks (the intervals may be 1 month, 1 year, 10 years, 100 years). Marks are added to the line at the appropriate time place to designate significant events, and each event is given a brief description in words (e.g., 1993: my little sister is born).
- Picture timelines use illustrations for historical people, places, and events. For example, a timeline of the history of flight could include a drawing of Lindbergh's plane, *The Spirit of St. Louis*.
- Object timelines use real things. The activity with old buttons described earlier included an opportunity for children to make a timeline with the buttons they were examining.
- Other timelines do not use paper. It is possible to make a "clothesline" timeline. A string is stretched across a space, clothespins are placed on the line at appropriate points to designate historical events, and written descriptions or illustrations can be attached to the line with the clothespins.
- Finally, good news! Computer software has made it much easier to produce accurate, neat timelines.

Geography in the Elementary School

Although there is universal agreement that geography is an essential component of the school curriculum, geography has struggled to find a significant place in the schools (Geography Education Standards Project, 1994; Gregg & Leinhardt, 1994; Salter, 1989; Stoltman, 1991). In most classrooms, geographic teaching and learning are a small part of social studies as activity is limited to memorizing the names and locations of a few geographic features, such as oceans, rivers, lakes, and capital cities (Rallis & Rallis, 1995). A broader range view of geography is needed. A simple definition is that geography is the study of place, just as history is the study of the past. Gregg and Leinhardt (1994) provide a definition that we should consider:

Geography uses the language of maps to communicate ideas about the context and distribution of phenomena and processes important for human decision making, issues of scale, the dynamic nature of phenomena, and cultural perspective. (p. 328)

This definition, though complex, provides a basis for understanding the geographic component of the social studies. Geography requires that students know how to read and make several types of *maps*. Through geographic lessons, students should understand how people, resources, and products are *distributed* over the earth. Geographic study should provide a *context* for understanding events as students see how the *decisions* people make are influenced by their physical surroundings. Finally, students should learn how people interact with the environment, and as a result, both people and place *change*.

Apparently, we must do a great deal to increase the level of geographic knowledge our students have. The first national assessment of geography among students in Grades 4, 8, and 12 revealed that only 3% were "advanced" in their level of geographic understanding and that only 20% were "proficient." A staggering 30% did not have even a "basic" level of achievement (Williams et al., 1995a).

Research on Geographic Learning and Teaching

To date, Gregg and Leinhardt's (1994) analysis of the research on geographic learning and teaching is the most comprehensive (see also Forsythe, 1995; Rice & Cobb, 1978; Rushdoony, 1968; Stoltman, 1991). They concluded that "little research has been done on issues of learning geography outside of learning about maps" (p. 330). The relevant research has looked at the relationship between map-reading tasks and human development, and the thinking processes required to read maps.

Jean Piaget investigated the map-reading abilities of children (Piaget & Inhelder, 1969). He thought that children go through three stages in their ability to see things from a different perspective, an ability that is prerequisite to reading maps. At first, children are in a "topographical" stage, unable to use directional labels (e.g., north, south). Then, children pass through a "projective" stage, when they can determine location in relation to their own position (they know what is to the right and left of them). The final stage, usually reached between ages 10 and 12, Piaget labeled as "Eucledian," as children have an accurate perception of spatial relationships. As is so often the case in developmental studies, other researchers have challenged Piaget's conclusions. Using different methods (e.g., familiar cartoon characters), researchers have shown that children are able to do more at an earlier age than Piaget thought they could.

A body of research is available on the child's ability to read symbols. Some amusing studies have shown that children tend to interpret symbols literally, stating that the urban centers colored yellow on a map were eggs or firecrackers (Liben & Downs, 1989). Children, however, can understand that symbols on maps represent things. The more difficult task for children is to see the relationships among the items represented on a map. Generally, the ability of children to understand symbols on a map is influenced by the "degree of abstractness of the symbol and the amount of detail on the map" (Gregg & Leinhardt, 1994, p. 333).

Geography is the study of place. In this classroom, the teacher has used multicultural literature to introduce her students to several fascinating places.

Likewise, several studies have been conducted on the ability of children to understand scale. Gregg and Leinhardt (1994) concluded that three things are necessary for a child to read and use scale. First, the child must have developed proportional reasoning; she or he must have a sense that the relationships among items remain constant even if the unit of comparison has shrunk. Second, the child must be able to measure in the units used on the map; on the simplest maps, this involves inches and miles or centimeters and kilometers. Finally, the child must have a sense of the frame of reference of the map. Maps are selective in what they reveal. No map can show everything about a place, and to understand scale the child must understand the level of detail in the map.

Research on the cognitive processes involved in map reading is complex. Researchers have investigated how the information on a map is recognized, how the images of maps are stored in memory, and how that information is recalled. Gregg and Leinhardt (1994) concluded, "From a cognitive perspective, it is not easy to make sense of the symbols and letters superimposed on the complex visual fields that are referred to as maps" (p. 343). Maps, through the use of symbol and scale, can convey large amounts of important information. Map reading is not easy; it places unique demands on the developing thinking abilities of children. Muir and Frazee (1986) noted that a significant cognitive challenge for young map readers is understanding that maps require a "bird's-eye," rather than a "ground-level," perspective. Some children, when asked to read maps, have great difficulty because they are not able to make this shift in perspective.

Unfortunately, few studies shed much light on how to teach geography. J. W. Miller (1974, 1982) did show that the design of maps makes a difference. Children find it easier to read maps with a limited number of different typefaces, clearly differentiated symbols, a compass rose, a grid system of latitude and longitude, boldly marked boundaries, and all labels in a horizontal format. Atkins (1981) found that young children can be taught to read simple maps if the instruction is presented in a clear and structured manner. In conclusion, it is important to note that at least one authority reached the same conclusion about the child's capacity to learn geography that others have reached about history. Karen Trifonoff (1997) stated that "many early geographic educators believed children to have a poorly developed sense of space. Most modern studies suggest the opposite. Students do have well-developed spatial understanding, and they continue to astound researchers with their advanced mapping behaviors" (p. 17). Although it is essential that our teaching be developmentally appropriate and not ask children to perform tasks that are beyond their abilities, it also appears that, regarding history and geography, educators have underestimated the capacity of children to learn essential concepts.

Geography in the Elementary School: Content

Geography includes the physical characteristics (elevation of land, types of vegetation), geopolitical information (boundaries, capital cities), demographics (size, density, identity of population), and economic information (type and volume of agricultural and manufactured products) of places. Students should learn the relationships among this information, especially how places change over time. Two schemes for organizing geographic content, each with considerable merit, have categorized what students should know about geography. Five fundamental themes were developed by the Geography Education National Implementation Project (GENIP; Boehm & Petersen, 1994; GENIP, 1987, 1989): (a) Location, (b) Place, (c) Human-Environment Interactions, (d) Movement, and (e) Region. These five themes have been used as the foundation for elementary social studies textbooks, state curriculum frameworks, and school district curriculum guides. They have played a significant role in improving geographic education (Petersen, Natoli, & Boehm, 1994). The national standards for geography are organized under six elements: (a) the world in spatial terms, (b) places and regions, (c) physical systems, (d) human systems, (e) environment and society, and (f) the uses of geography (Freese, 1997; Geography Education Standards Project, 1994). Because they are more current and have the potential to shape the curriculum we teach, let's look at the elements. Eighteen standards are organized across these six elements:

1. *The World in Spatial Terms*. The national standards seek to develop the "geographically informed person." Such a student is expected to have basic map-reading skills and the ability to produce maps that summarize geographic information. Students should be able to read and make maps that show the spatial relationships of people, places, and environments.

2. *Places and Regions*. The world's resources, both human and natural, are not evenly distributed over the earth. Each place is unique, and the earth's land masses can be divided into regions with clearly defined characteristics. Students should learn the physical and human characteristics of places. They should know, for example, what makes Hawaii and Alaska different.

3. *Physical Systems*. This is a part of social studies that overlaps science. Students should understand the physical processes that shape the earth's surface (e.g., floods, volcanoes, earthquakes) and the concept of an ecosystem.

4. *Human Systems*. This element looks at the three ways human beings relate to the surface of the earth: (a) People shape the surface of the earth by consuming resources and altering natural patterns, (b) people build structures that become a part of the surface of the earth, and (c) people compete for control of the surface of the earth.

5. *Environment and Society*. People modify the physical environment of the earth. An easy example for students to understand is how the construction of a dam creates a lake. Sometimes the relationship between nature and people is the reverse as nature "strikes back" and physical systems alter those things that people have constructed. For example, a hurricane destroys buildings; over a longer period of time, persistent drought leads to mass migration.

6. *The Uses of Geography*. The sixth and final element states that students should know how to apply geographical knowledge to interpret the past, understand the present, and plan for the future.

Geography in the Elementary School: Processes

The five sets of geographic skills proposed in *Guidelines for Geographic Education: Elementary and Secondary Schools* (Joint Committee on Geographic Education, 1984), listed below, are widely accepted as an outline of what students should be able to do in geography. The national standards in geography incorporate them:

1. *Asking Geographic Questions.* Students must learn how to ask questions in geographic terms. "Where is something located?" "How did it get there?" "Why is it located where it is?" "How is one place different from another?" Specifically, students should be able to:

   • Ask geographic questions about current events
   • Distinguish between questions that can be answered with geographic data and those that cannot

2. *Acquiring Geographic Information.* As with history, geographic data can be found in both primary and secondary sources. Primary data are gathered through fieldwork as students distribute surveys, take photographs, and record their observations on field trips. Secondary data are maps, databases, and books. Specifically, students should be able to:

   • Make records of geographic data on field trips
   • Use their mathematical skills to count and measure
   • Read maps, charts, graphs, and tables with geographic data

3. *Organizing Information.* Geographic data can be organized in several ways. Maps, of course, are the primary tool for organizing what students learn about a place. Students should also learn how to construct charts, graphs, and tables. Specifically, students should be able to:

   • Prepare maps, charts, graphs, and tables with geographic data
   • Write concise summaries of geographic data

4. *Analyzing Geographic Information.* It is often difficult to distinguish the processes of gathering and analyzing geographic data. They tend to occur simultaneously. Specifically, students should be able to:

   • Interpret data in maps, graphs, charts, and tables
   • Discover trends, relationships, and patterns in geographic data

5. *Answering Geographic Questions.* Finally, students should see the relationships among the data they have gathered and analyzed. They should reach generalizations that are true across time and place. Specifically, students should be able to:

   • Present oral and written reports accompanied by maps, charts, graphs, and tables
   • Apply geographic knowledge to interpret the past, understand the present, and predict the future

Teaching Geography in the Elementary School

Geography presents a unique challenge to us as teachers, primarily because geographic information is presented in an unfamiliar format. Maps and globes require a different type of reading from the expository text students read in textbooks and encyclopedias. Further, elementary students will work with a variety of maps, each with its own category of information. For example, one type of "climate" map shows precipitation for South America, whereas another, "historical," map shows European colonies in South America during the early 19th century. Another complicating factor with world maps is the difference between "conformal" maps and "equal area" maps. The *Mercator projection* produces a *conformal map;* all the land masses retain their appropriate shapes. Unfortunately, this type of map is distorted; Greenland appears larger than Africa. *Equal-area maps,* in contrast, show land areas with proper relative sizes. Unfortunately, this requires a distortion of the earth's land masses. The good news is that most social studies textbooks present maps that are developmentally appropriate for the children who read them. Further, schools should have globes and maps specially designed for young learners. For example, globes at many levels of sophistication are available. The simplest ones avoid detail, include only the names of nations and their capital cities, and use bright colors to distinguish boundaries.

The Internet is rapidly replacing hard-copy atlases as the best source for teachers and students looking for maps. Excellent Web sites are too numerous to mention here, but, for example, students could click on the "Mapquest" Web site *(http://www.mapquest.com)* and request a street map for any location in the United States. This site will be a valuable resource for students studying their neighborhood and community. Maps of every sort are available on the Internet. For example, a site developed by the Department of Geography at California State University, Northridge, has maps showing the distribution of the population of the United States on the basis of ancestry *(http://130.166.124.2/uspage1.html)*. Here, students would learn that the cities with the largest numbers of Czech Americans are Chicago and Cleveland, although more Czech Americans per capita live in Eastern Nebraska than anywhere else in the United States.

As with many social studies processes, map-reading skills should be developed through both repeated practice and direct instruction. Students will become geographically literate if they are *repeatedly* asked to use maps; there is no substitute for practice. At the same time, we as teachers should plan *developmental* lessons to help our students understand the special language of maps. All geography teaching with children should move from the concrete to the abstract, from the simple to the complex. If possible, developmental map-reading activities should use the following progression:

1. First, children should participate in activities that use their bodies as points of reference.

2. Next, children should use three-dimensional maps.
3. Then, children should use maps that are simplified for use in the elementary classroom.
4. Finally, children should be asked to complete activities with maps that are real and have been produced for use outside the classroom. The mini-unit presented later in the chapter on using a grid system follows this progression.

Symbols, Scale, Grid, and Direction. To both gather and report geographic information, elementary children must become sophisticated with four aspects of maps: symbols, scale, grid, and direction.

Symbols. Maps use symbols to report information. Some symbols represent things with a fixed, physical presence, such as highways and rivers; others reveal patterns of data, such as levels of unemployment. Consider the challenge children face. Material that is written, such as a textbook, uses a single, unvarying set of symbols— the 26 letters of the English alphabet. Most maps, in contrast, have their own set of symbols. A red circle on one map may represent a city with a population of 100,000, whereas on another map, a red circle may represent the location of a water treatment plant. The key concept for children to understand is that once a certain symbol stands for something on a map, it will always have the same meaning for that map. The *legend* on a map tells what the symbols mean.

Our youngest learners should be exposed to maps with three-dimensional symbols that look a great deal like what they represent. A three-dimensional map of the neighborhood, for example, might have milk cartons represent houses and a large shoe box, with doors and windows painted on it, represent the school. Next, students work with maps with symbols that are pictographs (or "pictorial" symbols); the symbols are drawings for what they represent. The next level of abstraction are "semi-pictorial" symbols, which look something like, or retain a single feature of, what they represent (e.g., a church is represented by a cross). When symbols no longer "look" like what they represent (e.g., the symbol for the state capital is a star), then the maps should be simplified and include very few symbols. Following are some activities that teach children to understand map symbols:

- *Group symbols*. If students are seated in groups, have each group of students choose a symbol to represent themselves. The symbols cannot have any writing; they may be pictorials, but eventually they should be abstract— for example, blue circles, red triangles. Use the symbols in class schedules and on charts.
- *Symbols in the community*. Develop a lesson with symbols that are used in the community and in the media. Students will recognize some commercial

symbols (e.g., the golden arches for McDonald's, the Nike "swoosh") and others used in public places (e.g., symbols for men and women on bathroom doors, symbols for railroad tracks).

- *Matching symbols with what they represent.* Prepare simple pictorial symbols for a set of photographs. For a picture of school, the symbol could be a simple drawing of a building with a flag; for a picture of a forest, the symbol could be a triangular treetop with a narrow, rectangular trunk, like a stylized Christmas tree. Shuffle the symbols and the photographs and then have students match each symbol to its photograph.
- *Simplified maps.* If the textbook does not have them, then make some maps that (a) have few places represented (few details) and (b) use pictorial symbols. Students will need repeated practice with these simplified maps (see Figure 12.1 for an example).

Scale. Our youngest students should work with some maps that are life-size. For example, it is possible to create a life-size map of the top of a teacher's desk. Eventually, the possibilities for life-size maps are exhausted, and students will have to understand scale to use maps. My experience is that this is a very difficult concept for young children. Most maps that I have seen primary-level children produce, prior to a good unit on maps, are more illustrations than maps. The problem is that the scale on these maps produced by primary-age children is inconsistent. I recall that, when I asked them to draw a map of the neighborhood, for example, most children drew houses that were grossly out of scale and covered an area that should represent an entire block. Our older students, in contrast, should be able to calculate the exact distance between two places on a map. Following are some activities that will help children understand scale:

- Compare the furniture in a first-grade classroom with the furniture in a fifth-grade classroom. The chairs the children use will make the point dramatically. Then, have the children think about the relative sizes of first graders and fifth graders. Help the children see that the furniture has been "built to scale"—smaller chairs for smaller children, larger chairs for larger children.
- Have the children draw maps of the classroom. Focus on scale. The children must represent their desks in a way that makes them smaller than the teacher's desk (assuming the teacher's desk is larger than the students'). Then, have the children try making maps of the school. First, you may want to measure the size of some of the buildings in the school complex. Help the children see that the smaller buildings at the school must look that way on their maps.
- When you think the children are ready, teach a series of lessons on using the scale of miles. The goal should be to have the children calculate actual

distances between places by using the scale. Following is a lesson plan for this type of lesson.

Grade 4: Using a Scale of Miles to Calculate Distance—A First Lesson

The first time students use a scale of miles to calculate the distance between two points on a map, it helps if they are not confronted with distances in fractions of inches. If 1 inch equals 100 miles, then it is easy to figure out how far apart two places are if they appear 3 inches apart on the map (3 inches × 100 miles/inch = 300 miles). It is quite another task if they are 1¾ inches apart.

Overview: This lesson is for a small group of fourth graders, six students.

Resources and Materials: Beforehand, make a map of either your state or the United States; cities should be placed on the map so that each city is exactly 1, 2, 3, or 4 inches from the other cities (no fractional distances). This will involve minor adjustments in placing some cities. Base the scale of miles on 1 inch (1 inch equals 50 miles or 100 miles, whichever is appropriate). Then, have available (a) a plastic transparency of the map, (b) six copies of the map, (c) six sets of colored pencils, and (d) six rulers.

Content Objectives: Students will calculate the actual distance between two points on a map by using scale.

Process Objectives: Students will *calculate* the actual distance between cities on the map.

Teaching Sequence
1. Display the plastic transparency of the simplified map. Explain that each student will receive a copy of this map. Point out the scale of miles.
2. Using the distance between any two cities as an example, (a) draw a straight line between two cities (e.g., from Kansas City to Detroit), (b) measure the line, (c) multiply the distance by 100 (or whatever distance is equivalent to 1 inch on this map).
3. Ask students to use their red pencils to draw a line between two other cities on their own copies of the map. Next, have students measure the line. Help them set up the multiplication problem and do the calculation.
4. Present other combinations of cities for students to calculate. For each pair of cities, have the class use a different-colored pencil. Help students with the standard process: Draw the line, measure the line, and multiply to find the real distance.

Evaluation: Your observation of the students will tell you who is having difficulty using a scale of miles. Collect each student's map for further analysis.

Effective Teaching in Today's Diverse Classroom: This lesson is planned for a small group of students. I have planned this as a first lesson on using a scale of miles. Although some of your more able students will find this an easy task, most elementary students find it challenging. Students will need a great deal of your attention to be successful. One more thing: Although you probably realize this, students cannot use a scale of miles to calculate distance on a map if they cannot perform the required multiplication (in this lesson, multiplying two-digit numbers by one-digit numbers).

Grids. The more detailed the map, the more important it is for the map reader to use a grid system. To locate a street on a detailed map of a city, for example, requires the map reader to find the street name in an index and then use the *coordinates* (e.g., E5) to narrow the search. Latitude and longitude constitute the grid system for maps and globes. Use of a grid system allows the map reader to find the *absolute location* of a place. Following is a mini-unit designed to help third graders learn how to use grids to find places on maps.

Grade 3: Using Grid Systems to Find Places on Maps

MINI-UNIT

The organizing framework for this unit comes from the national geography standards (Geography Education Standards Project, 1994).

Part I: Organizing Framework

Geographic Skills and Perspectives

Skill Set 2: Acquiring Geographic Information. Students should be given the opportunity to locate, gather, and process information from a variety of primary and secondary sources, including maps.

This mini-unit answers one question:

Unit Question: How can we use the grid system to help us locate things on maps?

Part II: Instructional Activities

Unit Question: How can we use the grid system to help us locate things on maps?

Activity 1: The Grid Game

Content Objectives: Using the classroom as an example, children will understand how a grid system works.

Process Objectives: Children will *identify* coordinates for several locations in the room and *use* coordinates to find the absolute location of several classmates.

Arrange the classroom so that the children are seated in rows. Label each row: if you have six rows, they should be labeled A, B, C, D, E, and F. Then label the position of each chair in each row. If each row has five chairs, the first chair would be 1, the second chair would be 2, and so on. Now each child has an absolute location with a set of coordinates (e.g., the child sitting in the fourth chair in the first row would be A4). Attach large signs in front of each row with the correct label (A, B, C, etc.) and do the same for the position of the chairs (you might have to use easels so that the children can see the labels). To begin, stand next to a child and ask the class what the coordinates are ("I am standing next to José. What are his coordinates?") If José is in the last seat of the fifth row, the answer is E5!) On a set of index cards, print all the possible coordinates (A1–A5, B1–B5, etc.). Shuffle the cards and pull out one at a time. Then ask, "Who is seated in D3?" (B2? A5? etc.).

Activity 2: Locating a Place on a Map of a Model City

Content Objectives: Children will understand how a grid system can be "placed" on a three-dimensional map.

Process Objectives: Children will *construct* a three-dimensional map of a hypothetical city, use yarn to *create* a grid system for the city, and *locate* places on the three-dimensional map by using the grid system.

Have the class make a three-dimensional map of a model city. This will require milk cartons, shoe boxes, and other paper containers that can be modified to resemble structures. The model should include businesses, parks, hospitals, houses, apartment buildings, and schools. After the children have finished this three-dimensional map, place a grid system "over" it with yarn. This is somewhat tricky, but be sure the spaces between the vertical and horizontal pieces of yarn are equivalent. Then, label the grid. Again, the vertical rows can be labeled A, B, C, and so on, and the horizontal rows 1, 2, 3, and so on. First, help children see that every place on the model city map can be identified by a set of coordinates (e.g., the hospital is in C4). Ask the children what they see in a variety of places (e.g., "What is in B3?"). Then, give the class a list of places and have them identify the proper coordinates.

Activity 3: A Simplified Map

Content Objectives: Children will move from a three-dimensional map to a two-dimensional map and understand how a grid system can be used on a flat map.

Process Objectives: Children will *locate* places on a simplified map of a city by using a grid system.

Have children work with simplified grid systems. Many social studies textbooks include these. If yours does not, it is easy to develop your own. Figure 12.1 shows a simplified grid system one teacher created for his third-grade class.

First, the simplified map should have a limited number of coordinates (no more than four vertical and four horizontal). Thus, the "squares" defined by the grid system are large. Second, the map should have a limited number of places represented on the map. The simplified map in Figure 12.1 includes only seven symbols. Challenge the class to find places by using the grid system. Ask them, "Where are the two parks?" (C1 and C4). You can also ask more difficult questions, like, "Do the people who live in B4 have a church nearby?" (Yes, one is in B4). A final important activity with the simplified map: Prepare an index of locations. This should list the coordinates for the places on the map (e.g., City Hall—A4; Churches—A1 and B4; Schools—A2, C3). Have children verify the information on the index.

Activity 4: A Real Map of Your City

Content Objectives: Children will now see how a grid system on a real map of their city can be used to locate places.

Process Objectives: Children will *locate* places on a real map of their city by using a grid system.

Third graders will appreciate the challenge of using a real city map, as their parents do. Obtain several copies of a map of your city, but be sure the map has a good grid system. Have the children work in groups. Because this activity is difficult, you may want to have cross-age helpers from the sixth grade come to your room to help each group. Give children a list of 10 places to find on the map. These should include a school, a park, and a library. First, have the children use the index to find the coordinates for each place. Then, ask the children to find the place by using the coordinates on the map. Finally, for a real challenge, give each group a set of cross streets to locate (e.g., Adams and Elm). They will need to find both streets on the index and then locate their intersection.

Effective Teaching in Today's Diverse Classroom: James Cummins has described how skills learned in one language transfer to another (1979, 1986a, 1986b, 1989, 1992). Because reading maps is dependent on symbols unrelated to English, the geographic processes described in this section of the textbook can be learned in any language. If a student learns to use symbols, a scale of miles (or kilometers), and a grid system in any language, then those skills can be used to read maps written in other languages. Admittedly, most English language learners attend schools where too few, if any, teachers and aides can provide primary-language instruction. When the possibility exists, however, it makes sense to use the primary language to teach map-reading skills to English language learners who speak little English.

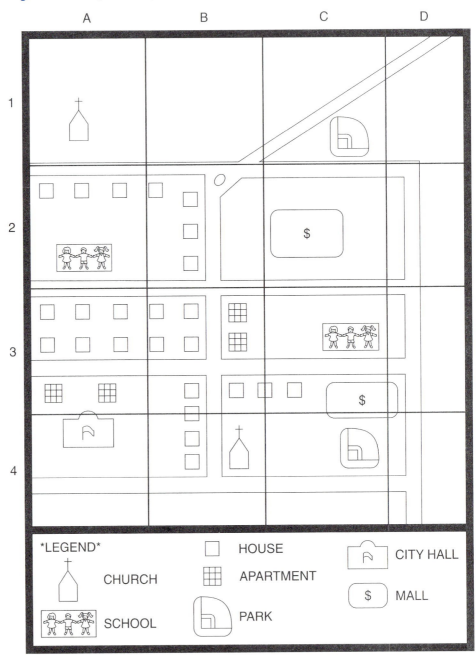

Figure 12.1 Simplified Map to Teach Children How to Use a Grid System

Direction. Children need to understand directionality to know the *relative location* of something. For example, where is San Antonio in relation to New Orleans? With our youngest students, it is a good idea to start with familiar directions of left-right and up-down before moving to the compass rose. Following are some activities that will help your students understand relative location and directionality:

- *Directions in the classroom.* Challenge your students to describe something in the classroom by using references to other things in the room, and the other students try to guess what the item is. For example, "This thing is in the front of the room. As I look at it, it is to the left of the flag and to the right of the pencil sharpener. It is below the clock" (the item was a wall thermometer). The person describing the thing may *not* reveal physical characteristics (e.g., it is red and large).
- *Compass rose on the playground.* Once students have been introduced to the compass rose and north, south, east, and west, take the class outdoors for a simple activity. On the playground, ask students to move according to instructions you give. Make sure all the instructions use north, south, east, and west; for example, "Take three steps north and two steps south," "Take two steps south and three steps east."
- *Relative location on a real map.* Present to the class a simple map of the United States. Have students answer some simple questions involving relative location; for example, "Which state is north of Missouri?" "Which states border Utah?" "Which state is closer to Arizona—California or Louisiana?" "If you were going from Chicago to Seattle, in which direction would you travel?"

Reporting Geographic Data: Student-Made Maps. Reading maps is one thing; making them is another. Here are several types of maps your students should make:

Mental Maps. The national geography standards suggest that students use mental (or sketch) maps to answer geographic questions (Geography Education Standards Project, 1994, pp. 146–147). A *mental map* is a map "inside your head" and is drawn without reference to other resources. When students draw their mental maps, these can be referred to as "sketch maps." Mental maps can be used in several ways:

- Mental maps can be used as a diagnostic tool. They reveal what students know about the region being mapped. More important, they reveal the map maker's attitude toward the places represented. The familiar and the important tend to be drawn larger than the less familiar and the less important.
- For some geographic tasks, a sketch map serves us well. *Sketch maps* can help us recall the relative locations and relative sizes of places. A sketch map could help us remember what nations a person must travel through to go from Paris to Moscow or to show someone how to get from school to the airport.

Relief Maps. For more than 100 years, elementary school children have made three-dimensional relief maps. *Relief maps* reveal the topography of a region because mountain ranges and valleys can be shown. To help your students be successful, consider conducting the following activity:

1. Build an outline map on an inflexible surface, such as plywood (cardboard tends to buckle; don't use it).
2. Start with a good "outline" map. An *outline map* shows some geographic features but omits others. Commercially produced outline maps of the world, the continents, the United States, and each of the 50 states are available. The outline map used for a relief map must be either drawn or projected on the surface. Do not make the outline map too small; a relief map must be large enough to show the important physical features of the region.
3. Sketch the outline of the features in the model (e.g., mountains, rivers, valleys) on the surface. Students will need an easy-to-read map to show the physical geography of the region they are mapping. It is essential that students have a good idea of the scale of things (e.g., how tall one mountain is in relation to another).
4. There are many recipes for making relief maps. The old tried-and-true recipe is salt and flour. Mix equal parts of salt and flour and add a minimal amount of water—just enough to keep the glob together. I prefer to use clay, but it is more expensive.
5. Have patience! It is not easy to make a mountain. Work with students to consider scale, and expect some initial efforts that will need to be reshaped.
6. Relief maps look better if they are painted (e.g., mountains, brown; valleys, green; rivers, blue). Tempera paints work fine.

Thematic Maps. In her excellent article, Trifonoff (1997) challenges primary-level teachers to allow their students to make thematic maps. Almost all the maps that elementary students read or make are location maps, which show where things are. Thematic maps, in contrast, "illustrate a single idea, distribution, or relationship" (p. 17). An example of a thematic map is a map of the United States showing the rate of coronary-related deaths among 100 people. States are divided into four categories based on the data on coronary-related deaths. Each category is assigned a color, and on the thematic map of coronary-related deaths in the United States, each state is colored according to the data. Anyone looking at the map can easily compare the data on any two states, and more important, regional trends (if any) are easy to spot.

To make a thematic map, start with a "blank" map of a region (e.g., your school, neighborhood, city, state). The map must have clearly defined subregions (e.g., the map of the state must show counties, the map of the school must show each classroom). Next, students need to gather data and compile it in a table. For example, students could do a survey to determine how frequently students in each classroom eat in the cafeteria. Then, students would have to organize the data so that they fall into four or five categories. Each classroom must fit into one of the categories based on the average number of students who eat in the cafeteria each day; for example: On the average, (a) more than 75% of students in the classroom eat in the cafeteria, (b) 50% to 74% of students in the classroom eat in the cafeteria, (c) 25% to 49% of students in the classroom eat in the cafeteria, and (d) less than 24% of students in the classroom eat in the cafeteria. A color must be assigned to each category (e.g., over 75%, red; 50%–74%, blue; 25%–49%, green; and 24% and under, yellow). A legend must be added that explains what the colors mean, and students would have to color each classroom on the map accordingly.

SUMMARY OF KEY POINTS

▶ History always has been an important part of the elementary school curriculum. Publication of the national history standards generated considerable debate about what historical content students should learn.

▶ Children have the cognitive capacity to learn historical concepts if they receive appropriate instruction.

▶ Elementary students should learn about the history of their families, schools, communities, and state; the history of the United States; the history of people living in other nations; and the historical contributions of women, people of color, and common people.

▶ Students should develop to think and act like historians; the "doing" of history is an important part of teaching history.

▶ Throughout the book, I have presented teaching ideas that are essential to teach history in a diverse classroom; these include contextual support, multiple lesson formats, cooperative learning, critical thinking, and a variety of resources.

▶ Three types of lessons are essential to teach history to children: (a) those using primary sources, (b) those incorporating children's fiction, and (c) those using timelines.

▶ We as teachers should adopt a broad definition of geography so that our students do more than memorize geographic data.

▶ Maps are difficult to read because information is presented in an unfamiliar format.

▶ Research on the cognitive development of children and geography shows that children can learn geographic concepts, although there are developmental limits.

- ▶ Geography is the study of place, including physical characteristics, geopolitical information, demographics, and economic information.
- ▶ The processes of geography include the ability to ask and answer geographic questions by acquiring, organizing, and analyzing geographic information.
- ▶ To read maps, children must understand symbols, scale, grid, and direction.

FOR FURTHER READING

History

- ▶ Read the study by Keith Barton and Linda Levstik (1996). Unlike much published research, it is relatively easy to read and full of fascinating detail. Downey and Levstik's chapter in the *Handbook of Research on Social Studies Teaching and Learning* (1991) is a good summary of the research on the teaching and learning of history. Downey's (1985) older bulletin for the NCSS, *History in the Schools,* presents four fine articles on the status of history in the schools. Virtually every issue of *The Social Studies, Social Education,* and *Social Studies and the Young Learner* has at least one article on teaching historical content. Some special issues devoted to teaching and learning history are Simpson (1995a, 1995b) and Alter (1994). For a full discussion of the controversy over the national history standards, see the January 1996 edition of *Social Education* and its articles by Saxe, R. Cohen, and Whelan. One interesting article on the psychology of teaching history is by Duis (1996), who explores history teaching and schema theory. An excellent resource in the form of a timeline for our better students (Grades 5+) who are studying the ancient world is the *Smithsonian Timelines of the Ancient World* (Scarre, 1993).
- ▶ Many articles have been published on teaching history with children's books. See the synthesis article by T. M. McGowan et al. (1996) in *Social Education.* Also of note are three books published by the Social Science Education Consortium: *C Is for Citizenship: Children's Literature and Civic Understanding* (Singleton, 1997); *G Is for Geography: Children's Literature and the Five Themes* (Singleton, 1993); and *H Is for History: Using Children's Literature to Develop Historical Understandings* (Singleton, 1995). Hoelscher (1997) writes about using the popular *American Girls Collection* to teach history to third graders.
- ▶ One curriculum project that is worth a look is *History Alive,* developed by Teachers Curriculum Institute (1995). *History Alive* uses slides, experiential exercises, and problem solving (Bower & Lobdell, 1998).

Geography

- ▶ Results of the 1994 National Assessment of Educational Progress in Geography are very interesting in terms of both results and methodology (Williams et al., 1995a). Gregg and Leinhardt's (1994) research review is difficult reading but well worth the effort. The journals regularly publish many articles on geography teaching and learning. For example, Carroll, Knight, and Hutchinson (1995) discuss how the computer software Where in the World is Carmen Sandiego? can teach geographic concepts. Rogers and Bromley (1995) list children's books that can be used to develop geographic literacy; Stremme (1993) addresses the same topic. Labbo, Field, and Brook (1995) write about using the national geography standards to teach about South Africa. Hollister (1994) shows how to use old maps, and Maier (1993) explores the use of globes and maps as advance organizers.

Chapter 13

The Other Social Sciences and Topics of Special Interest: Completing the Social Studies Curriculum

Two years ago, a curriculum committee in Darlene Hoyer's school district decided that key concepts from psychology should be a part of the social studies curriculum. For each grade level, projects or units were designed to help students learn how to develop positive interpersonal relationships. Mrs. Hoyer engaged her fifth-grade students in an anger management project. Students in Mrs. Hoyer's classroom were expected to learn about how they could limit and control their anger. During this project, some students conducted a survey of their classmates to find out what made them angry; others interviewed the school psychologist to find out what coping mechanisms could be used to exercise control over anger; and a third group read information books and health textbooks to learn about the causes and control of anger.

The goal of the project was to produce a video that could be used with other classes. Once informed about anger management, members of Mrs. Hoyer's class would write the video script, shoot the necessary footage, and edit the tape. Students determined that they should make two versions of the video: one for children in the primary grades, and one for students in the upper elementary grades. Much of the video would be simulated scenarios, with Mrs. Hoyer's students playing the roles. The simulations would illustrate how to decrease the chances someone would get angry and, if anger did come to the surface, how to cope with the hostile feelings. This project on anger management is an example of how the social science disciplines can be used to enrich the elementary social studies curriculum.

▲   ▲   ▲

In this chapter, you will read about:

- ▶ How anthropology can be an important part of elementary social studies
- ▶ How our students can participate in an archaeological dig
- ▶ Integrating economic concepts into the social studies curriculum
- ▶ A six-step process our students can use when they analyze economic problems
- ▶ How concepts from psychology and sociology will help our students better understand themselves and other people
- ▶ How concepts and concerns about global education, environmental education, and current events are essential for our students to learn as we enter the 21st century

Completing the Social Studies Curriculum

Citizenship education, history, and geography traditionally have been the main focus in the elementary social studies curriculum. Content from the other social sciences (anthropology, economics, sociology, psychology, and political science), however, also must be included in the elementary curriculum. Content from these areas is essential because, without it, our students will have a partial understanding of the world they live in. In this chapter, we look at anthropology, economics, psychology, and sociology (political science is covered in chap. 11, on citizenship education).

It is important to note that each social science includes both a body of knowledge (content) and a way of learning about people (process). For example, the content of anthropology includes information about ancient cultural groups of the Americas, like the Maya and the Aztec. Our students should learn this information. At the same time, the social studies curriculum should help our students understand how practitioners in each discipline gather information. For example, anthropologists who study ancient cultures learn about the Maya and the Aztec through several processes, primarily by analyzing artifacts obtained through excavation. If our students understand how social scientists gather and analyze data, they will have a better sense of how these experts reached their conclusions. In this chapter, we also examine two emerging fields of study in social studies: global education and environmental education. The chapter concludes with a discussion of how to teach current events.

Anthropology

Several authorities have written about how teachers can make anthropology a part of elementary social studies: Barnes (1991), Chilcott (1977), Dynneson (1986), Jantz and Klawitter (1991), Laney and Moseley (1990), Little Soldier (1990), M. R. Nelson and Stahl (1991), Owen (1982), and White (1989). *Anthropology* is the study of the physical and cultural characteristics of people. Jane White (1989) stated the goal of this discipline:

> The central goal of anthropologists is to explain why groups of people are different from each other; to explain why they have different physical characteristics, speak different languages, use different technologies, and why they think, believe, and act so differently. (p. 31)

Anthropology comprises two broad fields: physical anthropology and cultural anthropology. *Physical anthropology,* which explores the evolution and physical differences of people, is rarely a part of the elementary curriculum. Some sixth-grade social studies curricula, however, do cover the origins of humankind, introducing students to the work of Mary and Richard Leakey in East Africa (human paleontology is part of physical anthropology). *Cultural anthropology,* which is the study of the culture, should be an integral part of social studies in the elementary curriculum. When we plan and present units on the Navajo or ancient Rome, we are teaching cultural anthropology. Many aspects, or "manifestations," of culture can serve as the focus of elementary social studies lessons:

- *Food getting.* How is food gathered or produced? How is food distributed? Most elementary students assume that all other people—both those living today and those who lived in the past—live the same way the students do. It may never occur to a third grader, for example, that some people do not get their food in a grocery store. Social studies should teach students about groups who depend on hunting, agriculture, or trade for food.

- *Economic systems*. What resources does the cultural group use? How are resources converted to useful things? What must they trade for? How are resources allocated? What system of money is used for exchange?
- *Social stratification*. What social groups exist within the cultural group? What advantages are reserved for members of some groups (economic, power, prestige)? What is denied to other groups?
- *Patterns of residence*. Who lives with whom? What determines where a person lives? Although it is worthwhile to learn about different human dwellings, it is more important to consider the cultural rules that determine who resides in a home.
- *Political organization*. Who makes the laws? Who enforces the laws? How are conflicts resolved?
- *Religion*. What religions are practiced by members of the cultural group? What are the fundamental beliefs? What rituals are religious in nature?
- *Arts*. What forms of visual arts are produced and valued by members of the cultural group? What media are preferred? What types of performing arts are practiced by members of the cultural group?

Social studies units that introduce children to a cultural group do have a "bottom line," however. What is most important? *Curriculum Guidelines for Multicultural Education* (NCSS Task Force on Ethnic Studies Curriculum Guidelines, 1992) states that we want students to learn a cultural group's "ideas, ways of thinking, values, symbols" (p. 276). White (1989) summarizes this point:

All too often, well-intentioned teachers will teach about "our neighbors across the border" by having their class, for example, break a piñata or eat tamales. They may not realize these events are the tips of a cultural iceberg . . . these isolated experiences do not really capture the more central values of how the Mexicans make meaning out of their own culture. (p. 35)

Single Group Studies

A *single group study* is a unit on one cultural group (e.g., the Kikuyu, the Nez Percé, modern Germany). In another book, I stated some important points to consider when teaching about cultural groups (Zarrillo, 1994):

- *Don't lump groups of people together.* For example, if a teacher presents a unit on the "American Indian," students will be left with the impression that all Native groups shared a common culture. This, of course, is far from the truth. The Huron and the Hopi are as different as the Swedes and the Greeks. At the very least, a unit should cover a small group of tribes who inhabited a common physical region (e.g., "Natives of the Pacific Northwest"). A unit on a single tribe will provide depth of understanding and diminish the chances that students will learn inaccurate information about a cultural group.

- *Be specific about the historical period.* All cultural groups change over time, and so our units of study must have chronological boundaries. For example, the Chinese of the Han dynasty (206 B.C. to A.D. 220) share many cultural traits with the Chinese of the present day, yet there are some striking differences. Thus, well-defined units should state a time span—for example, "Mexico in the 20th Century," "Medieval Japan," "Ancient Egypt."

- *Avoid stereotyping.* This can be difficult because anthropologists describe a norm, and it is easy for children to assume that all members of a cultural group conform to the norm. Every cultural group, however, contains variation.

- *Use as many resources as possible:* videos, laser discs, the Internet, software, study prints, information books, biographies, reference books. The more resources we use, the better the chances that our students will acquire more than a superficial understanding of the cultural group. What if a resource is guilty of bias? Biased materials should be either excluded or presented as biased. Materials created by members of the cultural group being studied are a significant addition to any unit.

- *Include lessons on many facets of the cultural group.* For example, it should be clear to students what roles men and women fill. As I noted earlier, it is essential that students become aware of the values and beliefs of the cultural group, so lessons on religion are important. The students I taught, for example, were fascinated with the marriage and courtship rituals of other cultural groups.

- *Do some background work on the group of people to be studied.* No one should expect us to become experts; our teaching will be more successful, however, if we take time to read about the cultural group our students will study.

One final point: Students should make comparisons among cultural groups, contrasting the way we live with the ways of other groups. The purpose of a cultural comparison is to learn about ourselves and others, not to judge whether one group of people is better or worse than another. *Curriculum Guidelines for Multicultural Education* (1992) states that study of different cultural groups should help students see that

each individual and each ethnic group has worth and dignity. Students should be taught that persons from all ethnic groups have common characteristics and needs, although they are affected differently by certain social situations and may use different means to respond to their needs. (p. 286)

Doing Anthropology: A Dig

One activity that will give students some sense of how anthropologists work is a "dig." This is one way that *archaeologists,* those anthropologists investigating cultural groups from the past, gather data. During a dig, archaeologists excavate a site in search of artifacts. Several articles can help us in planning a dig with our students: Andel (1990), Carroll (1987), Hightshoe (1997), Morris (1998), Ovoian and Gregory (1991), Owen (1982), and Passe and Passe (1985). I also recommend two children's books: *Going on a Dig,* by Velma Morrison (1981), and *Digging to the Past: Excavations in Ancient Lands,* by W. John Hackwell (1986). Some Internet resources to help children understand how archaeologists conduct a dig are excellent. The "History/Social Studies Web Site for K–12 Teachers," through its "Archaeology/Anthropology" link, can connect to Web sites of several current projects *(http://execpc.com/~dboals/boals.html).* One that had excellent descriptions and photographs of a real dig was the Web site for the excavation of a 4th-century Coptic church in Wadi Natrum, Egypt (Center for Christian Antiquities, *http://www.scriptorium.org/theDigSite).*

Students who participate in a dig will learn how knowledge of a past culture is pieced together from the available evidence. We can plan two types of digs for our students. The first type is a *simulation.* We and a small group of our students gather old coins, pieces of inexpensive jewelry, old tools, and perhaps animal bones (e.g., from last night's roasted chicken). Then we bury these items in a sandbox on the playground. (Hightshoe, 1997, recommends constructing excavation boxes, which are 1 meter square and 15 centimeters deep.) The members of the class then conduct the excavation. They collect the items and analyze them for information on the hypothetical civilization that created them.

The other type of dig is an *excavation* of some part of the school grounds or an area in the community. It is best to conduct this type of dig with the assistance of an anthropologist. (Anthropologists are not difficult to find; almost every college has some!) The simplest example is an excavation of an area where children have played for a long time. One teacher I worked with conducted a successful dig of the bench area where children sat when their team was at bat during softball games. Other school and community digs are a more serious matter, must be conducted with an anthropologist, and commence only after receiving permission from the owners of the site. Susan Hightshoe (1997) describes a good combination of the two types of digs: Students study a local area that may have artifacts. The actual dig is a simulation, and the planted artifacts are representative of what might have been found at the actual site (this requires cooperation from a local history center or museum).

Here are some steps to consider when planning a dig for a class:

1. *Make sure students understand why archaeologists conduct excavations.* Young children do not understand why things get buried over time. Earthquakes, volcanic eruptions, and the gradual accumulation of mud, sand, and gravel bury the remains of a civilization.

2. *Provide students with an outline of the process before they start digging.* Students must understand why certain sites are selected for excavation. Explain that the actual physical act of digging must be performed with the utmost care. Students should realize that once artifacts are unearthed, their work is just beginning. The exact location of each artifact must be recorded. Once removed from their burial places, the artifacts must be cleaned, measured, and weighed. Each artifact must be analyzed to determine what it is and how it was used. Finally, artifacts should be displayed with an accompanying explanation.

3. *Prepare the excavation site.* Excavations on school grounds must be approved by the school principal before any digging begins. Excavations at off-school sites must be approved by the principal and the owner of the property. For a simulation, bury the fake artifacts ahead of time. Bury one set of artifacts at one level (e.g., 12 inches deep), and another set, belonging to an earlier culture, even deeper (e.g., 30 inches). This would approximate the layers of artifacts that archaeologists often find at a single site. Then "square" the excavation by using wooden stakes and lengths of strings to create a grid. Make each square in the grid large enough for two or three students to work within it (at least 5 feet square). Label each square by using a grid system (make horizontal spaces A, B, C, D, etc; make vertical spaces 1, 2, 3, etc.). Thus, students will be able to determine and record the precise location of each artifact they discover.

4. *Train students in excavation techniques.* Students must be careful. They should wear gloves for safety and use garden tools, kitchen utensils, and even whisk brooms to excavate the artifacts. Students must be cautious so that they do not break an item. When students discover something, its exact location should be recorded before the item is moved. Then it should be removed and placed into a plastic bag and labeled with the following information: date, time, coordinates of the square where it was found, approximate depth where it was found, and name of the person who found it. Students can also sift for artifacts. A simple sifter can be made by nailing 1/8-inch screen to a wooden frame. Students pour dirt through the sifter so that small items are caught on the screen.

5. *Analyze each artifact in a laboratory setting.* First, artifacts should be cleaned, usually with an old toothbrush. Then, each item should be measured and weighed. Items recovered intact are easy to identify (e.g., most coins). Other items are pieces of something else (a *shard,* for example, is a broken piece of pottery). Students should identify the item, speculate on what it reveals about the people who made it or used it, and try to figure out how old the item is. The whole group needs to share findings because the discovery of any item sheds light on all others.

6. *Consider creating a classroom museum.* An exciting way to share the results is on a "virtual" tour of a classroom museum (Ricchiuti, 1998). Students could create the tour on a school or classroom Web site or on a CD-ROM. A "real" museum is fun to create and would require only a corner of a classroom. Students write descriptions of each item, listing the measurements of the item, where it was found, its age, what it is, and how it was used.

Economics

Economics is the study of the production, distribution, and consumption of goods and services. Although economics has been called the "dismal science" by those who find it dull, economics can be an exciting part of an elementary social studies program (Armento, 1991; Kourilsky, 1977, 1987; Schug, 1985, 1996; Schug & Armento, 1985; Schug & Walstad, 1991; Van Fossen, 1998). Traditional primary-level units with an economic focus have included some elementary school classics, like "The Farm" or "The Market." In the upper grades, economics usually has been presented as a part of historical units or area studies. For example, during a unit on the American Colonies, students learn about triangular trade routes; during a unit on Saudi Arabia, students learn about oil production. Recently, interest has increased in linking school and 21st-century careers so that students learn about the world of work and acquire skills they will need after they leave school. Several organizations promote economic education, including the National Council on Economic Education, the Foundation for Teaching Economics, and the National Association of Economic Educators. These three groups formed a partnership to develop national standards for economics—the voluntary *National Content Standards in Economics* (National Council on Economic Education, 1997). Our discussion of economic education examines research on the development of economic thinking, the content and processes of economics that should be included in the elementary curriculum, and some teaching ideas.

Several researchers have examined how children acquire economic concepts: Armento (1991), Berti and Bombi (1988), Danziger (1958), Jahoda (1979), Schug (1983, 1994), and Schug and Walstad (1991). Most researchers posed economic problems to children and then interviewed them about their proposed solutions. This body of research leads to the following two conclusions:

1. *Children's economic thinking becomes more abstract and flexible with age.* Younger children are very concrete and literal in the way they view economic activity. For example, when asked to explain the exchange of money in a market, young children state that this is a form of ritual without economic meaning, that the exchange is required by law, or that the store is the place where money was produced (Armento, 1991). Young children have expressed the misconception that the

price of a good is determined by the size of the price tag and that the value of money is determined by the size and color of the currency or coin (Schug, 1994).

2. *Children's mature reasoning does not emerge at the same rate for all economic concepts.* Abstract thinking comes sooner for some aspects of economics than for others. For example, although young children usually are aware of their relative poverty or affluence, they often fail to grasp the relationship between work and income. At the same time they understand that they will receive 50¢ if they perform a household chore, many children fail to comprehend that their parents' jobs are linked to the household's financial status. As children mature, the economic relationship of labor and compensation becomes clearer and is generalized to all jobs. Our oldest students can understand the relationships among the parties in an economic system (e.g., jewelry salespersons depend on goldsmiths, who depend on gold miners), provide explanations for economic phenomena (e.g., why an airline slashes fares), and state the implications of economic policies (e.g., a temporary embargo on Japanese-manufactured cars could lead to fewer jobs in U.S. automobile dealerships).

Economics: The Curriculum

Almost all social studies textbooks have economic content. As I noted earlier, primary texts have focused on the production and distribution of common goods, such as food available in supermarkets and clothing in department stores. Upper grade texts have included economics as part of historical units or area studies. Two curriculum developers, however, have played a significant role in bringing economics to the elementary classroom. Lawrence Senesh (1963) and Marilyn Kourilsky (1977, 1987) have shown that basic economic concepts can be taught to young children. Senesh was the author of a popular series of texts titled *Our Working World*. Kourilsky wrote curriculum based on classroom mini-societies, simulated economies in which students developed their own laws, money, and government. Eventually, each class created a unique economic system, including entrepreneurial enterprises and taxes.

One of the most influential national documents in K–12 economics education was *A Framework for Teaching Economics: Basic Concepts,* published in 1977 under the sponsorship of the Joint Council on Economic Education (Hansen, Bach, Calderwood, & Saunders, 1977). The framework defined a K–12 economic curriculum with basic concepts from *microeconomics* (the working of specific markets), *macroeconomics* (the working of the national economy), and international economics. The framework was revised in 1984 and, despite its significant contribution to the social studies curriculum, was criticized by several leading economists (Saunders, Bach, Calderwood, & Hansen, 1984).

In 1997, the voluntary *National Content Standards in Economics* were published under the leadership of the National Council on Economic Education. These standards were authorized and funded by the Goals 2000 legislation of 1994. The 20 standards are written in plain English and provide "benchmarks" at Grades 4, 8, and 12. The benchmarks are objectives that state what students are expected to know and be able to do (Mezaros, 1997; Mezaros & Engstrom, 1998). Earlier, in 1994, *Expectations of Excellence: Curriculum Standards for the Social Studies,* produced by the NCSS, also attempted to define the scope of economic content that children should learn. Of the 10 strands in the NCSS standards, one (Strand 7, Production, Distribution, & Consumption) is devoted entirely to economics.

Both sets of standards expect elementary children to acquire a great deal of basic economic knowledge and to perform economic analysis. For example, Content Standard 11 in the national economic standards is "Students will understand that money makes it easier to trade, borrow, save, invest, and compare the value of goods and services." One knowledge objective in the benchmarks for this standard is that, by the completion of fourth grade, "students will know that money makes trading easier by replacing barter with transactions involving currency, coin, or checks." One performance objective for this standard is that fourth graders will be able to "decide whether they would rather have a suitcase full of money or one full of food when stranded on a deserted island" (National Council on Economic Education, 1997, pp. 20–21).

Both sets of standards expect children to know (a) that resources are limited and that people must choose to have some things and not have others; (b) that economic decisions require an analysis of costs and benefits; and (c) that economic systems are complex and involve several institutions, such as households, corporations, banks, and labor unions. In addition, children are to know (d) the nature of various economic systems; (e) how supply and demand, prices, incentives, and profits function in a market system; (f) the difference between private and public sectors of the economy; (g) how jobs become specialized; (h) various forms of exchange and money; (i) how income is determined by market conditions; (j) the nature of investment and entrepreneurship; and (k) the impact of government policy on a market system.

Both sets of standards also expect children to think critically about the economic content they learn. For example, children should be able to (a) compare economic systems according to who determines what is produced and distributed; (b) explain historical events from an economic perspective; and (c) use economic reasoning to evaluate policy proposals for contemporary issues like unemployment and pollution. Lessons with economic content should present opportunities for children to both gather and produce data in tables, charts, and graphs.

Teaching Ideas for Economics

Schug (1996) provides a framework for elementary students to use as they analyze economic problems or conditions. Use of the framework helps students grasp a fundamental concept: Economic decisions are the result of choices that people make on the basis of expected costs and expected benefits. The teacher presents a question ("Why do people save money?") or makes a statement ("We have cars in the United States that were made in many different nations"). Working in small groups or as a whole group, students then apply the six statements of Schug's framework:

1. *People choose to do things they think are best for them.* Children need to understand that economic events are not accidental or random. A third-grade class studying their local airport must see that the decision to build the airport was a difficult choice for citizens of the community. After a long debate, the airport was approved by voters because the majority thought the airport would help them. At this point, it is important for us to help children see the rationale behind economic choices.

2. *People's choices have costs.* The decision to build the new airport had costs. Children should realize the full range of costs beyond the money needed to acquire the land and pay for the terminal, runways, and supporting structures. Other costs included the relocation of people living on the land purchased for the airport, the "quality of life" costs to the airport's new neighbors, and the cost of not using for other purposes the resources allocated for the airport.

3. *People choose to do things for which they are rewarded.* Incentives encourage people to act. Wentworth and Schug (1994) note that "incentives may involve an increase in expected benefits, a decrease in expected costs, or some combination of the two" (p. 11). We might help children understand the nature of an incentive by noting some incentives that are used at school (e.g., rewards for positive behavior). To encourage people to vote for the airport, supporters offered the incentive of easier access to airline flights because the nearest other airport was 83 miles away.

4. *People create rules that affect their choices and actions.* Economic choices can only be made within the context of the existing laws governing economic activity. Construction of the airport was possible because of federal laws that allow for the private ownership of airlines and state laws that permit local governments to purchase private land for a public purpose. For each economic condition children study, they should see that the choices people make are restricted, or enabled, by laws.

5. *People gain when they decide to trade freely with others.* The key here is for children to understand that voluntary trade helps both traders. In the case of the airport, airline travel is a trade. Passengers exchange money for a ride on the airplane. Both sides benefit: The passenger reaches his or her destination, and the airline makes money. Children should understand that not all trade is voluntary. When children study the European colonization of North America and examine the economic relationships among the Native tribes and the Europeans, they will see an example of involuntary or *exploitative trade,* in which only one side benefited.

6. *People's immediate choices today have future results.* The construction of the new airport changed the community. New people arrived because of the jobs

created by the airport. Some members of the community living near the airport, however, continued legal action because of increased noise and traffic. Speculation is an important part of economic analysis, and we should encourage children to predict what they think the future will be like if an economic decision is made. Another, simpler way to help children analyze an economic decision is to prepare a two-column chart. On one side, list the benefits that will come from the decision, and on other side, list the costs. Challenge children to consider both short-term and long-term benefits and costs. Sometimes it is worthwhile to have children make a choice before doing the analysis and then to see how many have changed their minds after the cost benefit analysis.

School to Career. Recent interest has been shown in reforming the K–12 school curriculum so that students are prepared for the world of work in the emerging information age. This is sometimes called *school-to-career* or *workforce education*. Much of the focus at the secondary level has been on reforming the high school curriculum to fit the expectations of the contemporary workplace. At the elementary level, initiatives have expanded coverage of the requirements and responsibilities of contemporary jobs. Students are curious about "grown-up jobs," and we should plan some of the following activities for our classes:

- *Job shadowing*. Students spend time with someone while at work (e.g., a student spends a day with a dental hygienist).
- *Career inquiries*. Students find out all they can about a job: required schooling, scope of the tasks the job entails, special challenges of the job, tools used by people holding the job, and so on.
- *Career days*. Members of the community come to school to share information about their jobs.
- *Career opportunities*. Students use the classified section of the newspaper to learn about the jobs available in their community. Following is an example of this type of lesson.

Grade 6: Jobs Offered—The Classified Ads

LESSON PLAN

This lesson was part of a sixth-grade unit on careers. The lesson examined an advertisement in the classified section of the local newspaper that read as follows:

CONTROLLER
High-energy, top-notch accounting person needed for a manufacturer of office furniture. Handle management reporting, financial analysis, and internal control. Supervise employees in payroll, payables, and receiving. Should have BA/BS degree with emphasis in accounting; CPA is a plus; heavy computer exposure, experience managing people. FAX resume and salary history.

Social studies incorporates content from all the social science disciplines, including psychology and sociology. Social studies activities should help students abandon prejudicial attitudes and form lasting friendships with their classmates.

Overview: This lesson is for a sixth-grade class of 30 students.

Resources and Materials: (a) 30 copies of the same issue of the local newspaper and (b) a chart with six focus questions you prepare ahead of time.

Content Objectives: Students will understand the specialized nature of jobs, how each job has unique requirements and responsibilities.

Process Objectives: Students will *identify* the responsibilities and requirements for the position of controller, *identify* the responsibilities and requirements for any other position advertised in the want ads, and *compose* an ad for one of the jobs at their school.

Teaching Sequence

1. Acquire 30 copies of the same issue of the local newspaper (most newspapers will provide teachers with copies, especially day-old papers); circle the same want ad in each of the 30 newspapers. (If you cannot obtain these, make up your own or make copies of the ad for the controller shown above.)
2. Prepare the chart with the focus questions (see Step 5 below).

3. Review with the class the previous week's activities, all on careers, and distribute the newspapers. Tell students to open the paper to the page where the circled ad is located.
4. Explain that businesses that have open jobs often advertise them in the newspaper. The classified ads have many sections, and the section with available jobs is often called "Jobs Offered." Explain that the newspaper charges the employer to run the ad, usually by the number of words, so the text of the ads will appear "choppy" and have lots of abbreviations to keep them short.
5. Direct students to the ad for the controller. Help them answer the six questions you wrote on the chart paper:

What is the name of the job?
What type of business has placed the ad in the paper?
What are the responsibilities of the person who will fill the job? What will the successful applicant do?
What requirements must applicants fulfill?
How much will the job pay?
How do applicants contact the employer?

You will need to explain some of the vocabulary in the ad (e.g., *internal control, CPA*). Also, point out that all ads do not include an answer to each question on the chart.

6. Tell students that they may work individually, with a partner, or in small groups. Tell them to select a different ad and to answer the questions on the chart. If this appears too challenging, then select simple ads for each group to examine. Circulate among the students and ask, "How are the requirements for the job you selected different from the requirements for the job of controller?"
7. Extend the lesson by presenting a project. A group of students could write an ad for one of the jobs at school (e.g., teacher, principal, custodian, secretary). This would require students to do some research on the requirements and responsibilities of the job. Be sure to give students a word limit; for example, each ad must not exceed 50 words.

Evaluation: Collect and review students' answers to the six questions when they selected an ad in the paper. As you circulate among the students, note how many understand the different requirements for jobs.

Effective Teaching in Today's Diverse Classroom: *Scaffolding* is a word used by many educators to describe the help teachers provide to students. The use of *scaffold* is a metaphor. Just as a scaffold helps workers reach heights they could not reach on their own, an instructional scaffold helps students accomplish things they could not do on their own. The word was first used in the area of language development as a descriptor for the ways adults helped children expand their oral language (Cazden, 1983). Now, the concept has taken on a broader meaning and is often used to describe what teachers do to help English language learners succeed in mathematics, science, and social studies. Theoretically, instructional scaffolds place a learner in Vygotsky's zone of proximal development. Or, to use Cummins's ideas, scaffolds provide more contextual support for the learner. The words are not important, but the concept is. In this lesson, what would you do to help English language learners be successful and achieve the lesson's objectives? Of all the lessons presented so far, this one has the potential to be the most challenging for students who do not have advanced English language skills. Even the best sixth-grade readers will have difficulty understanding the newspaper ad for the controller position. Remember, though, all students need challenges, and it is important to plan activities that push your students. The "scaffolding" you provide your English language learners could be each of the following:

- In the second part of the lesson, when students select an ad and respond to the questions, be sure your English language learners are in a group with someone who can help them understand the text of the ad (the help can be provided by you, an aide, or a classmate who is a good reader).
- Help English language learners select an ad that is relatively easy to read.
- Be prepared to work with each group that has an English language learner. You may have to paraphrase the content of the ad in words your English language learners can understand.

Focus on the Consumer. A variety of interesting social studies activities can be built on the economic concept of consumption. Following are examples.

- *Best buys.* Challenge older children to gather comparative price data on similar products. Most markets now include unit prices beneath items (e.g., 16¢/oz). Students should look at several brands of a product, such as orange juice, paper plates, or ice cream. For each, they should conclude which is the "best buy." Remind students, of course, that price is only one feature a consumer considers.
- *Analysis of television advertisements.* The economic concept of distribution includes advertising and marketing. For this activity, videotape commercials that appear on television. Then challenge students to explain, for each commercial, how the advertiser has tried to make the product more appealing. Some television ads mention price or specific features of the product, but most use other factors to sell the product.
- *Budgets.* Preparation of a budget requires choices and economic analysis. Ask students to prepare proposed budgets for real situations. For example, if a fund-raiser has provided each classroom with $100 to spend on instructional materials, what should be purchased? Young children can prepare a

sample budget for a set of economic conditions. For example: You have $300 to spend on new clothes. You must purchase shoes, pants, a shirt, and a jacket. How will you spend your money? Older students can work with more complicated hypothetical budgets. For example: Prepare a yearly budget for a family of five with an annual income of $45,000. This is a difficult project, requiring students to investigate the actual costs of daily living.

- *Economize*. Students live in an era of corporate and governmental "downsizing" as families, schools, businesses, and all levels of government have made cuts in their expenditures. *Economizing* is economic analysis with the goal of saving money. Challenge students to think of ways money could be saved in the classroom, the school, their community, and in state and federal governments.

Psychology and Sociology

Psychology and sociology have played relatively minor roles in the elementary social studies curriculum (M. R. Nelson & Stahl, 1991). Six major areas of psychology could be included in a social studies curriculum: (a) psychological research methods, (b) growth and development, (c) cognition and learning, (d) personality, (e) mental health, and (f) social psychology (Baum & Cohen, 1989). Most of the area related to psychology focus on the personal identity of each child and how children can deal with emotions like anger, fear, and jealously. *Sociology,* the study of human society and how individuals relate to each other, examines group behavior. Attempts to infuse sociological content into the social studies curriculum have focused on the high school (Angell, 1981; Gray, 1989; Jantz & Klawitter, 1991; Switzer, 1986). Our students should examine several aspects of group behavior and understand the roles people play in primary groups, like their families, and secondary groups, like a church choir or softball team. Attitudes toward other groups, especially stereotyping and prejudice, should be addressed in the social studies curriculum (Walsh, 1992).

Expectations of Excellence (NCSS, 1994), the national social studies standards, have incorporated important concepts from psychology and sociology in Strand IV, "Individual Development and Identity" and Strand V, "Individuals, Groups & Institutions." Strand IV states that "social studies programs should include experiences that provide for the study of individual development and identity" (p. 57). Strand V proposes that "social studies programs should include experiences that provide for the study of interactions among individuals, groups, and institutions" (p. 57). The content of these two strands asks students to learn about the following:

- Personal changes, both in terms of physical growth and personal interests; personal connections to place, like home and school

- Unique features of families; how learning and physical development affect behavior; how families, groups, and community influence a person's daily life
- Factors that contribute to one's personal identity; how to work independently and cooperatively
- Roles people fill as members of groups
- Group and institutional influences on people and events
- Tensions between individuals and groups
- Tension between an individual's beliefs and government policies and laws
- How groups and institutions work to meet individual needs and the common good

Following are some activities that incorporate psychology and sociology:

- Suggest that students write autobiographies, using photographs of themselves as illustrations. The photographs will show how the students have changed physically. Have students complete "then and now" surveys to identify changing interests and attitudes. If your school has a Web site, then the autobiographies could become part of it.
- A very interesting activity is to have students continue their autobiographies as speculative works of fiction. Ask them to write about themselves at each of the following ages: 18, 25, 35, 50, and 70. Where will they live? What jobs will they have?
- Have students make a mini-mural showing the significant places in their lives. Each student can make one by dividing a piece of 12 × 18-inch drawing paper into four or eight sections. Then the student adds to each section an illustration of the significant places in his or her life (e.g., home, classroom, baseball field, Grandma's house).
- Have students make a list of the things they can do now that they could not do when they were younger (e.g., compare age 3 and age 8). This list should include physical tasks (e.g., shoot a basket), academic performance (e.g., add large numbers), home chores (e.g., dry the dishes), and other daily activities (e.g., answer the telephone).
- Suggest that a group of students interview their classmates and make a chart with three columns of activities: those best done individually, those best done in a small group, and those best done as a whole class.
- Help students see that they belong to many groups and understand their role within each group. Request that students complete a chart listing the groups to which they belong, identifying their roles in the group, and describing their responsibilities in that role. The chart should have three columns: "Group," "Role," and "Responsibilities." For example, a student would write "Group: Chavez School Student Council," "Role: representative and treasurer," and "Responsibilities: represent class, keep track of council

budget." Students would make other entries for other groups, such as Mr. Kim's class, my family, the East Park Rangers (soccer team), Temple Beth Torah.

- Help students consider the consequences of yielding to peer pressure. Tell small groups to report on how peer pressure affects the way their classmates dress, the slang they use, and the out-of-school activities they consider worthwhile. Students should discuss the importance of maintaining a strong sense of self.

- Allow interested students to prepare a multimedia display on "America's Dissenters." The national standards state that students should be able to "identify and describe examples of tension between an individual's beliefs and government policies and laws" (NCSS, 1994, p. 60). The display could be stored on CD-ROM and could include political leaders who opposed adoption of the Constitution (e.g., Patrick Henry), early practitioners of civil disobedience (e.g., Henry Thoreau), Native Americans who fought the expansion of the United States (e.g., Geronimo), abolitionists (e.g., Frederick Douglass), advocates of women's suffrage (e.g., Susan B. Anthony), prohibitionists (e.g., Carrie Nation), civil rights leaders (e.g., Medgar Evers), and consumer advocates (e.g., Ralph Nader).

- Invite students to go into the community to find out more about organizations that promote the common good, such as the Red Cross, service clubs, and groups that raise money to battle diseases. A group could write a book for their classmates on these groups. Or, invite the community to come to your classroom as representatives of these organizations visit your room to make presentations to your students.

Reducing Stereotyping and Prejudice

Aspects of psychology and sociology come into play when we try to reduce stereotypical and prejudicial attitudes in our classrooms. Gloria Ladson-Billings (1992) provides excellent suggestions:

1. *Assess our teaching.* Ladson-Billings asks us as teachers to consider what conclusions an observer would reach after spending time in our classroom. We would hope that people with overt biases never enter our profession, and I think that teachers as a group are among the most sensitive and least prejudiced people in our society. Nonetheless, many of us do things that are biased. For example, what is the seating pattern in the room? Are members of minority groups clustered together? Are boys and girls intermixed? Do we, in fact, have different discipline procedures for some students, and if so, are those students disproportionately members of a minority group? What does our room environment reveal? Are images of successful people from all groups displayed?

2. *Check our teaching materials.* Although textbooks, films, videos, children's books, and other resources have come a long way in the last 20 years to remove stereotyped and biased portrayals, it is a good idea to assess the materials we use.

3. *Transform the curriculum.* We should incorporate diverse content and perspectives.

4. *Strive for integration.* Students of both genders, of challenging conditions, of all ethnic groups, and of each social class should work together during the year. If we allow our students to select the projects they will complete, we must be sure that a pattern does not develop of some groups having only girls, or only African Americans, and so on. Consistent, positive interactions through cooperative learning can improve intergroup relations (Kagan, 1985, 1989).

5. *Do not ignore incidents of student prejudicial behavior.* When some students express stereotypical or biased feelings toward other students, whether through words or actions, we should intervene. We should work with students to find the source of these attitudes and then provide information to show a better picture of the group that was disparaged. Students who use racial slurs need to know the full impact of those words. A student who says that all members of a group behave in one way should be taught about intragroup diversity. Finally, we should make it clear to our students that prejudiced behavior on campus will not be tolerated.

Families and Friendship

The traditional social studies curriculum in the early grades has devoted attention to families and friendship, two topics that can help children learn key concepts in sociology and psychology. With some political and religious groups advocating that only one type of family be promoted in the schools, discussion of the diversity of family composition has become a hot issue. My suggestion is to take an anthropological view: The definition of family varies widely from cultural group to cultural group, and any cultural group will always contain variations from the norm. Children know the other members of their nuclear family, and in contemporary America, families will include a variety of people other than Mom and Dad, Brother and Sister. I think the goals of family-related lessons should be to (a) show how families contribute to each child's identity and (b) help children see how the cooperative efforts among family members can serve as a model for classrooms, schools, communities, states, and nations. Remember, lessons on the family should be preceded by a letter to parents describing the activities that will take place in our classroom. Not all information should be revealed in the classroom, and parents should be aware of what we are going to cover. The focus on friendship should help children understand the challenges and rewards of being a good friend. Friendship comes easily to many children, but other children will benefit from an exploration of the characteristics and responsibilities of friends. The opening vignette in chapter

2 described how one teacher implemented the unit "Families and Friends." Following are some other activities that could be a part of a unit on families and friends:

- *Compile family trees.* This project requires students to interview parents, grandparents, and other family members. You will need to help students develop the survey questions and provide a model for the actual family tree that is completed.
- *Make a class quilt.* The beautiful children's book *The Patchwork Quilt* (Flournoy, 1985) provides a perfect introduction to making a family quilt. Some elementary teachers have the expertise to help their students make real, sewn quilts. Most of us, though, will have to settle for helping our students make quilts with sections of paper pasted together. Like any quilt, each section of each student's quilt should be special and, in this case, represent something about the student's family. (McCall, 1994, discusses the use of quilts in elementary social studies. Her article focuses on the significance of quilting in people's lives and portrayals of history through quilts.)
- *Make semantic maps.* Create a semantic map with the word *Friend* in the middle. Ask students what makes a good friend. Record what the students say, linking common characteristics.
- *Sing songs about families and friends.* One of my favorites is "Five People in My Family" from *The Sesame Street Song Book* (Raposo & Moss, 1971). Another of my favorites is the song, "I Live in the City," by Malvina Reynolds. This song expresses multicultural cooperation as people of many colors build a city. "I Live in the City" can be found in many kindergarten, first-, or second-grade music textbooks.
- *Read books about families and friends.* Some of the best children's picture books address themes related to families and friends (Zarrillo, 1994). I provide a list of multicultural children's picture books focusing on families and friendship in Figure 13.4 (at the end of this chapter).
- *Tell family stories.* Give students the opportunity to tell the stories of their families, through timelines, chronologies, murals, and biographies. Following is a writing project that challenged children to discover some of the special aspects of their families.

Grade 2: "A Mini-Book on My Family"

Description of a PROJECT

As part of a unit on the family, several classes of children wrote and illustrated four-page books, including the covers, on their families.

Phase I

In the first phase of the project, each child surveyed her or his family by using the data retrieval chart reproduced as Figure 13.1. The chart was titled "3 Fascinating,

Figure 13.1 Data Retrieval Chart: Mini-Book on My Family

3 Fascinating, funny, incredible, wonderful, heroic, commendable, or ordinary things someone in *my family did.*

1. Who, what, when?

2. Who, what, when?

3. Who, what, when?

Funny, Incredible, Wonderful Heroic, Commendable, or Ordinary Things Someone in My Family Did." The three cells are labeled 1, 2, and 3, and each cell contains the questions "Who, What, When?" The teachers stressed that everything recorded on the charts had to be true and that it was OK to include things that were less than extraordinary. Funny events were definitely to be included! Children took their charts home and talked with members of their families. More able children wrote the information down; other children had their parents do the writing.

In one second-grade classroom, the completed charts made great reading. One child recorded "My grandfather met Clark Gable in a restaurant in 1938." Another student noted "My sister, Elva, scored three goals last Saturday." A third wrote, "Uncle Luis can make it sound like a frog singing 'Happy Birthday'."

Phase 2

In the second phase of the project, teachers handed out a template for the book. Each page would be half of an 8½ × 11-inch sheet of paper. Each book would be four pages, including a cover. (Templates are included as Figures 13.2 and 13.3.)

Figure 13.2 Mini-Book on My Family: Cover and Page 1

ONE
1   1

THREE

BY

Figure 13.3 Mini-Book on My Family: Pages 2 and 3

The children colored the numeral 3 at the top of their covers and then added, in their own writing, the title "Fascinating, Funny, Incredible, Wonderful, Heroic, Commendable, or Ordinary Things Someone in My Family Did." On each page, children provided an illustration and a description of the noteworthy event.

Effective Teaching in Today's Diverse Classroom: This would be a good opportunity to use a variation of the *language experience approach (LEA).* The LEA is a method of teaching children to read. The child tells the story of a personal experience to an adult, who writes down what the child says. Then, the child and the adult read the dictation aloud. Children who are not yet ready to do the writing required in this project could dictate their descriptions to an adult. The child would first draw the illustrations and then dictate a description. The adult would transcribe what the child said. Finally, the child and the adult would read aloud the dictated description.

Global Education, Environmental Education, and Current Events

Global Education

Revolutionary advances in technology and transportation have brought the people of the world closer together. "Global education" should be more than a slogan; the elementary social studies curriculum must be international in scope (Anderson, 1982; Case, 1993; Collins, Czarra, & Smith, 1998; Hanvey, 1976; Kniep, 1986, 1989; Lamy, 1987; Massialas, 1991; E. G. Miller & Jacobson, 1994; National Council for the Social Studies Ad Hoc Committee on Global Education, 1987; Simpson, 1996; K. E. Tye, 1990; B. B. Tye & Tye, 1992). Global education has meant different things to different people. Robert Hanvey (1976) and Willard Kniep (1985) were early and influential advocates of global education, and each provided a definition frequently cited by other writers. Case (1993) synthesized Hanvey's and Kniep's work and argued for two dimensions to global education: a *substantive* dimension, "knowledge of various features of the world and how it works," and a *perceptual* dimension, which is "an outlook or orientation" (p. 318).

The substantive dimension includes five categories of content:

1. *Universal and cultural values and practices.* Our students should learn about the many cultural groups that inhabit the earth and discover the similarities and differences among groups.
2. *Global connections.* Our curriculum should include units and lessons that show how people are linked by global economic, political, ecological, and technological systems.

In the 21st century, modern technology will continue to bring the world's people closer together. Teachers should help their students understand the global implications of the topics they study.

3. *Contemporary worldwide concerns and conditions.* Our students should learn about issues and problems that are global in scope and that require international solutions.
4. *Origins and past patterns of worldwide affairs.* This category requires a curriculum that helps our students understand the history of international current events.
5. *Alternative future directions in worldwide affairs.* Among the essential activities in global education are those that require speculation and that challenge our students to predict the global consequences of political and economic decisions.

Case's (1993) perceptual dimension is more difficult to define. This dimension is part of the affective domain; the goal is a social studies program that leads students to adopt a perspective that includes "open-mindedness, anticipation of complexity, resistance to stereotyping, inclination to empathize, and nonchauvinism" (p. 320). To Case, open-mindedness is crucial to global education. After all, it makes little sense to develop units of study that present global content if students will ignore the information because of previous biases or prejudices.

Social studies can help students learn about other people and places, but only if they are willing to accept that their preconceptions may be inaccurate. Global systems in economics, ecology, politics, communication, and transportation are complex. It should go without saying that our social studies programs should help students resist stereotyping. We as teachers inadvertently lead to stereotyping by using descriptors that fail to distinguish the differences among nations, groups, and people (e.g., "The Third World"). Repeated references to "Eastern Europe," for example, can lead students to conclude that there are no differences between life in the Czech Republic and Bulgaria; in fact, the status of those two nations in the post-Soviet era is not at all alike. Likewise, lessons and units that cover a topic superficially can result in stereotyping. For example, a short unit on Egypt could lead students to think that this nation is "a museum or curiosity piece as the land of pyramids and sphinxes" (Case, 1993, p. 322).

The national social studies standards (NCSS, 1994) emphasize the importance of "internationalizing" the social studies curriculum. One of the 11 strands is "Global Connections" (Strand 10). The standards are ambitious and call for students in the upper elementary grades to learn about a wide range of global topics and issues, such as the following:

- How aspects of culture, such as language, the arts, and belief systems, can both facilitate and impede global understanding
- Examples of conflict and cooperation among nations and cultural groups
- Effects of technology on the global community
- Causes and possible solutions of global issues, such as health, security, and environmental quality
- The relationship between national sovereignty and global interests
- Standards and concerns related to universal human rights
- The purpose and status of international organizations

Teaching Global Education

The traditional expanded environments framework leads to a social studies curriculum that lacks global content (Akenson, 1989; Larkins & Hawkins, 1990). The primary grades focus on awareness of self, primary social groups like the school and family, the neighborhood, and the community. Fourth grade focuses on the geography and history of the state. Fifth grade is a survey of U.S. history. Not until sixth grade does the curriculum become international. Alternatives, however, place greater emphasis on global education. If you recall, in chapter 1, the social studies framework adopted by Gwinnett County, Georgia, was presented as an "internationalized" alternative (Blankenship, 1994). Social studies at every grade level should include lessons and units that take a global perspective (Diaz, Massialas, & Xanthopoulos, 1999).

With global education, environmental education, and current events, we can adopt three approaches: (a) address it as a "stand alone" component of the social studies curriculum, with separate units of study; (b) "integrate" topics into the units we teach; or (c) a combination of the stand-alone and the integration approaches. Global education units include those on other places, both in historical and contemporary context (e.g., "South Africa Today," "The Aztec"), cross-cultural units (e.g., "Going to School in Colombia, Kenya, and Indonesia"), thematic units (e.g., "Cooperation and Conflict Among Nations"), units on events with global implications (e.g., "The Persian Gulf War"), and units on global problems (e.g., "Famines: Causes and Solutions"). Whether or not the curriculum includes separate units of study, every social studies unit should explore global connections. For example, a unit on families can introduce children to families in other nations. If the fourth-grade curriculum is the geography and history of our state, then we can incorporate considerable global content. For example, a unit on the early history of North Carolina should include information on a slave economy closely linked to Africa and the Caribbean. A unit on contemporary North Carolina should help students understand how many jobs in the state are either with foreign-owned companies or with firms dependent on foreign trade.

Following are some specific teaching ideas for global education:

- Suggest that your students become electronic pen pals with students living in other countries. The easiest way to find e-mail pen pals for your students is to use the "ePALS Classroom Exchange" *(http://www.epals.com/index.html)*. Formerly known as the "Email Classroom Exchange," this service began in 1996 and currently has e-pals in 96 countries. In the spring of 1999, more than 850,000 students had e-pals!

- Globalize your curriculum with another Internet resource—a "virtual interactive field trip." The "California SCORE" Web site *(http://score.rims.k12.ca.us)*, the NCSS site *(http://www.ncss.org/online)*, and the "History/Social Studies Web Site for K–12 Teachers" *(http://execpc.com/~dboals/boals.html)* all have links to virtual field trips. The most successful example of this type of experience is MayaQuest (Hefte, 1995). In 1995, 1996, 1997, and 1998, more than 1 million students and teachers joined a group of explorers who bicycled through Mexico and Central America in an attempt to find out why ancient Maya civilization collapsed. As the explorers toured sites and talked with experts from several fields, they completed daily reports that could be read in classrooms that joined the project. The reports included photographs, maps, and commentary.

- Use many topics that lend themselves to cross-cultural comparison (e.g., clothing, shelter, school, government, sports, food). For example, if students in a third-grade class take part in a unit on transportation in Los Angeles, they should also learn about transportation systems in other places. Students in Los Angeles would learn about freeways, the metropolitan bus system, and plans for Southern California's emerging light rail system. They would also become acquainted with historical means or transportation in Southern California, such as horse-powered wagons, early automobiles, and the efficient system of light rail "red cars" that was discontinued in the 1950s. To internationalize this unit, their teacher could select another large city for investigation, such as Beijing, where urban transit is not based on the automobile.

- Conduct this common global activity with your class: Have them gather data on the source of products in their homes or at school. For example, you could ask your students to select three shirts or blouses. On a data retrieval chart, the students would note where each item was produced (found on the clothing labels). Tally class totals and have students use maps to locate the places where the clothes were made. In most situations, students will see that almost everyone has clothes that were made overseas, especially in Asia and the Spanish-speaking Americas. Students should explore the economic factors that have led U.S. corporations to build factories in other nations and consider the consequences for workers here and abroad.

- Plan a unit on international organizations for your upper grade students. This is a good Jigsaw project, as small groups gather information on different organizations and then share what they have learned with their classmates. Students could learn about the United Nations (UN), the Organization of American States (OAS), the International Red Cross, Amnesty International, the North Atlantic Treaty Organization (NATO), the World Health Organization (WHO), or the International Olympic Committee (IOC).

- Use people in your community as resources for global education. Some of your students, their parents, or grandparents are immigrants and can share information about their native lands. An increasing number of "local" businesses actually are international in scope and include employees who can talk about their work with colleagues overseas. Almost every university in the United States has faculty and students who are citizens of other countries. In addition to encyclopedias, books, films, the Internet, and other computer-based resources, people in your city with global experience can help your students with global projects.

- Teach more elementary units that look at foreign nations in a contemporary context. So often, students only study places like China or Mexico as history. Learning about life today in another nation can be important learning experiences for your students. Ensure that the resources you use are accurate. Fortunately, several excellent nonfiction children's books on other nations are available with updated information presented through a well-researched text and attractive photographs. When planning these units, take time to avoid superficial coverage and misunderstandings. Topics should include the economics, the arts, recreation, education, and religion.

- Challenge your students to create an atlas for a region. This is a challenging task because students will have to make several maps. These student-made books make an excellent group project. For example, an atlas on Southeast Asia would include a world map highlighting the region, a map of the region itself, a map of each nation in Southeast Asia, maps of large cities in the region, topographical maps, economic maps, and historical maps showing the political boundaries of the past.
- Suggest that your students create a "virtual tour" of a nation or region. Virtual tours can be a part of a Web site or be recorded on CD-ROM. Photographs and maps can be "clipped" from Internet sites as long as they have no copyright restriction. Students would write the text and organize the sequence of the tour.
- Assign your class a similar project, the "travel brochure." This is an old social studies favorite. Students design a document promoting a nation or a region as a travel destination. To avoid superficial coverage, I suggest that each brochure promote a tour that will last at least 15 days. Then, students will have to include information about several locations in the nation. Stress to students that these brochures should highlight the places tourists would want to visit.

Environmental Education

Environmental education is highly interdisciplinary. Much of what students learn about their environment is a part of science, as they study the plants and animals and other organisms that share the planet. Many traditional elementary school learning activities, like nature study and outdoor education, are a part of environmental education. As a part of social studies, the focus is how the actions of people affect the air, water, and other living things (Charles, 1985; Simmons, 1994, 1995; Wilkie, 1993). Simmons (1995) provides a summary of the content of environmental education:

- An affective component, sensitivity and appreciation of environmental issues and topics
- Ecological knowledge, a part of the science curriculum, including the biology of plants and animals, and the relationships within an ecosystem
- Sociopolitical knowledge, how human activities influence the environment
- Knowledge of current environmental issues
- Environmental skills, including the ability to use primary and secondary sources to learn about environmental topics and issues
- Environmental responsibility and citizenship, an understanding of what individuals and groups can do to preserve and protect the environment

As with the other topics covered in this chapter, environmental topics can either be integrated with existing units of study or serve as the basis for separate units. Following are some teaching ideas for the social studies part of environmental education:

- Ask students to examine the contents of school wastebaskets. This is sometimes recommended as an exercise in anthropology, as students examine the contents as artifacts that reveal aspects of our culture. With an environmental focus, students classify the items according to whether or not they could be reused or recycled. This task helps students see that they can play a role in conserving our natural resources.
- Plant a tree. This is an activity full of educational potential. Students will become botanists as they learn about the structure of the tree and how it lives. They will also see how people determine whether or not the tree survives. Initially, the tree will need to be nurtured and protected. As the tree grows stronger, both single incidents of irresponsibility and the long-term effects of human-made pollution will threaten the tree. In addition to the science-related activities surrounding the tree planting, ask students to provide complete answers to the questions "What can we do to help the tree grow?" and "What may people do that will harm the tree?"
- Suggest reading. Many excellent children's books address environmental issues. For example, Lynn Cherry's *The Great Kapok Tree* (1990) helps students realize the full impact of cutting down a tree in the Amazon rain forest.
- Urge older students to analyze the consumption of energy at home and school. What appliances use the most energy? What use is essential? What use can be reduced? Challenge students to develop precise energy conservation plans for home, school, and classroom.
- Suggest that students share information on several endangered species. This is not only a good Jigsaw project but also a good mix of science and social studies. Assign each group of students a different species; each group is responsible for gathering information on that species and what actions by people have placed it at risk of extinction.
- See whether students can create pictorial flowcharts showing the process of converting crude oil to consumable energy. The chart should show drilling for oil, the work of an oil refinery, and the many products (e.g., gasoline, asphalt) ultimately produced from oil.
- Help students prepare a bulletin board display on some of the leading ecologists who have helped bring about changes in environmental policy (e.g., John Muir, Gifford Pinchot, Rachel Carson).
- Challenge older students to analyze contemporary environmental issues and consider policy alternatives. These can be local issues, such as the construction of a highway, or national and global issues, such as toxic waste, global warming, or ozone depletion.

- Help your youngest students learn about the plants and animals that share their immediate environment at school. This can begin with a simple inventory of all the living things that either live at the school (e.g., trees, grass, insects) or regularly visit (e.g., birds). This requires a nature walk around your school.

Current Events

Many of us can remember the dreadful chore of searching for a "current event" in the newspaper. Our time came, and we would find ourselves in front of our classmates, struggling to explain the content of our clipping. Fortunately, there are many alternatives for incorporating current events into the school day (Passe, 1988). As a separate part of social studies, one option is to schedule current events activities for a special time each week (e.g., every Friday morning). Another option is to integrate current events into our units of study; some important current events, however, will not fit our units. A third option is a combination approach. We would be ready to modify our unit plans to include current events and, at the same time, reserve a time each week for current events activities. Current events provide an opportunity for students to apply what they have learned about citizenship, history, geography, and the other social sciences.

The exploration of current events, if done properly, can be controversial. Our goal is to increase student understanding of the event, and this requires an effort to be sure we present multiple perspectives. The material on civil discourse in chapter 11 will help us have a fair, friendly, and thorough discussion of an event. The presentation and exploration of diverse views, however, is not as easy because attached to some topics is intense pressure to present only a popular view (Soley, 1996). We need to screen the news stories our students want to share. Some stories, such as many crimes, children are too young to discuss. For the most part, however, our students already have been exposed to major news events through television. The extra knowledge we help them acquire will often make them less anxious about troubling events.

In addition to television, radio, the Internet, and print media that are available to adults, several news resources are designed for children. Print media include *Weekly Reader, NewsCurrents,* and *Scholastic Newstime.* Technology has added software programs like World Classroom, a program that requires a modem and that links children by presenting social studies and science projects.

Following are teaching ideas for current events:

- Plan a unit or mini-unit on the news media. Writing about teaching media literacy, Passe (1994) stressed the importance of helping children understand the news they see presented in the media. Children need geographic and historical information to make sense of some events. Help students identify the major issues surrounding an event, which is often a challenge, given the amount of coverage major events receive. Also be sure that students learn to look for balance in coverage, detecting bias in the perspectives of advocates of certain positions. Involve students in news production as they make classroom or school newspapers. Work with students to produce videotaped news broadcasts, complete with news anchors, on-the-spot reporters, and commentators.

- Teach students how to use the newspaper as a data source (Rhoades, 1994). Like an encyclopedia or a Web site, the newspaper is a tremendous source of information. Have older students identify the sections of a major newspaper, use the index to find a desired section, and distinguish commentary from news reporting. (By the way, the Internet provides access to all the nation's major newspapers [e.g., the *Los Angeles Times* at *http://www.latimes.com*; the *New York Times* at *http://www.nytimes.com*; and the *Washington Post* at *http://www.washingtonpost.com*].)

- As for the "stand alone" approach, reserve a time for activities relating to current events. The use of student newspapers, like *Weekly Reader*, will help. Encourage, but don't require, students to bring in clippings of news stories they find interesting. Videotape portions of televised newscasts for use later in the week. Assign a small group of students to keep an "In the News" bulletin board up to date.

- Encourage small groups of interested students to "follow" a story and keep their classmates up to date. Members of the group will need to watch television newscasts and read newspapers to obtain information for their daily or weekly reports to the class. One interesting activity is to have a group of students follow each candidate during a political campaign. Each group could trace their candidate's travels on a map, follow the candidate's changing fortune as reflected in the polls, and make a display of the candidate's position on the major issues.

- Use current events as the catalyst for further study by students. Some events will stimulate students to complete written, artistic, or dramatic projects. For example, after reading a story about homeless people, interested students could read any of a number of excellent children's books about homelessness (Hofbauer & Prenn, 1996; Patton, 1996).

SUMMARY OF KEY POINTS

▶ Anthropology should have a prominent place in the elementary social studies curriculum, as students learn about other cultural groups and participate in anthropological data-gathering activities, like a dig.

▶ National standards in economics emphasize the importance of economic content and analysis in elementary social studies.

▶ Instructional activities drawing content from psychology and sociology will help students learn more about themselves and the people around them.

▶ Global education, environmental education, and current events are essential components of social studies; content from these areas should be integrated into all units of study and should serve as the focus for separate units.

FOR FURTHER READING

▶ Black (1998) describes how archaeology can be a part of the elementary social studies curriculum. She recommends the Society for American Archaeology's Web site as "probably the best sources of lesson plans as well as information about archaeology education programs across the United States" (p. 13). The society's Web site address is *http://www.saa.org*. Yell (1998) describes a series of lessons that would help students "think like an archaeologist."

▶ The National Council on Economic Education's curriculum project, called "EconomicAmerica," has produced units and lessons to accompany the *National Content Standards in Economics* (1997; contact the National Council at 1140 Avenue of the Americas, New York, NY 10036). A good Web site for teaching resources is the "Economic Education" Web site *(http:ecedweb.unomaha.edu)*. Rader (1995) reflects on the innovative elementary economics curriculum that he and others developed at the University of Chicago in the 1960s.

▶ Of the many resources on global education, consult the American Forum for Global Education *(http://www.globaled.org)* and the Global Education Network of the Association for Supervision and Curriculum Development (ASCD), whose newsletter, *Global Connections,* is a good source. The September 1998 issue of *Social Education* is devoted to global education (Collins et al., 1998). Cangemi and Aucoin (1996) describe a third-/fourth-grade thematic unit called "It's a Small World After All," a separate unit with a global focus (I think their unit should be expanded to provide deeper coverage). My colleague at Cal State Hayward, Jean Easterly (1994), edited the book *Promoting Global Teacher Education: Seven Reports,* which has some interesting chapters.

▶ For resources on environmental education see the Web sites for the North American Association for Environmental Education *(http://www.naaee.org)* and the Environmental Education Network *(http://www.environlink.org)* O'Brien and Stoner (1987) write about increasing environmental awareness through children's literature. Imeson and Skamp (1996) describe a unit integrating environmental education and social studies; Imeson implemented it in his classroom in Australia. The October 1997 issue of *Social Education* includes a special section: "Economics and the New Environmentalism" (Simpson, 1997).

Figure 13.4   **Families and Friends: A List of Multicultural Picture Books**

Baylor, Byrd. *Hawk, I Am Your Brother.* This is a story of the friendship of a boy and an animal.

Bunting, Eve. *The Wall.* A Mexican American boy and his father visit the Vietnam Veterans' War Memorial.

Clifton, Lucille. *My Friend Jacob.* This is the story of a friendship between an African American boy and another who is mentally challenged.

Crews, Donald. *Bigmama's.* African American author-illustrator Crews reminisces about trips to his grandparents' farm.

Dorros, Arthur. *Abuela.* A Latina girl and her grandmother fly above New York; some text is in Spanish.

Flournoy, Valerie. *The Patchwork Quilt.* An African American girl helps her mother make a quilt.

Friedman, Ina. *How My Parents Learned to Eat.* The book tells how a boy's father, a U.S. sailor, and his Japanese mother met.

Garza, Carmen Lomas. *Family Pictures.* This book, with text in English and Spanish, tells about growing up in a small Texas town.

Grifalconi, Ann. *Osa's Pride.* An African girl alienates friends with stories about her dead father.

Havill, Juanita. *Jamaica Tag-Along.* An African American brother thinks his little sister is a nuisance.

Keats, Ezra Jack. *Peter's Chair.* An African American boy decides to run away because of the arrival of his new sister.

Miller, Montazalee. *My Grandmother's Cookie Jar.* A Navajo girl and her grandmother eat cookies and share stories.

Morris, Ann. *Loving.* This is an information book that shows parents, friends, siblings, and pets from all over the world.

Polacco, Patricia. *Chicken Sunday.* A European American girl and her African American friends figure out a way to get a hat for Grandma Eula.

San Souci, Robert. *The Faithful Friend.* A retelling of a folktale from the island of Martinique, two friends break the spell of a wizard.

Say, Allen. *The Lost Lake.* A Japanese American boy and his father go backpacking.

Soto, Gary. *Too Many Tamales.* A Mexican American girl loses her mother's diamond ring on Christmas Eve.

Steptoe, John. *Stevie.* An African American boy deals with his foster brother.

Turkle, Brinton. *Thy Friend, Obadiah.* This book is a good introduction to religious minorities. A Quaker boy befriends a duck.

Uchida, Yoshiko. *Sumi's Special Happening.* A Japanese girl must find a gift for a 99-year-old relative.

Williams, Sherley Anne. *Working Cotton.* The author recalls her African American family's life as migrant workers in California's central valley.

Williams, Vera. *A Chair for My Mother.* (See the lesson plan in chap. 1.)

▶ Main et al. (1996) describe a 16-week unit on family and home culture for bilingual (Spanish/English) first graders. Morin (1997) shows how software can be used for the graphics in a primary unit on the family. Swearingen (1996) discusses how to promote tolerance among teacher credential candidates. The children's books listed in Figure 13.4 are useful resources for integrating multiculturalism.

Children's Literature to Support Social Studies Instruction

Accrosi, W. (1992). *My name is Pocahontas*. New York: Holiday House.

Adler, D. (1989). *A picture book of Martin Luther King, Jr.* New York: Holiday House.

Ancona, G. (1985). *Freighters: Cargo ships and the people who work them*. New York: Crowell.

Atkin, S. B. (Ed.). (1993). *Voices from the fields: Children of migrant farmworkers tell their stories*. Boston: Little, Brown.

Baker, O. (1981). *Where the buffaloes begin*. New York: Frederick Warne.

Barton, B. (1968). *Boats*. New York: Crowell.

Baylor, B. (1976). *Hawk, I am your brother*. New York: Scribner.

Bernard, C. (1974). *The book of fantastic boats*. New York: Golden Press.

Berry, E. (1952). *Sybil Ludington's ride*. New York: Viking.

Bourne, M. A. (1983). *Uncle George Washington and Harriet's guitar*. New York: Coward.

Brenner, B. (1994). *If you were there in 1776*. New York: Bradbury.

Brown, D. (1993). *Ruth Law thrills a nation*. New York: Ticknor & Fields.

Brown, D. P. (1985). *Sybil rides for independence*. Niles, IL: Albert Whitman.

Brown, M. (1949). *Henry-fisherman*. New York: Scribner.

Brown, M. W. (1988). *Homes in the wilderness*. New York: William Scott (Original work published 1939)

Bunting, E. (1990). *The wall*. New York: Clarion.

Bunting, E. (1994). *A day's work*. New York: Crown.

Carter, K. (1963). *Ships and seaports*. Chicago: Childrens Press.

Cherry, L. (1990). *The great Kapok tree*. San Diego: Harcourt Brace Jovanovich.

Choi, S. N. (1991). *The year of impossible goodbyes*. Boston: Houghton Mifflin.

Clapp, P. (1977). *I'm Deborah Sampson: A soldier in the War of Revolution*. New York: Lothrop, Lee & Shepard.

Cleaver, E. (1985). *Enchanted caribou*. New York: Atheneum.

Clifton, L. (1980). *My friend Jacob*. New York: Dutton.

Collier, J. L., & Collier, C. (1974). *My brother Sam is dead*. New York: Four Winds.

Collier, J. L., & Collier, C. (1981). *Jump ship to freedom*. New York: Delacorte.

Collier, J. L., & Collier, C. (1983). *War comes to Willy Freeman*. New York: Delacorte.

Collier, J. L., & Collier, C. (1984). *Who is Carrie?*. New York: Delacorte.

Creech, S. (1994). *Walk two moons*. New York: HarperCollins.

Crews, D. (1991). *Bigmama's*. New York: Greenwillow.

Crisman, R. (1993). *Racing the Iditarod Trail*. New York: Dillon.

Cushman, K. (1995). *The midwife's apprentice*. New York: Clarion.

D'Aulaire, I., & D'Aulaire, E. P. (1946). *Pocahontas*. New York: Doubleday.

Walt Disney Company. (1989). *Ships* [Videocassette]. Burbank, CA: Author.

Dorris, M. (1992). *Morning girl*. Boston: Hyperion.

Dorros, A. (1991). *Abuela*. New York: Dutton.

Fisher, L. E. (1991). *Sailboat lost*. New York: Macmillan.

Flack, M. (1946). *Boats on the river*. New York: Viking.

Flournoy, V. (1985). *The patchwork quilt*. New York: Dial.

Forbes, E. (1943). *Johnny Tremain*. Boston: Houghton Mifflin.

Frank, A. (1967). *The diary of a young girl* (Rev. Ed., B. M. Mooyart, Trans.). New York: Doubleday.

Freedman, R. (1987). *Lincoln: A photobiography*. New York: Clarion.

Freedman, R. (1988). *Buffalo hunt*. New York: Holiday House.

Freedman, R. (1990). *Franklin Delano Roosevelt*. Boston: Houghton Mifflin.

Freedman, R. (1991). *The Wright Brothers: How they invented the airplane*. New York: Holiday House.

Freedman, R. (1993). *Eleanor Roosevelt: A life of discovery*. New York: Clarion.

Friedman, I. R. (1987). *How my parents learned to eat*. Boston: Houghton Mifflin.

Fritz, J. (1967). *Early thunder*. New York: Coward McCann.

Fritz, J. (1969). *George Washington's breakfast*. New York: Coward McCann.

Fritz, J. (1992). *The great adventure of Christopher Columbus*. New York: Putnam & Grosset.

Garson, E. (Ed.). (1968). *The Laura Ingalls Wilder songbook*. New York: Harper & Row.

Garza, C. L. (1990). *Family pictures* (As told to Harriet Rohmer, Spanish text by R. Zubizarreta.) San Francisco: Children's Book Press.

Gibbons, G. (1991). *Surrounded by sea: Life on a New England fishing island*. Boston: Little, Brown.

Giblin, J. C. (1993). *Be seated: A book about chairs*. New York: HarperCollins.

Goble, P. (1978). *The girl who loved wild horses*. Scarsdale, NY: Bradbury.

Goble, P. (1984). *Buffalo woman*. Scarsdale, NY: Bradbury.

Goble, P. (1988). *Her seven brothers*. New York: Bradbury.

Goble, P., & Goble, D. (1973). *Lone Bull's horse raid*. Scarsdale, NY: Bradbury.

Goldstein, P. (1991). *Lóng is a dragon: Chinese writing for children*. San Francisco: China Books.

Grifalconi, A. (1990). *Osa's pride*. Boston: Little, Brown.

Hackwell, W. J. (1986). *Digging to the past: Excavations in ancient lands*. New York: Scribner.

Hall, D. (1979). *Ox-cart man*. New York: Viking.

Hartford, J. (1986). *Steamboat in a cornfield*. New York: Crown.

Harvey, B. (1986). *My prairie year: Based on the diary of Elinore Plaisted.* New York: Holiday House.

Harvey, B. (1987). *Immigrant girl: Becky of Eldridge Street.* New York: Holiday House.

Harvey, B. (1988). *Cassie's journey: Going West in the 1860s.* New York: Holiday House.

Hautzig, E. (1968). *The endless steppe.* New York: Crowell.

Havill, J. (1989). *Jamaica tag-along.* Boston: Houghton Mifflin.

Hodges, M. (1989). *The arrow and the lamp.* Boston: Little, Brown.

Houston, J. (1965). *Tikta Liktak: An Eskimo legend.* New York: Harcourt.

Houston, J. (1967). *The white archer.* New York: Harcourt.

Hoyt-Goldsmith, D. (1992). *Arctic hunter.* New York: Holiday House.

Humble, R. (1991). *Ships, sailors, and the sea.* New York: Franklin Watts.

Huynh, Quang Nhuong. (1982). *The land I lost: Adventures of a boy in Vietnam.* New York: Harper.

Keats, E. J. (1967). *Peter's chair.* New York: Harper & Row.

Krull, K. (Ed.). (1992). *Gonna sing my head off: American folk songs for children.* New York: Knopf.

Lasky, K. (1977). *Tugboats never sleep.* Boston: Little, Brown.

Lasky, K. (1978). *Tall ships.* New York: Scribner.

Leeming, J. (1946). *Toy boats to make at home.* New York: Appleton-Century.

Lester, J. (1968). *To be a slave.* New York: Dial.

Levine, E. (Ed.). (1993). *Freedom's children: Young civil rights activists tell their own stories.* New York: Putnam's Sons.

Loeb, R. H. (1979). *Meet the real Pilgrims: Everyday life on Plimoth Plantation in 1627.* Garden City, NY: Doubleday.

Loeper, J. J. (1973). *Going to school in 1776.* New York: Atheneum.

Lord, B. B. (1984). *In the year of the boar and Jackie Robinson.* New York: Harper & Row.

Lowery, L. (1987). *Martin Luther King Day.* Minneapolis: Carolrhoda.

Lowry, L. (1989). *Number the stars.* Boston: Houghton Mifflin.

Macauley, D. (1973). *Cathedral.* Boston: Houghton Mifflin.

Macauley, D. (1977). *Castle.* Boston: Houghton Mifflin.

Macauley, D. (1993). *Ship.* Boston: Houghton Mifflin.

MacLaughlin, P. (1985). *Sarah, plain and tall.* New York: Harper & Row.

McGovern, A. (1975). *The secret soldier: The story of Deborah Sampson.* New York: Four Winds.

Meltzer, M. (Ed.). (1984). *The Black Americans: A history in their own words.* New York: Harper & Row.

Meltzer, M. (1986). *George Washington and the birth of our nation.* New York: Franklin Watts.

Meltzer, M. (1987). *The American revolutionaries: A history in the their own words, 1750–1800.* New York: Crowell.

Meltzer, M. (1991). *Thomas Jefferson: The revolutionary aristocrat*. New York: Franklin Watts.

Miller, M. (1987). *My grandmother's cookie jar*. Los Angeles: Sloan.

Mitchell, B. (1986). *Shoes for everyone: A story about Jan Matzeliger*. Minneapolis: Carolrhoda.

Molloy, A. S. (1965). *Shaun and the boat: An Irish story*. New York: Hasting House.

Morris, A. (1990). *Loving*. New York: Lothrop, Lee & Shepard.

Morrison, V. F. (1981). *Gong on a dig*. New York: Dodd, Mead.

Mosel, A. (1968). *Tikki Tikki Tembo*. New York: Holt, Rinehart & Winston.

Nabakov, P. (Ed.). (1978). *Native American testimony: An anthology of Indian and White relations*. New York: Crowell.

O'Dell, S. (1960). *Island of the blue dolphins*. Boston: Houghton Mifflin.

Olney, R. R. (1985). *Ocean-going giants*. New York: Atheneum.

Patrick, D. (1990). *Martin Luther King, Jr.* New York: Franklin Watts.

Patterson, L. (1989). *Martin Luther King, Jr. and the freedom movement*. New York: Facts on File.

Penner, L. R. (1991). *Eating the plates: A Pilgrim book of food and manners*. New York: Macmillan.

Perl, L. (1977). *Hunter's stew and hangtown fry: What pioneer America ate and why*. New York: Clarion.

Polacco, P. (1992). *Chicken Sunday*. New York: Philomel.

Rachlis, E. (1960). *Indians of the Plains*. New York: American Heritage.

Raposo, J., & Moss, J. (1971). *The Sesame Street song book*. New York: Simon & Schuster.

Reiss, J. (1976). *The upstairs room*. New York: Crowell.

Rosenblum, R. (1976). *Tugboats*. New York: Holt, Rinehart & Winston.

San Souci, R. D. (1995). *The faithful friend*. New York: Simon & Schuster.

Say, A. (1982). *The bicycle man*. Boston: Houghton Mifflin.

Say, A. (1989). *The lost lake*. Boston: Houghton Mifflin.

Say, A. (1993). *Grandfather's journey*. Boston: Houghton Mifflin.

Scarry, H. (1982). *Life on a barge: A sketchbook*. Upper Saddle River, NJ: Prentice Hall.

Scott, G. (1981). *Egyptian boats*. Minneapolis: Carolrhoda.

Soto, G. (1993). *Too many tamales*. New York: G. P. Putnam.

Speare, E. G. (1958). *The witch of Blackbird Pond*. Boston: Houghton Mifflin.

Speare, E. G. (1961). *The bronze bow*. Boston: Houghton Mifflin.

Spier, P. (1970). *The Erie Canal*. New York: Doubleday.

Stanley, D. (1986). *Peter the Great*. New York: Four Winds Press.

Stanley, D. (1991). *The last princess: The story of Princess Ka'iulani of Hawai'i*. New York: Four Winds Press.

Stanley, D. (1994). *Cleopatra*. New York: Morrow Junior.

Stanley, D., & Vennema, P. (1988). *Shaka: King of the Zulus*. New York: Morrow.

Stanley, D., & Vennema, P. (1990). *Good Queen Bess: The story of Elizabeth I of England*. New York: Four Winds Press.

Stanley, D., & Vennema, P. (1992). *Bard of Avon*. New York: Morrow.

Stephens, B. (1984). *Deborah Sampson goes to war*. Minneapolis: Carolrhoda.

Steptoe, J. (1969). *Stevie*. New York: Harper & Row.

Stokes, J. (1978). *Let's make a toy sailboat*. New York: David McKay.

Toppin, E. A. (1973). *The black Americans in U. S. history*. Boston: Allyn & Bacon.

Tunis, E. (1952). *Oars, sails, and steam: A picture book of ships*. Cleveland: World.

Tunis, E. (1957). *Colonial living*. Cleveland: World.

Tunis, E. (1961). *Frontier living*. Cleveland: World.

Tunis, E. (1979). *Indians* (Rev. ed.). New York: Crowell.

Turkle, B. (1969). *Thy friend, Obadiah*. New York: Viking.

Uchida, Y. (1966). *Sumi's special happening*. New York: Scribner.

Uchida, Y. (1971). *Journey to Topaz*. New York: Scribner.

Uchida, Y. (1978). *Journey home*. New York: Atheneum.

Van Allsburg, C. (1983). *The wreck of the Zephyr*. Boston: Houghton Mifflin.

van Tol, R. (1984). *Submarines*. New York: Franklin Watts.

Waters, K. (1989). *Sarah Morton's day: A day in the life of a Pilgrim girl*. New York: Scholastic.

Wibberly, L. (1959). *Johnny Treegate's musket*. New York: Farrar, Straus.

Wilder, L. I. (1935). *Little house on the prairie*. New York: Harper & Row.

Williams, S. A. (1992). *Working cotton*. San Diego: Harcourt Brace Jovanovich.

Williams, V. B. (1982). *A chair for my mother*. New York: Greenwillow.

Winter, J. (1988). *Follow the drinking gourd*. New York: Knopf.

Wolf, D. (1975). *Chinese writing: An introduction*. New York: Holt, Rinehart & Winston.

Woodford, S. (1983). *The Parthenon*. Minneapolis: Lerner.

Wormfeld, H. H. (1988). *Boatbuilder*. New York: Macmillan.

Yolen, J. (1992). *Encounter*. New York: HarperCollins.

Zeck, P. & Zeck, G. (1982). *Mississippi steamwheelers*. Minneapolis: Carolrhoda.

Ziner, F. (1961). *The Pilgrims of Plymouth Colony*. New York: American Heritage.

References

Adams, D. M., & Hamm, M. E. (1992). Portfolio assessment and social studies: Collecting, selecting, and reflecting on what is significant. *Social Education, 56,* 103–105.

Akenson, J. E. (1989). The expanding environments and elementary education: A critical perspective. *Theory and Research in Social Education, 27,* 33–52.

Alabama State Department of Education. (1992). *Aviation and space curriculum guide K–3* (Rev. ed.). Montgomery: Author. (ERIC Document Reproduction Service No. ED 363 506)

Alleman, J., & Brophy, J. (1994a). Taking advantage of out-of-school opportunities for meaningful social studies learning. *The Social Studies, 85,* 262–267.

Alleman, J., & Brophy, J. (1994b). Trade-offs embedded in the literary approach to early elementary social students. *Social Studies and the Young Learner, 6*(3), 6–8.

Alleman, J., & Brophy, J. (1998). Assessment in a social constructivist classroom. *Social Education, 62,* 32–34.

Alleman, J. E., & Rosaen, C. L. (1991). The cognitive, social-emotional, and moral development characteristics of students: Basis for elementary and middle school social studies. In J. P. Shaver (Ed.), *Handbook of research on social studies teaching and learning* (pp. 121–133). New York: Macmillan.

Alter, G. (Ed.). (1994). History and the young learner [Special issue]. *Social Studies and the Young Learner, 7*(2).

Alter, G. (Ed.). (1995a). Technology and social studies [Special issue]. *Social Studies and the Young Learner, 7*(3).

Alter, G. (Ed.). (1995b). Variations on "ten themes": Applying the social studies standards to the elementary classroom [Special issue]. *Social Studies and the Young Learner, 8*(1).

Alter, G. (Ed.). (1995c). Varieties of literature and elementary social studies [Special issue]. *Social Studies and the Young Learner, 8*(2).

Alter, G. (Ed.). (1996). Moral, social, and civic issues [Special issue]. *Social Studies and the Young Learner, 8*(4).

Alter, G. (1997). The emergence of a diverse, caring community: Next steps in responsive curriculum design for elementary social studies. *Social Studies and the Young Learner, 10*(1), 6–9.

Andel, M. A. (1990). Digging for the secrets of time: Artifacts, old foundations, and more. *Social Studies and the Young Learner, 3*(1), 9–11.

Anderson, C., Avery, P. G., Pederson, P. V., Smith, E. S., & Sullivan, J. L. (1997). Divergent perspectives on citizenship education: A Q-method study and survey of social studies teachers. *American Educational Research Journal, 34,* 333–364.

Anderson, C. C. (1982). Global education in the classroom. *Theory Into Practice, 21,* 168–176.

Angell, R. C. (1981). Reflections on the project Sociological Resources for the Social Studies. *American Sociologist, 16,* 41–43.

Apple, M. (1993). *The politics of official knowledge.* New York: Routledge.

Archbald, D. A., & Newmann, F. M. (1988). *Beyond standardized testing: Assessing authentic academic achievement in the secondary school.* Reston, VA: National Association of Secondary School Principals.

Armento, B. J. (1991). Learning about the economic world. In V. A. Atwood (Ed.), *Elementary school social studies: Research as a guide to practice* (pp. 85–101). Washington, DC: National Council for the Social Studies.

Armento, B. J., Nash, G. B., Salter, C. L., & Wixson, K. K. (1991). *America will be* (Teacher's edition). Boston: Houghton Mifflin.

Aronson, E., Blaney, N., Stephan, C., Sikes, J., & Knapp, M. (1978). *The Jigsaw classroom.* Beverly Hills, CA: Sage.

Atkins, C. L. (1981). Introducing basic map and globe concepts to young children. *Journal of Geography, 80,* 228–233.

Atwood, V. A. (Ed.). (1991). *Elementary school social studies: Research as a guide to practice* (2nd ed.). Washington, DC: National Council for the Social Studies.

Au, K. H. (1980). Participation structures in a reading lesson with Hawaiian children: Analysis of a culturally appropriate instructional event. *Anthropology and Education Quarterly, 11,* 91–115.

Au, K. H. (1993). *Literacy instruction in multicultural settings.* Ft. Worth, TX: Harcourt Brace.

Au, K. H., & Kawakami, A. J. (1994). Cultural congruence in instruction. In E. R. Hollins, J. E. King, & W. C. Hayman (Eds.), *Teaching diverse populations: Formulating a knowledge base* (pp. 5–24). Albany: State University of New York Press.

Avery, P. G., & Graves, M. F. (1997). Scaffolding young learners' reading of social studies texts. *Social Studies and the Young Learner, 9*(4), 10–14.

Banks, D. (1997). The human face of immigration: A literary approach. *Social Education, 61,* 197–202.

Banks, J. A. (1997a). Approaches to multicultural curriculum reform. In J. A. Banks & C. A. M. Banks (Eds.), *Multicultural education: Issues and perspectives* (3rd ed., pp. 229–250). Boston: Allyn & Bacon.

Banks, J. A. (1997b). Multicultural education: Characteristics and goals. In J. A. Banks & C. A. M. Banks (Eds.), *Multicultural education: Issues and perspectives* (3rd ed., pp. 3–31). Boston: Allyn & Bacon.

Banks, J. A., & Banks, C. A. M. (Eds.). (1997). *Multicultural education: Issues and perspectives* (3rd ed.). Boston: Allyn & Bacon.

Barnes, B. R. (1991). Using children's literature in the early anthropology curriculum. *Social Education, 55,* 17–18.

Baron, J. B., & Sternberg, R. J. (1987). *Teaching thinking skills: Theory and practice.* New York: Freeman.

Barr, J. B., Barth, J., & Shermis, S. (1977). *Defining the social studies.* Washington, DC: National Council of the Social Studies.

Barron, R. F. (1969). The use of vocabulary as an advance organizer. In H. L. Herber & P. L. Sanders (Eds.), *Research in the content areas: First-year report* (pp. 29–39). Syracuse, NY: Reading and Language Arts Center.

Barth, J. L. (1993). Social studies: There is a history, there is a body, but is it worth saving? *Social Education, 57,* 56–57.

Barth, J. L., & Shermis, S. (1970). Defining the social studies: An exploration of three traditions. *Social Education, 34,* 743–750.

Barton, K. C. (1997). History—it can be elementary: An overview of elementary students' understanding of history. *Social Education, 61,* 13–16.

Barton, K. C., & Levstik, L. S. (1996). "Back when God was around and everything": Elementary children's understanding of historical time. *American Educational Research Journal, 33,* 419–454.

Baum, C. G., & Cohen, I. S. (1989). Psychology and the social science curriculum. In *Charting a course: Social studies for the 21st century* (pp. 65–69). Washington, DC: National Commission on Social Studies in the Schools.

Beatty, A. S., Reese, C. M., Persky, H. R., & Carr, P. (1996). *NAEP 1994 U.S. history report card: Findings from the National Assessment of Educational Progress.* Washington, DC: U.S. Department of Education.

Beck, I. L., & McKeown, M. G. (1988). Toward meaningful accounts in history texts for young learners. *Educational Researcher, 17*(6), 31–39.

Beck, I. L., & McKeown, M. G. (1991a). Research directions: Social studies texts are hard to understand: Mediating some of the difficulties. *Language Arts, 68,* 482–489.

Beck, I. L., & McKeown, M. G. (1991b). Substantive and methodological considerations for productive textbook analysis. In J. P. Shaver (Ed.), *Handbook of research on social studies teaching and learning* (pp. 496–512). New York: Macmillan.

Beck, I. L., McKeown, M. G., & Worthy, J. (1995). Giving a text voice can improve students' understanding. *Reading Research Quarterly, 30,* 220–239.

Bennett, C. T., & Dawson, K. (1998). Software reviews: 3D Atlas 97 and America Rock. *Social Education, 62,* 161–164.

Benniga, J. S. (Ed.). (1991). *Moral education and civic education in the elementary school.* New York: Teachers College Press.

Berti, A. E., & Bombi, A. S. (1988). *The child's construction of economics.* Cambridge, UK: Cambridge University Press.

Bestor, A. (1953). *Educational wastelands: The retreat from learning in our public schools.* Urbana: Illinois University Press.

Bestor, A. (1955). *Restoration of learning.* New York: Knopf.

Beyer, B. K. (1985). Critical thinking: What is it? *Social Education, 49,* 270–276.

Beyer, B. K. (1987). *Practical strategies for the teaching of thinking.* Boston: Allyn & Bacon.

Beyer, B. K., & Gilstrap, R. L. (Eds.). (1982). *Writing in elementary school social studies.* Boulder CO: Social Science Education Consortium.

Beyer, B. K., & Penna, A. (Eds.). (1971). *Concepts in the social studies.* Washington, DC: National Council for the Social Studies.

Bigelow, W. (1992). Once upon a genocide: Christopher Columbus in children's literature. *Language Arts, 69,* 112–120.

Bjorklun, E. C. (1995). Teaching about personal injury law: Activities for the classroom. *The Social Studies, 86,* 78–84.

Black, M. S. (1998). Using archaeology to explore cultures of North America. *Social Studies and the Young Learner, 11*(1), 11–16.

Blais, D. M. (1988). Constructivism: A theoretical revolution in teaching. *Journal of Developmental Education, 11*(3), 2–7.

Blankenship, G. (1994). Social studies curriculum renewal. *Social Studies and the Young Learner, 6*(4), 14–16.

Bloom, B. S. (Ed.). (1956). *Taxonomy of educational objectives: The classification of educational goals. Handbook 1: The cognitive domain.* New York: David McKay.

Boehm, R. G., & Petersen, J. F. (1994). An elaboration of the fundamental themes in geography. *Social Education, 58,* 211–218.

Boggs, S. T., Watson-Gegeo, K., & McMillen, G. (1985). *Speaking, relating, and learning: A study of Hawaiian children at home and at school.* Norwood, NJ: Ablex.

Boldt, D. J., Gustafson, L. V., & Johnson, J. E. (1995). The Internet: A curriculum warehouse for social studies teachers. *The Social Studies, 86,* 105–112.

Bower, B., & Lobdell, J. (1998). History alive! Six powerful constructivist strategies. *Social Education, 62,* 50–53.

Boykin, A. W. (1982). Task variability and the performance of Black and White schoolchildren: Vervistic explorations. *Journal of Black Studies, 12,* 469–485.

Bradley Commission on History in the Schools. (1988). *Building a history curriculum: Guidelines for teaching history in the schools.* Washington, DC: Educational Excellence Network.

Brandt, R. (Ed.). (1992). Using performance assessment [Special issue]. *Educational Leadership, 49*(8).

Braun, J. A., & Cook, M. L. (1985). Making heritage experiences come alive for elementary school social studies students. *The Social Studies, 76,* 216–219.

Breen, K. (Ed.). (1988). *Index to collective biographies for young readers* (4th ed.). New York: Bowker.

Brooks, D. (Ed.). (1997). Character education [Special issue]. *Social Studies Review, 37*(1).

Brophy, J. (1985). Classroom management as instruction: Socializing self-guidance in students. *Theory Into Practice, 24,* 233–240.

Brophy, J. (1990). Teaching social studies for understanding and higher order application. *Elementary School Journal, 90,* 351–417.

Brophy, J. (1999). Elementary students learn about Native Americans: The development of knowledge and empathy. *Social Education, 63,* 39–45.

Brown, B. B., Malepe, L., & Sullivan, J. (1996). Selecting books on Africa: A response to "Safari Sojourns." *Social Studies and the Young Learner, 8*(4), 12–14.

Bruner, J. (1960). *The process of education.* Cambridge, MA: Harvard University Press.

Bruner, J. (1961). The act of discovery. *Harvard Educational Review, 31,* 21–32.

Bruner, J. (1966). *Toward a theory of instruction.* Cambridge, MA: Belknap.

Bruner, J. (1983). *In search of mind: Essays in autobiography.* New York: Harper & Row.

Bruner, J., Goodnow, J., & Austin, G. (1956). *A study of thinking.* New York: John Wiley.

California Department of Education. (1992a). *Handbook for teaching Korean American students.* Sacramento: Author.

California Department of Education. (1992b). *With history-social science for all: Access for every student.* Sacramento: Author.

California Department of Education. (1997). *History-social science framework for California public schools kindergarten through Grade 12.* Sacramento: Author.

Camperell, K., & Knight, R. S. (1991). Reading research and social studies. In J. P. Shaver (Ed.), *Handbook of research on social studies teaching and learning* (pp. 567–577). New York: Macmillan.

Cangemi, J., & Aucoin, L. (1996). Global thematic units are passports to learning. *Social Education, 60*(2), 80–82.

Caplan, N. S., Choy, M. H., & Whitmore, J. K. (1991). *Children of the boat people: A study of educational success.* Ann Arbor: University of Michigan Press.

Cardis, R. J., & Risinger, C. F. (1994). Contemporary trends in social studies. *Social Studies and the Young Learner, 6*(3), 4–5, 22.

Carrol, R. F. (1987). Schoolyard archaeology. *The Social Studies, 78,* 69–75.

Carroll, T., Knight, C., & Hutchinson, E. (1995). Carmen Sandiego: Crime can pay when it comes to learning. *Social Education, 59,* 165–169.

Carter, J. M. (1995). "Grandma Books": Writing to discover your past. *Social Education, 2–59,* 92–94.

Case, R. (1993). Key elements of a global perspective. *Social Education, 57,* 318–325.

Cazden, C. (1983). Adult assistance to language development: Scaffolds, models, and direct instruction. In R. P. Parker & F. A. Davis (Eds.), *Developing literacy: Young children's use of language* (pp. 3–18). Newark, DE: International Reading Association.

Center for Civic Education. (1994). *National standards for civics and government.* Calabasas, CA: Author.

Charles, C. (1985). Using the natural world to teach and learn globally. *Social Education, 49,* 213–215.

Charney, R. S. (1993). *Teaching children to care: Management in the responsive classroom*. Greenfield, MA: Northeast Foundation for Children.

Cherryholmes, C. H. (1990). Social studies for which century? *Social Education, 54,* 438–442.

Chilcott, J. H. (1977). Curriculum models for teaching anthropology. *Anthropology and Education Quarterly, 8,* 14–18.

Chung, C. H. (1992). Teaching LEP students in the content areas: A sheltered English approach. *Social Studies Review, 32*(1), 29–38.

Clark, T. (Ed.). (1997). Service learning [Special issue]. *Social Studies Review, 36*(2).

Clarke, J. H. (1990). *Patterns of thinking: Integrating learning skills in content teaching*. Boston: Allyn & Bacon.

Clements, H. M., Fielder, W. R., & Tabachnick, B. R. (1966). *Social study: Inquiry in elementary classrooms*. Indianapolis, IN: Bobbs-Merrill.

Cohen, E. G. (1986). *Designing groupwork: Strategies for the heterogeneous classroom*. New York: Teachers College Press.

Cohen, R. (1996). Moving beyond name games: The conservative attack on the U.S. history standards. *Social Education, 60,* 49–54.

Collins, H. T., Czarra, F. R., & Smith, A. F. (Eds.). (1998). Global education: Challenges, cultures, and connections [Special issue]. *Social Education, 62*(5).

Cooper, B. L. (1989). Popular records as oral evidence: Creating an audio time line to examine American history, 1955–1987. *Social Education, 53,* 34–40.

Cordier, M. H., & Perez-Stable, M. A. (1996). Latino connections: Family, neighbors, and community. *Social Studies and the Young Learner, 9*(1), 20–22.

Cort, H. R., & Peskowitz, N. (1977). *A longitudinal study of man: A course of study, summary report*. Washington, DC: National Science Foundation. (ERIC Document Reproduction Service No. ED 151 275)

Cowan, G. (1997). How the Internet works. *Social Education, 61.*

Cox, C. (1996). *Teaching language arts: A student- and response-centered classroom* (2nd ed.). Boston: Allyn & Bacon.

Cremin, L. (1961). *The transformation of the school: Progressivism in American education*. New York: Knopf.

Cuban, L. (1984). *How teachers taught: Constancy and change in American classroom, 1890–1980*. New York: Longman.

Cuban, L. (1991). History of teaching in social studies. In J. P. Shaver (Ed.), *Handbook of research on social studies teaching and learning* (pp. 197–209). New York: Macmillan.

Cullinan, B. E. (Ed.). (1993). *Fact and fiction: Literature across the curriculum*. Newark, DE: International Reading Association.

Cummins, J. (1979). Linguistic interdependence and the educational development of bilingual children. *Review of Educational Research, 49,* 222–251.

Cummins, J. (1986a). Empowering minority students: A framework for intervention. *Harvard Educational Review, 56,* 18–36.

Cummins, J. (1986b). The role of primary language development in promoting educational success for language minority students. In *Schooling and language minority students: A theoretical framework* (pp. 3–49). Los Angeles: CSULA Evaluation, Dissemination, and Assessment Center.

Cummins, J. (1989). *Empowering minority students.* Sacramento: California Association for Bilingual Education.

Cummins, J. (1992). Language proficiency, bilingualism, and academic achievement. In P. A. Richard-Amato & M. A. Snow (Eds.), *The multicultural classroom: Readings for content-area teachers* (pp. 16–26). White Plains, NY: Longman.

Cunningham, J. W., Cunningham, P. M., & Arthur, S. V. (1981). *Middle and secondary school reading.* New York: Longman.

Curtis, C. K. (1991). Social studies for students at risk and with disabilities. In J. P. Shaver (Ed.), *Handbook of research on social studies teaching and learning* (pp. 57–174). New York: Macmillan.

Danziger, K. (1958). Children's earliest conceptions of economic relationships. *Journal of Social Psychology, 47,* 231–240.

Darling-Hammond, L., Ancess, J., & Falk, B. (Eds.). (1995). *Authentic assessment in action: Studies of schools and students at work.* New York: Teachers College Press.

Davis, B. H., Rooze, G. E., & Runnells, M. K. T. (1992). Writing-to-learn in elementary social studies. *Social Education, 56,* 393–397.

Davis, J. E., & Fernlund, P. M. (1995). Civics: If not, why not? *The Social Studies, 86,* 56–59.

De Avila, E. A., Duncan, S. E., & Navarrete, C. J. (1987a). *Cooperative learning: Integrating language and content-area instruction.* Wheaton, MD: National Clearinghouse for Bilingual Education.

De Avila, E. A., Duncan, S. E., & Navarrete, C. J. (1987b). *Finding out/Descubrimiento: Teacher's resource guide.* Northvale, NJ: Santillana.

Delisle, J. R. (1991). Gifted students and social studies. In J. P. Shaver (Ed.), *Handbook of research on social studies teaching and learning* (pp. 175–184). New York: Macmillan.

DePauw, L. G. (1994). Roles of women in the American Revolution and the Civil War. *Social Education, 58,* 77–79.

Dewey, J. (1900). *The school and society.* Chicago: University of Chicago Press.

Dewey, J. (1902). *The child and the curriculum.* Chicago: University of Chicago Press.

Dewey, J. (1933). *How we think.* Boston: Heath. (Original work published 1910).

Dewey, J. (1976). The university elementary school: History and character. In J. A. Boydston (Ed.), *John Dewey: The middle works, 1899–1924. Vol. 1: 1899–1901* (pp. 325–338). Carbondale: Southern Illinois University Press. (Original work published 1897)

Diaz, C. F., Massialas, B. G., & Xanthopoulos, J. A. (1999). *Global perspectives for educators.* Boston: Allyn & Bacon.

Diaz-Rico, L. T., & Weed, K. Z. (1995). *The cross-cultural, language, and academic development handbook: A complete K–12 reference guide*. Boston: Allyn & Bacon.

Dimmitt, J. P., & Van Cleaf, D. W. (1992). Integrating writing and social studies: Alternatives to the formal research paper. *Social Education, 56,* 382–384.

Donaldson, M. (1978). *Children's minds*. New York: Norton.

Dougan, A. (1988). The search of a definition of social studies: A historical overview. *International Journal of Social Education, 3*(3), 13–36.

Douglass, M. P. (1967). *Social studies from theory to practice in elementary education*. Philadelphia: J. B. Lippincott.

Douglass, M. P. (1989). *Learning to read: The quest for meaning*. New York: Teachers College Press.

Dow, P. B. (1976). MACOS: Social studies in crisis. *Educational Leadership, 34,* 112–117.

Dow, P. B. (1991). *Schoolhouse politics: Lessons from the Sputnik era*. Cambridge, MA: Harvard University Press.

Downey, M. T. (Ed.). (1985). *History in the schools*. Washington, DC: National Council for the Social Studies.

Downey, M. T., & Levstik, L. S. (1988). Teaching and learning history: The research base. *Social Education, 52,* 336–342.

Downey, M. T., & Levstik, L. S. (1991). Teaching and learning history. In J. P. Shaver (Ed.), *Handbook of research on social studies teaching and learning* (pp. 400–410). New York: Macmillan.

Downs, J. R. (1993). Getting parents and students involved: Using survey and interview techniques. *Social Studies, 84*(3), 104–106.

Drake, J. J., & Drake, F. D. (1990). Using children's literature to teach about the American Revolution. *Social Studies and the Young Learner, 3*(2), 6–8.

Drew, M. A. (1992). African American literature for young people. *Social Education, 56,* 334–337.

Drisko, J. (1993). The responsibilities of schools in civic education. *Journal of Education, 175,* 105–119.

Duis, M. (1996). Using schema theory to teach American history. *Social Education, 60,* 144–146.

Dynneson, T. (1986). Trends in precollegiate anthropology. In S. Wronski & D. Bragaw (Eds.), *Social studies and social sciences: A 50-year perspective* (pp. 153–163). Washington, DC: National Council for the Social Studies.

Easterly, J. E. (Ed.). (1994). *Promoting global teacher education: Seven reports*. Reston, VA: Association of Teacher Education.

Echevarria, J., & Graves, A. (1998). *Sheltered content instruction: Teaching English-language learners with diverse abilities*. Boston: Allyn & Bacon.

Eggen, P. D., Eggen, P., & Kauchak, D. (1995). *Strategies for teachers: Teaching content and thinking skills* (3rd ed.). Boston: Allyn & Bacon.

Ehman, L. H., & Glenn, A. D. (1991). Interactive technology in social studies. In J. P. Shaver (Ed.), *Handbook of research on social studies teaching and learning* (pp. 513–522). New York: Macmillan.

Eisner, E. (1991). Art, music, and literature within social studies. In J. P. Shaver (Ed.), *Handbook of research on social studies teaching and learning* (pp. 551–558). New York: Macmillan.

Ember, C. R., & Ember, M. (1990). *Cultural anthropology* (6th ed.). Upper Saddle River, NJ: Prentice Hall.

Engle, S. H. (1986). Late night thoughts about the New Social Studies. *Social Education, 50,* 20–22.

Engle, S. H., & Ochoa, A. S. (1988). *Education for democratic citizenship: Decision making in the social studies.* New York: Teachers College Press.

Epstein, T. L. (1994). Sometimes a shining moment: High school students' representation of history through the arts. *Social Education, 58,* 136–141.

Evans, M. D. (1995). Exchanging opinions through letters and editorials: A social studies activity. *Social Education, 59,* 158.

Evans, R. W. (1989a). Diane Ravitch and the revival of history: A critique. *The Social Studies, 80,* 85–88.

Evans, R. W. (1989b). A dream unrealized: A brief look at the history of issue-centered approaches. *The Social Studies, 80,* 178–184.

Evans, R. W. (Ed.). (1992). Defining issues-centered social studies education [Special issue]. *The Social Studies, 83*(3).

Faltis, C. J. (1993). *Joinfostering: Adapting teaching strategies for the multilingual classroom.* Upper Saddle River, NJ: Merrill/Prentice Hall.

Farivar, S. (1993). Continuity and change: Planning an integrated history-social science/English language arts unit. *Social Studies Review, 32*(2), 17–24.

Felton, R. G., & Allen, R. F. (1990). Using visual materials as historical resources. *Social Studies, 81,* 84–87.

Fenton, E. (1967). *The New Social Studies.* New York: Holt, Rinehart & Winston.

Fenton, E. (1991). Reflections on the New Social Studies. *The Social Studies, 82,* 84–90.

Ferguson, P. (1988). Modernization in Meiji, Japan: A Jigsaw lesson. *Social Education, 52,* 392–394.

Field, S. L. (1997). Teaching young citizens [Special issue]. *Social Studies and the Young Learner, 10*(1).

Field, S. L. (1998). Social studies: Gateway to literacy [Special issue]. *Social Studies and the Young Learner, 10*(4).

Fine, M. (1995). *Habits of mind: Struggling over values in America's classrooms.* San Francisco: Jossey-Bass.

Finklestein, J. M., Nielsen, L. E., & Switzer, T. (1993). Primary elementary social studies instruction: A status report. *Social Education, 57,* 64–69.

Finn, C. E., & Ravitch, D. (1988). No trivial pursuit. *Phi Delta Kappan, 69,* 559–564.

Flouris, G. (1988). Teaching about ancient Greece: A model teaching unit. *The Social Studies, 79,* 25–31.

Forsythe, A. S. (1995). *Learning geography: An annotated bibliography of research paths.* Indiana, PA: National Council for Geographic Education.

Fraenkel, J. R. (1992). Hilda Taba's contributions to social studies education. *Social Education, 56,* 172–178.

Freeland, K., & Smith, K. (1993). A thematic teaching unit on flight. *Social Studies and the Young Learner, 5*(4), 15–17.

Freeman, D., & Freeman, Y. (1988). *Sheltered English instruction.* Washington, DC: ERIC Clearinghouse on Language and Linguistics. (ERIC Document Reproduction Service No. ED 301 070)

Freeman, D. E. & Freeman, Y. S. (1991). "Doing" social studies: Whole language lessons to promote social action. *Social Education, 55,* 29–32.

Freeman, E. B., & Person, D. G. (Eds.). (1992). *Using nonfiction trade books in the elementary classroom: From ants to zeppelins.* Urbana, IL: National Council of Teachers of English.

Freese, J. R. (1997). Using the National Geographic standards to integrate children's social studies. *Social Studies and the Young Learner, 10*(2), 22–24.

Fry, P. G., Phillips, K., Lobaugh, G., & Madole, S. (1996). Halliday's functions of language: A framework to integrate elementary-level social studies and language arts. *The Social Studies, 87,* 78–80.

Fulbright-Hays Seminars Abroad Program. (1993). *China: Tradition and transformation (curriculum projects).* New York: National Committee on United States-China Relations. (ERIC Document Reproduction Service No. ED 358 003)

Gallavan, N. P. (1997). Achieving civic competence through a DRAFT writing process. *Social Studies and the Young Learner, 10*(2), 14–16.

Garcia, E. (1994). *Understanding and meeting the challenge of student cultural diversity.* Boston: Houghton Mifflin.

Gardner, H. (1983). *Frames of mind: The theory of multiple intelligences.* New York: Basic Books.

Gardner, H. (1991). *The unschooled mind: How children think and how school should teach.* New York: Basic Books.

Gavrish, M. J. A. (1995). The historian as detective: An introduction to historical methodology. *Social Education, 59,* 151–153.

Gay, G. (1991). Culturally diverse students and social studies. In J. P. Shaver (Ed.), *Handbook of research on social studies teaching and learning* (pp. 144–156). New York: Macmillan.

Gay, G. (1997). Educational equity for students of color. In J. A. Banks & C. A. M. Banks (Eds.), *Multicultural education: Issues and perspectives* (3rd ed., pp. 171–194). Boston: Allyn & Bacon.

Gay, G., & Banks, J. A. (1975). Teaching the American Revolution: A multiethnic approach. *Social Education, 39,* 461–465.

Geographic Education National Implementation Project (GENIP) (1987). *K–6 geography: Themes, key ideas, and learning opportunities.* Washington, DC: Author.

Geographic Education National Implementation Project (GENIP) (1989). *7–12 geography: Themes, key ideas, and learning opportunities.* Washington, DC: Author.

Geography Education Standards Project. (1994). *Geography for life: National geography standards.* Washington, DC: Author.

Gilligan, C. (1982). *In a different voice.* Cambridge, MA: Harvard University Press.

Gilliland, H. (Ed.). (1992). *Teaching the Native American.* Dubuque, IA: Kendall/Hunt.

Gilstrap, R. L. (1982). Writing in elementary social studies: Report of a personal search. In B. K. Beyer & R. L. Gilstrap (Eds.), *Writing in elementary school social studies* (pp. 19–29). Boulder, CO: Social Science Education Consortium.

Gilstrap, R. L. (1991). Writing for the social studies. In J. P. Shaver (Ed.), *Handbook of research on social studies teaching and learning* (pp. 578–587). New York: Macmillan.

Ginsburg, H., & Opper, S. (1979). *Piaget's theory of intellectual development* (2nd ed.). Upper Saddle River, NJ: Prentice Hall.

Goldenberg, C. (1991). *Instructional conversations and their classroom application.* Washington, DC: Center for Applied Linguistics.

Goldenberg, C. (1992 / 1993). Instructional conversations: Promoting comprehension through discussion. *The Reading Teacher, 46,* 316–326.

Goodlad, J. I. (1984). *A place called school.* New York: McGraw-Hill.

Goodman, J. (1992). *Elementary schooling for critical democracy.* Albany: State University of New York Press.

Goodman, K. (1986). *What's whole in whole language?* Portsmouth, NH: Heinemann.

Grant, S. G. (1997). Appeasing the Right, missing the point? Reading the New York state social studies framework. *Social Education, 61,* 102–107.

Grant, S. G., & Vansledright, B. A. (1996). The dubious connection: Citizenship education and the social studies. *The Social Studies, 87,* 56–59.

Gray, P. S. (1989). Sociology. In *Charting a course: Social studies for the 21st century* (pp. 71–75). Washington, DC: National Commission on Social Studies in the Schools.

Greenbaum, P. E. (1985). Nonverbal differences in communication style between American Indian and Anglo elementary classrooms. *American Educational Research Journal, 22,* 101–115.

Greenstein, F. I. (1969). *Children and politics.* New Haven, CT: Yale University Press.

Gregg, M., & Leinhardt, G. (1994). Mapping out geography: An example of epistemology and education. *Review of Educational Research, 64,* 311–361.

Griffith, B. (1991). The abandonment of social studies? *Theory and Research in Social Education, 19,* 136–151.

Gronlund, N. E. (1991). *How to write and use instructional objectives* (4th ed.). New York: Macmillan.

Grossman, H. (1984). *Educating Hispanic students: Cultural implications for instruction, classroom management, counseling, and assessment.* Springfield, IL: Charles C Thomas.

Gunter, M. A., Estes, T. H., & Schwab, J. (1995). *Instruction: A models approach* (2nd ed.). Boston: Allyn & Bacon.

Haas, J. D. (1986). Is the social studies curriculum impervious to change? *The Social Studies, 77,* 61–65.

Hale-Benson, J. E. (1986). *Black children: Their roots, culture, and learning styles* (Rev. ed.). Baltimore: Johns Hopkins University Press.

Halliday, M. A. K. (1976). *System and function in language.* London, UK: Oxford University Press.

Handley, L. M., & Adler, S. (1994). Standards in social studies: Curriculum concerns. *Social Studies and the Young Learner, 6*(3), 17–19.

Hanna, P. R. (1963). Revising the social studies: What is needed. *Social Education, 27,* 190–196.

Hanna, P. R. (Ed.). (1987a). *Assuring quality for the social studies in our schools.* Stanford, CA: Hoover Institution Press.

Hanna, P. R. (1987b). Society-child-curriculum. In P. R. Hanna (Ed.), *Assuring quality for the social studies in our schools* (pp. 11–19). Stanford, CA: Hoover Institution Press. (Original work published 1956)

Hansen, W. L., Bach, G. L., Calderwood, J. D. & Saunders, P. (1977). *A framework for teaching economics: Basic concepts.* New York: Joint Council for Economic Education.

Hanvey, R. G. (1976). *An attainable global perspective.* New York: Global Perspectives in Education.

Harms, J. M., & Lettow, L. J. (1994). Criteria for selecting picture books with historical settings. *Social Education, 58,* 152–155.

Harvey, K. D. (1993). Native Americans: The next 50 years. *Social Studies and the Young Learner, 5*(3).

Hatcher, B., & Olsen, M. (1984). Sidewalk social studies. *Social Education, 48,* 473–474.

Hattler, J. A., & Ledford, C. C. (1996). More than mock elections: Using the Internet to connect children to the '96 election. *Social Studies and the Young Learner, 9*(1), 30–32.

Heath, J. A., & Vik, P. (1994). Elementary school Student Councils: A statewide study. *Principal, 74*(1), 31–32.

Heath, S. B. (1986). Sociocultural contexts of language development. In *Beyond language: Social and cultural factors in schooling language-minority students* (pp. 143–186). Los Angeles: California State University Evaluation, Dissemination, and Assessment Center.

Hefte, R. (1995). MayaQuest: A student expedition. *Social Studies and the Young Learner, 7*(3), 4–7.

Herlihy, J. G. (1974). Man: A course of study, an exemplar of the New Social Studies. *Social Education, 38,* 442–443.

Herman, W. L. (1988). Development in scope and sequence: A survey of school districts. *Social Education, 52,* 385–388.

Hertzberg, H. W. (1981). *Social studies reform 1880–1980*. Boulder, CO: Social Science Education Consortium.

Hickey, G. M. (1990). Mock trials for children. *Social Education, 54,* 43–44.

Hickey, G. M. (1991). "And then what happened, Grandpa?": Oral history projects in the elementary classroom. 216–217.

Hicks, K., & Austin, J. (1994). Experiencing the legal system: Fairy-tale trials for fifth graders. *The Social Studies, 85,* 39–44.

Hicks, S. J. (1996). Promoting civic competence using children's trade books: Ideas for pre K–4 classrooms. *Social Education, 60,* 216–219.

Hightshoe, S. (1997). Sifting through the sands of time: A simulated archaeological dig. *Social Studies and the Young Learner, 9*(3), 28–30.

Hirshfield, C. (1991). New worlds from old: An experience in oral history at the elementary school level. *Social Studies, 82*(3), 110–114.

Hittleman, C. G., & Hittleman, D. R. (1998). Bringing grandparents into social studies: A unit of study. *Social Studies and the Young Learner, 10*(2).

Hoelscher, K. (1997). The American Girls Collection history project: A third-grade and teacher education collaborative. *Social Studies and the Young Learner, 10*(2), 17–24.

Hofbauer, D., & Prenn, M. (1996). A place to call one's own: Choosing books about homelessness. *Social Education, 60,* 167–169.

Hoge, J. D., & Saye, J. W. (1994). Social studies educators' awareness of CD-ROM and on-line databases. *Computers in the Schools, 11*(2), 103–113.

Hollins, E. R., King, J. E., & Hayman, W. C. (Eds.). (1994). *Teaching diverse populations: Formulating a knowledge base*. Albany: State University of New York Press.

Hollins, E. R., Smiler, H., & Spencer, K. (1994). Benchmarks in meeting the challenges of effective schooling for African American youngsters. In E. R. Hollins, J. E. King, & W. C. Hayman (Eds.), *Teaching diverse populations: Formulating a knowledge base* (pp. 163–174). Albany: State University of New York Press.

Hollister, V. G. (1994). Arriving where we started: Using old maps in a middle school social studies classroom. *Social Education, 58,* 279–280.

Honey, M. (1994). NII roadblocks: Why do so few educators use the Internet? *Electronic Learning, 14*(2), 14–15.

Hoone, C. (1989). Teaching timelines. *Social Studies and the Young Learner, 2*(2), 13–17.

Hoover, R. L., & Kindsvatter, R. (1997). *Democratic discipline: Foundation and practice*. Upper Saddle River, NJ: Merrill/Prentice Hall.

Huck, C. S., Hepler, S., Hickman, J., & Kiefer, B. Z. (1997). *Children's literature in the elementary school* (6th ed.). Dubuque, IA: Brown & Benchmark.

Hunter, M. (1984). Knowing, teaching, and supervising. In P. L. Hosford (Ed.), *Using what we know about teaching* (pp. 169–192). Alexandria, VA: Association for Supervision and Curriculum Development.

Imeson, J., & Skamp, K. R. (1996). A novel use of literature to integrate environmental education with social studies. *The Social Studies, 86,* 215–220.

Inkpen, T. D. (1974). A selected bibliography on man: A course of study. *Social Education, 38,* 456–457.

Irvin, J. L., Lunstrum, J. P., Lynch-Brown, C., & Shepard, M. F. (1995). *Enhancing social studies through literacy strategies.* Washington, DC: National Council for the Social Studies.

Jahoda, G. (1979). The construction of economic reality by some Glaswegian children. *European Journal of Social Psychology, 19,* 115–127.

James, M., & Zarrillo, J. (1989). Teaching history with children's literature: A concept-based, interdisciplinary approach. *The Social Studies, 80,* 153–158.

James, M. E. (1985). Teaching the American myth: George Washington and the cherry tree. In M. P. Douglass (Ed.), *Claremont Reading Conference 49th yearbook* (pp. 180–192). Claremont CA: Claremont Reading Conference.

Jantz, R. K., & Klawitter, K. (1991). Anthropology and sociology. In V. A. Atwood (Ed.), *Elementary school social studies: Research as a guide to practice* (pp. 102–118). Washington, DC: National Council for the Social Studies.

Jenness, D. (1990). *Making sense of the social studies.* New York: Macmillan.

Jennings, T. E., Crowell, S. M., & Fernlund, P. F. (1994). Social justice in the elementary classroom. *Social Studies and the Young Learner, 7*(1), 4–6.

Johnson, D. W., & Johnson, R. T. (1986). *Learning together and alone* (2nd ed.). Upper Saddle River, NJ: Merrill/Prentice Hall.

Johnson, D. W., & Johnson, R. T. (1989 / 1990). Social skills for successful group work. *Educational Leadership, 47*(4), 29–33.

Johnson, D. W., & Johnson, R. T. (1992a). Approaches to implementing cooperative learning in the social studies classroom. In R. J. Stahl & R. L. VanSickle (Eds.), *Cooperative learning in the social studies classroom: An introduction to social study* (pp. 44–51). Washington, DC: National Council for the Social Studies.

Johnson, D. W., & Johnson, R. T. (1992b). Encouraging thinking through constructive controversy. In N. Davidson & T. Worsham (Eds.), *Enhancing thinking through cooperative learning* (pp. 120–137). New York: Teachers College Press.

Johnson, D. W., Johnson, R. T., & Holubec, E. (1984). *Circles of learning: Cooperation in the classroom.* Alexandria, VA: Association for Supervision and Curriculum Development.

Johnson, D. W., Maruyama, G., Johnson, R. T., Nelson, D., & Skon, L. (1981). Effects of cooperative, competitive, and individualistic goal structures on achievement: A meta-analysis. *Psychological Bulletin, 89,* 47–62.

Joint Committee on Geographic Education. (1984). *Guidelines for geographic education: elementary and secondary schools.* Washington, DC: Association of American Geographers and National Council for Geographic Education.

Jones, D. H. (1993). Using authentic assessment in elementary social studies. *Social Science Record, 30*(2), 17–24.

Joyce, B. R., & Weil, M. (1980). *Models of teaching* (2nd ed.). Upper Saddle River, NJ: Merrill/Prentice Hall.

Joyce, W. W., Little, T. H., & Wronski, S. P. (1991). Scope and sequence, goals, and objectives: Effects on social studies. In J. P. Shaver (Ed.), *Handbook of research on social studies teaching and learning* (pp. 321–331). New York: Macmillan.

Kagan, S. (1985). Dimensions of cooperative classroom structures. In R. Slavin, S. Sharan, S. Kagan, R. Hertz-Lazarowitz, C. Webb, & R. Schmuck (Eds.), *Learning to cooperate, cooperating to learn* (pp. 67–96). New York: Plenum.

Kagan, S. (1989). *Cooperative learning resources for teachers.* San Juan Capistrano, CA: Resources for Teachers.

Kagan, S. (1989 / 1990). The structural approach to cooperative learning. *Educational Leadership, 47*(4), 12–15.

Katt, B. (1992). Abraham Lincoln: Deified martyr, flesh and blood hero, and a man with warts. *Children's Literature in Education, 23,* 119–129.

Keefe, S. E., & Padilla, A. M. (1987). *Chicano ethnicity.* Albuquerque: University of New Mexico Press.

Kellough, R. D. (Ed.). (1995). *Integrating language arts and social studies for intermediate and middle school students.* Upper Saddle River, NJ: Merrill/Prentice Hall.

Kerckhoff, A. C. (1986). Effects of ability grouping in British secondary schools. *American Sociological Review, 51,* 842–858.

Key, D. M. (1995). Operationalizing the thematic strands of social studies for young learners. *Social Studies and the Young Learner, 8*(1), 12–15.

Kilpatrick, W. H. (1918). The project method. *Teachers College Record, 19,* 319–333.

Kilpatrick, W. H. (1925). *Foundations of method.* New York: Macmillan.

Kim, C. Y., & Garcia, J. (1996). Diversity and trade books: Promoting conceptual learning in social studies. *Social Education, 60,* 208–211.

King, M., Bratt, B. F. T., & Baer, R. (1992). Social studies instruction. In P. A. Richard-Amato & M. A. Snow (Eds.), *The multicultural classroom: Readings for content-area teachers* (pp. 287–299). White Plains, NY: Longman.

King, R., & King, J. (1998). Is group decision making in the classroom constructive or destructive? *Social Education, 62,* 101–104.

Kirp, D. L. (1990, August 12). The classroom according to Hunter. *Los Angeles Times Magazine,* pp. 16–23, 37–39.

Kirschenbaum, H. (1977). *Advanced value clarification.* La Jolla, CA: University Associates.

Kleg, M. (1993). On the NCSS curriculum guidelines for multicultural education. *Social Education, 57,* 58–59.

Kniep, W. M. (1985). *A critical review of the short history of global education: Preparing for new opportunities.* New York: Global Perspectives in Education.

Kniep, W. M. (1986). Defining a global education by its content. *Social Education, 50,* 437–446.

Kniep, W. M. (1989). Social studies within a global education. *Social Education, 53,* 385, 399–403.

Kochman, T. (1981). *Black and White styles in conflict.* Chicago: University of Chicago Press.

Koeller, S. (1992). Social studies research writing: Raising voices. *Social Education, 56,* 379–382.

Kohlberg, L. (1981). *The philosophy of moral development: Moral stages and the idea of justice.* New York: Harper & Row.

Kon, J. H., & Martin-Kniep, G. O. (1992). Students' geographic knowledge and skills in different kinds of tests: Multiple-choice versus performance assessment. *Social Education, 56,* 95–98.

Kornfeld, J. (1994). Using fiction to teach history: Multicultural and global perspectives of World War II. *Social Education, 58,* 281–286.

Kourilsky, M. (1977). The kinder-economy: A case study of kindergarten pupils of economic concepts. *Elementary School Journal, 77,* 182–191.

Kourilsky, M. (1987). Children's learning of economics: The imperative and the hurdles. *Theory Into Practice, 26,* 198–205.

Krashen, S. (1981). *Second-language acquisition and second-language learning.* Oxford, UK: Pergamon Press.

Krashen, S. (1982). *Principles and practices of second-language acquisition.* Oxford, UK: Pergamon Press.

Krashen, S. (1985). *Inquiries and insights.* Hayward, CA: Alemany Press.

Krashen, S. (1986). Bilingual education and second-language acquisition theory. In *Schooling and language minority students: A theoretical framework* (pp. 51–79). Los Angeles: California State University Evaluation, Dissemination, and Assessment Center.

Krashen, S., & Biber, D. (1988). *On course: Bilingual education's success in California.* Sacramento: California Association for Bilingual Education.

Krashen, S. D., & Terrell, T. D. (1983). *The natural approach.* Hayward, CA: Alemany.

Krathwohl, D. R., Bloom, B. S., & Masia, B. B. (1964). *Taxonomy of educational objectives: The classification of educational goals. Handbook II: Affective domain.* New York: David McKay.

Krey, D. M. (1998). *Children's literature in social studies: Teaching to the standards.* Washington, DC: National Council for the Social Studies.

Labbo, L. D., & Field, S. L. (1997). Wish you were here: Picture postcard explorations in children's books. *Social Studies and the Young Learner, 9*(4), 19–23.

Labbo, L. D., Field, S. L., & Brook, D. L. (1995). Safari sojourns: Exploring South Africa with the new geography standards. *Social Studies and the Young Learner, 8*(2), 8–12.

Ladson-Billings, G. (1992). I don't see color, I just see children: Dealing with stereotyping and prejudice in young children. *Social Studies and the Young Learner, 5*(2), 9–12.

Ladson-Billings, G. (1995). Toward a theory of culturally relevant pedagogy. *American Educational Research Journal, 32,* 465–492.

Lamme, L. L. (1994). Stories from our past: Making history come alive for children. *Social Education, 58,* 159.

Lamy, S. L. (1987). *The definition of a discipline: The objects and methods of analysis in global education.* New York: Global Perspectives in Education.

Laney, J. D., & Moseley, L. (1990). Who packed the suitcase? Playing the role of an archaeologist/anthropologist. *Social Studies and the Young Learner, 2*(3), 17–19.

Langer, J. A. (1981). From theory to practice: A prereading plan. *Journal of Reading, 25,* 106–110.

Langer, J. A., Applebee, A. N., Mullis, I. V. S., & Foertsch, M. A. (1990). *Learning to read in our nation's schools: Instruction and achievement in 1988 at Grades 4, 8, and 12.* Washington, DC: U.S. Department of Education.

Language mirrors immigration. (1993, April 28). *USA Today,* p. 11A.

Lankiewicz, D. (1987). Our museum of American life. *Clearing House, 60,* 256–257.

Lara, J. (1994). Demographic overview: Changes in student enrollment in American schools. In K. Spangenberg-Urbschat & R. Pritchard (Eds.), *Kids come in all languages: Reading instruction for ESL students* (pp. 9–21). Newark, DE: International Reading Association.

Larkins, A. G., & Hawkins, M. L. (1990). Trivial and noninformative content in primary grade social studies texts: A second look. *Journal of Social Studies Research, 14,* 25–32.

Laughlin, M., Black, P., & Loberg, M. (1991). *Social studies readers' theater for children: Scripts and script development.* Englewood, CO: Teacher Idea Press.

Laughlin, M., & Kardaleff, P. (1991). *Literature-based social studies: Children's books and activities to enrich the K–5 curriculum.* Phoenix AZ: Oryx.

Lechner, J. V. (1997). Accuracy in biographies for children. *New Advocate, 10,* 229–242.

LeRiche, L. W. (1987). The expanding environments sequence in elementary social studies: The origins. *Theory and Research in Social Education, 5,* 137–154.

Levstik, L. (1986). The relationship between historical response and narrative in a sixth-grade classroom. *Theory and Research in Social Education, 21*(1), 1–15.

Levstik, L. (1989). Historical narrative and the young reader. *Theory Into Practice, 28,* 114–119.

Levstik, L. (1990). Mediating content through literary texts. *Language Arts, 67,* 848–853.

Levstik, L. (1991). Teaching history: A definitional and developmental dilemma. In V. A. Atwood (Ed.), *Elementary school social studies: Research as a guide to practice* (pp. 68–84). Washington, DC: National Council for the Social Studies.

Liben, L., & Downs, R. (1989). Educating with maps: Part I. The place of maps. *Teaching Thinking and Problem Solving, 11*(1), 6–9.

Lickona, T. (1991). *Educating for character: How our schools can teach respect and responsibility.* New York: Bantam.

Little Soldier, L. (1990). Making anthropology a part of the elementary social studies curriculum. *Social Education, 54,* 18–19.

Losey, K. M. (1995). Mexican American students and classroom interaction: An overview and critique. *Review of Educational Research, 65,* 283–318.

Lou, Y., Abrami, P. C., Spence, J. C., Poulson, C., Chambers, B., & D'Apollonia, S. (1996). Within-class grouping: A meta-analysis. *Review of Educational Research, 66,* 423–458.

Louie, B. Y. (1993). Using literature to teach location. *Social Studies and the Young Learner, 5*(3), 17–18.

Lybarger, M. (1991). The historiography of social studies: Retrospect, circumspect, and prospect. In J. P. Shaver (Ed.), *Handbook of research on social studies teaching and learning* (pp. 3–15). New York: Macmillan.

Lyman, F. T. (1992). Think-Pair-Share, Thinktrix, Thinklinks, and weird facts: An interactive system for cooperative thinking. In N. Davidson & T. Worsham (Eds.), *Enhancing thinking through cooperative learning* (pp. 169–181). New York: Teachers College Press.

Lyman, L., Foyle, H. C., & Azwell, T. S. (1993). *Cooperative learning in the elementary classroom.* Washington, DC: National Educational Association.

Mager, R. F. (1984). *Preparing instructional objectives* (Rev. 2nd ed.). Belmont, CA: Lake.

Magnuson, P. (1996). If we were in charge . . . Students debate the ideal school at Concordia Language Village. *Social Studies and the Young Learner, 8*(3).

Mahood, W. (1980). The land of milk and honey: Simulating the immigrant experience. *Social Education, 44,* 22–27.

Maier, J. (1993). Relating here to there: Globes and world maps as advance organizers. *Social Studies and the Young Learner, 5*(3), 9–11.

Main, M., Wilhelm, R. W., & Cox, A. R. (1996). Mi communidad: Young children's bicultural explorations of the meaning of family. *Social Studies and the Young Learner, 9*(1), 7–9, 14.

Mandeville, G. K., & Rivers, J. L. (1988 / 1989). Effects of South Carolina's Hunter-based PET program. *Educational Leadership, 46*(4), 63–66.

Martorella, P. H. (1991a). Knowledge and concept development in social studies. In J. P. Shaver (Ed.), *Handbook of research on social studies teaching and learning* (pp. 370–384). New York: Macmillan.

Martorella, P. H. (1991b). Strategies for aiding students in comprehending social studies subject matter. *The Social Studies, 81,* 131–134.

Massialas, B. G. (1991). Education for international understanding. In J. P. Shaver (Ed.), *Handbook of research on social studies teaching and learning* (pp. 448–458). New York: Macmillan.

Massialas, B. G., & Cox, C. B. (1966). *Inquiry in social studies.* San Francisco: McGraw-Hill.

Mayhew, K. C., & Edwards, A. C. (1936). *The Dewey School: The Laboratory School of the University of Chicago 1896–1903.* New York: Appleton-Century.

McBee, R. H. (1996). Can controversial topics be taught in the early grades? The answer is yes! *Social Education, 60,* 38–41.

McCall, A. L. (1994). Including quilters' voices in the social studies curriculum. *Social Studies and the Young Learner, 7*(1), 10–14.

McCall, A. L. (1996). Making a difference: Integrating social problems and social action in the social studies curriculum. *The Social Studies, 87,* 203–209.

McCracken, H. (1959). *George Catlin and the old frontier.* New York: Dial.

McGowan, M. J., & Powell, J. H. (1996). An annotated bibliography of resources for literature-based instruction. *Social Education, 60,* 231–232.

McGowan, T. M. (Ed.). (1996). Telling the story of citizenship [Special issue]. *Social Education, 60*(4).

McGowan, T. M., Erickson, L., & Neufeld, J. A. (1996). With reason and rhetoric: Building the case for the literature-social studies connection. *Social Education, 60,* 203–207.

McKeown, M. G., Beck, I. L., Sinatra, G. M., & Loxterman, J. A. (1991). The contribution of prior knowledge and coherent text to comprehension. *Reading Research Quarterly, 27,* 79–93.

McLaren, P. (1994). *Life in schools: An introduction to critical pedagogy in the foundations of education.* New York: Longman.

McLaughlin, B. (1987). *Theories of second-language learning.* London, UK: Edward Arnold.

McPeck, J. (1981). *Critical thinking and education.* Toronto: Oxford University Press.

McPeck, J. (1990). *Teaching critical thinking.* New York: Routledge.

Mehaffy, G., Sitton, G., & Davis, O. L. (1979). *Oral history in the classroom.* Washington, DC: National Council for the Social Studies.

Meltzer, M. (1994). *Nonfiction for the classroom: Milton Meltzer on writing history and social responsibility.* Newark, DE: International Reading Association.

Mezaros, B. (1997). Economic standards: A guide for curriculum planners. *Social Education, 61,* 324–328.

Mezaros, B., & Engstromn, L. (1998). The voluntary national content standards in economics: From standards to classroom implementation. *Social Studies and the Young Learner, 11*(2), 7–12.

Miel, A. (1952). *Cooperative procedures in learning.* New York: Teachers College Press.

Miller, E. G., & Jacobson, M. G. (1994). Teaching for global-mindedness. *Social Studies and the Young Learner, 6*(4), 4–6.

Miller, J. W. (1974). Comparisons of conventional "subdued" to vivid "highly contrasting" color schemes for elementary school maps: Report of an experiment. *Journal of Geography, 73*(3), 41–45.

Miller, J. W. (1982). Improving the design of classroom maps: Experimental comparison of alternative formats. *Journal of Geography, 81*(2), 51–55.

Mitchell-Powell, B. (1995). More than just a pretty interface: Access, content, and relevance in computer technology. *Social Studies and the Young Learner, 7*(3), 11–13.

Mohan, B. (1986). *Language and content.* Reading, MA: Addison-Wesley.

Monahan, B. D., & Dharm, M. (1995). The Internet for educators: A user's guide. *Educational Technology, 35*(1), 44–48.

Moore, A. W. (1985). A question of accuracy: Errors in children's biographies. *School Library Journal, 31*(6), 34–35.

Moore, D. W., & Moore, S. A. (1986). Possible sentences. In E. K. Dishner, T. W. Bean, J. E. Readence, & D. W. Moore (Eds.), *Reading in the content areas: Improving classroom instruction* (2nd ed., pp. 174–179). Dubuque IA: Kendall/Hunt.

Morin, J. A. (1997). Software enhancement for a diverse family unit. *Social Studies and the Young Learner, 9*(3), 24–26.

Morris, R. V. (1998). Using artifacts as a springboard to literacy. *Social Studies and the Young Learner, 10*(4), 14–17.

Mosher, R., Kenney, R., & Garrod, A. (Eds.). (1994). *Preparing for citizenship.* Westport, CT: Prager.

Muir, S. P., & Frazee, B. (1986). Teaching map-reading skills: A developmental perspective. *Social Education, 50,* 199–203.

Murphy, C. (Ed.). (1993). Rethinking the holidays [Special issue]. *Social Studies and the Young Learner, 6*(2).

Nash, G. B., & Dunn, R. E. (1995). History standards and culture wars. *Social Education, 59,* 5–7.

National Center for History in the Schools. (1996). *National standards for history: Basic edition.* Los Angeles: Author.

National Commission on Social Studies in the Schools. (1989). *Charting a course: Social studies for the 21st century.* Washington, DC: National Council for the Social Studies.

National Council for the Social Studies (NCSS). (1994). *Expectations of excellence: Curriculum standards for the social studies.* Washington, DC: Author.

National Council for the Social Studies Ad Hoc Committee on Ability Grouping. (1992). Ability grouping in social studies. *Social Education, 56,* 268–270.

National Council for the Social Studies Ad Hoc Committee on Global Education. (1987). Global education: In bounds or out? *Social Education, 51,* 242–249.

National Council for the Social Studies Task Force on Early Childhood/Elementary Social Studies. (1989). Social studies for early childhood and elementary school children preparing for the 21st century. *Social Education, 53,* 14–23.

National Council for the Social Studies Task Force on Ethnic Studies Curriculum Guidelines. (1992). Curriculum guidelines for multicultural education. *Social Education, 56,* 274–294.

National Council for the Social Studies Task Force on Scope and Sequence. (1989). In search of a scope and sequence for social studies: Report of the National Council for the Social Studies Task Force on Scope and Sequence. *Social Education, 53,* 375–387.

National Council for the Social Studies Task Force on Standards for Teaching and Learning in the Social Studies. (1993). A vision of powerful teaching and learning in the social studies: Building social understanding and civic efficacy. *Social Education, 57,* 213–223.

National Council on Economic Education. (1997). *National content standards in economics.* New York: Author.

National standards for history for Grades K–4: Expanding children's world in time and space. (1994). Los Angeles: National Center for History in the Schools.

National standards for United States history: Exploring the American experience. (1994). Los Angeles: National Center for History in the Schools.

National standards for world history: Exploring paths to the present. (1994). Los Angeles: National Center for History in the Schools.

Natoli, S. J. (Ed.). (1992). Integrating language arts and social studies [Special issue]. *Social Education, 56*(7).

Nelson, J. L. (1991). Discipline, knowledge, and social education. *International Journal of Social Education, 6*(2), 41–50.

Nelson, M. R., & Stahl, R. J. (1991). Teaching anthropology, sociology, and psychology. In J. P. Shaver (Ed.), *Handbook of research on social studies teaching and learning* (pp. 420–426). New York: Macmillan.

Neuenschwander, J. A. (1976). *Oral history as a teaching approach.* Washington, DC: National Education Association.

Newmann, F. M. (1990a). Higher order thinking in social studies: A rationale for the assessment of classroom thoughtfulness. *Journal of Curriculum Studies, 22,* 41–56.

Newmann, F. M. (1990b). Qualities of thoughtful social studies classes: An empirical profile. *Journal of Curriculum Studies, 22,* 253–275.

Newmann, F. M. (1991). Promoting higher order thinking in social studies: Overview of a study of 16 high school departments. *Theory and Research in Social Education, 19,* 324–340.

Newmann, F. M., & Associates. (1996). *Authentic achievement: Restructuring schools for intellectual quality.* San Francisco: Jossey-Bass.

Newmann, F. M., Secada, W. G., & Wehlage, G. G. (1995). *A guide to authentic instruction and assessment: Vision, standards, and scoring.* Madison: Wisconsin Center for Education Research.

Nickell, P. (Ed.). (1992). Student assessment in social studies [Special issue]. *Social Education, 56*(2).

Northrup, T., & Rooze, G. E. (1990). Are social studies teachers using computers? A national survey. *Social Education, 54,* 212–214.

Norton, D. E. (1999). *Through the eyes of a child: An introduction to children's literature* (5th ed.). Upper Saddle River, NJ: Merrill/Prentice Hall.

Norton, J. (1992). The state vs. the Big Bad Wolf: A study of the justice system in the elementary school. *Social Studies and the Young Learner, 5*(1), 5–9.

Oakes, J. (1985). *Keeping track: How schools structure inequality.* New Haven, CT: Yale University Press.

O'Brien, K., & Stoner, D. K. (1987). Increasing environmental awareness through children's literature. *The Reading Teacher, 41,* 14–19.

Ochoa, A. S. (1986). Are social studies educators impervious to change? *The Social Studies, 77,* 66–68.

O'Day, K. (1994). Using formal and informal writing in middle school social studies. *Social Education, 58,* 39–40.

Ogle, D. (1986). K-W-L: A teaching model that develops active reading of expository text. *The Reading Teacher, 39,* 564–570.

Oliver, D. W., & Shaver, J. P. (1966). *Teaching public issues in the schools.* Boston: Houghton Mifflin.

Olmedo, I. M. (1993). Junior historians: Doing oral history with ESL and bilingual students. *TESOL Journal, 2*(4), 7–10.

Olmedo, I. M. (1996). Creating contexts for studying history with students learning English. *The Social Studies, 87,* 39–43.

Olsen, D. G. (1995). "Less" can be "more" in the promotion of thinking. *Social Education, 59,* 130–134.

Onosko, J. T. (1992). An approach to designing thoughtful units. *Social Studies, 83,* 193–196.

O'Reilly, K. (1998). What would you do? Constructing decision-making guidelines through historical problems. *Social Education, 62,* 46–49.

Ouzts, D. T. (1998). Enhancing literacy using the question-answer relationship. *Social Studies and the Young Learner, 10*(4), 26–28.

Ovoian, G., & Gregory, D. (1991). Can you dig it? *Social Studies Review, 30*(3), 83–88.

Owen, R. C. (1982). Anthropology and a social science/social studies: One more plea. *Social Studies, 73,* 207–211.

Paley, V. G. (1979). *White teacher.* Cambridge, MA: Harvard University Press.

Palinscar, A. S., & Brown, A. L. (1984). Reciprocal teaching of comprehension-fostering and comprehension-monitoring activities. *Cognition and Instruction, 2,* 117–175.

Palmer, J. J. (1988). The electoral college: A Jigsaw lesson. *Social Education, 52,* 306–307.

Parker, F. W. (1883). *Talks on teaching.* New York: Kellogg.

Parker, F. W. (1894). *Talks on pedagogics.* New York: Kellogg.

Parker, W., & Jarolimek, J. (1984). *Citizenship and the critical role of the social studies.* Washington, DC: National Council for the Social Studies.

Parker, W. C. (1991). Achieving thinking and decision-making objectives in social studies. In J. P. Shaver (Ed.), *Handbook of research on social studies teaching and learning* (pp. 345–356). New York: Macmillan.

Parker, W. C. (1995). Assessing civic discourse. *Educational Leadership, 52*(5), 84–85.

Parker, W. C., & Kaltsounis, T. (1991). Citizenship and law-related education. In V. A. Atwood (Ed.), *Elementary school social studies: Research as a guide to practice* (pp. 14–33). Washington, DC: National Council for the Social Studies.

Passe, J. (1988). Developing current events awareness in children. *Social Education, 52,* 531–533.

Passe, J. (1994). Media literacy in a global age. *Social Studies and Young Learner, 6*(4), 7–9.

Passe, J., & Passe, M. (1985). Archaeology: A unit to promote thinking skills. *Social studies, 76,* 238–239.

Patrick, J. J., & Hoge, J. D. (1991). Teaching government, civics, and law. In J. P. Shaver (Ed.), *Handbook of research on social studies teaching and learning* (pp. 427–436). New York: Macmillan.

Patton, M. M. (1996). Where do you live when you don't have a house? Learning about houses, homes, and homelessness. *Social Studies and the Young Learner, 8*(4), 14–17.

Pearson, P. D., & Fielding, L. (1994). Comprehension instruction. In R. Ruddell, M. R. Ruddell, & H. Singer (Eds.), *Theoretical models and processes for reading* (4th ed., pp. 815–860). Newark, DE: International Reading Association.

Perez-Stable, M. A. (1996). A kaleidoscope of perspectives in children's literature about slavery and the Civil War. *The Social Studies, 87,* 24–31.

Petersen, J. F., Natoli, S. J., & Boehm, R. G. (1994). The guidelines for geographic education: A 10-year retrospective. *Social Education, 58,* 206–210.

Pezone, M., & Singer, A. (1997). Empowering students through democratic dialogues. *Social Education, 61,* 75–79.

Phillips. S. U. (1972). Participant structures and communicative competence: Warm Springs children in community and classroom. In C. B. Cazden, V. P. John, & D. Hymes (Eds.), *Functions of language in the classroom* (pp. 370–394). New York: Teachers College Press.

Piaget, J., & Inhelder, B. (1969). *The psychology of the child.* (H. Weaver, Trans.). New York: Basic Books.

Poplin, M. S. (1988). Holistic/constructivist principles of the teaching/learning process: Implications for the field of learning disabilities. *Journal of Learning Disabilities, 21,* 401–416.

Powe, F. (1998). Perspectives on the American landscape. *Social Education, 62,* 126–133.

Pratt, L., & Beaty, J. J. (1999). *Transcultural children's literature.* Upper Saddle River, NJ: Merrill/Prentice Hall.

Proctor, D. R., & Haas, M. E. (1993). Social studies and school-based community service programs: Teaching the role of cooperation and legitimate power. *Social Education, 57,* 381–384.

Qin, Z., Johnson, D. W., & Johnson, R. T. (1995). Cooperative versus competitive efforts and problem solving. *Review of Educational Research, 65,* 129–143.

Quigley, C. N., & Bahmueller, C. F. (Eds.). (1991). *Civitas: A framework for civic education.* Calabasas, CA: Center for Civic Education.

Rader, W. (1995). The Elementary School Economics Project at the University of Chicago. *The Social Studies, 86,* 85–90.

Rallis, D. N., & Rallis, H. (1995). Changing the image of geography. *The Social Studies, 86,* 167–168.

Ramirez, M., & Castaneda, A. (1974). *Cultural democracy, bicognitive development, and education.* New York: Academic Press.

Raphael, T. E. (1982). Question-answering strategies for children. *The Reading Teacher, 36,* 186–191.

Raphael, T. E. (1986). Teaching question-answer relationships, revisited. *The Reading Teacher, 39,* 516–523.

Raths, L. E., Harmin, M., & Simon, S. B. (1978). *Values and teaching: Working with values in the classroom* (2nd ed.). Upper Saddle River, NJ: Merrill/Prentice Hall.

Ravitch, D., & Finn, C. E. (1987). *What do our 17-year-olds know?* New York: Harper & Row.

Rhoades, L. (1994). Quick-start ideas for teaching current events with newspapers. *Social Education, 58,* 173–174.

Rice, M. J., & Cobb, R. L. (1978). *What can children learn in geography? A review of the research.* Boulder, CO: SSEC.

Ricchiuti, L. (1998). Hanging in the Louvre: Virtual museum. *California Council for the Social Studies, 38*(1), 57–63.

Risinger, C. F. (1996). Webbing the social studies: Using Internet and World Wide Web resources in social studies instruction. *Social Education, 60,* 174–175.

Risinger, C. F. (1998). Separating the wheat from the chaff: Why dirty pictures are not the real dilemma in using the Internet to teach social studies. *Social Education, 62,* 148–150.

Risinger, C. F., & Garcia, J. (1995). National assessment and the social studies. *Clearing House, 68*(4), 225–228.

Ritchie, D. A. (1995). *Doing oral history.* New York: Twayne.

Roberts, P. L. (1996). *Integrating language arts and social studies for kindergarten and primary children.* Upper Saddle River, NJ: Merrill/Prentice Hall.

Rogers, L. K., & Bromley, K. (1995). Developing geographic literacy: An annotated list of children's literature. *Social Studies and the Young Learner, 8*(2).

Rose, S. A., & Fernlund, P. M. (1997). Using technology for powerful social studies learning. *Social Education, 61,* 160–167.

Rosenshine, B., & Meister, C. (1994). Reciprocal teaching: A review of the research. *Review of Educational Research, 64,* 479–530.

Ross, D. D., & Bondy, E. (1993). Classroom management for responsible citizenship: Practical strategies for teachers. *Social Education, 57,* 326–328.

Rossi, J. A. (1992). Uniformity, diversity, and the "New Social Studies." *The Social Studies, 83,* 41–45.

Rossi, J. A. (1996a). Creating strategies and conditions for civil discourse about controversial issues. *Social Education, 60,* 15–21.

Rossi, J. A. (Ed.). (1996b). Teaching controversial issues [Special issue]. *Social Education, 60*(1).

Rothwell, J. T. (1997). History making and the Plains Indians. *Social Education, 61,* 4–10.

Ruggiero, V. R. (1988). *Teaching thinking across the curriculum.* New York: Harper & Row.

Rule, A. C., & Sunal, C. S. (1994). Buttoning up a hands-on history lesson: Using everyday objects to teach about historical change. *Social Studies and the Young Learner, 7*(2), 8–11.

Rushdoony, H. A. (1968). A child's ability to read maps: Summary of the research. *Journal of Geography, 67,* 213–222.

Sahr, D. E. (1997). Native American governments in today's curriculum. *Social Education, 61,* 308–315.

Salter, G. (1989). Geography. In *Charting a course: Social studies for the 21st century* (pp. 43–47). Washington, DC: National Commission Social Studies in the Schools.

Saunders, P., Bach, G. L., Calderwood, J. D., & Hansen, W. L. (1984). *A framework for teaching economics: Basic concepts* (2nd ed.). New York: Joint Council on Economic Education.

Saxe, D. (1991). *Social studies in schools: A history of the early years.* Albany: State University of New York.

Saxe, D. W. (1992). Framing a theory for social studies foundations. *Review of Educational Research, 62,* 259–278.

Saxe, D. W. (1996). The national history standards: Time for common sense. *Social Education, 60,* 44–48.

Scarre, C. (1993). *Smithsonian timelines of the ancient world: A visual chronology from the origins of life to A.D. 1500.* New York: Dorling Kindersley.

Schaffarzick, J. (1979). Federal curriculum reform: A crucible for value conflict. In J. Schaffarzick & G. Sykes (Eds.), *Value conflicts and curriculum issues: Lessons from research and experience* (pp. 1–26). Berkeley, CA: McCutchan.

Scheurman, G. (1998). From behaviorist to constructivist teaching. *Social Education, 62,* 6–9.

Scheurman, G., & Yell, M. A. (Eds.). (1998). Constructing knowledge in social studies [Special issue]. *Social Education, 62*(1).

Schiever, S. W. (1991). *A comprehensive approach to the teaching of thinking.* Boston: Allyn & Bacon.

Schimmel, D. (1997). Traditional rule making and the subversion of citizenship education. *Social Education, 61,* 70–74.

Schug, M. C. (1983). The development of economic thinking in children and adolescents. *Social Education, 47,* 141–145.

Schug, M. C. (Ed.). (1985). *Economics in the school curriculum, K–12.* Washington, DC: Joint Council on Economic Education and the National Education Association.

Schug, M. C. (1994). How children learn economics. *International Journal of Social Education, 8,* 25–34.

Schug, M. C. (1996). Introducing children to economic reasoning: Some beginning lessons. *The Social Studies, 87,* 114–118.

Schug, M. C., & Armento, B. J. (1985). Teaching economics to children. In M. C. Schug (Ed.), *Economics in the school curriculum, K–12* (pp. 33–43). Washington, DC: Joint Council on Economic Education and the National Education Association.

Schug, M. C., & Walstad, W. B. (1991). Teaching and learning economics. In J. P. Shaver (Ed.), *Handbook of research on social studies teaching and learning* (pp. 411–419). New York: Macmillan.

Selwyn, D. (1995). *Arts and humanities in the social studies.* Washington, DC: National Council for the Social Studies.

Semrau, P., & Boyer, B. A. (1995). Social studies lessons integrating technology. *Social Studies and the Young Learner, 7*(3), 16 / 1–16 / 5.

Senesh, L. (1963). *Our working world: Families at work.* Chicago: Science Research Associates.

Shade, B. J. (1986). Is there an Afro-American cognitive style?: An explanatory study. *Journal of Black Psychology, 13,* 13–16.

Shade, B. J., & New, C. A. (1993). Cultural influences on learning: Teaching implications. In J. A. Banks & C. A. M. Banks (Eds.), *Multicultural education: Issues and perspectives* (pp. 317–331). Boston: Allyn & Bacon.

Shaftel, F., & Shaftel, G. (1967). *Role playing for social values: Decision making in the social studies.* Upper Saddle River, NJ: Merrill/Prentice Hall.

Sharan, S., & Sharan, Y. (1976). *Small-group teaching.* Englewood Cliffs, NJ: Educational Technology Publications.

Sharan, Y., & Sharan, S. (1989 / 1990). Group investigation expands cooperative learning. *Educational Leadership, 47*(4), 17–21.

Shaver, J. P. (Ed.). (1991). *Handbook of research on social studies teaching and learning.* New York: Macmillan.

Short, D. J. (1994). The challenge of social studies for limited-English-proficient students. *Social Education, 58,* 36–38.

Short, D. J., Mahrer, C. A., Elfin, A. M., Liten-Tejada, R. A., & Montone, C. L. (1994). *Protest and the American Revolution: An integrated language, social studies, and culture unit for middle school American history.* Washington, DC: National Center for Research on Cultural Diversity and Second Language Learning & Center for Applied Linguistics.

Simmons, D. (1994). "Think globally, acting locally": Using the local environment to explore global issues. *Social Studies and the Young Learner, 6*(4), 10–13.

Simmons, D. (1995). Environmental education, social studies, and education reform: Why is environmental education essential education? *Social Studies and the Young Learner, 8*(1), 9–11.

Simpson, M. (Ed.). (1995a). Teaching history creatively [Special issue]. *Social Education, 59*(1).

Simpson, M. (Ed.). (1995b). Teaching students to think [Special issue]. *Social Education, 59*(3).

Simpson, M. (Ed.). (1996). The world around us: Global education [Special issue]. *Social Education, 60*(7).

Simpson, M. (Ed.). (1997). A new view of the world: Using technology in social studies education [Special issue]. *Social Education, 61*(3).

Simpson, M. (Ed.). (1998). Technology 101: Teaching in the information age [Special issue]. *Social Education, 62*(3).

Singleton, L. (1993). *G is for geography: Children's literature and the five themes.* Boulder, CO: Social Science Education Consortium.

Singleton, L. (1995). *H is for history: Using children's literature to develop historical understandings.* Boulder, CO: Social Science Education Consortium.

Singleton, L. (1997). *C is for citizenship: Children's literature and civic understanding.* Boulder, CO: Social Science Education Consortium.

Slavin, R. E. (1978). Student teams and achievement divisions. *Journal of Research and Development in Education, 12,* 39–49.

Slavin, R. E. (1980). Cooperative learning. *Review of Educational Research, 50,* 315–342.

Slavin, R. E. (1986). *Using student team learning* (3rd ed.). Baltimore: Johns Hopkins University Center for Research on Elementary and Middle Schools.

Slavin, R. E. (1987). Ability grouping and achievement in elementary school: A best evidence synthesis. *Review of Educational Research, 60,* 471–499.

Slavin, R. E. (1989). PET and the pendulum: Fadism in education and how to stop it. *Phi Delta Kappan, 70,* 752–758.

Slavin, R. E. (1989 / 1990). Research on cooperative learning: Consensus and controversy. *Educational Leadership, 47*(4), 52–55.

Slavin, R. E. (1990a). *Cooperative learning: Theory, research, and practice.* Boston: Allyn & Bacon.

Slavin, R. E. (1990b). On making a difference. *Educational Researcher, 19*(3), 30–34.

Slavin, R. E. (1992). Cooperative learning in the social studies: Balancing the social and the studies. In R. J. Stahl & R. L. VanSickle (Eds.), *Cooperative learning in the social studies classroom: An introduction to social study* (pp. 21–25). Washington, DC: National Council for the Social Studies.

Sloyer, S. (1982). *Readers' theatre: Story dramatization in the classroom.* Urbana, IL: National Council of Teachers of English.

Smagorinsky, P. (1994). Bring the courtroom to the classroom: Develop civic awareness with simulation activities. *The Social Studies, 85,* 174–180.

Smith, F. (1986a). *How education backed the wrong horse.* Victoria, BC: Abel Press.

Smith, F. (1986b). *Insult to intelligence: The bureaucratic invasion of our classrooms.* Portsmouth, NH: Heinemann.

Smith, F. (1988). *Understanding reading: A psycholinguistic analysis of reading and learning to read.* Mahwah, NJ: Lawrence Erlbaum.

Smith, J. A., Monson, J. A., & Dobson, D. (1992). A case study on integrating history and reading instruction through literature. *Social Education, 56,* 370–375.

Smith, K. A., Johnson, D. W., & Johnson, R. T. (1981). Can conflict be constructive? Controversy versus concurrence seeking in learning groups. *Journal of Educational Psychology, 73,* 651–663.

Smitherman, G. (1977). *Talkin' and testifyin': The language of Black America.* Boston: Houghton Mifflin.

Snow, J. S. (1990). *Transportation transformation: A writing project for at-risk students.* New York: New York Institute of Technology. (ERIC Document Reproduction No. ED 326 892)

Soley, M. (1996). If it's controversial, why teach it? *Social Education, 60,* 9–14.

Spagnoli, C. (1995). These tricks belong in your classroom: Telling Asian trickster tales. *Social Studies and the Young Learner, 8*(2), 15–16.

Stahl, R. J., & VanSickle, R. L. (1992a). Cooperative learning as effective social study within the social studies classroom: Introduction and invitation. In R. J. Stahl & R. L. VanSickle (Eds.), *Cooperative learning in the social studies classroom: An introduction to social study* (pp. 1–7). Washington, DC: National Council for the Social Studies.

Stahl, R. J. & VanSickle, R. L. (1992b). *Cooperative learning in the social studies classroom: An introduction to social study.* Washington, DC: National Council for the Social Studies.

Stallings, J., & Krasavage, E. M. (1986). Program implementation and student achievement in a 4-year Madeline Hunter follow-though project. *Elementary School Journal, 87,* 117–138.

Steffe, L. P., & Gale, J. (Eds.). (1995). *Constructivism in education.* Mahwah, NJ: Lawrence Erlbaum.

Sternberg, R. J. (Ed.). (1994). *Thinking and problem solving* (2nd ed.). San Diego: Academic Press.

Stiggins, R. J. (1994). *Student-centered classroom assessment.* Upper Saddle River, NJ: Merrill/Prentice Hall.

Stokes, S. M. (1997). Curriculum for Native American students: Using Native American values. *The Reading Teacher, 50,* 576–584.

Stoltman, J. P. (1991). Research on geography teaching. In J. P. Shaver (Ed.), *Handbook of research on social studies teaching and learning* (pp. 437–447). New York: Macmillan.

Stone, L. (1991). Intercultural and multicultural education: In V. A. Atwood (Ed.), *Elementary school social studies: Research as a guide to practice* (pp. 34–54). Washington, DC: National Council for the Social Studies.

Strang, R. (1958). *Group work in education.* New York: Harper.

Stremme, R. (1993). Great geography using notable trade books. In M. Zarnowski & A. F. Gallagher (Eds.), *Children's literature and social studies: Selecting and using notable books in the classroom* (pp. 12–150). Washington, DC: National Council for the Social Studies.

Study Group on Law-Related Education. (1978). *Final report of the U.S. Office of Education Study Group of Law-Related Education.* Washington, DC: Government Printing Office. (ERIC Document Reproduction No. ED 175 737)

Stull, A. T., & Ryder, R. J. (1999). *Education on the Internet: A student's guide.* Upper Saddle River, NJ: Merrill/Prentice Hall.

Suchman, R. (1962). *The elementary school training program in scientific inquiry: Report to the U.S. Office of Education Project Title VII, Project 216.* Urbana: University of Illinois.

Suchman, R. (1966). *Inquiry development program: Developing inquiry.* Chicago: Science Research Associates.

Sullivan, J. (1996). Implementing a cooperative learning research model: How it applies to a social studies unit. *The Social Studies, 87,* 210–216.

Swearingen, J. (1996). Promoting tolerance in preservice teachers. *Social Education, 60,* 152–154.

Switzer, T. (1986). Teaching sociology in K–12 classrooms. In S. Wronski & D. Bragaw (Eds.), *Social studies and social sciences: A 50-year perspective* (pp. 124–138). Washington, DC: National Council for the Social Studies.

Taba, H. (1967). *Teachers' handbook for elementary social studies.* Palo Alto, CA: Addison-Wesley.

Taylor, H. E., & Larson, S. (1998). Using cooperative learning activities with students who have attention deficit learning disorder. *Social Studies and the Young Learner, 10*(4).

Teachers Curriculum Institute. (1995). *History alive!* Mountain View, CA: Author.

Terwilliger, J. (1997). Semantics, psychometrics, and assessment reform: A close look at "authentic" assessments. *Educational Researcher, 26*(8), 24–27.

Thelan, H. (1960). *Education and the human quest.* New York: Harper & Row.

Thornton, S. J., & Vukelich, R. (1988). Effects of children's understanding of time concepts on historical understanding. *Theory and Research in Social Education, 16,* 69–82.

Tierney, R. J., Readance, J. E., & Dishner, E. K. (1995). *Reading strategies and practices: A compendium* (4th ed.). Boston: Allyn & Bacon.

Trifonoff, K. M. (1997). Introducing thematic maps in the primary grades. *Social Studies and the Young Learner, 11*(1), 17–22.

Trueba, H. T. (1989). *Raising silent voices: Educating the linguistic minorities of the 21st century.* New York: Newbury House.

Tunnell, M. O. (1993). *The story of ourselves: Teaching history through children's literature.* Portsmouth, NH: Heinemann.

Tunnell, M. O., & Ammon, R. (1996). The story of ourselves: Fostering multiple historical perspectives. *Social Education, 60,* 212–215.

Turnbull, A., Turnbull, R., Shank, M., & Leal, D. (1999). *Exceptional lives: Special education in today's schools* (2nd ed.). Upper Saddle River, NJ: Merrill/Prentice Hall.

Turner, T. N., & Hickey, G. M. (1991). Using radio tapes to teach about the past. *Social Studies and the Young Learner, 3*(4), 6–8.

Tye, B. B., & Tye, K. E. (1992). *Global education: A study school change.* Albany: State University of New York Press.

Tye, K. E. (Ed.). (1990). *Global education*. Alexandria, VA: Association for Supervision and Curriculum Development.

U.S. Department of Education. (1991). *America 2000: An education strategy*. Washington, DC: Author. (ERIC Document Reproduction No. ED 327 009)

U.S. Department of Education. (1992). *American education at a glance*. Washington, DC: Author.

Vacca, R. T., & Rasinski, T. V. (1992). *Case studies in whole language*. Ft. Worth, TX: Harcourt Brace Jovanovich.

Vacca, R. T., & Vacca, J. L. (1998). *Content area reading: Literacy and learning across the curriculum*. Reading, MA: Addison-Wesley.

Van Fossen, P. (Ed.). (1998). Economics in elementary schools [Special issue]. *Social Studies and the Young Learner, 11*(2).

Van Meter, V. (1990). *American history for children and young adults: An annotated bibliographic index*. Littleton, CO: Libraries Unlimited.

Van Meter, V. (1991). *World history for children and young adults*. Littleton, CO: Libraries Unlimited.

Vermette, P. J. (1998). *Making cooperative learning work: Student teams in K–12 classrooms*. Upper Saddle River, NJ: Merrill/Prentice Hall.

Virginia State Department of Education. (1989). *Social studies: Standards of learning objectives for Virginia public schools*. Richmond: Author. (ERIC Document Reproduction Service No. ED 316 466)

Voluntary national content standards in economics. (1997). New York: National Council on Economic Education.

Vuyk, R. (1981). *Piaget's genetic epistemology 1965–1980* (2 vols.). London: Academic Press.

Vygotsky, L. S. (1962). *Thought and language* (E. Hanfmann & G. Vakar, Trans.). Cambridge: MIT Press. (Original work published 1934)

Vygotsky, L. S. (1978). *Mind in society: The development of higher psychological processes* (M. Cole, V. John-Steiner, M. Lopez-Morillas, A. R. Luria, S. Scribner, E. Souberman, & J. Wartsch, Trans.). Cambridge, MA: Harvard University Press. (Original works published 1935–1966)

Wade, R. C. (1993). Content analysis of social studies textbooks: A review of 10 years of research. *Theory and Research in Social Education, 21,* 232–256.

Wade, R. C. (1994). Community service-learning. *Social Studies and the Young Learner, 6*(3).

Wade, R. C., & Everett, S. (1994). Civic participation in third-grade social studies textbooks. *Social Education, 58,* 308–311.

Walsh, H. M. (Ed.). (1992). Dealing with stereotypes and prejudices [Special issue]. *Social Studies and the Young Learner, 5*(2).

Wasta, S., & Scott, M. (1998). Building bridges to China. *Social Studies and the Young Learner, 11*(1), 6–10.

Wentworth, D. R., & Schug, M. C. (1994). How to use an economic mystery in your history course. *Social Education, 58,* 10–12.

Whelan, M. (1996). Right for the wrong reasons. *Social Education, 60,* 55–57.

White, J. J. (1988). Searching for substantial knowledge in social studies texts. *Theory and Research in Social Education, 16,* 115–140.

White, J. J. (1989). Anthropology. In *Charting a course: Social studies for the 21st century* (pp. 31–36). Washington, DC: National Commission on Social Studies in the Schools.

Wiggins, G. (1989). A true test: Toward more equitable assessment. *Phi Delta Kappan, 70,* 703–713.

Wiggins, G. (1992). Creating tests worth taking. *Educational Leadership, 49*(8), 26–33.

Wiggins, G. (1993). *Assessing student performance.* San Francisco: Jossey-Bass.

Wiggins, G. (1998). *Educative assessment: Designing assessments to inform and improve student performance.* San Francisco: Jossey-Bass.

Wilen, W. W., & Phillips, J. A. (1995). Teaching critical thinking: A metacognitive approach. *Social Education, 59,* 135–138.

Wilen, W. W., & White, J. J. (1991). Interaction and discourse in social studies classrooms. In J. P. Shaver (Ed.), *Handbook of research on social studies teaching and learning* (pp. 483–495). New York: Macmillan.

Wilkie, R. (Ed.). (1993). *Environmental education teacher resource handbook.* Milwood, NY: Kraus.

Williams, P. L., Reese, C. M., Lazer, S., & Shakrani, S. (1995a). *NAEP 1994 geography: A first look.* Washington, DC: U.S. Department of Education.

Williams, P. L., Reese, C. M., Lazer, S., & Shakrani, S. (1995b). *NAEP 1994 history: A first look.* Washington, DC: U.S. Department of Education.

Willison, S., & Ruane, P. (1995). Promoting acceptance of diversity and service to others. *The Social Studies, 86,* 91–92.

Wilson, E. K., & Marsh, G. E. (1995). Social studies and the Internet revolution. *Social Education, 59,* 198–202.

Wilson, J. (1995). Social studies online resources. *Social Studies and the Young Learner, 7*(3), 24–26.

Wilton, S. (1993). New biographies are "better than before." In M. Zarnowski & A. F. Gallagher (Eds.), *Children's literature and social studies: Selecting notable books in the classroom* (pp. 16–19). Washington, DC: National Council for the Social Studies.

Winitzky, N. E. (1991). Classroom organization for social studies. In J. P. Shaver (Ed.), *Handbook of research on social studies teaching and learning* (pp. 530–549). New York: Macmillan.

Wise, N., & Kon, J. H. (1990). Assessing geographic knowledge with sketch maps. *Journal of Geography, 89,* 123–129.

Wolfgang, C. H., & Kelsay, K. L. (1995). Discipline and the social studies classroom, Grades K–12. *The Social Studies, 86,* 175–182.

Wright, I. (1995). Making critical thinking possible: Options for teachers. *Social Education, 59,* 139–143.

Wunder, S. (1995). Addressing the standards for social studies with children's literature. *Social Studies and the Young Learner, 8*(2), 4–7.

Wyner, N. B., & Farquhar, E. (1991). Cognitive, emotional, and social development: Early childhood social studies. In J. P. Shaver (Ed.), *Handbook of research on social studies teaching and learning* (pp. 109–120). New York: Macmillan.

Yager, S., Johnson, R. T., Johnson, D. W., & Snider, B. (1986). The impact of group processing on achievement in cooperative learning. *Journal of Social Psychology, 126,* 389–397.

Yell, M. M. (1998). The time before history: Thinking like an archaeologist. *Social Education, 62*(1), 27–31.

Young, K. A. (1994). *Constructing buildings, bridges, and minds: Building an integrated curriculum through social studies.* Portsmouth, NH: Heinemann.

Young, T. A., & Vardell, S. (1993). Weaving readers' theater and nonfiction into the curriculum. *The Reading Teacher, 46,* 396–406.

Zarnowski, M. (1990). *Learning about biographies: A reading and writing approach for children.* Urbana, IL: National Council of Teachers of English.

Zarnowski, M., & Gallagher, A. F. (Eds.). (1993). *Children's literature and social studies: Selecting and using notable books in the classroom.* Washington, DC: National Council for the Social Studies.

Zarrillo, J. (1989). History and library books. *Social Studies and the Young Learner, 2*(2), 17–19.

Zarrillo, J. (1994). *Multicultural literature, multicultural teaching: Units for the elementary grades.* Ft. Worth, TX: Harcourt Brace.

Zimmerman, B. (1992). *How to tape instant oral biographies: Recording your family's life story in sound and sight.* New York: Bantam.

Index